THE CLASSICS
OF WESTERN
SPIRITUALITY

THE CLASSICS OF WESTERN SPIRITUALITY
A Library of the Great Spiritual Masters

𝔚alter 𝔥ilton

THE SCALE OF PERFECTION

TRANSLATED FROM THE MIDDLE ENGLISH,
WITH AN INTRODUCTION AND NOTES BY
JOHN P.H. CLARK AND ROSEMARY DORWARD

PREFACE BY
JANEL MUELLER

PAULIST PRESS
NEW YORK • MAHWAH

Cover art: MOTHER PLACID DEMPSEY, O.S.B. is a Benedictine nun of the Abbey of Regina Laudis in Bethlehem, Connecticut. A sculptress and painter currently working on murals of the Life of St. Benedict, she is also a book illustrator whose work for the Classics of Western Spirituality series includes: Hadewijch of Brabant, Hildegard of Bingen, Birgitta of Sweden, and now Walter Hilton. Of this new work she has this to say: "To me the striking thing about Hilton is his great interior luminosity; something at once rugged and refined, a characteristic, perhaps, that is peculiarly English. For it is a kind of 'native paradox' that one finds everywhere in their literature and art. Nowhere is it more apparent than in the lofty mystical sweep yet grounded homey solidity of the square gothic towers that enhance so many English medieval churches. One such tower appears behind Hilton on the cover of this book. It is that of the Augustinian Church of Thurgarton in Nottinghamshire, the very priory where Hilton entered the Canons of St. Augustine and where he died many years later in 1396. The tower is depicted not merely because of its historical relevance to Hilton but because of its symbolic significance as well. In itself it is a kind of ladder or 'scale'—a structural embodiment of the stages of vertical ascent and aspiration so essential to Hilton's spirituality."

Acknowledgment for photographs of historical material pertinent to the cover illustration are made to Historic Buildings and Monuments, Scotland, particularly to Chris Tabraham, Principal Inspector of Ancient Monuments and to the Reverend Canon Richard Kirton, Vicar of Thurgarton, for photographs of the church tower.

Library of Congress Cataloging-in-Publication Data

Hilton, Walter, d. 1396.
    The scale of perfection/by Walter Hilton: translated from the Middle English with introduction and notes by John P.H. Clark and Rosemary Dorward.
        p.   cm.—(The Classics of Western spirituality)
    Includes bibliographical references and index.
    ISBN 0-8091-0440-7 (cloth)
    ISBN 0-8091-3194-3 (pbk.)
        1. Spiritual life—Catholic authors. I. Clark, John P. H. II. Dorward, Rosemary,
    1921-   . III. Title. IV. Series.
    BX2349.H54   1991
    248.8—dc20   90-21618
                                                                                    CIP

Published by Paulist Press
997 Macarthur Boulevard
Mahwah, New Jersey 07430

Printed and bound in the United States of America

Contents

Editors of this Volume

JOHN P.H. CLARK is Vicar of Longframlington, Northumberland. He was born at Horsham, Sussex, in 1937, and studied French and German at St. Catharine's College, Cambridge, and theology at St. Stephen's House and Worcester College, Oxford. In 1974 he received a B.D. from Oxford University for work on Walter Hilton. He is the co-editor of *Walter Hilton's Latin Writings* (with Cheryl Taylor, Salzburg, 1987) and is currently collaborating with Dr. James Hogg on an edition of *The Latin Versions of "The Cloud of Unknowing."* He has contributed numerous articles to theological journals on the fourteenth-century English contemplative writers, especially Walter Hilton, and has made some related explorations into late-fourteenth-century Cambridge theology. In 1989 he was awarded the degree of D.D. (Lambeth) by the Archbishop of Canterbury.

ROSEMARY DORWARD (née Birts) went up to St. Hilda's College, Oxford, after wartime service in the W.R.N.S., to take an honors degree in English language and literature. She was taught by Helen Gardner, who encouraged her to continue her own work on *The Scale of Perfection* by editing a section of Book 1 in a B. Litt. (later M. Litt.) dissertation (1951). Dorward's studies were then interrupted by marriage and a long sojourn in remote parts of Africa, where she reared a family and at times taught in secondary schools. In 1983 the SLG Press (Oxford) published her modern English version of *Angels' Song* together with the *Eight Chapters on Perfection*, which Walter Hilton translated from an undiscovered work by Dom Luis de Fontibus.

Author of the Preface

JANEL MUELLER is Professor of English and Humanities at the University of Chicago, and the editor of *Modern Philology*. Since publishing *The Native Tongue and the Word: Developments in English Prose Style, 1380–1580* (Chicago, 1984), she has continued to work on the literature of English spirituality from Lollardy through the Reformation.

Acknowledgments

Our deep indebtedness to other workers in this field is reflected in the bibliography and notes. We should like to acknowledge in particular the help we have received from the late Professor A. J. Bliss, whose edition of *The Scale of Perfection*, Book 1, is to be published by the Early English Text Society, and from Dr. M. G. Sargent, who is seeing that edition through the press; likewise that given by Professor S. S. Hussey, who is editing Book 2 for the Society. We also wish to thank the Right Reverend L. E. Stradling and Dr. Stephen Medcalfe for reading parts of Book 1 and offering constructive suggestions.

The Cambridge University Library kindly allowed us to use their MS. Add. 6686 as the basis of the version of Book 1, and the British Library similarly allowed us the use of MS. Harley 6579 for Book 2.

We should like to thank Professor Valerie Lagorio, who gave the initial stimulus to this edition; we are grateful too for the support we have received from our families, and particularly to Frank Dorward for helping in ways too numerous to mention.

In this edition the modern English version was made by Rosemary Dorward, who is also responsible for that section of the Introduction dealing with the English text. The remainder of the Introduction, and the notes, were written by John Clark. Each editor has read the other's work, and they have consulted freely with each other, so that this is a collaborative effort.

Foreword

Walter Hilton's *Scale of Perfection* is generally considered the crown of his spiritual writing. The work is in fact a diptych, consisting of two books that are intimately related, but which were written on different occasions and in some measure for different needs. In this respect—and indeed in some others—the combined work may be compared with *The Ascent of Mount Carmel* and *The Dark Night of the Soul* by St. John of the Cross.

The first book is addressed to an anchoress and describes the renewal or "reforming" of the image of God in man, defaced by sin, to the "likeness" of God in Christ. Despite its ostensibly limited readership, its eminently sane and practical counsel soon ensured that it was widely read by people living in the world as well as by vowed religious.

The second book takes up points made in Book 1, but leads the reader considerably further along the road to contemplative union with God. Here Hilton deals carefully with the sacraments of baptism and confession, and then takes up at greater length the point already made in Book 1, that the way to union with God entails the costly taking up of the cross—that there are no short cuts to perfection. In this second book he gives careful attention to the theology of grace. The contemplative Christian life is now no longer seen as an "extra," available to a few chosen souls in the vowed religious life, but as something that may and should be sought by all Christians, because it represents the proper development of the baptismal life, in which "those who are led by the Spirit of God are the sons of God" (Romans 8.14).

Hilton's perception is sharpened at many points by the religious controversies of his day as he seeks to discover and demonstrate where true "liberty of spirit" lies. Some of the problems he addresses are not far removed from those encountered by Christians today, so that the wisdom of the past has an "actuality" for us.

Preface

Our age—the late twentieth century—is an ecumenical one. The fact itself needs no establishing, for its signs are familiar and abundant. We find ourselves frequently uncertain, however, about the significance and potential of this ecumenism for the future of Christianity. It is clear that factors of spirit and outlook have much to do with how issues of differences and perceptions of limits are approached and handled. When we ask and try to imagine how and how far Christian cooperation might extend toward Christian reunification, our thinking typically runs along two tracks at once. We think in a personalized way, trying to gauge the interplay of openness, flexibility, and principle among those who lead and speak for various churches and confessions. We also think in a thematic way, seeking possibilities for containing and yet honoring the divergent understandings and disparate emphases that bear on the fundamentals of the Christian religion. Since the questions we ask about ecumenism are intrinsically hard and inevitably speculative, we could easily despair of them and of ourselves if we confined our search for answers only to a contemporary focus. Fortunately there is no need for us to do this. The richly documented history of Christianity offers recurrent instances of persons of great spirituality and great humanity for whom the challenge of being a true Christian—apprehended as the mystery of becoming Christlike—figured as primary in their lives and writings. Although their historical junctures cannot be collapsed with ours or reoccupied from our own, the interworkings of personality and positionality among these individuals of the Christian past may yield sources of insight and intimations of possibilities that would otherwise be closed to us, simply because we would never manage to envision them for ourselves.

Walter Hilton, a late fourteenth-century monk of the Augustinian priory of Thurgarton in Yorkshire, is one such person of significance for contemporary questions of Christian ecumenism. I find Hilton significant in both of the ways indicated above—as the authorial personality he projects in his surviving works, chief among them *The Scale of Perfection,* and as the negotiator of positions that can accommodate alternative stances on issues still recognized as essential by Christians today. First to be registered, perhaps, among features of Hilton's personality is his sane and sensitive acknowledgment of how we as humans are individually constituted—that our bodies and their needs are to be respected, that we cannot force our spiritual progress for there is no such forced progress, but that our will can take a role in leading our affections (*Scale* 1, chs 72, 33, 19). The second striking element in Hilton's personality is his warm acceptance of others. Since he writes as a spiritual director, we expect an authority figure. What we get is rather more of a friend and companion who, for example, admits that he does not fully know how to distinguish venial from deadly sin (*Scale* 1, ch 56) but is certain that for us all the hardest thing is to hate the sin and love the sinner (*Scale* 1, chs 64–65). The *Scale* gives us an extraordinary implementation of Hilton's understanding that the basic relation of Christian to Christian is a mutual humanity constituted in equality before God—a relation expressively denoted as that of "even-christians" in the English of his day. As the term "even-christian" echoes through his work, considerations of status, vocation, and gender are constantly subordinated to this equality as the essential aspect of being Christlike: hence the characteristic discussion of the "tokens" by which to know if we love our "even-christian" and the example to take from Christ in doing so (*Scale* 1, ch 70; cf. *Scale* 2, chs 37–38).

Undergirding the positions taken by Hilton in which I find significance for ecumenism there is, first, the continual mediation that his writings perform on the respective claims of institutional and evangelical Christianity, the authority of church and the authority of scripture. The chief outcome of this mediation in the *Scale* is a very strong position on the authority of scripture within the institutional framework of the church. The position is explicitly theorized and defended in one of Hilton's climactic chapters (*Scale* 2, ch 43). Closely dependent in turn on his biblicism are the positions he takes on "reforming," "faith," and "feeling" as fundamental religious terms and the definitions he makes of them. In the space available to me in this preface, I wish to reflect on the appeal of Hilton's tone, tactics, and outlook while addressing his suggestiveness on issues of Christian understanding and experience in the late twentieth century.

Before positions of such a nature can be addressed, we need to begin by registering, at least in outline, Hilton's historical context in the late fourteenth century. Unless we begin with historical circumstances, we may well curtail our possibilities of appreciating either the personality or the positions that emerge in Walter Hilton's writings. A degree holder in civil and canon law who was thereby eminently qualified to assist his priory in its assigned task of prosecuting Lollards in the 1390s, Hilton was a wholly loyal and orthodox adherent of the medieval Catholic Church. In this frequently disillusioned and thus often rancorous era, Lollard writings were a conduit for a much broader anti-clericalism but they inscribed their specific character in virulent, obsessive attacks on the corruption of the clergy, the fraudulence of the friars, and the damnable lust for power manifested by the papacy. These are not at all Hilton's tonalities. We find him in the *Scale of Perfection* building outward from a firm but very sparingly elaborated grounding in the sacramental authority of the church. From this grounding Hilton moves—chiefly by way of extended meditations on scripture—into an outreach, flexibility, and openness to his own developing spiritual insights that are remarkable and original for his age. His was the gift, we can now see, to be creative and even prophetic for Christianity in his orthodoxy.

That the church was for Hilton a uniquely sacred and supremely authoritative institution registers with memorable intensity in his assertion that "God and holy church are so united and agreed together that whoever acts against the one, is acting against both" (*Scale* 1, ch 58). The church attests its sacredness and authoritativeness in its sacraments, which stand in relation to God's grace and forgiveness as a king's charter stands to the king's oral pardoning of a capital offender—an analogy that sheds equal light on its own contents and its author's legal background (*Scale* 2, ch 6). Yet *The Scale of Perfection* has strikingly little else to say about the sacraments (nothing on the Eucharist, a few observations on baptism and penance) and is altogether silent on the powers of the papacy and the ecclesiastical hierarchy. By contrast, the work has a very great deal to say, on the basis of scripture, about knowing, loving, and serving God. Of the four brief passages on heretics, only one mounts a sacramentalist defense against the identifiable Lollard objection that confessing to and being absolved by a bad priest can secure no grace (*Scale* 2, ch 7). The other three passages (*Scale* 1, chs 4, 20, 57) represent heretics as pridefully self-blinding against the plain sense of scripture—failing to recognize in themselves the pharisee in the parable of the pharisee and the publican, or failing to attend to St. Paul who said nothing profited him unless he had charity (1 Corinthians 13) and that it was death to live according to carnal, worldly desires (Romans 8.13). This is typical proceeding on Hilton's part. His biblicism is a brilliant, courageous stroke—the sole effective answer that orthodoxy could make to the challenge of Lollardy. At the very time that the *Scale* was being written, the Lollards were proclaiming open access by the laity to vernacular scripture as the core of their anti-papal, reformist program. Hilton declares himself through his method of composition. He refuses to consign vernacular scripture to the heretics, but instead makes endlessly productive his own recourse to it.

Early in the *Scale* an ostensible problem arises for the view of Hilton that I have just sketched. Addressing the anchoress for whom he is writing, he speaks of her as having to depend on prayer and meditation rather than on Bible reading which "is not practicable" for her (*Scale* 1, ch 15). This, however, must be a remark about the anchoress's material circumstances, not about what she is permitted to do, for Hilton throughout the *Scale* repeatedly and amply cites scripture from the Vulgate and then translates it for her to use in her prayers and meditations. There is more corroboration of Hilton's biblicism to be had in his small tract *On Mixed Life* dating from the same period as the *Scale*'s first book. Here Bible reading is urged upon another addressee who is under no religious vow and is firmly counseled against one. Hilton writes to a wealthy layman—the head of a great house and family—to be true to his worldly responsibilities and to utilize scripture in his devotions. While the institutional church of his day maintained categorical and hierarchical distinctions between the vowed religious life and lay life, and among contemplative life, active life, and the "mixed" life partaking of both, Hilton's human and spiritual understanding underwent an evolution as he wrote the *Scale*. He was finally unable to set much stock by these distinctions and certainly unwilling to correlate with them the capacity or potential for communion with God.

"I accuse no one, neither do I condemn any state, for in every state some are good and some are otherwise," remarks Hilton in his typically mingled tones of mildness and intense seriousness. "But one thing I say to every man or woman . . . whether he is religious or secular, or whatever degree he is in. So long as love and his affection is bound, fastened, and as it were entangled with the coveting of earthly goods that he has or would like to have, he cannot truly have or feel the pure love and clear sight of spiritual things" (*Scale* 1, ch 71). "For what is a man but his thoughts and his loves?" Hilton exclaims at another point. "If you want to know what you have, look at what you think about; for where the love is, there is the eye, and where the pleasure is, there is the heart thinking most. . . . As much as you love God and know him, so large is your soul" (*Scale* 1, ch 87). The biblical echo appears catalytic: "Where your treasure is, there your heart is also" (Matthew 6.21). Despite these clues in the *Scale*'s first book as to the direction that Hilton's insights are taking, it is still as surprising as it is gratifying to find Hilton in the *Scale*'s second book, written after the lapse of some years, expressly representing contemplation—the highest reach of religious experience defined by the terms of late fourteenth-century orthodoxy—as the Zion toward which all of God's chosen souls are bound, whatever their state or manner of life (*Scale* 2, ch 19; contrast *Scale* 1, ch 9, end). It is small wonder, then, that *The Scale of Perfection* became a favorite book of the English laity and found its way into print before any of the other notable spiritual writings in English from this period. From the perspective of ecumenism, however, what remains especially significant is the role played by scripture; it is the source that authorizes Hilton's forthright representation of universalism and egalitarianism as the heart of Christian religion. His most constant prototype both for spiritual instruction and for spiritual experience is the apostle Paul, who cast himself variously as the chiefest of sinners, as filled with the Holy Spirit, and as being all things to all men, if by any means he might win them to Christ. Hilton's apprehension of Pauline theology, which in turn is refracted through his study of Augustine (especially *De Trinitate*), shapes and imbues the project of the *Scale*.

It is helpful to bear in mind that *The Scale of Perfection* is an editorial, not an authorial title. Its aptness is expressly confirmed in just one passage on the necessarily gradual, cumulative process of receiving and responding to God's grace, which Hilton compared to needing to climb a ladder one rung at a time (*Scale* 2, ch 19). However, a manuscript now in the British Library carries the title, *The Reforming of Man's* (that is, *the Human*) *Soul*. This is the one I would favor, as much more descriptive, if the choice could be made over again. For Hilton's great subject is to consider how the soul, once formed in the image of God but now both defaced and debased by sin, can be re-formed to God's image. At every

5

key point, from the announcement of this subject through the anatomizing of sins and the projections of redemption and transformation under grace, formulations drawn from the Pauline epistles figure centrally in the style and content of Hilton's work. After using this source in his opening chapters to identify mistaken or inadequate conceptions of his subject, Hilton makes it the basis of a better representation: a soul is reformed by becoming Christlike in knowing and perfectly loving God and being filled with all virtue. "Saint Paul says this of such union and conforming: *Qui adhaeret deo unus spiritus est cum illo*. That is to say, If anyone is fastened to God, . . . then God and the soul are not two, but both are one—not in flesh but in one spirit" (*Scale* 1, ch 7, citing 1 Corinthians 6.17). Now further quotations spring up as guideposts for a more considered entry into this main subject: Paul's reference to seeing God as in a glass or mirror points to our need for introspection and self-assessment, his exhortation to be rooted and grounded in charity signals the preeminence of a life of love, his yearning to put behind all that is past and press forward to his supreme reward sets the course of our spiritual desire and direction (*Scale* 1, chs 9, 12, 13). And the first recapitulatory passage on the Christward orientation that should govern the whole of one's life turns on 1 Corinthians 10.31 as translated by Hilton: "Whether you eat or drink, or whatever kind of work you do, do it all in the name of our Lord Jesus Christ, forsaking yourself, and offer it up to him" (*Scale* 1, ch 23).

The next significant concern in Book 1 of the *Scale* is Hilton's careful and celebrated critique of Richard Rolle and others (we might think of the yet uncomposed *Book of Margery Kempe* by Hilton's younger contemporary) who wrote of mystical experience as if it consisted in physical sensations and was identifiable by them. No, says Hilton, the one true bodily locus for Christians lies nowhere in ourselves. It lies in the flesh and blood of the sinless Jesus as he suffered beating, verbal abuse, mutilation, and public crucifixion, and in the compassion, pity, love, and remorse that his sufferings evoke in us. This passage only hints at the theological representation that might have had special appeal for the historical Hilton with his legal training—the necessity of the Incarnation as a specific means of satisfying the capital penalty of criminal justice that humankind incurred by sinning—but consideration of this rationale is postponed to a later passage (*Scale* 2, ch 2). Here, in this earlier passage, he collects and cites three major texts from Paul as his authority both for reproving the misguided mystics and for asserting a cardinal principle of Christian spirituality—that apprehension of Christ's divinity can proceed only by way of his humanity (*Scale* 1, ch 35). As the *Scale* continues, moreover, Hilton continues to draw authority from Paul on key points. In one extended discussion remarkable for the wit and finesse applied to a hot topical issue, he appropriates—by thoroughly reinterpreting in a Pauline light—in that Lollard rallying cry that idolatrous images be dishonored and destroyed. Hilton identifies idolatry not with the veneration of images in churches (which he elsewhere explicitly defended) but with the "body of sin and death," the worldly, carnal self from which Paul cried out to be delivered and whose members he sought to break apart (*Scale* 1, chs 42, 53, 84–85, 87, 89). The productive outcome of this destructive struggle is the soul's rebirth to a new Christlike life, again as envisaged by the apostle (ch 91, end).

Hilton's central project in *The Scale of Perfection* is to locate the true essentials of what it means to be a Christian and to distinguish these from mere approaches or approximations to them. His key texts for this purpose (in his own translations) are 1 Corinthians 11.7, "Man is the image of God" (*Scale* 2, ch 1); Romans 7.24, 25: "Ah, who shall deliver me from this body and this image of death? The grace of God by Jesus Christ" (*Scale* 1, ch 54); and 1 Corinthians 15.49, "As we have hitherto borne the image of the earthly man, the first Adam, that is, the image of sin, so let us now bear the image of the heavenly man Jesus, which is the image of virtues" (*Scale* 1, ch 86). The primacy of this concern with the restoration of the human image to its divine likeness is what makes the title *The Reforming of Man's Soul* so fitting for Hilton's work. Under the pressure of this concern Hilton develops and sharpens what becomes for him an utterly crucial distinction between "reforming in faith" and "reforming in feeling."

"Reforming in faith alone," we are told, "may be gained easily and in short time," but it "is sufficient for salvation" because it involves hating and repudiating one's "image of sin" (*Scale* 2, ch 5). Reforming in faith consists in casting oneself on God's mercy and imploring salvation by Christ's passion while submitting to the sacraments of the church, and such faith may be embraced even at the very end of an evil life (*Scale* 1, ch 44). "Reforming in feeling," however, "destroys the old feelings of this image of sin and brings into the soul new gracious feelings through the working of the Holy Spirit." Its signs are a complete moral and spiritual renovation whereby the soul "drives out the enjoyment and feeling of fleshly stirrings and worldly desires and allows no such spots to remain in this image" (*Scale* 2, ch 5). Reforming in feeling is a cooperative enterprise in which divine grace is primary and actuating, the human will subordinate and responsive: "God . . . does all. He forms and reforms: He forms by himself alone, but he reforms us with us; for all this is done by the giving of grace, and by applying our will to grace. And the way in which he does that is stated by Saint Paul: *Quos Deus praescivit fieri conformes imaginis Filii eius, hos vocavit: et quos vocavit, hos justificavit; et quos justificavit, hos magnificavit; et quos magnificavit, hos et glorificavit.* These that God knew before, that were to be made to conform to the image of his Son; these he called; these he corrected; these he magnified; and these he glorified" (*Scale* 2, ch 28, citing Romans 8.29, 30).

In the context of this distinction, Hilton elaborates on faith as the antithesis of feeling, performing a startling extension on the characterization of faith in Hebrews 11:1 as "the evidence of things not seen." "Just as the property of faith is to believe what you do not see, so it is to believe what you do not feel. But someone who is reformed to the image of God in his soul by the sacrament of penance feels no change taking place in himself. . . . He feels the same stirrings of sin and the same corruption of his flesh in passions and worldly desires rising in his heart, as he did before; yet he is nonetheless to believe that through grace he is reformed to the likeness of God, even though he may neither feel it nor see it" (*Scale* 2, ch 8). The sinner's redemption by virtue of the sacrament—penance in this quotation, but baptism later in the passage—figures here as involuntary, mechanical, and thus, for Hilton, as a distinctly subordinate spiritual modality. Yet he defends reforming by faith as all that many ordinary Christians can ever attain; heaven would be too empty of souls without it (*Scale* 2, ch 10). In a very interesting passage he also lays out his scriptural warrant for his understanding: "Saint Paul speaks thus about this reforming in faith: *Justus ex fide vivit.* The righteous man lives in faith. That is, someone who is made righteous by baptism or penance lives in faith, which is sufficient for salvation and for heavenly peace, as Saint Paul says: *Justificati ex fide pacem habeamus ad Deum.* That is, we who are justified and reformed through faith in Christ have peace and accord made between God and ourselves, notwithstanding the vicious feelings of our body of sin" (*Scale* 2, ch 9, citing Hebrews 10.38 and Romans 5.1).

Because, I think, of the explicit biblical citations that Hilton offers his readers to weigh and consider for themselves, the crucial distinction between reforming in faith and reforming in feeling underwent an active subsequent history of appropriation, splintering, and reformulation in the period that separated his work from the onset of the sixteenth-century Reformation. We find the later opponent of the Lollards, Reginald Pecock, in *The Book of Faith* (1456) distinguishing between "believing to be" (believing that someone or something merely exists) and "believing to" (believing in as authoritative). While Pecock's "believing to" corresponds quite nicely to Hilton's reforming in faith, it is indicative of the richness of Hilton's position that Pecock offers no analogue whatever for reforming in feeling. Later still, in his *Answer to Sir Thomas More's Dialogue* (1530) the Protestant activist, William Tyndale, elaborated a basic distinction between "historical faith" and "feeling faith." Historical faith appears to correlate closely with Pecock's "believing to be" (Tyndale's example is the belief that there is a city Constantinople although one has never been there) while feeling faith is an immediate experience of actuality that engages deeply with one's emotions and course of life (Constantinople as affirmed by a man who was wounded and taken prisoner while risking his life in its defense). Although it is hard to be sure about correspondences in meaning where definition by illustration is involved, Tyndale's feeling faith seems to share important features with Hilton's reforming in feeling. Yet by this date the Catholic defender, Thomas More, was content to disparage and implicitly dismiss this distinction in his *Confutation of Tyndale's Answer* (1533) by claiming that Tyndale cribbed it from Luther's associate, Melanchthon. More was unquestionably correct, nevertheless, in his larger implication that faith redefined in feeling—even redefined as feeling— had been affirmed by Luther as the crucial experience of a Christian.

A century and a quarter after Hilton wrote his *Scale of Perfection*, another Augustinian monk, Martin Luther, confronted Hilton's central question of the reforming of the human soul and searched his scripture. In the autobiographical rehearsal at the end of the preface to Luther's Latin works (1545) that has become well known as the "tower experience," Luther cited as warrant for his apprehension of justifying faith the same two texts—Hebrew 10.38 and Romans 5.1—that Hilton cited to define his reforming in faith. Yet the two men meant obviously different things by faith. Luther was persuaded, and he has persuaded many others, that he retrieved the apostle Paul's meaning, but we owe to Krister Stendahl a brilliant and sensitive caution on the historical difficulties with taking Luther's claim at face value.[1] The note on which I wish to end this preface is different from Stendahl's, but not in opposition to it. When we consider Hilton on reforming in faith and reforming in feeling, his biblical citations point for us the direction of his attempt to delineate a spectrum of reforming in Christlikeness which will be inclusive for life in this world—from a minimum of embracing the means of salvation offered in the church to a maximum of the advanced moral and spiritual state that English Puritans would still later distinguish and greatly emphasize as "sanctification." In doing so, the Puritans, like Hilton, built on Paul in Romans 8.29–30 as their warrant while translating differently from Hilton (who instead of "sanctified" reads "magnified" following the Vulgate).

Still practicing our historical hindsight, we now can see where Luther intervenes upon this spectrum: somewhere between reforming in faith and reforming in feeling as characterized by Hilton. No whit less a student of Paul than Hilton, Luther insisted, moreover, on the necessity of a conversion experience modeled on the apostle's own—the visionary encounter with Christ on the Damascus road. Is a conversion experience both paradigmatic and obligatory for a Christian? Edmund S. Morgan has given us an engrossing account of how early eighteenth-century Connecticut Valley congregations found their way from a "yes" to a "not necessarily" answer in response to this question and their concern with the intergenerational perpetuation of their churches.[2] Like Hilton, these congregations came to an emphasis on baptism when they thought about an entry point on the spectrum of Christlikeness.

What I would like to stress, however, is that Hilton's spectrum from faith to feeling accommodates both positions on conversion experience—Luther's and the position contradictory to his. Here, then, is a large and compelling instance of the positionality that makes the author of *The Scale of Perfection* so suggestive for concerns of contemporary ecumenism. It is surely going too far to claim that there would have been less perceived impetus toward the sixteenth-century Reformation if *The Reforming of Man's Soul*—to use, now, this alternative title for Hilton's work—had been more widely read and more deeply assimilated. But I think that if the century following his had produced better students of Hilton, the Reformation would have had far less occasion for divisiveness and rupture on the issues of the rival authority of scripture and the church as well as the interpretation of "reforming," "feeling," and "faith." The study of Hilton, fortunately, remains an open opportunity to this day. I am happy to herald what will be for its readers the welcome arrival of a new translation of the *Scale* by John Clark and Rosemary Dorward.

Notes

1. Krister Stendahl, "The Apostle Paul and the Introspective Conscience of the West," *Harvard Theological Review* 56 (1963): 199–215.
2. Edmund S. Morgan, *Visible Saints: The History of a Puritan Idea* (New York, 1963).

Introduction

Walter Hilton: His Life and Writings

It has long been known that Walter Hilton, author of *The Scale of Perfection*, died as a Canon of the Augustinian Priory of Thurgarton, between Nottingham and Newark, on the Eve of the Annunciation to our Lady (March 24) 1396.[1] Research over the last fifty years[2] has illuminated something of his earlier career—an unusual one.

There is a manuscript tradition that Hilton was an Inceptor in Canon Law, that is, one who (like the *Venerabilis Inceptor* William of Ockham in the discipline of theology) had qualified for the doctorate but had not actually taken it.[3] Hilton's legal background is confirmed by a reference in a Latin letter, where he alludes to what had once been a promising legal career.[4] In such a renunciation there is a certain parallel with William Flete, the Cambridge Austin Friar and Bachelor of Divinity who in 1359 left the University behind and began a new life overseas at the hermitage of Lecetto in Italy, where he became one of the group closely associated with Catherine of Siena, William Flete's book, *Remedies Against Temptations* (*De Remediis contra Tentationes*) exists in various versions and has been translated from Latin into English; it was familiar to Hilton, but whether Hilton knew the identity of the author and his story is not clear, since the memory of Flete's authorship was in time lost and only one extant manuscript of the book bears Flete's name.[5]

Short of absolute proof, there is very strong presumptive evidence that Hilton himself was educated at Cambridge University. A Walter de

Hilton, Bachelor of Civil Law, clerk of Lincoln diocese, was granted the reservation of a canonry and prebend of Abergwili, Carmarthen, in January 1371. There is a reference to Walter Hilton, still a Bachelor of Civil Law rather than of Canon Law—the study of civil law preceded that of canon law—who was present at the Ely Consistory Court in 1375. If this was our Walter Hilton, then in order to have studied arts and then civil law, and graduated B.C.L. by 1370, he must have come up to Cambridge by 1357; since fourteen years was the minimum age for entry, he can hardly have been born later than 1343.[6]

Where was he born and brought up? Carthusian James Grenehalgh (d. 1529/30), a devoted student and annotator of Hilton's *Scale*, of *The Cloud of Unknowing* and of other contemplative writings, and himself a Lancastrian, refers to Hilton as coming "from the same region," and there is indeed a Hulton (formerly Hilton) in the Salford hundred of Lancashire. But Grenehalgh wrote long after the event, and for all his importance and interest in the history of the English spiritual tracts, he is not an infallible guide, as his ascription of the *Cloud* to Hilton shows.[7] Among the many other places called Hilton, there is one in the archdeaconry of Huntingdon and another seven miles southwest of Derby. One of Hilton's correspondents, to whom Hilton addressed the letter *On the Usefulness and Prerogatives of Religion* (*De Utilitate et Prerogativis Religionis*) was Adam Horsley, who very possibly took his name from the Horsley in Derbyshire. Adam Horsley became a Carthusian monk of Beauvale Priory, within striking distance of the Community at Thurgarton where Hilton found his home. If Walter and Adam had originated from the same part of the country, this would account in part for their association, but Adam Horsley was only one of Hilton's many associates, and we are in the realms of conjecture.

None of Hilton's writings is extant in autograph, and medieval copyists often applied their own dialect, so the linguistic evidence of the English manuscripts remains inconclusive. The language of the best manuscripts does suggest their origin in the Northeast Midlands,[8] but perhaps this is simply what we might expect in view of Hilton's residence at Thurgarton in the later part of his life.

If Hilton was still Bachelor of Civil Law in 1375, but was then appearing in an ecclesiastical court rather than a civil one, he had presumably gone on to the study of canon law in the meantime. He could have been Bachelor of Canon Law in 1376 and ready to incept as Master or Doctor of Canon Law in 1381/2. In a recent study various links have been adduced between Hilton and a circle of northern clerks who were retained by Thomas Arundel (Bishop of Ely, 1374–88) in his administration at Ely, and who were given preferment at Peterhouse, a college with a strong bias towards Hilton's own subject of canon law. Just as Arundel and his clerks at Cambridge and Ely were active in the orthodox response to incipient Lollardy, so after Arundel's translation to York in 1388 Hilton and others were to become instrumental in carrying out his policy of imposing rule and structure upon a piety that was deeply influenced by the eremitical movement of which Richard Rolle was an outstanding example, but where "liberty of spirit" seemed to open the way to unruliness.[9] Thurgarton Priory, where Hilton was to spend his latter years, was in the York diocese in the fourteenth century. Within that diocese Arundel's policy of pastoral education was to mark the continuation and strengthening of a process already clearly discernible during the episcopate of John Thoresby (1353–73).

Perhaps after abandoning academic life Hilton continued to practice law while reflecting on his future. It has been suggested that he was at Cambridge until about 1384,[10] but he could well have left the university and city before then.

What seems to be his earliest extant work is the Latin letter *On the Image of Sin* (*De Imagine Peccati*). This is addressed to a solitary. Hilton remarks that at the time of writing he too is a solitary and expresses some dissatisfaction with his state; he feels that he has renounced the world, but is being of little practical service to God and to the church.[11]

His letter to Adam Horsley, *On the Usefulness and Prerogatives of Religion* (*De Utilitate et Prerogativis Religionis*), provides a next vital clue. Horsley was an official of the Exchequer in the King's service—in 1375 he was appointed Controller of the Great Roll—who eventually entered the Community of Beauvale in 1386.[12] This letter is intended not only to encourage Adam in his purpose but also to give a reasoned and carefully laid-out (if at times somewhat truculent) defense of the vowed religious life in community in the face of contemporary controversies (among the opinions distilled from Wyclif's writings and condemned at the famous Blackfriars Synod held in London in 1382 had been "that the religious living in private religions are not of the Christian faith"[13]).

In this letter Hilton says that he is himself open to the possibility of joining a religious community, but is not yet certain of his vocation.[14] We do not know whether Horsley's difficulties were resolved before Hilton's, but it is reasonable to suppose that Hilton was at any rate not far behind Horsley in joining a community, and to suggest 1386 as the date of his entry into Thurgarton Priory.

It is significant that Hilton chose to join the Augustinian Canons rather than a Charterhouse. While his writings came to be highly regarded by the Carthusian Order (MS Harley 6579—the manuscript that has caused such problems to editors of the *Scale*, Book 1, was a "working copy" belonging to the London Charterhouse), his own spirit found its fulfilment in the very different regime of an order that stood for a "mixed life."[15] This accords with the range of his sympathies in his writings, in partial contrast to the author of the *Cloud*.[16]

There is still incomplete agreement on the canon of Hilton's writings; more will be said of this later. But is has been persuasively argued that he engaged in the religious controversies of his day, not only in defense of the religious life, but also in defense of the veneration of images. In the course of the 1380s this too was a matter of dispute, and the call for destruction of religious images became a Lollard characteristic.[17] *Conclusiones de Imaginibus* (*Conclusions Concerning Images*) is attributed in one manuscript to Hilton, and the present writer believes that the attribution may be supported on internal evidence.[18] In 1388 the Prior of the Augustinian house at Thurgarton was authorized, with others, to arrest, examine and imprison heretics.[19] Assuming that Hilton was now a member of the community, it is understandable that his expertise should have been used in the orthodox cause.

It could well be during the early years at Thurgarton that Hilton wrote another letter, *Epistola de Lectione, Intentione, Oratione, Meditatione, etc.* (*On Reading, Intention, Prayer, Meditation, etc.*) The letter implies that he was now an established spiritual guide, and concerned once more to uphold the orthodox faith and practice of the church in the face of singularity and a purported "liberty of spirit," which sat lightly by the common prayers of the church for the sake of a "higher" illumination.[20] Whether the English tract *Of Angels' Song* should be placed at this point or a few years later in Hilton's life is not absolutely clear; the teaching of this tract, together with elements from *De Imagine Peccati*, *Epistola de Utilitate* and *Epistola de Lectione*, is all matched within the broader and more systematic framework of *The Scale of Perfection*, Book 1. But there are also some elements in *Of Angels' Song* that accord rather with points made in *The Scale of Perfection*, Book 2,[21] so the matter should perhaps be left open.

Complementary at many points to *Scale* 1, and no doubt written at about the same time, is the little tract *Mixed Life*. It has been argued that Hilton also made the English version (*The Pricking of Love*) of the popular *Stimulus Amoris* (a much expanded form of a book of that name by the thirteenth-century Franciscan James of Milan, which had come by this time to pass under the name of Bonaventure). The Hilton attribution is not certain, though J. P. H. Clark believes that from the evidence of the theological modifications as well as the style it may be upheld.[22] If Hilton did make this translation, this too would seem to date from his early years at Thurgarton.

Three, or perhaps four, other writings of Hilton should be placed intermediately between *Scale* 1 and *Scale* 2, taking it that the latter was written some time after *Scale* 1, at the end of Hilton's life.

The Latin *Letter to Someone Wanting to Renounce the World* (*Epistola ad Quemdam Seculo renuntiare Volentem*) is written to a lawyer who has experienced a religious awakening, apparently following imprisonment, after a career of worldliness and search for self-advancement. The purpose of the letter is to reassure him on certain points concerning which he has scruples, while dissuading him from entering the religious life for which he is unfitted.[23] Closely related in subject matter, though not, apparently, written to the same man, is a little piece beginning *Firmissime crede*, perhaps a fragment from something bigger.[24]

Reference has been made to the claim that Hilton translated one Franciscan work. If there are some doubts about his responsibility for the English *The Prickynge of Love*, there are none as to his authorship of the English version of *Eight Chapters on Perfection*. The eight chapters were "found" in the book of Master Luis de Fontibus at Cambridge; presumably they are part of something bigger, but we do not possess the original. Luis de Fontibus, an Aragonese Franciscan, was sent to read the *Sentences* of Peter Lombard at Cambridge in 1383; if his academic career followed the normal prescribed course, his regency as Master or Doctor in Theology at the University may be dated 1391–93 or 1392–94. The colophon in the manuscripts of Hilton's English version of his writing refers to him as Master, so the implication is that the book was passed on to Hilton after Luis had left Cambridge, that is, not before 1393, assuming that Luis completed the full customary two years of his regency. Such a date would accord with the similarities found at some points between *Eight Chapters* and *Scale* 2 (as distinct from *Scale* 1).[25] The matter illustrates how, long after he had left the university, Hilton was still in touch with people there. A further pointer to his continuing links with those who had been his contemporaries, or near contemporaries, at Cambridge will be adduced later.

An English commentary on Psalm 90, *Qui Habitat*, is unascribed in the manuscripts but appears in close association with established works of Hilton and has particularly close links, again, with some of the distinctive subject matter of *Scale* 2. In the opinion of J. P. H. Clark, it should almost certainly be ascribed to Hilton, and to the last phase of his life.[26]

A lost letter of Hilton's, apparently to a Gilbertine nun, is known only from a commentary upon it.[27] A few other works have been tentatively assigned to him by some modern editors. A commentary on Psalm 91, *Bonum Est*, associated with *Qui Habitat* in some manuscripts, is in Clark's opinion unlikely to be his. It is built around Peter Lombard's *Gloss* on the psalm, and has none of Hilton's distinctive marks. Likewise the English commentary on the *Benedictus* is of indeterminate authorship and has no firm ties with Hilton.[28]

One fifteenth-century manuscript ascribes the "drawing" or translation of William Flete's *De Remediis*—in one of its various English versions—to Hilton, but there is nothing in the style or specific theological presentation to support this. In fact, this English version was made from a Latin text of the same family as a Bodleian manuscript, which ascribes the Latin original to Hilton—a recognition of the affinity between Hilton's and Flete's work, when the memory of Flete himself had faded.[29] The Carthusian James Grenehalgh, and even some modern scholars, have pleaded for Hilton's authorship of *The Cloud of Unknowing*,[30] but for all the undoubted points of similarity and—it will be argued—even of contact, this attribution is to be rejected on theological grounds.[31]

The two books of the *Scale* won the accolade of being translated into Latin, probably by 1400 and possibly in Hilton's lifetime, although there are grounds to believe that Hilton himself did not check the translation.[32] The Latin version is of interest, not only because it provides a check for the difficult textual tradition of *Scale* 1, but also because in *Scale* 2, chapters 20 to the end intensify further the Christocentric—and indeed Trinitarian—bias already present in that part of the English text, reusing and developing phrases lifted from other parts of the *Scale*.[33]

The translation is also of interest for the further light that it throws upon Hilton's contacts and sphere of influence. The translator, Thomas Fishlake, was a Carmelite, and Bachelor of Divinity at Cambridge in about 1375.[34] One copy of the translation, now in the Chapter Library at York Minster, was written for John Pole, another Carmelite who had studied at Cambridge, and who was Master of Theology there in 1381.[35] It is commonplace to point out the esteem in which Hilton was held by the Carthusians. It is worth noting also that he was well-regarded by the

Carmelites, including some who must have known him at Cambridge. The mendicants, and the Carmelites in particular, became firm opponents of Wyclif and his followers,[36] and Hilton's alignment with the orthodox party on such matters as the religious life and the sacraments commended him to the Carmelites too.

The Scale of Perfection in its relation to Hilton's other Writings

The name *Scale of Perfection* is editorial; half the manuscripts containing *Scale* I have this title, in Latin (*Scala Perfectionis*) or in English, and it is from this point that it has been passed on to the two books taken together.[37] But there are other titles too, for instance, *De Vita Contemplativa* (British Library Add, MS 11748) and *The Reformyng of Mannys Soule* (British Library, MS Harley 2397). Some of the earliest and best manuscripts—including Cambridge University Library Add, MS 6686 containing *Scale* I, and York Minster Chapter Library MS XVI K 5, containing Thomas Fishlake's Latin translation of both books—give no title.

In fact, the two books are a diptych. *Book 1* is addressed in the first instance to an anchoress, though whether she is a real or a notional figure is unclear; at the end of the book Hilton says that his words are intended for her or anyone else who is vowed to the contemplative life.[38] Hilton's *Scale* I is one of a whole genre of books addressed to anchoresses; among other works so addressed in England are St. Ailred's *De Vita Inclusarum*, *Ancrene Wisse*, and Richard Rolle's *The Form of Living*.

As already indicated, an interval of some little time must be allowed between the completion of the two books. *Book 2* refers to a request to learn more about the "image" that has been described earlier.[39] This might just conceivably be taken to refer to the "image of sin" of *De Imagine Peccati*, but is more likely to refer to *Scale* I, since both books are written in English and there is a very real continuity of subject-matter between the two. Time and again, *Scale* 2 takes up a point made in *Scale* I, developing at a deeper level the teaching given in the earlier book.

As to whether *Scale* 2 is addressed to the same individual as *Scale* I, this raises again the question of whether the addressee is a distinct person or a convenient literary fiction representing a whole class of reader. What is significant is the shift of emphasis between the two books; *Scale* I envisages the contemplative life as the preserve, in principle, of those vowed to the contemplative religious state, while *Scale* 2 sees "contemplation," or (as it is there called) "reforming in feeling," as something to which every Christian should aspire, whatever his or her state in life. This is part of a shift in the understanding of what actually constitutes "contemplation."

Closely related to *Scale* 1 is the little tract *Mixed Life*. While *Scale* 1 is addressed to an anchoress and deals with the means to be used by vowed religious in aspiring toward contemplation, *Mixed Life* is addressed to a wealthy layman with family, tenants and dependents, who has received the call to "devotion." Once again, it is not clear whether the recipient is a particular individual, or whether he is a notional figure intended to represent a whole class of reader. An introductory chapter is present in some manuscripts and absent in others (as is the conclusion). It was at one point suggested that the introduction was added after a letter originally addressed to a particular individual was then made available for more general circulation; the recent editor has argued that the introduction was always part of the tract, and that its omission in some manuscripts is fortuitous; perhaps the last word on this has yet to be said.[40] It is in any case clear that *Mixed Life* is conceived as complementary to *Scale* 1 and must have been completed at about the same time; there are many similarities in both subject matter and expression. But whereas *Scale* 1 sees contemplation as the supreme goal, *Mixed Life* is concerned to dissuade the reader from trying to ape the life of a vowed religious; he should use the religious exercises appropriate to his state and commitments, and hold a balance between the direct service of God in himself and the practical service of God in responding to the needs of others, even though this may mean that the contemplative element in his "mixed life" is less purely spiritual than that of a vowed religious.

Both books of the *Scale* take up within their more systematic frameworks points which have been handled elsewhere in response to particular needs. *Scale* 1 includes matter from *De Imagine Peccati, Epistola de Utilitate et Prerogativis Religionis*, and *Epistola de Lectione*; it also includes material that is closely matched in *Of Angels' Song*, although, as noted, the chronology of this last is not absolutely clear.

There are also some few points of similarity between *Scale* 1 and *The Prickynge of Love*—assuming the latter to be Hilton's[41]—and *Conclusiones de Imaginibus* has some points of similarity with both *Scale* 1 and *Scale* 2,[42] but neither of these works is a specifying influence in either part of the *Scale*. *Scale* 2 not only develops further points made in *Scale* 1, but includes material (on sacramental confession and absolution) from *Epistola ad Quemdam Saeculo Renunciare Volentem*. In chapters 20 to the end it also has a number of points of contact with *Eight Chapters*, and especially with *Qui Habitat*.

Sources

While the intellectual crosscurrents of the day bring some aspects of Hilton's theology into sharper relief, and a better knowledge especially of the theology centered on Cambridge University would be rewarding and helpful, it is above all to the mainstream of ascetic and spiritual theology as represented through the monastic tradition that he is indebted. Sometimes Hilton names his sources in order to underline a point. But time and again an expression or illustration that strikes the reader with conciseness and force can be shown, on closer examination, to be derived from a traditional source. Hilton felt no need, as modern writers do, to name his sources on every occasion when he used them; he assumed that his readers would pick up his allusions.

Both *The Cloud of Unknowing* and Julian of Norwich are full of biblical allusions even where they do not quote scripture verbatim. Hilton's writing is more obviously and expressly biblical. In his English writings he quotes the Latin text first—sometimes rather loosely—then gives an English paraphrase or translation. Very often the English goes beyond the strict meaning of the text to emphasise a particular point he is making in line with his characteristic theology.[43]

To attempt an exhaustive analysis of Hilton's sources would go far beyond the scope of this introduction.[44] However, the most important influences among ecclesiastical writers may be indicated. It is not always clear how far Hilton had read these authors *in extenso*, and how much he is simply drawing on extracts from *florilegia* or indicated by liturgical readings in service-books or picking up references suggested by such text-books as the *Sentences* of Peter Lombard or the *Decretum* of Gratian. As a canon lawyer, he would have been familiar with the latter, as well as with the standard books on theology proper, which he came to study.

Echoes of John Cassian[45] and of the *Vitae Patrum*[46] can come as no surprise. It is overwhelmingly the three Latin doctors of Abbot Cuthbert Butler's *Western Mysticism*[47]—Augustine, Gregory the Great and

Bernard—whom Hilton explicitly invokes, and on whom he constantly draws even when he does not name them. The evidence of their influence in the *Scale* and in *Mixed Life* is equalled in the Latin letters.

The area of Augustine's writing is so vast, and his influence so pervasive, that simply to list borrowings from him would be wearisome; some indication of Hilton's debt to him may be gathered from the footnotes. But perhaps particular emphasis should be laid on his great *De Trinitate,* in which the doctrine of the Trinity is integrated with the whole theological perspective of creation and redemption. Again and again Hilton recalls points found in this book. Gregory the Great, above all a pastor rather than a speculative theologian, popularized many elements derived from Augustine's theology. Among his writings, the *Homilies on Ezekiel,* the *Moralia on Job* and the *Pastoral Rule,* were constant resource books for medieval churchmen, and certainly for Hilton.

In the Latin *Epistola de Utilitate,* Hilton names Gregory as an authority on the religious life, together with Anselm, Bernard, Hugh of St. Victor, and especially (*specialiter*) St. Thomas Aquinas.[48] Though Anselm is named only on this occasion, his influence is considerable, not least (in conjunction with Augustine) for Hilton's emphasis on "understanding" as the outcome of faith and of the recovery of purity of heart.[49]

Hilton is by no means alone in his immense debt, direct and indirect, to the religious movements of the twelfth century.[50] The writers of this century, with their emphasis upon the psychology of the religious life in conjunction with the renewal of the *imago Dei* in humanity, upon the importance of interior intention, liberty of choice, self-knowledge and love, give a fresh direction, a fresh nuance, to Christian spirituality in the West. Emphasis on individual religious experience becomes increasingly bound up with an imaginative, loving and emotional attention to the details of Christ's human life, and as an extension of this, to the life of Mary. At a more popular level, such a tendency in time crystallized in such devotions as the Rosary and the Stations of the Cross. Julian of Norwich distilled profound theological reflection from vivid consideration of the physical appearance of Jesus and Mary, obviously inspired in part by the religious art of her day. In the twelfth century, and in such fourteenth-century writers as Hilton and Julian, such motifs are still profoundly integrated in the corporate and sacramental life of the church. We shall see that Hilton, for all his emphasis on devotion to Christ's humanity, is chary of undue exuberance in devotion, and does

his best to curb undue attachment to religious sensation. The reverberations of the movement focussed in the twelfth century carried beyond
the Middle Ages, and such diverse figures as Martin Luther and St.
Ignatius Loyola drew inspiration from Bernard.

Bernard's influence is pervasive throughout Hilton's writings. In
particular, the debt to him is explicit when Hilton deals with the "carnal" and "spiritual" love of Christ.[51] Hilton knows something of Bernard's *De Gradibus Humilitatis.*[52] Bernard's *Sermons on the Song of Songs*,
together with *De Diligendo Deo*, contribute something to Hilton's appre-
ciation of true liberty of spirit within contemplation.[53] Bernard is particularly influential for Hilton's view of "fluctuation" within contemplation
—of progress toward an ever closer union with God, which can never
be fully and finally realized on earth.[54] He is also named as an authority,
together with Richard of St. Victor, in *Epistola de Lectione*, where Hilton is dealing with the distinction between truth and deception in religious experience.[55]

In Hilton's day the *Epistola ad Fratres de Monte Dei*, by the Cistercian William of St. Thierry, commonly passed under the name of St.
Bernard.[56] This too is a pervasive influence, not least for Hilton's close
integration in *Scale* 2 of the theology of contemplation with that of the
Trinity and of grace, and for his understanding of true freedom in conformity to the Holy Spirit. A further important Cistercian source (un-
named by Hilton) is the continuation by Gilbert of Hoyland of St. Bernard's exposition of *The Song of Songs.*[57] There is no clear indication of
direct dependence on Ailred of Rievaulx, important as the latter was for
the background especially of Northern English monastic spirituality.
Some echo of Hugh of St. Victor's *De Arca Noe Morali* will be noted in
Scale 1,[58] and some commonplaces are derived from Richard of St. Victor,[59] though it would be too much to say that he is a specifying influence. Hilton seems, like the author of the *Cloud*, to have known the
Carthusian Guigo II's *Scala Claustralium.*[60] Actually, in the Middle Ages
this little book was much more commonly ascribed to Bernard, Augustine or others.[61]

Reference has been made to Hilton's appeal to St. Thomas. A number of the arguments in *Epistola de Utilitate* are in line with St.
Thomas;[62] so—assuming it to be Hilton's—are some of those in *Conclusiones de Imaginibus.*[63] On another matter where Hilton stands close to
the Angelic Doctor—on the theology of grace, and the careful distinction between the modes of its operation[64]—there is of course no reason
why he should not have read St. Thomas firsthand. It is also possible that

the precisions in *Scale* 2, reflecting these distinctions, may have been worked out partly with the help of the *Cloud* or even through discussion with its author. More will be said on this point.

It must be borne in mind that in the fourteenth century the theology of St. Thomas was only one element, albeit an important one, in the material available to theologians. On some points the varying strands of Franciscan theology might prevail, whether the conservative Augustinianism associated with Alexander of Hales and Bonaventure or the more recent perspectives opened up by Duns Scotus and even by Ockham. It is worth noting that Hilton's theology of sacramental absolution is in line with the older tradition upheld by many of the Franciscans in contrast to St. Thomas.[65]

If Hilton's authorship of the English version of the *Stimulus Amoris* is allowed, then this very popular work must be taken into account in searching for the sources of the *Scale*. The occasional similarity may be noted,[66] though how far these are specific and how far they are commonplace may be debated.

There are some convergences, at least, with points made in the influential thirteenth-century manual of moral teaching, the *Somme le Roy*, of which a number of medieval English translations exist, though it is not clear whether Hilton is directly using this book.[67]

Hilton criticizes some aspects of Rolle.[68] He must have known some of Rolle's writing firsthand. While it is the ebullience of the younger Rolle he implicitly questions—an ebullience Rolle never entirely lost, though it became tempered in his maturity—there is much in Rolle's later writing, for instance in *The Form of Living*, that stands close to Hilton.[69] *De Remediis contra Tentationes* by the Austin Friar William Flete has a widespread influence in many of Hilton's works, and is an important contributor toward his handling of spiritual aridity.[70]

Finally, there is the problem of the relationship between Hilton and *The Cloud of Unknowing*—with the latter's attendant corpus, including the very important *Book of Privy Counselling*. The *Cloud*, and Hilton, cover the same ground at very many points, allowing for the deliberately restricted concentration of the *Cloud* on the proximate approach to contemplation, by comparison with Hilton's more widespread interests. There is, for instance, the same concern for the twin virtues of humility and charity with their "inclusive" and mutually dependent role, so that together these two virtues are seen as the best means of breaking down sin and conforming the soul to God, implying as they do the whole Christian moral life.[71] There is the same distinction (common to the

Cloud and *Scale* 2) between "imperfect" and "perfect" humility;[72] the same criticism of attachment to sensible "heat, sweetness and song";[73] the same distinction between the working of grace in its "co-operant" and its "operant" mode.[74]

At the same time there is a profound difference between Hilton and the *Cloud*. In *Scale* 2 Hilton refers to the "luminous darkness"—the expression derived from Pseudo-Dionysius, the fifth-century Syrian monk to whose writings in Latin dress the *Cloud*'s author had so great an attachment. But, as we shall see, Hilton applies the expression in a very different way from that of the *Cloud*'s author.[75] Thus he implicitly by-passes a vital area of the *Cloud*'s theology, even while indicating his awareness of it.

All this becomes explicable if we suppose that there was some degree of interchange, and of mutual criticism and enlightenment, between Hilton and the author of the *Cloud*. The *Cloud* refers at three points to "another man's work": the first, on reading, meditation and prayer as means to contemplation; the second, on the discernment of good and evil in regard to sensory religious experience; the third (in a spirit of mild criticism) to argue against possible misunderstanding of the language of recollection and introversion, as if this implied that God was in some way to be "localized."[76] All these points touch on matter which may be found in *Scale* 1.[77] It is true that the same material, or material very closely related, is found in Hilton's *Epistola de Lectione*,[78] but this was a *letter* written to a particular man for a particular need—and in Latin—rather than a *book* written in English, as the *Cloud* is written in English. So we should suppose that if it is a writing of Hilton's that is meant, it is the English book rather than the Latin letter. There does not seem to be any other book extant which deals with all three points. It is true that the references need not be all to the same book, but the coincidence of all three points in *Scale* 1 remains highly suggestive.

The earliest extant manuscripts of the *Cloud* corpus, belonging to the early fifteenth century, are in a North-East Midland dialect,[79] indicating that at this time the texts were circulating in the very area where Hilton ended his days. James Walsh, in his translation of the *Cloud*, explored the possibility that the author may have been a Carthusian of Beauvale.[80] Hilton's link with Adam Horsley provides one point of contact between himself and Beauvale. If the *Cloud*'s author were indeed a Beauvale Carthusian, this would be a point from where he and Hilton could have been in touch.

While there is much in common between *Scale* 1 and the *Cloud*, the more "advanced" teaching of the *Cloud*—for instance, on imperfect and perfect humility, and on "operant" grace—is matched only in *Scale* 2. If we do assume some kind of interchange between Hilton and the *Cloud*'s author, it is hard to believe that Hilton would have omitted some reference to this teaching in his preview of the "third part of contemplation" in *Scale* 1, if it had been available to him. The suggestion is that *Scale* 1 was written before the *Cloud*, and that the latter takes up some of the points made in *Scale* 1. In turn, it may be suggested that *Scale* 2 is influenced by the *Cloud* and is in some measure a response to criticisms of Hilton's earlier book made by the *Cloud*'s author, for instance, in that section of *Scale* 2 where Hilton gives a careful explanation of what is meant by the statement that God, or Christ, is "within" or "above" the soul.[81] In turn, Hilton takes over the Dionysian expression "luminous darkness," but uses it for his own purpose.

This last point indicates that criticism and enrichment was not a one-way process, but—assuming that there was interchange between the two authors—was mutual: Hilton may have helped the *Cloud*'s author too. *The Book of Privy Counselling* is apparently designed as a sequel to the *Cloud*,[82] to clarify points made earlier and perhaps to meet objections that had been made. It emphasizes strongly what the *Cloud* largely, though not entirely, takes for granted: The only way to that union with God in Christ where distinct and consciously meditated images are left behind is through a previous habit of meditation on the humanity of Christ and on the Passion and through conformity to the human life of Christ. In making this point forcefully *The Book of Privy Counselling* echoes the saying of Christ that he is the "door" (John 10.9, with 10.1), in terms that stand close to Hilton in *Scale* 2, and, indeed, in part in *Scale* 1.[83] Likewise, *The Book of Privy Counselling* cites Augustine on the withdrawal of Christ's bodily form, in order that the love of his divinity may grow in us, recalling John 16.7, *Expedit vobis ut ego vadam* ("It is expedient for you that I go away").[84] This is one of the passages in Augustine which anticipate in some measure the more developed teaching of St. Bernard on the transition from the "carnal" to the "spiritual" love of God in Christ, teaching with which Hilton was so familiar.[85] Hilton, and no doubt his contemporaries, were well able to go behind Bernard to Augustine in this area.[86] The more explicitly Christocentric emphasis of *The Book of Privy Counselling*, by comparison with the *Cloud*, could well have been intended to meet the criticisms which Hilton might have made of the earlier book.

Again, though here we are on progressively speculative ground, it is possible that Hilton may have felt the need to counterbalance the "Dionysian" and "theocentric" emphasis of the *Cloud* by a deepened Christocentric emphasis of his own. There is no point, indeed, when he is not Christocentric, but *Scale* 2, chapters 20 to the end in particular, is full of references to "Jesus." These chapters are, of course, not only Christocentric; they become more and more explicitly Trinitarian also. But the point is worth considering.

Hilton in His Setting

The fourteenth century saw a flowering of vernacular religious writing, not only in England but also in Germany and the Low Countries, in which elements derived from the monastic tradition were fused with the theology of the schools. To appreciate the writing of Hilton or of the *Cloud* author—to say nothing of the writings of Ruysbroeck or the sermons of Eckhart and Tauler—it is necessary to feel some sympathy with the theological world in which they moved and to have some understanding of its long traditions. In the Middle Ages, Latin terminology was deployed with considerable precision to express abstract as well as concrete ideas; words or phrases from the Latin Bible and the Church Fathers colored men's thinking and form of expression in much the same way as the King James version of the English Bible for so long permeated English culture. No small part of the achievement of the English contemplative writers, as well as of those on the Continent, was to evolve exact and clear expressions to convey the precisions of Latin theology in the vernacular.

English contemplative writers of this period saw themselves as a part of an international church, and also as heirs to a long tradition of writing of which the greater part, including most of that in their own country, was in Latin. Among the medievals, Anselm, Bernard and St. Thomas Aquinas were theologians of international standing, but the English religious tradition includes as equals such figures as Gilbert of Hoyland and Ailred of Rievaulx among the writers on monastic themes, and it gave to the international church Duns Scotus and William of Ockham among the scholastics.

The fourteenth century also saw change and unrest in both the political and the intellectual or spiritual spheres: The Black Death ravaged the population of Europe; the Hundred Years' War between England and France dragged on, a source of strain and weakness to both sides; in England itself social unrest culminated in the Peasants' Revolt of 1381; and the spiritual unity of Western Christendom was fractured by the Avignon Schism.

In the area of academic theology the synthesis of reason and faith, which had seemed possible in the thirteenth century, when the foundations laid by reason were apparently ready to underpin a structure of supernatural faith and life, had been broken apart. In contrast to the perspective of St. Thomas, Neo-Augustinian theologians of the early fourteenth century, among them Duns Scotus and Ockham, held that theology could not be considered a science in the sense of knowledge derived from self-evident first principles, since it depended on specifically Christian faith. Theologically, truths that could be conceived naturally, such as God's existence, were held to be inevident to humanity in its actual (fallen) condition, while those that were beyond rational comprehension, such as the Trinity and the Incarnation, could not even be conceived naturally. The function of reason came to be seen as the elucidation of revealed truths, rather than as providing a natural theology in the thirteenth-century sense of finding natural arguments for revealed truths.[87] In such an intellectual climate, it would not be surprising if some were to turn to a more experiential and less dialectical quest for Christian truth. It is perhaps no coincidence that the last great flowering of the traditional monastic wisdom in conjunction with the resonances of high scholasticism came in the century where the intellectual edifice of medieval theology was coming to be dissected.

The contemplative life stands for "liberty of spirit" in the sense of which Christ speaks when he refers to his easy yoke (Matthew 11.29–30), or of which St. Paul speaks when he says that where the Spirit is, there is liberty (2 Cor. 3.17). Throughout the Middle Ages, within and sometimes on the fringes of the institutional church, there were movements claiming the inspiration of the Spirit, the truth or falsehood of whose claim to divine inspiration had to be tested by the fruit of the lives which they inspired. Movements toward poverty of spirit and simplicity could lead men outside the church, as in the case of the Waldensians, or, as with the Franciscans, they could become powerful forces for renewal within it.

The problematic status of movements claiming "liberty of spirit" has a long history. In particular, the movement of the "Free Spirit," which came to be associated with the Beguines and Beghards had long been a source of disquiet to the ecclesiastical authorities. The condemnation of Margaret Porete at Paris in 1310, and of a series of Beghard doctrines at the Council of Vienne in 1311–12, are incidents in a long campaign against a heresy that, in the name of perfection and contemplation, regarded the church's means of grace as superfluous. These heretics aspired to a state where God and the soul were held to be indistinguishable, where the exercise of acts of virtue was left behind, and, in the guise of love, morality—including especially sexual morality —might be abandoned.[88] The controversy surrounding Eckhart illustrates how the lines of demarcation between authentic Christian spirituality and its deviations were by no means always clear.[89] In the event, Eckhart's place as a great Catholic teacher of spiritual theology has been abundantly vindicated.

Just as in the age of the Church Fathers it was the heretical or inadequate statements of Christological or Trinitarian doctrine that evoked an orthodox reply, delivered with increased clarity, so now it was the perceived danger of perversion or heresy which evoked a clearer statement of the true theology of the spiritual life. In particular, Suso, Tauler and Ruysbroeck incorporate many elements from Eckhart's own teaching (as well as from the wisdom of the monasteries and Schools) in their theology, while taking pains both to give a definitive answer to the proponents of false "liberty of spirit" and to avoid any looseness or ambiguity of expression such as had led to Eckhart's condemnation.

Probably nothing of Eckhart and Tauler's sermons, and but little of the writing of Ruysbroeck and Suso, were known in late fourteenth-century England.[90] But there is plenty of evidence that the spread of such a movement as that of the "Free Spirit" was feared in England, and that vigorous steps were taken by the authorities to forestall it.[91] It may be suggested that some of Hilton's careful teaching on the contemplative life—more especially in *Scale* 2, though there are traces in his minor writings too—was sharpened by the perceived need to combat error and prevent any possibility of the misunderstanding of his own views.[92]

Curiously, Margaret Porete's *Mirror of Simple Souls*, with its authorship and antecedents forgotten, established itself as acceptable reading in some devout circles in England. The extant copies of the English version of this book all date from the fifteenth century, but it may very well have circulated earlier. The suspect character of some of the book's teaching could not be allowed to pass, and so the English version carries glosses by a mysterious "M.N.," whose purpose is to explain the book's teaching in an orthodox way, in terms of the normal Thomist theology of grace and the supernatural. We do not know who "M.N." was, and in the absence of clear dating it is unwise to speculate as to the exact relationship between "M.N." and Hilton's writings, but many of the corrective points made by M.N. are very close to Hilton's teaching in *Scale* 2, and, indeed, in part to that of *The Cloud of Unknowing*.[93]

The "Movement of the Free Spirit," with its affinities to Neo-Platonism, was perhaps an attitude of mind rather than in all cases a settled body of doctrine.[94] There are indications—not least in Hilton himself —of its presence in England in the late fourteenth century.[95] But other more characteristically English movements were distinctly subversive of the ecclesiastical order. Reference has been made to Wyclif's opinions—opinions expressed by an academic, but which served as fuel for a wider unrest—and to the active part Hilton took in combating Lollard views. Wyclif's challenge to Catholic polity included attacks on the sacramental system of the church, an assault on the common doctrine of the Eucharist, and on the necessity and value of sacramental confession.[96] When Hilton takes issue with the Lollards on these matters, he is defending the Eucharist as a focus of worship,[97] and sacramental confession and absolution as a powerful instrument in the process of spiritual renewal.[98]

From a twentieth-century standpoint, we tend to see the different strands in medieval thought, including the different strands in heretical thought, as distinct entities. But, in fact, the categories are not always so distinct and would not have appeared so distinct to contemporaries who saw matters from a nearer perspective. So there are some passages in Hilton where "heresy" or "liberty of spirit" (taken in a pejorative sense) seem to refer to something with Lollard characteristics, other places to something more distinctly antinomian. Those engaged in the actual situation would see one subversive tendency as opening the door to another.

We have spoken of "heresy" in some of its aspects. There were other movements which might be characterized as "enthusiastic," but were in themselves not heretical, although "enthusiasm" might on occasions become suspect and be seen as opening the way to that singularity which is one mark of the heretic.

In particular, Hilton takes issue with the kind of "enthusiasm" associated especially with the "heat, sweetness and song" of the great Yorkshire hermit Richard Rolle (d. 1349). In Hilton's day there were moves afoot for Rolle's canonization,[99] and no one would have spoken of him as a heretic. Hilton himself, when correcting a possible misunderstanding about Rolle's teaching on devotion to the Holy Name of Jesus, speaks of "sayings of certain holy men."[100] Indeed, those who would judge Rolle simply on the basis of his attachment to sensible, perceptible "heat, sweetness and song," and on the basis of some of his more intolerant remarks in *The Fire of Love* (*Incendium Amoris*) do him less than justice. It is true that Rolle set great store by perceptible feelings of warmth in the breast, quasi-physical sensations of sweetness, and perception of angelic song and visions of the citizens of heaven, and that his intolerance and over-sensitivity toward those who misunderstood him or let him down, together with his fearfulness of women, indicate a certain immaturity and insecurity. Rolle never lost his attachment to sensible feelings in religion, but the fierce misogynist became the valued spiritual director of the nuns of Hampole, and in his later writings, such as *The Mending of Life* (*Emendatio Vitae*) and *The Form of Living,* he speaks in terms that are not far from Hilton of the purifying effect of trial and suffering and the supreme value of humility and charity.[101] The *Emendatio Vitae* must have been at least as popular as the *Incendium Amoris* in the Middle Ages; there are even more manuscripts of it extant.[102]

Hilton does not at once take issue with Rolle. It has been suggested that his own decision to become a hermit for a time may have been partly inspired by Rolle's example.[103] It is when "heresy" on other fronts becomes a live issue that he refers in a warning way to attachment to sensible feelings of heat in *Epistola de Lectione.*[104] Evidently he feared that undirected "enthusiasm" and singularity might lead to actual heresy. From this point on, he steadily warns against attachment to quasi-physical sensations in religion, often linking such references with further warnings against actual heresy. In the *Scale* he carefully indicates that such phenomena are occasional gifts of God for the edification or encouragement of the recipient, but are not to be confused with the supernatural union with God, which pertains to charity and sanctifying grace, in line with the distinction St. Thomas makes between *gratia gratis data* and *gratia gratum faciens.*[105]

Hilton's academic roots in Cambridge are of interest in relation to his theology. Although his higher education was in canon law rather than in theology as such, he must have been influenced by the theological environment in which he moved. Compared with Oxford, the theology of fourteenth-century Cambridge has been little studied; its exponents were less original and idiosyncratic than Ockham, Bradwardine and Wyclif. Since some scholars studied at both universities, one must of course avoid making too facile a distinction between the two; there will have been interplay. But there are indications that Cambridge theology in the fourteenth century had some conventional and conservative strands. The *Quaestiones* of John of Walsham, a Franciscan who studied and taught at Cambridge about 1360, have been remarked as independent in their attitude from Ockham, Duns Scotus, and indeed from Bradwardine, and as standing closer to the older tradition associated with Alexander of Hales and Bonaventure.[106] Nearer to Hilton, we are fortunate in possessing one identified academic work from the Cambridge of the 1370s which has a certain personal link, if an indirect one, with Hilton himself. Thomas Maldon, a Carmelite, was Prior of the Cambridge Carmelite house from 1369–72, and his period of teaching as regent master at the university may be placed at some point in the years following this. He may well have been known to Hilton, and would certainly have been known to his slightly younger confrère Thomas Fishlake, who translated the *Scale* into Latin. Where only one of Maldon's works has been identified, it would be precarious to build too much, but it is interesting that he shows familiarity and sympathy with Anselm and Gilbert of Hoyland (two of Hilton's important sources), and that he has a rather old-fashioned Augustinian theology, combined with an orthodox Augustinian/Thomist theology of grace.[107]

David Knowles, to whose insights all students of the English fourteenth-century contemplatives are indebted, made the interesting suggestion at one stage that Hilton and *The Cloud of Unknowing* owed their careful teaching on the supernatural life of grace, with its emphasis on the role of "operant grace," where all is perceived as God's work, to the influence of the great Rhineland teachers on contemplative prayer, Suso, Tauler and Ruysbroeck.[108] This suggestion was bound up with the assumption that both the Oxford and Cambridge schools of theology were heavily infiltrated with nominalism, and that the orthodox Thomist view of grace as an intrinsic principle of supernatural life in the soul had become excluded from the main English academic milieu.[109]

Suso's *Horologium Sapientiae* was in England in the last quarter of the fourteenth century,[110] and parts of Ruysbroeck's *Spiritual Espousals* are incorporated, in English, in *The Chastising of God's Children*, written at the end of the fourteenth or the very beginning of the fifteenth century.[111] But the parts of these works translated into English are commonplace aids to popular devotion and do not convey the distinctive contemplative and mystical teaching of the Rhineland writers. Bearing in mind the few straws that have been gathered of Cambridge theology, and the evidence of the limited reception of Continental mystical texts in this country, it seems likely that the Thomist theology on which

Hilton and the *Cloud* draw was accessible in at least some circles in England, and there is no reason to urge that the English writers depended on the Rhineland for this.

The Scale of Perfection as a Spiritual Classic

One modern writer has justly referred to the *Scale* as a *Summa* of the spiritual life.[112] It sets before the reader the program of ascetic theology that the author of *The Cloud of Unknowing* and Julian of Norwich would have taken for granted. It is the first book, or the first pair of books, written in English to cover the whole field of the spiritual life, integrating this closely with the doctrine of the Trinity, the fall and redemption, and the sacraments. It does so in such a way as to meet the needs of beginners and equally of souls who are very far along the spiritual journey. Although *Scale* 1 is ostensibly addressed to an anchoress, its very practical teaching soon ensured it a wide readership. On the evidence of the extant English manuscripts, it was more popular in the Middle Ages than *Scale* 2, with the latter's more advanced teaching, even though *Scale* 2 boldly holds out the call to "contemplation" to all Christians, and not only to vowed religious as in *Scale* 1. There are forty-five extant English manuscripts of *Scale* 1 known, as against only twenty-six of *Scale* 2.[113] Both books were read and copied in Charterhouses during the fifteenth century; James Grenehalgh, a Carthusian of Sheen, is known to have annotated three manuscripts as well as a copy of the first printed edition. This last he gave to a Brigittine nun, Joanna Sewell, probably on the occasion of her profession at the Brigittine convent of Syon in 1500.[114]

An instance of the early popularity of Hilton's writing outside the cloister as well as within is provided by MS. Lambeth Palace 472, containing both books of the *Scale* in English, together with *Mixed Life* and other closely related material. This was made for one John Killum, provisionally identified with a London grocer of that name who died in 1416. It was a "common profit" book: Killum directed that it be used by each owner for his lifetime and passed on until worn out.[115]

The English *Scale* was printed in London by Wynkyn de Worde in 1494 at the behest of Margaret Beaufort, mother of Henry VII; five extant copies also include *Mixed Life*.[116] Successive printings continued in England until the Reformation changed the pattern of church life. MS. Harley 6579 belonged to the London Charterhouse, as did Cambridge U.L. MS. Ee. iv. 30. The *Scale* must have formed part of the reading of the Carthusian martyrs who suffered under Henry VIII. The *Scale*, together with *The Cloud of Unknowing* and Julian of Norwich's *Revelations of Divine Love*, was taken abroad by English Catholic religious in exile following the dissolution of the monasteries. The Carthusians of Sheen Anglorum at Mechlin evidently owned or borrowed one of the early editions (possibly de Worde 1525) from which the MS. now in Brussels (Bib. Royale 2544-5) was copied in 1608 by Brother Abraham, provisionally identified with the *Conversus* Abraham Ellis who died in about 1620.[117] Father Augustine Baker (1575-1641) refers to the *Scale* in various places in *Holy Wisdom*, especially citing Hilton's parable of the pilgrim in *Scale* 2,[118] and this, with other passages from the *Scale*, is quoted at length in a book published in Paris in 1657, *The Holy Practises of a Devine Lover* or *The Sainctly Ideots Deuotions*. This was the posthumous work of Dame Geraldine More, great-granddaughter of Sir Thomas More and a nun of Cambrai. In 1659 the *Scale* and *Mixed Life* were reprinted together in London, "by the changing of some antiquated words rendred more intelligible." It has been suggested that this revision (often attributed to Serenus Cressy) was the work of Abraham Woodhead,[119] an attribution also recorded by William Smith, the historian of University College, Oxford, in a note added to a manuscript of the *Scale* in the college library.[120] Woodhead was a Fellow of University College and became a Roman Catholic.

With the revival of the Roman Catholic Church in England in the nineteenth century, a modernized version of the 1659 edition was issued by Fr. J. B. Dalgairns in 1870. Anglican interest in Catholic sources for the spiritual life led to Evelyn Underhill's edition of the *Scale* in 1923, which in the absence of a critical edition of the Middle English text has formed the basis of many subsequent modern English texts and studies, including the edition of Dom Gerard Sitwell (London: Orchard Books, 1952). The Orchard Books edition of 1927 (with a translation of Dom Noetinger's Introduction to the 1923 French edition) referred also to the printed edition (1494) of Wynkyn de Worde. A recent version by L. del Mastro, *The Staircase of Perfection* (New York, 1977), uses a combination of MSS. Harley 6579, CUL Add 6686 and TCC 354. The present edition is the first to be based specifically on CUL Add 6686 for Book 1 and to be checked throughout against Thomas Fishlake's Latin translation.

Hilton's roots in the classical sources of Latin Christianity have been indicated. He is ostensibly traditional and conservative, but he can also be creative and apply old principles in a new way, as in his teaching on the scope of the "mixed life."[121] In fact, the *Scale* is far more than a simple recapitulation of the wisdom of the past after the manner of a textbook. It is a creative synthesis, in which, for all his disclaimers, Hilton adds the fruits of his own experience and insights. The writing of the two books of the *Scale* answers to a development within Hilton himself in his understanding of crucial points, especially on the character and scope of "contemplation."

Standing within a living tradition, both Hilton and the author of *The Cloud of Unknowing* look forward to something of the teaching of St. John of the Cross on the "dark night" of the spiritual life in its various aspects. There is no reason to suppose that St. John of the Cross knew the writings of the fourteenth-century English contemplatives.[122] But the convergence of the English teaching with that of the Spanish saint witnesses to a comparable experience interpreted in the light of a closely related tradition.

At the present time Hilton is perhaps less widely read than the *Cloud* or Julian's *Revelations of Divine Love*. This may be due to elements in his writing that his contemporaries would have seen as a strength, and which, when due allowance is made for shifts of emphasis on points of detail between his day and ours, may once again be seen as a positive and indeed essential contribution. His ascetic, moral and theological teaching makes constant reference to scripture and is at all times closely integrated with the church's doctrinal formulations and with her practices. In the present intellectual and spiritual climate, the institutional church, viewed in its human aspects, is often an object of criticism. But Hilton sees the church as of divine institution, albeit an institution that in the conditions of this life embraces both saints and sinners. His sturdy emphasis on the corporate and sacramental aspects of the Christian life as a life within the church, of which Christ is the head and source, provides the setting in which the spiritual, moral and ascetic tradition he expounds so powerfully has always been most at home. His firm scriptural basis demands that he be taken seriously by evangelical as well as Catholic Christians.

The Spirituality of the Scale

The theme of both books of the *Scale* is the renewal or "reforming" of man, created in God's image and likeness (cf. Genesis 1.26), but damaged through Adam's fall. The "image" of God, man's rational nature by which he has the capacity to know and love God, remains ineradicable, however obscured or overlaid it may be. But the "likeness" to God in conformity to God's character as disclosed in Christ has to be regained through grace. In *Scale* 1 this theme is expressed in teaching on the Christian moral life, especially on the capital sins and the opposing virtues summed up in humility and charity. In *Scale* 2 it is also bound up with teaching on the sacraments of baptism and penance.

The human soul is a created trinity (*trinitas creata*) reflecting the uncreated Trinity of Father, Son and Holy Spirit. In Augustinian theology, based in part upon St. Paul, the characteristics of power, wisdom, and love or goodness are appropriated to the three Persons; these characteristics are not peculiar to any one of the three Persons, but they reflect the manner in which the threefold activity and life of the Trinity is disclosed to us. In turn, the human soul has three faculties, answering to the divine Persons: the memory (*memoria*), which really means "awareness"; the understanding (*intelligentia*), or, as Hilton has it, the reason; and the will or love. Through Adam's fall, human beings have lost the intuitive awareness of God and spontaneous conformity to God's will in which humanity was created; the memory is no longer attentive to the Father; the reason is no longer responsive to the Son, who is Wisdom; the love has become disordered and restless, and so no longer answers to the Holy Spirit.[123] It is the intuitive awareness of God and conformity to God's will which has to be recovered through the grace of Christ, and it is in this sense that the goal of the Christian life is a contemplative one, answering to the third and highest stage of the three parts of contemplation as set out in *Scale* 1.[124]

In *Scale* 1, Hilton follows tradition in describing the two lives of action and contemplation, seeing the contemplative life as that which is immediately directed to God, and the active life as precious and yet subordinate to the contemplative life. The active life has two aspects: the good practical life of service of God and of one's neighbor, and the life of discipline and preparation for the contemplative life.[125] The contemplative life in its fullest development on earth consists in perfect love of God and of neighbor as in interior reality.[126] Hilton takes it in *Scale* 1 (as he does in *Mixed Life*) that the highest degree of contemplation, which he terms "very [true] contemplation," is in principle beyond the reach of those whose calling in life is to be "active," and is the prerogative of vowed religious, though God may occasionally give it to actives.[127] The medieval tradition had increasingly tended to make such a restriction of the contemplative life to vowed religious, partly indeed on the basis of Augustine's and Gregory's teaching, but going beyond this and drawing also on intervening elements, which made a much more cut-and-dried equation of "life" with "state."[128]

Scale 1 lists three parts of contemplation. The first is simply rational knowledge of the truths of the faith. The second part, by contrast, consists in affection, with sensible feelings of "devotion." This is divided into a lower and a higher degree, as a peaceful and settled habit of affective devotion is formed. The third part, "very contemplation," holds the rational and affective elements together.[129] Contemplation and union (*unitas spiritus*) become complementary aspects of a single experience: *Qui adhaeret Deo, unus spiritus est cum Illo* (1 Cor. 6.17), "He who is united to the Lord becomes one spirit with Him." The contemplative wisdom Hilton describes is that of Augustine, who holds knowledge and love together. *Unitas spiritus* recalls more particularly the bridal imagery of St. Bernard and the other early Cistercians, inspired remotely by Origen's interpretation of the Song of Songs.[130]

True contemplation, *unitas spiritus* with God, is contrasted sharply with any sensible feelings of "devotion," and likewise with any corporal or imaginary representation of spiritual reality, or with sensible "heat, sweetness and song" or visions of angels such as "enthusiasts" might aspire to, fired by Richard Rolle's example and singling out certain aspects of his teaching. Standing close to the *Cloud,* Hilton consistently emphasizes that such *gratiae gratis datae* (occasional graces given for the edification of the recipient) are secondary to union with God by sanctifying grace and charity.[131] He repeatedly contrasts the immature religious enthusiasm of beginners, often marked by pride and intolerance of others, with the stillness and humility of contemplation.[132] He is at pains to emphasize that the "fire of love" is interior and spiritual and that any overflow of this into the bodily senses is a mark of the soul's weakness and immaturity, even though such an ebullient "fire of love" with its bodily expressions may be a real mark of the purification God is effecting inwardly in the spirit.[133] Again, with an eye to misunderstandings based on Rolle's teaching, he is careful to define what is meant by love of the name of Jesus. This is not to be identified simply with a song in the heart, but begins with the desire for salvation, since this is the meaning of the name of Jesus and this is itself sufficient for salvation. From this point there may indeed be a progression to greater love of God and forgetfulness of oneself, so that those who find spiritual song and joy in the holy name do indeed attain a special reward in heaven.[134]

Three means are commonly used to attain contemplation: reading (*lectio*), meditation and prayer.[135] Reading includes both the scriptures and recognized ecclesiastical writers.[136] Hilton assumes an "ecclesial" and Christological basis for bible reading. In *Scale* 1 he also assumes that bible reading will not be possible for his reader;[137] presumably he did not expect his anchoress to be able to read Latin. In *Scale* 2 he has no such inhibitions.[138] He refers in the latter book to the different levels of meaning in scripture, like a piece of music with varying reverberations and nuances. The Bible points to Christ, who is the Father's agent in creation and redemption. Hilton accepts the standard four meanings of scripture: the literal, straightforward and factual meaning; the moral meaning, what the passage is saying in terms of practical living; the allegorical meaning, as events (especially Old Testament events) are seen as pointing to Christ and the church; and the anagogical or heavenly meaning, as the passage points even now to the soul's participation in the heavenly realities.[139]

Speaking again of a threefold pattern, Hilton refers to a triple foundation of the Christian life. First of all there is humility, which enables us to have a proper perception of ourselves as we are before God, with a consequent openness to receive his gifts, as well as a right attitude toward other people.[140] Then there is firm faith: Hilton is in line with William Flete in emphasizing faith as an act of the will in the face of doubts and temptations.[141] Third, there is the wholehearted intention to serve God, an intention which is his gift and so is to be identified with the infused virtue of charity. Because this intention is God's gift to us, it is not lightly broken and enables us to return to our course after an involuntary fall.[142] Hilton's emphasis on the importance of humility and charity as means to conformity with God has an important corollary in his ascetic theology. He consistently emphasizes "discretion" in the use of bodily austerities, together with respect for the proper "need" of the body.[143] One is to think more about God, or Christ, than about the sin that one is trying to overcome, and in this way God is left free to break down sin.[144]

In *Scale* 1 Hilton goes on to describe various aspects of prayer. He insists forcefully on the importance of the common vocal prayer of the church, and especially on the canonical hours for those who are bound to them.[145] One's approach to God in Christ must be formed by the mind of the church. After this there is a freer, affective prayer, but one which still uses formulae derived from the church's liturgy, especially the Psalms. This answers to the second, affective part of contemplation.[146] Third, there is a still, interior prayer in the heart, without any distinct words.[147]

Hilton declines to lay down too hard and fast rules on meditation, since meditation is a gift of God.[148] There is meditation on Christ's humanity and passion, on the Blessed Virgin and the saints,[149] and on vices and virtues, the mercy of Christ and the joys of heaven.[150] At the beginning of conversion, meditation is likely to be concerned with one's previous sins and the mercy of God.[151]

Meditation on the humanity of Christ, with the sensible consolations that it brings, answers to the "carnal" love of God in Christ, as St. Bernard understands this. Christ comes to us at the point where we are able to receive him, in his humanity, but Christ's humanity appeals to that humanity, that "fleshliness" in us, which is tainted by Adam's fall. So we come to Christ in his humanity, but sensible consolations have to be withdrawn in order that we may be led to a more directly spiritual knowledge of him: *Expedit vobis ut ego vadam* (John 16.7), "It is to your advantage that I go away."[152]

The ramifications of Bernard's teaching on the transition from the carnal to the spiritual love find echoes at various points elsewhere in Hilton. In his twentieth sermon on the Song of Songs, where in particular this doctrine is set out, Bernard not only cites John 16.7, but at the same time Lamentations 4.20 in a form familiar through Origen's commentaries: "Christ the Lord is a spirit before our face; we shall live under his shadow among the Gentiles" (*Spiritus ante faciem nostram Christus Dominus; sub umbra eius vivemus inter gentes*). There is no point on earth at which we can outgrow devotion to the humanity of Christ, the "shadow" (*umbra*) under which the light of his divinity is set so long as we walk by faith and not by sight.[153] Lamentations 4.20 recurs in similar contexts elsewhere,[154] and Hilton echoes Bernard's use of it in other parts of his writings.[155]

Closely related to Bernard's teaching on this point in his sermons on the Song of Songs is that found in *De Diligendo Deo*, a text with which Hilton was also familiar. Here Bernard refers to 1 Corinthians 15.46: *Non prius quod spirituale est, sed quod animale est, deinde quod spirituale*, "It is not the spiritual which is first but the physical, and then the spiritual." The progression from attachment to God's benefits and consolations to level of the "disinterested" love of God for himself, in which his benefits are no longer the primary consideration, marches with progression from "servile" to "filial" fear and love of God, in which fear of punishment gives place to the fear of offending God's love (cf. 1 John 4.18). The truth of Christ's words, "My yoke is easy, and my burden is light" (Matthew 11.30) is realized, as the heavy yoke that is laid upon the sons of Adam

(Ecclesiasticus 40.1) gives place to the spontaneous service of Christ.[156] This further aspect of Bernard's teaching is echoed in *Scale* 2.[157]

Returning to *Scale* 1, Hilton's teaching on the positive value of the withdrawal of sensible devotion owes much to Bernard (and to his antecedents in Augustine). But this is fused with the teaching of William Flete in his *De Remediis contra Tentationes*. Hilton stands very close to Flete as he describes how God withdraws sensible devotion for our own good. Through the aridity that ensues, along with the violent temptations to flesh and spirit that accompany it, we remain united to God at a supernatural level through the life of the infused virtues, and this union is strengthened, issuing in a profounder illumination.[158]

The withdrawal of meditation on Christ revealed in his humanity through the bodily senses and imagination represents a call to find God at a deeper and more spiritual level through the process of introspection familiar since the *Noverim me, noverim te* ("When I know myself, I shall know you") of Augustine's *Soliloquies*.[159] This includes the realization of the soul's essential nature as created in the image of God, as well as of its present plight in consequence of the Fall, whereby the image of God is overlaid and obscured by the "image of sin" rooted in inordinate self-love,[160] in pride, and the attendant capital sins of anger, envy, covetousness, *accidie* (sloth), gluttony and lechery.[161] Hilton develops the theme of taking up the cross to follow Christ and speaks in Pauline terms of "mortifying" that element in human nature that is corrupted through the Fall.[162] He refers to the soul's search for Christ with a whole series of illustrations derived from scripture and ecclesiastical tradition.[163] He is mindful that if in one sense we can speak of our search for Christ, there is a profounder sense in which we should speak of Christ's search for us, since Christ's call to us always anticipates our response to him.[164]

The assault upon the foundation or "ground" of sin is a harder and more deliberate process than that involved in the initial call to follow Christ, accompanied as this was by the sweetness of devotion. Whereas one has previously been concerned to avoid simply the grosser sins, one now begins, by the grace of God, to strike at the very roots of sin, of which pride is the *fons et origo*.[165]

The likeness (*similitudo*) of God or of Christ is expressed above all in the twin virtues of humility and charity: "Learn of me, for I am meek and humble in heart" (Matthew 11.29): "This is my commandment, that you love one another as I have loved you" (John 13.34–5). Recalling the Pauline expression "to put on Christ" (Romans 13.14, etc.), Hilton speaks of them as Christ's "livery."[166] He emphasizes the inclusive and interdependent character of humility and charity, in which the whole Christian moral life is implied.[167]

Reference has been made to Hilton's preference for the inner dispositions of humility and charity rather than for excessive physical penance. In the *Scale* he shows a concern to respect the proper "need" (*necessitas*) of the body in sleep, food and drink.[168] That humility is the antidote to pride is obvious, but Hilton explains with some care how humility, in conjunction with that charity, which it disposes us to receive as a gift from God, is also the efficacious remedy not only for spiritual sins, but also for carnal sins, since misuse of our own bodies and of their senses is a breach of the proper "order of charity" (*ordo caritatis*). Hilton follows closely the teaching of Augustine (expressed particularly in *De Doctrina Christiana*) on the "order of charity." God is to be loved for himself, and he alone is to be "enjoyed" (*frui*). Other human beings—or oneself—are to be loved "in God," or else "for God." They are loved "in God" when their attractive qualities are referred to the Creator, so that love of them looks beyond the creature to God; they are loved "for God" when in the face of qualities that may be unattractive or sinful they are loved as those for whom Christ died and whose redemption and renewal is to be desired.[169] Hilton takes for granted the corollary in Augustine's teaching that the inanimate things of this world are to be "used" (*uti*) in relation to God.[170]

The wisdom and practicality of *Scale* 1 is shown also in its teaching about how vowed religious, especially anchoresses, should behave toward those whose calling in the church and in life is different from their own. The *Cloud*—much more of a "specialist" book—remarks that actives complain about contemplatives and is at some pains to defend contemplatives.[171] Hilton points out that vowed contemplatives should respect those of "active" state in the church; many of them would gladly be contemplatives if they might, and without their labors it would not be possible for the anchoress and her like to lead their contemplative life.[172] While accepting that the life of consecrated virginity gains an "accidental reward" in heaven, Hilton points out that this is secondary to the principal reward, the vision of God according to one's degree of love for him. It is perfectly possible for a man or woman living in the world, rich or poor, to have, by God's gift, more love of God than a vowed religious.[173] Hilton gives wise and practical advice on how anchoresses should behave toward visitors, emphasizing here as in other contexts the virtue of "discretion."[174]

Scale 1 is addressed to an anchoress. The little tract *Mixed Life*, addressed to a layman living in the world, was written at about the same time and is complementary to it. This book too is concerned with the importance of "discretion" in preserving the "order of charity," and with the giving of proper attention and service to God, and to one's neighbor for the sake of God.[75] Hilton urges the recipient not to try to live like a monk or a friar when his calling is to live in the world with proper regard for his family and dependents. Gregory the Great had written earlier of what would become known as the "mixed life" of action and contemplation for bishops and pastors, who, after the example of Christ, should divide their time between the direct service of God and the service of God in humanity. Hilton breaks apparently fresh ground in applying to lay people in the world with temporal and pastoral responsibilities the principles Gregory had enunciated for professional ecclesiastics. He urges his reader to lead just such a "mixed life,"[76] in which, as in *Scale* 1, "true contemplation" is in principle excluded.[77] Hilton has not yet reached the point of view found in *Scale* 2, that "contemplation," now understood more specifically as an awareness of the life of grace, itself opens the way to the fullness of love of God and of neighbor, and so should be sought by all, regardless of their state in life.

Scale 2, like *Scale* 1, is ostensibly addressed to a single reader and sets out to develop further points made in the earlier book. Whereas *Scale* 1 points the way to "very contemplation," but leaves this beyond the horizon, *Scale* 2 leads the reader to contemplation in the fullest sense attainable on earth. In this book there is a changed and deepened understanding of what constitutes contemplation. Hilton also has a far wider perception of who may be called to contemplation.

This second book begins by repeating Anselm's theory of the Atonement from *Cur Deus Homo*,[78] and goes on to describe how the redemptive work of Christ is applied to us. Original sin is put away through the sacrament of baptism,[79] while actual sin committed after baptism (more specifically mortal sin, through which communion between the soul and God is broken) is put away through the sacrament of penance. Hilton gives a careful apologia for the sacrament of penance, saying that God forgives us as soon as through his gift we are sorry for our sins. Going to confession is an act of humility and is done in order that our reconciliation to the church as well as to God may be expressed through absolution. This is a traditional understanding; such a "declaratory" theology of absolution was in Hilton's day still held by many theologians, but had begun to give ground to the view of St. Thomas, endorsed by the Council of Trent, that sacramental absolution is not merely declaratory, but is a truly efficacious sign, effecting in a real sense what it represents. Hilton's explanation has an eye to two fronts: first, to reassuring tender consciences, which may be doubtful about the reality of God's forgiveness; second, to answering those who held that the sacrament was superfluous by emphasizing (in line with tradition) the motive of humility in going to confession.[180]

Scale 1 had indicated three main stages in the evolution of the spiritual life. *Scale* 2 indicates at a number of points the conventional threefold classification,[181] though this is in any case not precisely what Hilton had in mind in *Scale* 1. Much more fundamental for *Scale* 2 is the basic division between "reforming in faith" and "reforming in feeling." Reforming in faith means that the benefits of Christ's redemption are applied to us, but that this is simply believed by faith, without interior and spiritual realization; this is the lot of beginners and proficients in terms of the conventional scheme, with the provision that within this basic phase there is also reforming by faith and imagination, entailing devotion to the humanity of Christ and imaginative representation of this.[182] Reforming in feeling means the interior awareness for oneself of what Christ has done, through the realization of the life of grace: it is, in Hilton's phrase, a "lively feeling of grace."[183] Reforming in faith means that one is indeed on the way to salvation, but old sinful impulses still press hard; reforming in feeling means that the power of the old impulses is broken. This pertains to "perfect" souls.[184]

The expression *feeling* suggests the terminology of the "spiritual senses," through which spiritual realities are perceived. There are conventionally taken to be five spiritual senses answering to the five bodily senses.[185] *Feeling* is a comprehensive term, including something of all the five senses taken together. It is also synonymous with understanding, which in the thought of Augustine and Anselm, among others, is that realization of the things of God that accompanies the recovery of purity of heart and is the fruit or reward of faith, mediating between the life of naked faith (*fides*) and the open vision of God (*species*) in the life to come. The contrast is famous through Anselm's *fides quaerens intellectum* (faith seeking understanding),[186] but it also runs through other writers in the Augustinian tradition with whose work Hilton was familiar, including Bernard and Gilbert of Hoyland.[187] The latter's work has been characterized as an interesting blend of Anselm and Bernard.[188] Among the various biblical texts used by Augustine and his successors in this connection, there is the Old Latin form of Isaiah 7.9, *Nisi credideri-*

tis, non intelligetis, "Unless you believe, you shall not understand," and Acts 15.9, *fide mundans corda eorum,* "cleansing their hearts by faith," both of which Hilton cites to make the point.[89]

The contrast between faith and understanding runs through much of Hilton's writing. It is already made in *Scale* 1, in close relationship with that other Augustinian contrast between desire (*desiderium*) and love of God.[190] But it is in *Scale* 2 that it is brought out with particular force.

The Full Development of the Baptismal Life

The Christian baptismal life has been described as a process of "becoming what we are." The tensions within the baptismal life, the process of making our own that death to sin and that new life in God that is a sharing in the passion and resurrection of Christ, are forcefully described in St. Paul's letter to the Romans, chapters 6 to 8, and in the letters to the Ephesians and Colossians. When Hilton comes to speak of the "luminous darkness" and of the "reforming" of God's image in man in greater detail, he refers to various texts from St. Paul that have a familiar connotation within the baptismal life.[191] He points to the same tension between the interior life of faith and the continuing impulses of human beings' sensual nature (*sensualitas,* "sensuality"), caught up as it still is in the effects of Adam's fall, employing a text familiar in this sense through the Cistercian tradition: "I am black, but comely, O daughters of Jerusalem" *Nigra sum, sed formosa, filiae Ierusalem* (Canticle 1.4).[192]

To stand still in the spiritual life is to be in imminent danger of regressing. Hilton emphasizes that while the way to "reforming in feeling" is long and arduous, and while there can be no shortcuts, any Christian who is content to stand still in the spiritual journey does so at his or her peril.[193] All spiritual progress depends upon the grace of Christ, yet it requires our response to grace too. There is no single blueprint for progress in the spiritual journey; Christ leads various souls by various ways according to their needs. Since God exceeds all our deserts, we cannot "earn" the perfect love of God, for this is in God's gift to give to whom he will. Nevertheless, we should dispose ourselves to the best of our powers to receive this gift.[194] To come to the perfect love of God, it is necessary to be perfectly humble, to be stripped of all pride in one's good deeds and to attribute them all to the grace of Christ.[195]

The spiritual journey is symbolized by the journey of a pilgrim to Jerusalem. While the image of the Christian life as a pilgrimage is biblical, suggested by the first letter of St. Peter (2.11), it would seem that Hilton is here influenced particularly by one of St. Bernard's Lenten sermons.[196] Poverty of spirit means that humility and desire for God go hand in hand; claiming nothing of one's own as of right, one may desire the love of God. It is necessary to advance with single-minded desire for God, and resist all assaults and distractions on the way, all temptations to either worldliness or despair.[197]

The desire for God is given us by God, or Christ, himself; he is both the author and the end of this desire; all is his work.[198] So the whole process of our purification, including its most painful aspects, is one in which God is present and active.

The journey from worldly love to love of God is compared to the passage from one day, through the intervening night, to the following day. Hilton echoes Gregory the Great when he applies Job 3.3, "May the day perish in which I was born" (*Pereat dies in qua natus sum*) to the false day into which the devil deluded Adam by promising him that his eyes would be opened (Genesis 3.5).[199] The passage through the "night" —a night in which God's light shines firmly—is termed a "good night" and a "luminous darkness," borrowing phrases from Gilbert of Hoyland and Pseudo-Dionysius. It is a process of stripping oneself of disordered loves in order to attain the love of God, a process which is at first painful but becomes progressively "restful" and luminous.[200]

Hilton's use of the phrase "luminous darkness" is significant for the adaptation of the term's connotation. It derives ultimately from the *huperphotos gnophos* described by Pseudo-Dionysius, whose teaching in turn draws in part on the *Life of Moses* by Gregory of Nyssa (c. 330–95). Gregory implies that Moses enters into a *lampros gnophos* at Sinai.[201] Pseudo-Dionysius speaks of the excess of God's light as a darkness. For him, the soul ascends toward union with God who in his preeminence over all created things, over all concepts that can fall under the cognizance of the imagination or the intellect, is beyond not only all affirmation but also beyond all denial of specific concepts.[202] The Pseudo-Dionysian writings, of which *Concerning Mystical Theology* (*De Mystica Theologia*) is perhaps the most important for our purpose, enjoyed a great vogue not only in the Greek church, but also in the Latin church. It is this Dionysian theology, with its Latin modifications, that the *Cloud* incorporates in a context which is deeply rooted in the Western tradition. Among the modifications the *Cloud*'s author inherits through such

Dionysian interpreters as Thomas Gallus, Abbot of Vercelli (d. 1246), is a more explicitly affective note and a marked emphasis on grace.[203]

Among the books of the *Cloud* corpus, the term "luminous darkness" is actually used in the *Book of Privy Counselling*.[204] In the *Cloud* itself, despite the various Augustinian modifications, the author is still close enough to Pseudo-Dionysius to speak of the overwhelming excess of God's light, which strikes the soul as darkness.[205] But whereas the Dionysian sense of the luminous darkness is retained by the *Cloud*'s author, for Hilton the luminous darkness does not refer to the effect of God's ontological transcendence on the soul, but rather to a condition considered as within humanity itself. This is in keeping with his consistent use of the approach to God by introspection and recollection, an approach concerning which the author of the *Cloud* has serious reservations because it might seem to suggest that God may be localized or otherwise limited.[206] In *Scale* 2 Hilton himself is concerned to defend the use of the terms *within* and *above* in relation to the soul.[207] So in *Scale* 2 Hilton adapts a commonplace Dionysian phrase to his own ends, but implicitly rejects or ignores the Dionysian "apophatic" approach to God, an approach which is still a powerful force in the *Cloud*, for all the modifications of Dionysian theology effected within the Latin tradition.

The discernment of spirits is an important theme in Hilton. He has touched on the matter in *Scale* 1 with reference to Rolle's "heat, sweetness and song,"[208] and now he reverts to the matter in *Scale* 2 with reference to the pride and presumption of "enthusiasts," who take a little religious zeal to be the perfection of the Christian, so that, once they avoid the carnal sins, they take it on themselves to despise and condemn others. Such spiritual pride is bound up with contempt of the church's laws and with heresy.[209] Hilton is at pains to emphasize that there can be no shortcuts to Christian perfection; he contrasts the heretics' pride and divisiveness with the humility and love of God that the church's traditional disciplines and sacramental practices are meant to develop. The midday devil, *daimonium meridianum* (Psalm 90.6), pride masquerading as sanctity, is set in antithesis to the illumination of the true sun of righteousness (Malachi 4.2).[210] Here and elsewhere Hilton is drawing especially on Bernard's thirty-third sermon on the Song of Songs, in which the abbot describes the various temptations represented by the nighttime dread (*timor nocturnus*), the arrow flying by day (*sagitta volans in die*) and the *daimonium meridianum* of this psalm.[211]

The need to obviate any suggestion that there can be a shortcut to contemplation certainly sharpens Hilton's emphasis on the importance

of entering into the "luminous darkness" of self-knowledge and mortification. One must be able to say with St. Paul, "The world is crucified
to me, and I to the world" (Galatians 6.14). Hilton takes up a passage
from *Scale* 1: Christ in his humanity and in the virtues of his humanity is
the door to contemplation; anyone who tries to enter by some other way
is a thief and a robber (cf. John 10.1).[212]

What Hilton has said in *Scale* 1 about the creative effect of trial and
testing at the hand of God is taken up in *Scale* 2, in another passage,
which still shows traces of William Flete's *De Remediis*, but also has
points of contact with *Eight Chapters*. Hilton emphasizes once more that
the whole process is initiated by God. There is now a certain difference
of emphasis, which accords with the different perception of what constitutes contemplation and with the fact that *Scale* 2 does actually intro-
duce the reader to contemplation as it is now understood. Basing his
description on Romans 8.29–30, *Quos Deus praescivit fieri conformes
imaginis Filii eius, hos vocavit; et quos vocavit, hos justificavit,* "For those
whom he foreknew he also predestined to be conformed to the image of
his Son . . . and those whom he called he also justified," Hilton passes
quickly over the initial phase of "calling" (*vocare*), with its sweetness of
devotion. This passes away for a time and is followed by the second
phase, that of justification, understanding *justificare* not in the sense of a
purely extrinsic imputation of Christ's righteousness, but in the sense of
making his righteousness progressively our own through sanctification.
We recognize what Hilton has described in *Scale* 1 in terms of the
withdrawal of devotion. But now, in partial contrast to *Scale* 1, the severe
trials that follow, in which one is sustained by God at a supernatural
level in the face of an ostensible dereliction, as fierce trials beset both
soul and body, is placed not at the beginning of the second phase, but
firmly within it, as one makes considerable further progress. It is seen to
open the way to the final stage of progress on earth, "magnifying" or
"reforming in feeling."[213]

At this point it is appropriate to make a comparison with *The Cloud
of Unknowing* on the one hand and with St. John of the Cross on the
other. Both of these use the imagery of light and darkness in the spiritual
life; both speak of more than one phase in this light and darkness; and
both distinguish between our own deliberate taking up of the cross by
the common grace and the more severe and terrifying "passive" purification brought upon us by God regardless of what we may resolve or do. It
has been noted that in *Scale* 2—though not in *Scale* 1—Hilton does use
the Dionysian phrase "luminous darkness," with which the author of

the *Cloud* would have been familiar, even while transforming its meaning. Whereas for Hilton terms such as *darkness* and *nought* (nothing) refer to a condition within man himself,[214] for the *Cloud*'s author they point to the transcendent "otherness" of God, to his excess of light, which strikes us as darkness.[215]

The Cloud of Unknowing itself speaks predominantly of what in the terminology derived from St. John of the Cross would be termed the "active" aspect of the night, that deliberate self-stripping of attachment to all that is less than God, which is achieved by human effort in conjunction with grace. It is a penetration by love into the "cloud of unknowing," which points to God's transcendent presence, as created things are left behind under the "cloud of forgetting."[216] It is *The Book of Privy Counselling* which speaks more eloquently of the "passive" aspect of the darkness and withdrawal of devotion.[217] It will already be apparent that Hilton holds the active and passive elements in interdependence.

Basing itself on Pseudo-Dionysius, the *Cloud* points to the fact that not only that which can appeal to the bodily senses, but also that which can be clearly apprehended by the spiritual senses must be left behind in order that union with God may be attained.[218] But the book does not develop a formal distinction between a night of the senses and a night of the spirit with all the rigor of St. John of the Cross.

The Spanish saint is more deliberately systematic in his treatment of the "night" than either of the English writers. It is hardly possible here to go into the full details of his exposition. He speaks of a night of the senses, a stripping from all that can appeal to our bodily appetites, and of a night of the intellect, so that in the absence of all distinct images one travels toward God by faith, while God himself is a "dark night" to us in this life.[219] Following the Latinized Dionysian tradition, he says that there are two complementary reasons why God's light appears as darkness to the soul: the excess of God's light and the lowliness and impurity of the soul.[220] He distinguishes formally between the "night" in its active and passive aspects.[221]

Within the scheme of St. John of the Cross, a key point is the "ligature" or "passive night of the senses," which marks the transition from the way of beginners to that of proficients. Following the initial phase of conversion and progress, God begins to pour his love and light more directly into the soul, which begins to be "bound" and unable to gain any consolation from meditation involving the bodily senses and imagination.[222] There are violent temptations to flesh and spirit.[223] This marks the call to detachment from all that is less than God, as one engages more directly against the roots of sin: the phase which in the terminology derived from St. John of the Cross may be termed the "active night of the spirit."[224] We recognize an almost exact parallel with the process Hilton describes in *Scale* 1 as accompanying and following the withdrawal of sensible devotion.

But St. John of the Cross recognizes a further and more severe form of the "passive night" that on the basis of his teaching his interpreters designate the "passive night of the spirit." He says that this is the lot of some who have for a long time gone forward in the way of proficients—the illuminative way—and that it is a necessary phase if God is at last to draw them to union with himself.[225] The distinction between the sensible and spiritual aspects of the passive night rests upon the assumption in Pseudo-Dionysius that both elements in humankind need successively to be purified. While the fact that there is more than one phase to the "passive night" is a matter of empirical observation, the assignment of one phase to the senses and the other to the spirit rests upon this Dionysian theoretical basis. So a modern interpreter of St. John of the Cross holds that it is probably best to think of a "lineal continuity, differentiated only by a greater or less intensity" between the two parts.[226]

We must refrain from trying to impose upon the medieval contemplatives a pattern derived from a sixteenth-century model. In fact, neither of the English writers makes a formal division between the purification of sense and that of spirit in the manner of St. John of the Cross. When Hilton comes to speak of the more severe experience of the passive "night" in *Scale* 2, he says that it impinges sharply on both sense and spirit, while *The Book of Privy Counselling*, in the passage referred to above, says that the desolation that is described is intended to lead to conformity to the will of God, but does not ask the question whether this is a night of the senses or of the spirit.[227]

Hilton is not alone among medievals in recognizing more than one phase of the "passive night"; John Tauler does as much, but he too avoids making the formal distinction between the passive nights of sense and spirit we find in St. John of the Cross.[228]

Emphasizing the interior and supernatural character of "reforming in feeling," Hilton again, as in *Scale* 1, distinguishes contemplation properly so-called from the sensible fervor of beginners and proficients, recalling, again, as in *Scale* 1, something of Bernard's distinction between the carnal and the spiritual love with its roots in Augustine.[229] In making this emphasis and in showing that "reforming in feeling" is to be effected in the human soul, which is itself the *imago Dei,* Hilton calls upon a series of Pauline texts already familiar through the tradition of Augustine's *De Trinitate,* beginning with Romans 12.2: "Do not be conformed to this world, but be reformed in the newness of your feeling" (*Nolite conformari huic saeculo, sed reformamini in novitate sensus vestri*).[230]

It is in *Scale* 2, from chapter 34 to the end, that Hilton powerfully describes the Trinitarian character of contemplation. He begins this section of the *Scale* by reiterating the interdependence of knowledge and love. The *Cloud* emphasizes that we may be united by love to the God whom we cannot apprehend by the intellect in this life. Hilton insists on the cognitive character of contemplation, while maintaining that it is through God's gift of love that we are brought to this knowledge. Hilton's emphasis on the role of love is not indeed absent elsewhere, but he may have had the *Cloud*'s teaching in mind.

In underlining the necessity of God's gift of love, Hilton repeats the common distinction between created and uncreated Charity. It is God's gift of himself—of that uncreated Love especially identified with the Holy Spirit—which is to be desired. In *Scale* 1 Hilton has made a few passing references to the work of the Holy Spirit,[231] but now he speaks more emphatically of the work of the Spirit in appropriating Christ's saving work to us and in disclosing to us the way by which we have been led.[232] Such a disclosure leads to self-forgetfulness and to a growing docility to the Spirit: "Those who are led by the Spirit of God, they are the sons of God" (Romans 8.14).[233] Hilton contrasts the labored and deliberate efforts of those who try to love God by common grace with the spontaneity of those who are directly led by the Spirit. His account clearly recalls the distinction made by St. Thomas between co-operant and operant grace, a distinction with which the author of the *Cloud* is also familiar.[234] In those who are led by the Spirit, and who indeed see that all good works are the work of Christ in the soul, there is no self-conscious striving to acquire virtues, but a growing and deepening conformity to Christ.[235]

This is developed once more in terms of the interrelation of love of God and humility. Developing hints he has thrown out earlier, Hilton makes a formal distinction between imperfect and perfect humility, again marching closely at this point with the *Cloud.* Imperfect humility is based on the sense of one's own sinfulness; this is good and necessary and indeed can never be entirely left behind on earth. Perfect humility looks beyond the self to God, in his immensity, love and grace.[236] It is this "perfect humility" that enables the soul to see itself and all other human beings as equally dependent on God and so opens the way to loving them fully "in God."[237] Perfect humility also strikes down pride in its various guises: the *timor nocturnus* (fear by night) and the *sagitta volans in die* (arrow flying by day) of Psalm 90, representing sensitivity to the blame and the praise of others, both of which are signs of a self-centered love.[238]

If love—in conjunction with the perfection of humility—strikes down pride at its root, then love can be said to destroy the remaining capital sins. What has been adumbrated in *Scale* 1 is now developed more fully.[239] In all this, Hilton obviates any suggestion of quietism; as he will say later, echoing a phrase of William of St. Thierry, reforming in feeling (contemplation) is a "holy idleness and a most busy rest."[240]

In *Scale* 1 there was a certain bookishness in Hilton's account of "very contemplation." In *Scale* 2 he still disclaims personal experience and takes over a whole series of standard expressions derived from others. But here his achievement is to insist that contemplation is too many-sided to be categorized under any single heading. The deliberately commonplace titles he uses are welded into a synthesis which is in fact his own. Among the descriptions of contemplation Hilton gives are: purity of spirit and spiritual rest, inward stillness and peace of conscience, highness of thought and solitude of soul, a lively feeling of grace and intimacy of heart, the waking sleep of the spouse and tasting of heavenly savor.[241] These, and the closely related list of titles in the following chapter, are rooted in the tradition of Gregory the Great, the early Cistercians and the Victorines, as the notes make clear.

Fear of punishment gives place to the assurance of salvation as servile fear gives place to filial fear and love: "The Holy Spirit himself bears witness to our spirit, that we are the sons of God" (Romans 8.16).[242] The "hidden manna" (*manna absconditum*) of Revelation 2.17 is identified with the "lively feeling of grace"[243] that is so essential to Hilton's deepened understanding of what constitutes contemplation.

In *Scale* 1 Hilton referred to the fleeting character of contemplation.[244] There are various points in *Scale* 2 where he already emphasized contemplation as a progressive habit and in this connection referred to "homeliness" (which is rendered as *familiaritas* by Fishlake), recalling the terminology of Richard of St. Victor.[245] Referring to Canticle 5.2, "I sleep, and my heart wakes"—a familiar verse in contemplative contexts —Hilton speaks of a progressive sleep of the senses to worldly things in order that the spiritual senses may be awake to God revealed in Christ. This is compared to the apostles' experience of the transfiguration.[246]

When Hilton speaks of the fluctuating experience of contemplation, he draws clearly on St. Bernard's descriptions of *vicissitudo* in the latter's sermons on the Song of Songs. *Revertere, dilecte mi!* (Canticle 2.17). The bridegroom hides his presence from time to time from the soul which is his bride; yet each apparent absence issues in deeper union. So one should not speak of a fixed and final union, but rather of a deepening habit of union, which becomes progressively more stable and constant.[247] But in all our life on earth—and here Hilton must have an eye to correcting the ideas of any who might suppose that permanent impeccability is possible on earth—there can be no absolutely unbroken "feeling of grace."[248]

Whereas in *Scale* 1 reading (*lectio*) and prayer are seen as means to contemplation, in *Scale* 2 these are seen rather as extensions of the contemplative process.[249] Referring to the different levels of understanding scripture, and including the various spiritual senses as well as the literal sense, Hilton declares that they are all a disclosure of Christ and that they give life to the soul just as the disclosure of Christ does in the life of grace.[250]

There is no final resting point in the spiritual journey on earth. If Hilton's account of the various aspects of contemplation draws on traditional sources, his account of the intellectual visions that may be associated with the highest levels of contemplation have points of contact not only with *Eight Chapters* and *Qui Habitat* but also with Gilbert of Hoyland's sermons on the Song of Songs. God's grace is to be seen in the holy souls and in the angels; the vindication of his justice—Hilton is not afraid to say—in the condemned.[251] There is an ascent of the mind from intellectual visions of the glorified humanity of Christ to some perception of the Holy Trinity.[252] But even these intellectual visions are but means to lead the soul to closer union with God.[253]

By comparison with *Scale* 1, *Scale* 2 has a different picture of contemplation and a wider vision of who may be called to it. There are a number of places where Hilton indicates that "reforming in feeling" is open not only to vowed contemplatives but to all who generously give themselves to God's service. Some of the ground for this has been prepared in *Epistola ad Quemdam Saeculo Renuntiare Volentem*, a letter which has other points of contact with *Scale* 2 as against *Scale* 1. In this letter, written to counsel a reader troubled in conscience and to dissuade him from seeking to join the vowed religious life for which he is unsuited, Hilton declares that there are "perfect" souls outside the cloister as well as within it and that a generous soul living in the world may aspire to as much fullness of charity and "of other spiritual gifts" as one living in the cloister.[254] It is because "reforming in feeling," identified with the "lively feeling of grace," leads to self-forgetfulness and entire openness to the grace of Christ and the leading of the Spirit, issuing in a far closer conformity to God's will than could be attained by one's own efforts in conjunction with common grace, that Hilton goes so far as to say not only that contemplation is a possibility for everyone (including even rich men living in the world,[255] not simply—as in *Scale* 1 and *Mixed Life*—for contemplatives living under vows), but that every rational soul created in the image of God should desire it and dispose himself or herself to receive it.[256] There is here a convergence with the point of view set out so eloquently on the basis of St. Thomas's theology by Reginald Garrigou-Lagrange in *Christian Perfection and Contemplation.* According to this view, the proper and full term of the Christian baptismal life issues in that docility to the leading of the Holy Spirit ascribed to the full operation of the gifts of the Spirit, and this docility or openness to God's inspiration should properly be called contemplative.[257] Hilton's experiential "reforming in feeling" answers to the connaturality with divine things that St. Thomas sees as the full development of charity and to the working of the gift of wisdom: *Non solum discens, sed et patiens divina,* "not only learning divine things, but also experiencing them."[258]

The Text

It was in the introduction to her 1923 edition that Evelyn Underhill mentioned "the much-needed critical edition of the *Scale.*" Sixty-five years later her own version, based on MS. Harley 6579 (H) and checked against MSS. Harley 2387 and Lambeth 472, remains (apart from some minor errors) the best-known and most reliable witness to Hilton's Middle English text. Although usually described as semi-modernized, it reproduces most of the vocabulary and all the syntax of the manuscript; only the spelling and punctuation have been changed and about forty obsolete words replaced. It gives the reader much of the archaic flavor of the original. We can look forward to the appearance of full critical editions of both books of the *Scale,* which are being actively prepared for the Early English Text Society by Dr. M. G. Sargent (completing the work of the late Professor A. J. Bliss on Book 1) and Professor S. S. Hussey (editing Book 2). The modern English text of the present volume is based on the manuscripts chosen for these editions, and it is the research of their editors which underpins that choice. A long and detailed examination of the textual problems would therefore be inappropriate here. Nevertheless, something needs to be said of the more important issues that have provoked discussion and of the complex and often baffling relationships linking the extant Hilton manuscripts.

In Book 1 the most conspicuous variations are visibly and obviously displayed in MS. Harley 6579 (H), which has for this reason become the starting point for all discussion of the text.[259] Written toward the middle of the fifteenth century, it belonged to the London Charterhouse, though some persistent Northern forms in its language suggest that it may not have been written there. It seems to be a kind of working exemplar with additions in several hands, untidily written, incompletely rubricated, and with indications of three different systems of chapter breaks and numbers. There is a *tabula* with headings and *incipits* that differ from those in the text, and two extra leaves, which have been bound in after f.27 as an addition to chapter 44, containing a long passage on the holy name of Jesus. A much shorter passage, on charity, has been written on a small slip of vellum sewn to the outer edge of f.48 to form part of chapter 70. A large number of interpolations have also been written into the margins and between the lines of the text, sometimes replacing words that have been deleted. These are the expansions described by Evelyn Underhill as "Christocentric" and regarded by her as evidence of a change of direction in Hilton's spiritual development. If H did serve as a storehouse of the most obvious variants noticed in the manuscripts acquired by or passing through the London Charterhouse, we can expect to find the same variants occurring in other manuscripts still extant, and it is indeed possible to trace evidence of all three systems of chapter division elsewhere, to find MSS. with or without the addition to chapter 44 (some showing the scribe's awareness that this passage was not always present), and to identify a few MSS. where the H interpolations form part of the text. Manuscripts invite easy classification on this basis, which can also take account of a few other conspicuous variants, such as "Gostely [spiritual] syster/brother/brother or suster" in the opening words of the book, and provide useful evidence of direct manuscript relationship in certain cases.

However, the appearance and evident function of H also convey a warning. If it were indeed used as an exemplar, copies made from it would incorporate these superficial features (possibly derived from several different textual traditions) into heavily conflated texts and further confuse the lines of descent, which should lead back to the archetype. A manuscript in the Cambridge University Library, Ee.iv.30 (E), is perhaps of this kind, with characteristics derived partly from a manuscript similar to H and partly from one like Lambeth 472. Meticulously written in a consistently southern dialect, it is delightful to handle and to read, with delicately ornamented initials and an ingenious *ex libris* inscription (one letter at the foot of each *recto*) showing that it too belonged to the London Charterhouse.

In spite of their contrasting appearance, a single aim inspired the compilation of H and E, that is, to produce as full, as edifying, and as readily intelligible a version of the *Scale* as possible, without enquiring into the authenticity of every addition or trying to preserve the local flavor of the original language. Whereas in H this purpose is seen only half achieved—the assembled material laid out in different hands and dialects, with erasures, interlinear additions and crowded margins—in E it is complete. Even more material has been incorporated, but the joins are no longer seen.

It has been shown that several other MSS. containing the "Christo-centric" interpolations of H were located in or near London in the fifteenth century, and that the text used by de Worde for his edition of 1494 was of this expanded type.[260] The majority of the expansions, which do not occur in the Latin translation of Book I, are not now generally thought to be authorial and have been aptly described as "formulaic" in character. The various systems of chapter division, with the chapter headings themselves and the tables of contents some manuscripts contain have proved extraordinarily complex. There is little evidence as to which formed part of the original book. The end of chapter 44, on the other hand, has been generally accepted as an authorial addition, despite Dame Helen Gardner's argument for its being part of the original text, lost through the accidental omission of a leaf and later restored in some copies.[261] In either case there is no doubt that both this and the passage on charity in chapter 70 are the work of Walter Hilton.

The affiliations of the main body of the text have been more reliably traced through the now standard method of collating minor and inconspicuous manuscript variants, since these are less likely to have invited conflation. Even so, among the forty-five manuscripts of Book I some show signs of mixed descent through detailed editorial conflation of two or more exemplars and the construction of a convincing stemma is likely to remain difficult. However, by distinguishing and evaluating groups of related manuscripts, it has been possible to recognize some traditions as more reliable than others and eventually to identify C (CUL Add 6686) as a competently written record of what seems to be an early and relatively uncontaminated text close to that translated into Latin by Thomas Fishlake, perhaps during Hilton's lifetime.[262] C also shows linguistic forms compatible with a North East Midland origin, not far from Thurgarton where Hilton died.

It is generally agreed that Book 2 was not originally planned as the second part of the treatise but written some time after Book 1 as a distinct sequel. This is implied both by its opening sentence and by the sometimes diverse paths along which the texts of the two books appear to have circulated. From the editorial point of view, therefore, they have to be approached as two separate works.

Here again MS. Harley 6579 shows additions and corrections in several hands, but these alterations, although numerous, are individually less remarkable than those in Book 1. A short section added at the end of the final chapter and absent in some other MSS. may simply have been lost from an early exemplar, while the alterations and additions are shown by Hussey to be mainly correctional and not comparable in content to Book 1's Christocentric interpolations.[263] Chapter headings are added inconsistently here and there, and (as in Book 1) differ in content and language from those of the complete *tabula* at the end of the work. Hussey has nevertheless chosen it as the best of the 26 extant versions of Hilton's text (including that used by the printer de Worde and his successors), since the uncorrected H is the best representative of the more primitive of the two textual traditions he has distinguished and the corrections have in fact removed most of the mechanical errors.

The text of Book 1 in the present edition is accordingly based on CUL Add 6686, corrected when necessary from the Latin version of York Cathedral Chapter Library MS. XVI K 5. These two manuscripts will be referred to as C and Y.

Book 2 has been translated from MS. Harley 6579 in its corrected state (referred to here as H) and similarly corrected from Y. The chapter headings are supplied from the *tabula* of H, written at the end of Book 2 in a different hand from that of the main text.

Thomas Fishlake and the Latin Version

Thomas Fishlake's Latin version of the *Scale* is of interest in its own right. It may have been made by 1400. If it was made actually within

Hilton's lifetime—and *Scale* 2 can have been completed only shortly before his death in 1396—it would seem that this Latin version was not checked by Hilton himself.[264] It is based on a manuscript that must have been close to MS. CUL Add. 6686 for *Scale* 1, while for *Scale* 2 Fishlake used a manuscript from the second branch of the stemma, with small divergences from the textual tradition represented by Harley 6579.[265] Fishlake's version is thus a valuable check on the English text, especially for *Scale* 1, after allowance is made for some duplication in the quest for synonyms, and for clarification or paraphrase where the Latin idiom differs from English.

The translation shows a sensitivity to the deep roots of Hilton's English terminology in Latin theology, so that Latin equivalents are chosen to convey the appropriate nuances and connotations. At the same time, this is not a "learned" translation. Where Hilton is citing ecclesiastical writers, as distinct from the Bible, Fishlake makes no effort to seek out the Latin originals of Hilton's quotations. One feature of Fishlake's version is of particular interest. In the English *Scale* 2, the Christocentric emphasis becomes progressively more marked from chapter 20 onward. In this section of the *Scale*, Fishlake introduces a number of Christocentric expansions even beyond what is in the English at this point. However, investigation shows that these are not simply his own invention, but are based on his wider reading of the *Scale*, and are an adaptation of phrases used by Hilton in other contexts.[266]

References

References to the Latin Bible are to *Biblia Sacra iuxta Vulgatam Versionem*, ed. B. Fischer, O.S.B., et al., *Deutsche Bibelgesellschaft*, ed. 3, (Stuttgart, 1983).

References to ecclesiastical writers before 1216 are in accord with Migne, *Patrologia Latina*, unless otherwise indicated. Where available, the *Corpus Scriptorum Ecclesiasticorum Latinorum*, the *Corpus Christianorum* (with *Continuatio Mediaevallensis*), or the *Sources Chrétiennes* give in many cases an improved text, but the divisions of the text itself are usually interchangeable among the editions. For St. Bernard, we have used the edition by Dom J. Leclercq, O.S.B., et al.

Among the Scholastics, the *Sentences* of Peter Lombard have been consulted in the *Spicilegium Bonaventurianum* edition, 2 vols. (Grottaferrata 1971, 1981). For St. Thomas we have used the various Leonine and

Marietti editions; for St. Bonaventure, the *Editio Minor* of Quaracchi (1934ff.).

The *Corpus Iuris Canonici,* including Gratian's *Decretum,* has been consulted in the edition by E. Friedberg, 2 vols. (Leipzig, 1879–81, reprinted).

Abbreviations

C	Cambridge University Library Additional Manuscript 6686
CCh	*Corpus Christianorum* (Tournai)
CChCM	*Corpus Christianorum Continuatio Mediaevallensis*
CSEL	*Corpus Scriptorum Ecclesiasticorum Latinorum* (Vienna)
EETS	Early English Text Society
EETS OS	Early English Text Society. Ordinary Series
H	British Library Manuscript Harley 6579
OED	*Oxford English Dictionary*
PG	*Patrologia Graeca* (ed. J.-P. Migne)
PL	*Patrologia Latina* (ed. J.-P. Migne)
SC	*Sources Chrétiennes* (Paris)
ST	Thomas Aquinas, *Summa Theologiae*
Y	York Cathedral Chapter Library Manuscript XVI K 5

Symbols Used in the Text

Words enclosed in square brackets [ ] have been supplied by the editor in order to complete the modern English sense indicated by the context, usually with the support of the Latin text (MS. Y), or (in Book 1) MS. H.

Notes

1. J. Russell Smith, "Walter Hilton and a Tract in Defence of the Veneration of Images," *Dominican Studies* 7 (1954), pp. 208–11.
2. See the studies of Helen Gardner, begun in 1933, continued by Joy Russell Smith. For studies by Gardner and Smith, and by J. P. H. Clark, see the Bibliography.

3. Smith, pp. 184f.
4. *Walter Hilton's Latin Writings*, ed. J. P. H. Clark and C. Taylor (Salzburg, 1987), p. 262.
5. On Flete, see B. Hackett, O.S.A., "William Flete and the *De Remediis Contra Temptaciones*," in *Mediaeval Studies Presented to Aubrey Gwynn, S.J.* (Dublin, 1961), pp. 330–48.
6. J. P. H. Clark, "Walter Hilton in Defence of the Veneration of Images and of the Religious Life," *Downside Review* 103 (1985), pp. 1f., with notes and references to J. Russell Smith, A. B. Emden and B. Hackett.
7. See M. G. Sargent, *James Grenehalgh as Textual Critic* (Salzburg, 1984), p. 75.
8. The language of the *Scale* will be discussed in the editions to be published by the Early English Text Society.
9. Jonathan Hughes, *Pastors and Visionaries: Religion and Secular Life in Late Mediaeval Yorkshire* (Woodbridge, Suffolk, 1988), esp. pp. 180ff.
10. A. B. Emden, *A Biographical Dictionary of the University of Cambridge to A.D. 1500* (Cambridge, 1963), s.v. Hilton.
11. Clark and Taylor, p. 90.
12. Sargent, *Grenehalgh*, pp. 580–81.
13. H. B. Workman, *John Wyclif* vol. 2 (Oxford, 1926), p. 417.
14. Clark and Taylor, p. 146.
15. On the Augustinian Canons, see J. H. Dickinson, *The Origin of the Austin Canons and Their Introduction into England* (London, 1950).
16. See p. 41.
17. Smith, pp. 200–4. See also Margaret Aston, "Lollards and Images," in *Lollards and Reformers* (London, 1984), pp. 135–92.
18. Clark, pp. 9–16.
19. Smith, pp. 202f.
20. Clark and Taylor, pp. 215–43.
21. Cf. *Scale* 2.44 (p. 298)–2.46 (p. 301) with notes. There is also the idea of a progress within the union of the soul with God. *Of Angels' Song*, ed. T. Takamiya (Tokyo, 1980), p. 10; ed. Dorward (Oxford: Fairacres, 1983), pp. 15–16. This is more developed in *Scale* 2 than in *Scale* 1. On Hilton's authorship of *Of Angels' Song*, see J. P. H. Clark, "The Problem of Walter Hilton's Authorship: *Bonum Est, Benedictus*, and *Of Angels' Song*," *Downside Review* 101 (1983), pp. 22–24. Though the attribution occurs in only one late manuscript and in the sixteenth-century printed edition, it may be upheld.
22. J. P. H. Clark, "Walter Hilton and the *Stimulus Amoris*," *Downside Review* 102 (1984), pp. 79–118.
23. Clark and Taylor, pp. 245–98.
24. Ibid. pp. 299–304.
25. Clark, "Walter Hilton in Defence of the Veneration of Images and of the Religious Life," p. 2.
26. J. P. H. Clark, "Walter Hilton and the Psalm Commentary *Qui Habitat*," *Downside Review* 100 (1982), pp. 235–62.

27. Clark and Taylor, pp. 327–33.
28. Clark, "The Problem of Walter Hilton's Authorship: *Bonum Est, Benedictus and of Angels Song*," pp. 15–29.
29. B. Hackett, E. Colledge and N. Chadwick, "William Flete's *De Remediis Contra Temptaciones* in Its Latin and English Recensions: The Growth of a Text," *Mediaeval Studies* 26 (1964), pp. 221–23.
30. The possibility is considered by W. Riehle, "The Problem of Walter Hilton's Possible Authorship of *The Cloud of Unknowing* and its related Tracts," *Neuphilologische Mitteilungen* 78 (1977), pp. 31–45.
31. J. P. H. Clark, "The 'Lightsome Darkness': Aspects of Walter Hilton's Theological Background," *Downside Review* 95 (1977), pp. 95–109.
32. J. P. H. Clark, "English and Latin in *The Scale of Perfection:* Theological Considerations," in *Spiritualität Heute und Gestern* (Salzburg, 1982), pp. 170–71. Cf. S. S. Hussey, "Latin and English in *The Scale of Perfection*," *Mediaeval Studies* 35 (1973), pp. 456–76.
33. Clark, "English and Latin in *The Scale of Perfection:* Theological Considerations," pp. 208–11.
34. J. P. H. Clark, "Thomas Maldon, O. Carm., a Fourteenth-Century Cambridge Theologian," *Carmelus* 29 (1982), p. 194, note 9.
35. H. L. Gardner, "The Text of *The Scale of Perfection*," *Medium Aevum* 5 (1936), p. 22.
36. D. Knowles, *The Religious Orders in England*, vol. 2 (Cambridge, 1961), pp. 70–73.
37. S. S. Hussey, "The Text of *The Scale of Perfection*, Book II," *Neuphilologische Mitteilungen* 65 (1964), p. 79.
38. *Scale* 1.92, p. 160.
39. *Scale* 2.1, p. 193.
40. *Walter Hilton's "Mixed Life edited from Lambeth Palace MS. 472,"* ed. S. Ogilvie-Thomson (Salzburg, 1986), pp. xxxix–xli. Ogilvie-Thomson bases her edition on MS. Lambeth Palace 472. Her full critical apparatus gives the material from which the reader can form his or her own opinion on the various textual problems.
41. Clark, "Walter Hilton and the *Stimulus Amoris*," pp. 88ff. See notes on *Scale* 1.17, p. 91; 1.91, p. 160.
42. J. P. H. Clark, "Walter Hilton in Defence of the Veneration of Images and of the Religious Life," pp. 9–16, with references in the notes.
43. For example, *Scale* 1.9 (p. 83) where the exposition of 2 Corinthians 3.18 includes characteristic references both to the opening of spiritual vision and to the progress from faith to understanding.
44. Some further indications of Hilton's sources may be found in the notes to Clark and Taylor and to S. Ogilvie-Thomson's edition of *Mixed Life*, as well as in J. P. H. Clark's articles listed in the Bibliography.
45. Clark and Taylor, pp. 373f. (notes).
46. *Scale* 1.16, p. 90; 1.41, p. 111.

47. Cuthbert Butler, *Western Mysticism* (London, 1922); 2nd edition, with "Afterthoughts," (London, 1926).
48. Clark and Taylor, p. 145.
49. J. P. H. Clark, "Augustine, Anselm and Walter Hilton," in *The Medieval Mystical Tradition in England: Dartington 1982*, ed. M. Glasscoe (Exeter, 1982), pp. 102–26.
50. On the abiding influence of the twelfth-century writers, see G. Constable, "Twelfth-Century Spirituality and the Later Middle Ages," in *Medieval and Renaissance Studies* 5 (1971 for 1969), pp. 27–60: for a qualification of some of the points of view expressed here, see C. Bynum, "Did the Twelfth Century Discover the Individual?," revised and reprinted in her *Jesus as Mother: Studies in the Spirituality of the High Middle Ages* (University of California Press, 1982), ch. 3, pp. 82–109. See also G. Constable, "The Popularity of Twelfth-Century Spiritual Writers in the Late Middle Ages," in *Renaissance Studies in Honor of Hans Baron*, ed. A. Melho and J. Tobaschi (Northern Illinois, 1971), pp. 5–28.
51. *Scale* 1.35, p. 106.
52. E.g. *Scale* 1.78, 79, 80, pp. 149–150, with notes.
53. *Scale* 2.40, pp. 281–282, with notes.
54. *Scale* 2.41, pp. 285–286.
55. Clark and Taylor, p. 227.
56. Guillaume de S. Thierry, *Lettre aux Frères du Mont-Dieu*, ed. J. M. Déchanet, *Sources Chrétiennes* 223, pp. 81–86.
57. *Scale* 2.24, p. 235; 2.45, p. 298.
58. *Scale* 1.49, p. 122.
59. E.g. *Scale* 2.31, p. 258, and 2.40, p. 282.
60. *Scale* 1.14–15, p. 87.
61. Guigues II le Chartreux, *Lettre sur la Vie Contemplative*, ed. E. Colledge and J. Walsh, *Sources Chrétiennes* 163, pp. 21–23.
62. Clark and Taylor, pp. 362–79 (notes).
63. Ibid. pp. 381–90 (notes).
64. *Scale* 2.35, pp. 268–269.
65. *Scale* 2.7, p. 201, with note 23.
66. *Scale* 1.17, p. 91; 1.30; 1.91, pp. 101, 160.
67. See *Scale* 1.4, p. 80; *Scale* 2.37, p. 271. Two versions of the *Somme le Roi* have been published by the Early English Text Society: *The Ayenbite of Inwit*, ed. R. Morris, (1866), rev. P. Gradon (1965), with notes (1979); and *The Book of Vices and Virtues*, ed. W. N. Francis (1942).
68. *Scale* 1.10; 1.44, pp. 83 and 115–116.
69. Cf. J. P. H. Clark, "Richard Rolle: A Theological Re-assessment," *Downside Review* 101 (1983), pp. 129–31.
70. *Scale* 1.37–38; *Scale* 2.28, pp. 107–109, 248.
71. See below, p. 38, with note 143.
72. See below, p. 50, with note 236.
73. See below, p. 37, with note 131.

74. See below, p. 50, with note 234.
75. See below, p. 46.
76. *The Cloud of Unknowing*, chs. 35, 48, 68 (in the edition by P. Hodgson, EETS [1944], pp. 71, 91, 121).
77. *Scale* 1, chs. 15, 10, 25 and 87, pp. 87–88, 83–84, 97–98, 156.
78. Clark and Taylor, pp. 221–43 passim, especially on the discernment of spirits, pp. 228f.
79. *The Cloud of Unknowing*, ed. Hodgson, pp. xlix–l.
80. *The Cloud of Unknowing*, ed. J. Walsh, Paulist Press (1981), pp. 2–9. Hughes, in *Pastors and Visionaries*, pages 349–51, suggests that the *Cloud*'s author may have been a Dominican, but this seems to rest on his supposed dependence on the theology of the Rhineland Dominicans.
81. *Scale* 2.33, p. 261–262.
82. *Cloud*, ed. Hodgson, ch. 74 (p. 130), promises a sequel to explain difficult points; on the probable chronology, cf. *Cloud*, p. lxxviii.
83. *The Book of Privy Counselling*, in *Cloud*, (Hodgson, p. 159). Cf. *Scale* 2.27, with *Scale* 1.91, p. 245 and p. 160.
84. *The Book of Privy Counselling*, Hodgson p. 171, citing Augustine, *Sermo* 143.4 (PL 38.786).
85. *Scale* 1.35. See the discussion in J. P. H. Clark, "Sources and Theology in *The Cloud of Unknowing*," *Downside Review* (1980), p. 96, with notes.
86. Cf. *Scale* 2.30 and Hilton's use of John 20.17 after Augustine.
87. Gordon Leff, *The Dissolution of the Mediaeval Outlook* (New York, 1976), ch. 1, esp. pp. 16–17.
88. See, for instance, Romama Guarnieri, *Il Movimento del Libero Spiritu*, (*Storia e Letteratura*, Rome, 1965); Gordon Leff, *Heresy in the Later Middle Ages* 2 vols., (Manchester, 1967) vol. 1, part 2, ch. 4 (pp. 308–407); R. E. Lerner, *The Heresy of the Free Spirit in the Later Middle Ages* (Berkeley, 1972).
89. For orientation on Eckhart, see, e.g., Leff, *Heresy in the Later Middle Ages*, vol. 1, part 2, ch. 3 (pp. 260–307). The papal bull *In Agro Dominico*, condemning propositions distilled from Eckhart's writings, is printed in H. Denifle, "*Meister Eckharts Lateinische Schriften und die Grundausschauung seiner Lehre*," *Archiv für Literatur und Kirchengeschichte des Mittelalters* 2 (1886), pp. 636–40. There is a translation of the Bull in *Meister Eckhart*, ed. E. Colledge and B. McGinn, Classics of Western Spirituality Series, (Paulist Press, 1981), pp. 77–81.
90. Advice from Dr. R. Lovatt of Peterhouse, Cambridge. See p. 32.
91. Cf. J. Bazire and E. Colledge, *The Chastising of God's Children* (Oxford, 1957), pp. 51ff.
92. J. P. H. Clark, "Walter Hilton and 'Liberty of Spirit'," *Downside Review* 96 (1978), pp. 61–78.
93. "*The Mirror of Simple Souls*," *a Middle English Translation*, ed. Marilyn Doiron, with an appendix, "The Glosses by 'M.N.' and Richard Methley," by E. Colledge and R. Guarnieri (Rome, 1968).

94. Cf. Leff, *Heresy in the Later Middle Ages*, vol. 1, pp. 400f.

95. A possible reference in Hilton, *Scale* 2.26 is noted by Guarnieri, *Il Movimento del Libero Spiritu*, p. 461. In the present edition it is suggested that the reference may not be precisely to the movement in question. However, cf. *Eight Chapters on Perfection*, ed. F. Kuriyagawa (Tokyo, 1971), pp. 21–22 (in modern English, ed. Dorward [Oxford: Fairacres, 1983], p. 7), and *Qui Habitat*, ed. B. Wallner (Lund, 1954), p. 22, both discussed by Clark, "Walter Hilton and 'Liberty of Spirit,'" p. 65. See also the indications given by R. A. Knox, *Enthusiasm: A History in the History of Religion* (Oxford, 1950), pp. 119–20, cited in Guarnieri, *Il Movimento del Libero Spiritu*, p. 464.

96. Workman, pp. 416f.

97. *Scale* 1.37 and 38, p. 108.

98. *Scale* 2.7, pp. 201–203.

99. See, e.g., H. E. Allen, *Writings Ascribed to Richard Rolle, Hermit of Hampole, and Materials for his Biography* (New York, 1927), ch. 3, pp. 51–61.

100. *Scale* 1.44, p. 115.

101. Clark, "Richard Rolle: A Theological Re-assessment," pp. 129–31.

102. Allen, pp. 231–45.

103. H. L. Gardner, "Walter Hilton and the Mystical Tradition in England," *Essays and Studies* 22 (1937), p. 110.

104. Clark and Taylor, pp. 228ff.

105. *Scale* 1.10, p. 83 with notes.

106. F. Pelster, "Die Quästionen des Johannes von Walsham, OFM," *Franziskanische Studien* (1952), pp. 129–46.

107. J. P. H. Clark, "Thomas Maldon, a Cambridge Theologian of the Fourteenth Century," *Carmelus* 29 (1982), pp. 206f.; 223ff.

108. D. Knowles, *The English Mystical Tradition* (London, 1961), pp. 38, 76.

109. Knowles, *Religious Orders in England*, vol. 2, p. 83.

110. R. Lovatt, "Henry Suso and the Mystical Tradition in England," in *The Medieval Mystical Tradition in England: Dartington 1982*, (ed. by Marion Glasscoe, Exeter, 1982), pp. 47f.

111. Bazire and Colledge, pp. 35ff.

112. M. Thornton, *English Spirituality* (London, 1963), p. 176.

113. Information from the late Professor A. J. Bliss, and from Professor S. S. Hussey.

114. M. J. Sargent, "Walter Hilton's *Scale of Perfection:* The London Manuscript Group Reconsidered," *Medium Aevum* 52 (1983), pp. 201ff.

115. *Minor Works of Walter Hilton*, ed. Dorothy Jones (London, 1928), pp. xii–xvi.

116. *Mixed Life*, Ogilvie-Thompson, p. xxii.

117. Cf. James Long, Prior of the English Charterhouse at Nieuport list of *Fratres conversi, Carthusianorum anglorum Notitia* (Brussels, Bibliothèque Royale MS. 555–56, p. 106.

118. Augustine Baker, *Holy Wisdom*, ed. Dom Gerard Sitwell, OSB (London, 1964), section 1, ch. 6, pp. 31–38.

119. *Mixed Life*, Ogilvie-Thomson, p. xxvi.
120. The hand recognized by the late Dr. R. W. Hunt. On William Smith see also R. W. Hunt, "The Manuscript Collection of University College," *Bodleian Library Record* III.29 (1950), p. 13. His note was probably written in the Long Vacation of 1700.
121. See below, p. 42.
122. J. Orcibal, *S. Jean de la Croix et les Mystiques Rhéno-Flamands* (Paris: Desclée Brouwer, 1966, *Présence du Carmel* No. 6), p. 117.
123. For all this, see notes on *Scale* 1.43, pp. 113–114.
124. *Scale* 1.45, p. 118.
125. *Scale* 1.2, p. 78.
126. *Scale* 1.3, p. 78.
127. *Scale* 1.9, p. 83.
128. See the discussion in J. P. H. Clark, "Action and Contemplation in Walter Hilton," *Downside Review* 97 (1979), pp. 259ff.
129. *Scale* 1.4–9, pp. 179–183.
130. *Scale* 1.8, p. 82.
131. *Scale* 1.10, pp. 83–84; cf. 1.47, p. 120. Also Ogilvie-Thomson, p. 43; and *Cloud*, ch. 48.
132. See further *Scale* 2.29, pp. 249–252.
133. *Scale* 1.26, p. 98.
134. *Scale* 1.44, p. 117.
135. *Scale* 1.15, pp. 87–88.
136. Cf. *Scale* 2.43, p. 296.
137. *Scale* 1.15, p. 88.
138. It may be worth noting that although English versions of the Bible came to be seen as "tainted" with Lollard tendencies and so were condemned by Archbishop Arundel in his Constitutions of 1407, recent investigation shows that as late as 1401 the question of biblical translation could still be debated openly, without accusations of heresy against the defenders of vernacular translation. See Anne Hudson, "The Debate on Bible Translation, Oxford 1401," in *Lollards and Their Books* (London, 1985), p. 83. Nowhere in his extant writings does Hilton insist on the use of the Latin Bible as distinct from any English version, although he habitually quotes the Bible in Latin, followed by a translation or paraphrase.
139. *Scale* 2.43, p. 294.
140. *Scale* 1.16ff., pp. 88ff.
141. *Scale* 1.21, p. 94. Cf. also *Scale* 2.22, p. 231.
142. *Scale* 1.22, pp. 95–96. Cf. also *Scale* 1.33, pp. 103–104 on distractions in prayer.
143. *Scale* 1.22, p. 96 and 1.72, pp. 144–145. There is similar emphasis in *The Cloud of Unknowing*, ch. 12.
144. *Scale* 1.90, p. 159 and *Scale* 2.24, pp. 236–238.
145. *Scale* 1.27, pp. 98–99.
146. *Scale* 1.29, pp. 100–101.
147. *Scale* 1.32, pp. 102–103.

148. *Scale* 1.33, p. 104.
149. *Scale* 1.34, p. 105.
150. Cf. *Mixed Life*, Ogilvie-Thomson, pp. 51–59.
151. *Scale* 1.35, p. 106.
152. *Scale* 1.35, 1.35–36, pp. 106–107.
153. Bernard, *In Cant.* 20.5.6–7 in *Opera*, vol. 1, ed. J. Leclercq, et al. (Rome, 1957ff.), pp. 118–19.
154. Bernard, *In Cant.* 31.3.8; 48.3.6 in Leclercq, et al., vol. 1, p. 224; vol. 2, pp. 70–71); *Sermo in Ascensione Domini* 3.3 in Leclercq, et al., vol. 5, pp. 132–33).
155. E.g., *Scale* 2.30, p. 255.
156. Bernard, *De Diligendo Deo* 13.36–15.40 in Leclercq, et al., vol. 3, pp. 150–53.
157. *Scale* 2.40, p. 281.
158. *Scale* 1.37–38, pp. 107–109 with notes.
159. *Scale* 1.40, p. 111.
160. *Scale* 1.42, p. 112.
161. *Scale* 1.55–77 passim.
162. *Scale* 1.42, p. 113.
163. *Scale* 1.48–50, pp. 120–122.
164. *Scale* 1.50, pp. 122–123.
165. *Scale* 1.52, pp. 123–124.
166. *Scale* 1.51, p. 123.
167. *Scale* 1.62, 1.77, pp. 134, 149.
168. *Scale* 1.22, p. 96, and 1.75, p. 148. Cf. 1.72, pp. 144–145.
169. *Scale* 1.70, pp. 139–142 with notes.
170. *Scale* 1.71, p. 143 with note 300.
171. *The Cloud*, ch. 18.
172. *Scale* 1.17, p. 91.
173. *Scale* 1.61, p. 132.
174. *Scale* 1.83, pp. 152–154.
175. *Mixed Life*, Ogilvie-Thomson, pp. 7–8.
176. Ibid. pp. 7–17, with notes.
177. Ibid. pp. 31–33, with notes.
178. *Scale* 2.2, pp. 194–195.
179. *Scale* 2.6, pp. 200–201.
180. *Scale* 2.7, pp. 201–203.
181. E.g. *Scale* 2.5, 2.28, 2.29, pp. 200, 247–249, 251–252.
182. *Scale* 2.5, pp. 199–200; 2.29, pp. 250–251.
183. *Scale* 2.5, p. 200; cf. *Scale* 2.40, p. 284.
184. *Scale* 2.5, pp. 199–200.
185. On the spiritual senses, see K. Rahner, "*Le Début d'une Doctrine des Cinq Sens Spirituels chez Origène,*" *Revue d'Ascétique et Mystique* 13 (1932), pp. 113–45; idem., "*La Doctrine des 'Sens Spirituels' au Moyen Age,*" *Revue d'Ascétique et Mystique* 14 (1933), pp. 263–99.
186. The original title of Anselm's *Proslogion*, as is made clear by the Prologue.

187. Clark, "Augustine, Anselm and Walter Hilton," pp. 102–26.
188. E. Gilson, *La Théologie Mystique de S. Bernard*, 3d ed. (Paris, 1969), pp. 84f., note 1.
189. Clark, "Augustine, Anselm and Walter Hilton," pp. 102–6.
190. *Scale* 1.9, p. 83.
191. *Scale* 2.27, pp. 244–245.
192. *Scale* 2.12, p. 211.
193. *Scale* 2.18, p. 221.
194. *Scale* 2.20, pp. 223–225.
195. *Scale* 2.20, pp. 225–226; 2.21, p. 229.
196. *Scale* 2.21, p. 227, with note 102.
197. *Scale* 2.21 and 22, pp. 227, 231–233.
198. *Scale* 2.24, p. 234.
199. *Scale* 2.24, p. 235.
200. *Scale* 2.24, pp. 235–236.
201. Gregory of Nyssa, *La Vie de Moïse* (*De Vita Moysis*), ed. J. Daniélou, *Sources Chrétiennes* 1 bis (Paris, 1987), pp. 210–12, comparing the Evangelist John to Moses. See *Gregory of Nyssa: The Life of Moses*, trans. A. J. Malherbe and E. Ferguson (New York: Paulist Press, 1978), pp. 94–97.
202. Pseudo-Dionysius, *De Mystica Theologia* (*On Mystical Theology*), ch. 1.3 (PG 3.1001); ch. 5 (PG 3.1048). See *Pseudo-Dionysius: The Complete Works*, trans. Colm Luibheid (New York: Paulist Press, 1987), pp. 136–37, 141.
203. Discussed by, for instance, Professor Hodgson in the introduction to her editions of *The Cloud* and in her *Deonise Hid Diuinite* (EETS 1955); see also Clark, "Sources and Theology in *The Cloud of Unknowing*," p. 86.
204. Hodgson, *The Cloud*, p. 154.
205. Ibid. p. 122.
206. Ibid. pp. 121–22.
207. *Scale* 2.33, pp. 261–262.
208. *Scale* 1, chs. 10ff.
209. *Scale* 2.26, pp. 240–241.
210. *Scale* 2.26, pp. 239, 241.
211. Clark, "Walter Hilton and the Psalm Commentary *Qui Habitat*," pp. 241ff.
212. *Scale* 2.27, pp. 244–245; cf. *Scale* 1.91, p. 160.
213. *Scale* 2.28, p. 247.
214. *Scale* 2.24, pp. 236–238; cf. *Scale* 1.53, pp. 124–125.
215. Hodgson, *The Cloud*, p. 122.
216. Ibid. p. 24.
217. Ibid. pp. 167–68.
218. Hodgson, *The Cloud*, pp. 11–12.
219. St. John of the Cross, *Ascent of Mount Carmel*, 1.2.1. (Hereafter *Ascent*.)

220. St. John of the Cross *Dark Night of the Soul,* 2.5.2. (Hereafter *Dark Night.*)
221. *Ascent,* 1.13.1.
222. Ibid. 2.13–14. For an analysis of the "ligature," see Dom J. Chapman, *Spiritual Letters* (London, 1935), pp. 316f.
223. *Dark Night,* 1.14.1–2.
224. Ascent, books 2 and 3 passim. See E. W. T. Dicken, *The Crucible of Love* (London, 1963), pp. 258–62.
225. *Dark Night,* 2.2.1; 2.5.1.
226. Dicken, pp. 265ff.
227. Hodgson, *The Cloud,* pp. 167–68.
228. E.g., John Tauler, Third Sermon for the Third Sunday after Trinity, in *Spiritual Conferences of John Tauler* (Herder, 1961), pp. 77f. Cf. Orcibal, p. 113.
229. *Scale* 2.30, p. 255, with note 200.
230. *Scale* 2.31, p. 257.
231. E.g. *Scale* 1.4, p. 80.
232. *Scale* 2.34, pp. 265–266.
233. *Scale* 2.35, p. 268.
234. *Scale* 2.35, pp. 268–269. Cf. Hodgson, *The Cloud,* pp. 70–71.
235. *Scale* 2.36, pp. 270–271.
236. *Scale* 2.37, pp. 271–273. Cf. Hodgson, *The Cloud,* pp. 40–41.
237. *Scale* 2.37, pp. 272–273, with 2.38 *passim.*
238. *Scale* 2.37, p. 274.
239. *Scale* 2.38 to 39, pp. 275–280.
240. *Scale* 2.40, p. 281.
241. *Scale* 2.40, pp. 280–281.
242. *Scale* 2.40, p. 282.
243. *Scale* 2.40, pp. 283–284.
244. *Scale* 1.9, p. 83.
245. *Scale* 2.25 and 29, pp. 238 and 252.
246. *Scale* 2.40, pp. 284–285.
247. *Scale* 2.41, p. 286, with references to sources in Bernard.
248. *Scale* 2.41, p. 287.
249. *Scale* 2.42 and 43, pp. 289–290 and 293.
250. *Scale* 2.43, pp. 294–295.
251. *Scale* 2.45, pp. 299–300.
252. *Scale* 2.46, p. 301.
253. *Scale* 2.44, p. 298.
254. Clark and Taylor, pp. 289–290.
255. *Scale* 2.27, p. 245, and especially *Scale* 2.39, p. 278.
256. *Scale* 2.41, pp. 287–288.
257. Reginald Garrigou-Lagrange, *Christian Perfection and Contemplation* (St. Louis, 1946). The original edition arose out of a series of lectures at the Angelicum in Rome and was published in French in 1922. St.

Thomas says that the effect of the gifts of the Spirit is to make a person *prompte mobilis ab inspiratione divina.* (ST 1–2, q.68, a.1).

258. ST 2–2, q.45, a.2.
259. See Evelyn Underhill, ed., *The Scale of Perfection* (London, 1923); Gardner, "The Text of *The Scale of Perfection*," pp. 11–30; R. Birts (Dorward), *The Scale of Perfection*, Book 1, chs. 38–52, M. Litt. diss., (Oxford, 1951); Hussey, "The Text of *The Scale of Perfection*, Book II," pp. 75–92; S. S. Hussey, "Editing the Middle English Mystics," *Spiritualität Heute und Gestern* 2 (Salzburg, 1982), pp. 167–73); Sargent, "Walter Hilton's *Scale of Perfection*," pp. 189–216.
260. Sargent, "Walter Hilton's *Scale of Perfection*," p. 189.
261. H. L. Gardner, "The Text of *The Scale of Perfection*," p. 29.
262. See below, pp. 56–57.
263. Hussey, "The Text of *The Scale of Perfection*," pp. 87–88.
264. Clark, "English and Latin in *The Scale of Perfection:* Theological Considerations," pp. 170–71.
265. Hussey, "Latin and English in *The Scale of Perfection*," pp. 465–66.
266. Clark, "English and Latin in *The Scale of Perfection*," pp. 208–11.

———— Book One ————

Book One

Table of Contents

cf. Love's Mirror

65. That it is very hard to love people truly in charity, and hate their sin.
66. That for the same outward works different people shall have different rewards.
67. That everyone's good works that have the appearance of good are to be approved, except those of the open heretic and the man publicly excommunicated.
68. That no good work can make one feel safe without charity; and that charity is obtained only by the gift of God to those who are humble; and who is perfectly humble.
69. How a person is to know how much wrath and envy is hidden in the bottom of his heart.
70. By what signs you are to know whether you love your enemy, and what example you shall take from Christ in order to love him in the same way.
71. How a person is to know how much covetousness is hidden in his heart.
72. How a person shall know when he does not sin in eating and drinking; and when he sins mortally, and when venially.
73. That the ground of lechery should be destroyed with the labor of the soul, not of the body.
74. That people should be careful to put away all stirrings of sin, but more careful over sins of the spirit than of the body.
75. That hunger and other pains of the body greatly hinder the work of the spirit.
76. What remedy is to be used against one's errors in eating and drinking.
77. That through diligent desire and labor in humility and charity one comes the sooner to other virtues, to labor in them.
78. What comes out of the darkness of the image of sin, and what comes through its windows.
79. That for lack of self-knowledge a soul journeys out by the five senses in search of pleasure.
80. That a soul should not search outside but ask Jesus within for all that it needs.
81. That the hole of the imagination needs to be stopped as well as the windows of the senses.
82. When the use of the senses and the imagination is mortal sin, and when venial.

Book One

1. How man's inward behavior should be like the outward.

   Spiritual Sister in Jesus Christ, I beseech you to be contented in the vocation through which our Lord has called you[1] to serve him, and in it to stand firm, toiling busily with all the powers of your soul; and by the grace of Jesus Christ to fulfil in true righteousness of living the state to which you have committed yourself in likeness and appearance. And as you have forsaken the world like a dead man,[2] your body turned to our Lord in the sight of men, so let your heart be as if dead to all earthly loves and fears, turned wholly to our Lord Jesus Christ. For you must know that a turning of the body to God, not followed by the heart, is only a figure and likeness of virtues, and not the reality. Therefore any man or woman is wretched who neglects all the inward keeping of the self in order to fashion only an outward form and semblance of holiness,[3] in dress, in speech and in bodily actions; observing the deeds of others and judging their faults; considering himself to be something when he is nothing at all; and so deceiving himself. Do not behave like that, but turn your heart together with your body first of all to God, and fashion yourself within to his likeness, through humility and charity and other spiritual virtues; and then you will truly have turned to him.

   I do not say that on the first day you can be turned to him in your soul through the full mastery of virtue as easily as you can be shut up with your body in a house, but that you should know that the cause of your bodily enclosure is that you may the better come to spiritual enclosure; and as your body is enclosed from bodily association with men, just so should your heart be enclosed from the fleshly loves and fears of all earthly things; and in this little book I shall tell you how best to come to it, as it seems to me.

You must understand that, as St. Gregory says,[4] there are two kinds of life in holy church in which Christians shall be saved. One is called active life and the other contemplative. Nobody can be saved without one of these.

2. Active life and its works.

Active life lies in love and charity shown outwardly in good bodily works, in the fulfilment of God's commandments and of the seven works of mercy—bodily and spiritual[5]—toward one's fellow Christians. This way of life belongs to all secular people who have riches and plenty of worldly goods, and also to all those with either standing, office, or charge over others and having wealth to spend, whether they are clergy or laity, temporal or spiritual. In general, all secular people are bound to fulfil this obligation according to their power and ability, as reason and discretion require; if anyone has a great deal, do a great deal; if he has little, do little; and if he has nothing, then let him have the will to do good. These are the works of active life, either bodily or spiritual.

Moreover, a part of the active life lies in great bodily work one does to oneself, such as great fasting and denial of sleep, and other sharp acts of penance, in order to chastise the flesh—with discretion—for previous trespasses, and by such penance to bridle its lusts and pleasures and make it prompt in obedience to the will of the spirit.

And although these works are active, nevertheless they greatly help a person and dispose him in the beginning to come to the contemplative life, if they are used with discretion.[6]

3. Contemplative life and its works.

Contemplative life lies in perfect love and charity,[7] felt inwardly through spiritual virtues and by a true knowledge and sight of God in spiritual things. This life belongs especially to those who for the love of God forsake all worldly riches, honors and outward business and give themselves entirely, body and soul, to the service of God through spiritual occupation, according to their strength and ability. Now, since it is the case that your state requires you to be contemplative—for that is the purpose and intention of your enclosure, that you might more freely and entirely give yourself to spiritual occupation—then it is your duty to be busy night and day, with labor of body and spirit, to come as near as you can to that life by such means as you think best for you.

Nevertheless, before I tell you of the means I shall first say a little more about this contemplative life, so that you can see something of what it is, and set it as an objective in the sight of your soul at which you will aim in everything you do.

4. The first part of contemplation.

Contemplative life has three parts.[8]

The first lies in the knowledge of God and the things of the spirit, acquired[9] by reason, by the teaching of man and by the study of holy scripture, without the spiritual affection or inward savor felt by the special gift of the Holy Spirit. This part belongs especially to some learned men and great scholars who by long study and labor in holy scripture come to this knowledge—more, or less, according to the subtlety of their natural wit and their perseverance in study, upon the basis of the general gift given by God to everyone who has the use of reason. This knowledge is good, and it may be called a part of contemplation in as much as it is a sight of truth and a knowledge of spiritual things. Nevertheless, it is only a figure and shadow of true contemplation, since it has no spiritual savor of God, or that inward sweetness of love no one can feel unless he is in great charity: for that is our Lord's own well to which no stranger comes.[10] Yet this kind of knowledge is common to good and bad, because it may be had without charity; and therefore it is not true contemplation, for often heretics, hypocrites and those living carnally have more such knowledge than many true Christian people; and yet these have no charity.

St. Paul speaks thus of this kind of knowledge. *Si habuero omnem scientiam et noverim mysteria omnia, caritatem non habeam, nihil sum.*[11] If I have had full knowledge of all things—yes, and if I have known all the mysteries—and have no charity, I am nothing.

Nevertheless, if those who have this knowledge keep themselves in such humility and charity as they have and flee worldly and carnal sins as they are able, it is a good way for them, strongly disposing them to true contemplation, if they desire and pray devoutly for the grace of the Holy Spirit. Others who have this knowledge turn it into pride and their own vain glory, or into covetousness, or a craving for worldly ranks, honors or riches; not humbly taking it in praise of God or spending it charitably for the benefit of their fellow Christians. Some of them fall either into errors and heresies or into other open sins by which they discredit themselves and the whole of holy church.

St. Paul said this about such knowledge, *Scientia inflat, caritas autem aedificat.*[12] Knowledge by itself puffs up the heart into pride, but mix it with charity and then it turns to edification. This knowledge by itself is only cold insipid water; and therefore if they were willing to offer it humbly to our Lord and prayed him for his grace, he would with his blessing turn the water into wine,[13] as he did when his mother prayed at the feast of Architriclin.[14] That is to say, he would turn insipid knowledge into wisdom, and the cold naked reason into spiritual light and burning love by the gift of the Holy Spirit.

5. The second part of contemplation.

The second part of contemplation lies principally in affection, without the understanding of spiritual things; this is commonly for simple and unlearned people who give themselves entirely to devotion,[15] and it is felt in the following way. Sometimes a man or woman meditating on God feels a fervor of love and spiritual sweetness in the remembrance of his passion, or any of his works in his humanity; or he feels great trust in the goodness and mercy of God for the forgiveness of his sins, and for his great gifts of grace; or else he feels dread in his affection, with great reverence for those secret judgments of God which he does not see, and for his righteousness; or else in prayer he feels the thought of his heart draw up from all earthly things, streamed together with all its powers as it rises into our Lord by fervent desire and with spiritual delight. Nevertheless, in that time he has no open sight for the understanding of spiritual things, or into the particular mysteries of holy scripture; only it seems to him for the time that nothing pleases him so much as praying or thinking as he does for the savor, delight and comfort that he finds in it. He cannot well explain what it is, but he feels it plainly; for from it spring many sweet tears, burning desires and still mournings, which scour and cleanse the heart from all the filth of sin and make it melt into a wonderful sweetness of Jesus Christ—obedient, supple and ready to fulfil all God's will—making him feel that he does not care what then becomes of him provided the will of God is fulfilled. With these come many other such stirrings, more than I have the knowledge or power to say. No one can have this feeling without great grace, and I suppose anyone who does have it is for the time in charity. Although the fervor of it may pass away, such charity cannot be lost or lessened except by a mortal sin; and to know that is comforting. This may be called the second part of contemplation.

6. The lower degree of the second part of contemplation.

Nevertheless, this part has two degrees. Men of active life may by grace have the lower degree of this feeling when they are visited by our Lord, just as strongly and as fervently as those who give themselves entirely to the contemplative life and have this gift; but it does not last so long. In the same way, this feeling in its fervor does not always come when one wishes, and it does not last very long: it comes and goes as he wills who gives it. Therefore whoever has it should humble himself and thank God; let him keep it secret except from his confessor and hold it as long as he can with discretion; and when it is withdrawn, let him not dread too much, [but[16]] stand in faith and in meek hope, with patient waiting until it comes again. This is a little tasting of the sweetness in the love of God, about which David speaks thus in the Psalter: *Gustate et videte quam suavis est Dominus.*[17] Taste and see the sweetness of our Lord.

7. The higher degree of the second part of contemplation.

But the higher degree of this part can be had and held only by people who are in great quietness of body and soul: those who by the grace of Jesus Christ and long labor in body and spirit feel rest of heart and cleanness in conscience, so that nothing pleases them so much as to sit still in bodily rest,[18] to pray to God always, and to meditate[19] on our Lord, sometimes also meditating on the blessed name of Jesus,[20] which is made so full of comfort and delight for them that through the remembrance of it they feel themselves fed by it in their affection. And not only are they nourished by that name, but all other prayers—such as the Our Father, Hail Mary, or hymns or psalms—and other devout sayings of holy church are turned as it were into spiritual melody and sweet song, by which they are encouraged and strengthened against all sins and greatly relieved of bodily disorders. St. Paul speaks thus of this degree: *Nolite inebriari vino, sed impleamini spiritu sancto loquentes vobismet ipsis in hymnis et psalmis et canticis spiritualibus, cantantes et psallentes in cordibus vestris Domino.*[21] Do not get drunk with wine, but be filled with

81

the Holy Spirit, speaking to one another in hymns, psalms and spiritual songs, with singing and psalmody in your hearts to our Lord. Whoever has this grace should keep himself lowly, always desiring to come to greater knowledge and feeling of God in the third part of contemplation.

8. The third part of contemplation.

The third part of contemplation, which is as perfect as can be here, lies both in cognition and in affection:[22] that is to say, in the knowing and perfect loving of God. That is when a person's soul is first cleansed from all sins and reformed to the image of Jesus by completeness of virtues, and afterward he is visited and taken up from all earthly and fleshly affections, from vain thoughts and imaginations of all bodily things, and is as if forcibly ravished[23] out of the bodily senses; and then is illumined by the grace of the Holy Spirit to see intellectually[24] the Truth, which is God, and also spiritual things, with a soft, sweet burning love for him—so perfectly that by the rapture of this love the soul is for the time united and conformed to the image of the Trinity. The beginning of this contemplation may be felt in this life, but the fullness of it is kept in the bliss of heaven. St. Paul says this of such union and conforming: *Qui adhaeret Deo, unus spiritus est cum illo.*[25] That is to say, if anyone is fastened to God by the rapture of love, then God and the soul are not two, but both are one—not in flesh, but in one spirit—and certainly in this union that marriage is made between God and the soul which shall never be broken.

9. The distinction between the third part of contemplation and the second, and the praise of it.

That other part may be called burning love in devotion, but this is burning love in contemplation; that is the lower, but this is the higher; that is the sweeter to the bodily feeling, but this is the sweeter to the spiritual feeling, since it is more inward, more spiritual, more worthy and more wonderful; for this truly [is] a tasting and as it were a sight of heavenly joy—not clearly but half in darkness—which shall be fulfilled and clearly revealed in the bliss of heaven, as St. Paul says: *Videmus nunc per speculum in aenigmate, tunc autem facie ad faciem.*[26] We see God now in a mirror, as if in darkness, but in heaven we shall see openly, face to face. This is the illumination of understanding in the delights of loving, as David says in the Book of Psalms: *Et nox mea illuminatio mea in deliciis meis.*[27] My night is my light in my delights. That other part is milk for children; this is whole meat for perfect people who have faculties tested in the discernment of good from evil, as St. Paul says: *Perfectorum est solidus cibus qui habent sensus exercitatos ad discretionem boni et mali.*[28] No one can have the practice and full use of this gift without being first reformed to the likeness of Jesus by fullness of virtue. I suppose no one living in a mortal body can have it often in its fullness, but occasionally, when he is visited; and as I conceive from the writings of holy men,[29] it is for a very short time, for soon afterward he lapses into sobriety of bodily feeling. All this is the work of charity. St. Paul spoke thus about himself, as I understand: *Sive excedimus Deo, sive sobrii sumus vobis, caritas Christi urget nos.*[30] Whether we pass beyond our bodily senses toward God in contemplation or are more sober in bodily feeling toward you, it is the charity of Christ that stirs us.

Of this part of contemplation and conforming to God, St. Paul speaks thus: *Nos autem revelata facie gloriam Dei speculamur, transformati in eandem imaginem, a claritate in claritatem tanquam a Domini spiritu.*[31] This is as much as to say, St. Paul says thus, speaking for himself and for perfect men: When we are first reformed by virtues to the likeness of God, and the face of our soul is uncovered by the opening of our spiritual eye, we look at heavenly joy as in a mirror; and we are conformed and made one with the image of our Lord, from the brightness of faith into the brightness of understanding, or else from the clarity of desire into the clarity of blessed love.[32] And all this is the work of our Lord's spirit in a person's soul, as St. Paul says.

This part of contemplation God gives wherever he wills, to clergy or laity, to men and women occupied in prelacy[33] and to the solitary as well; but it is a special gift and not a common one. Moreover, though a person in active life may have it by a special grace, I consider that no one can have the full use of it unless he is solitary and contemplative in life.

10. How showings to the bodily senses, and the feeling of them, may be both good and evil.

By what I have said you will to some extent understand that visions or revelations[34] of any kind of spirit, appearing in the body or in the imagination,[35] asleep or awake, or any other feeling in the bodily senses made in spiritual fashion—either in sound by the ear, or tasting in the mouth, or smelling to the nose, or else any heat that can be felt[36] like fire glowing and warming the breast or any other part of the body, or anything that can be felt by bodily sense, however comforting and pleasing it may be—these are not truly contemplation. They are only simple and secondary—though they are good—compared with spiritual virtues and the spiritual knowledge and loving of God.

For in virtues and in the knowledge of God with love there is no deceit, but all such feelings may be either good, the work of a good angel,[37] or they may be deceitful: the contrivance of a wicked angel when he transfigures himself into an angel of light.[38] Therefore, since they can be both good and evil, it seems that they are not the best. For you must know that the devil when he has leave can counterfeit in bodily feeling the likeness of the same things that a good angel may do: just as a good angel comes with light, so can the devil, and so with the other senses. Anybody who had felt both kinds should know how to tell which is good and which evil, but a person who never felt either, or only the one, can easily be deceived. They are alike in the way they are felt outwardly, but within they are very different, and therefore they are not to be greatly desired or carelessly received, unless a soul can by the spirit of discretion know the good from the evil, and so escape beguilement. St. John speaks in this way: *Nolite credere omni spiritui, sed probate si ex Deo sit.*[39] St. John tells us not to believe every spirit, but first to try whether he is from God or not. Therefore I shall tell you by one test, as it seems to me.

II. How you are to know when the showings to the bodily senses, and the feeling of them, are good or evil.

If it so happens that you see any kind of light or brightness with your bodily eye, or in imagination, other than everyone can see; or if you hear any pleasing and wonderful sound with your bodily ear; or if you have any sweet sudden savor in your mouth other than what is natural, or any heat in your breast as of fire, or any kind of pleasure in any part of your body; or if a spirit appears to you in bodily form like an angel to comfort and teach you; or you have any other such feeling which you well know does not come from yourself or from any bodily creature: be on your guard at that time or soon after. Wisely observe the stirring of your heart, in case you are stirred because of the pleasure you feel to withdraw your heart from spiritual occupation—from prayer, from thinking about yourself and your faults, from the inward desire of virtues and of the spiritual knowledge and feeling of God—in order to set the sight of your heart, your affection, your desire, and your rest mainly on this: supposing that feeling in the body to be a part of heavenly joy and of angels' bliss. And therefore you feel you should neither pray nor think of anything else, but give your whole attention to this, to keep it and delight in it. This feeling is suspect and from the Enemy, and therefore however pleasing and wonderful it may be, refuse it and do not consent to it; for this is the trick of the Enemy. When he sees that a soul wishes to give himself entirely to the work of the spirit he is extremely angry, for he hates nothing more than to see a soul in a body of sin[40] truly feel the savor of spiritual knowledge and the love of God, which he himself lost of his own will when not within the body of sin. And therefore if he cannot hamper him by obvious bodily sins he would like to hinder and beguile him by this vanity of bodily savors or sweetness in the senses, so as to bring him into spiritual pride and false self-confidence. This soul supposes himself to have by it a feeling of heavenly joy, and thinks he is half in paradise for the delight that he feels all about him, when he is nearly at hell's gates, and so by pride and presumption he can fall into errors or fantasies, or into other bodily or spiritual calamities.

Nevertheless, it may happen that this way of feeling does not hinder your heart from spiritual occupation, but makes you the more devout and more fervent in prayer, and wiser in thinking spiritual thoughts, and though it may upset you when it first begins to come, nonetheless afterward it turns and quickens your heart to greater desire for virtues, and increases your love both for God and for your fellow Christian. Also it makes you humbler in your own sight. By these tokens you may know then that it is from God, made by the presence and the comfort or touching of the good angel: and that is by the goodness of God, shown either for the comfort of simple devout souls in order to increase their trust in God and their desire for him, and to seek thereby the knowledge and love of God the more perfectly because of such bodily comfort; or else—if those who feel such delight are perfect—it seems then that it is an earnest and as it were a shadow of the glorifying the body shall have in the bliss of heaven. I do not know whether there is anyone like this living on earth. Mary Magdalene[41] had this privilege, as it looks to me, at the time when she was alone in the cave for thirty winters, each day borne up into the air by angels and fed in both body and soul by their presence: so we read in her history.

St. John speaks in his epistle of this way of testing the work of spirits, and teaches us: *Omnis spiritus qui solvit Jesum; hic non est a Deo.*[42] Every spirit that releases Jesus or unfastens him; he is not from God. These words may be understood in many ways; nevertheless in one way I can understand them with that meaning I have given.

12.   What knits Jesus to the human soul, and what loosens him
      from it.

Jesus is knitted and fastened to a person's soul[43] by a good will and a
great desire for him, to have him alone and to see him in his spiritual
glory. The greater this desire, the more firmly is Jesus knitted to the
soul; the less the desire, the more loosely is he joined. Then whatever
spirit or feeling it is that lessens this desire and wants to draw it down
from its natural ascent toward Jesus in order to set it upon itself, this
spirit will unknit and undo Jesus from the soul; and therefore it is not
from God but from the working of the Enemy. Nevertheless, if a spirit,
a feeling or a revelation by an angel increases this desire, knits firmer the
knot of love and devotion to Jesus, opens the sight of your soul more
clearly to spiritual knowledge, and makes it humbler in itself, this spirit
is from God.

Here you can partly see that you must not willingly allow your heart
to rest or find all its delight in any such feelings of comfort or sweetness
in the body even if they are good, but you shall hold them in your own
view as little or nothing compared with spiritual desire; and you shall not
fix your heart in them in thought, but forget them if you can and always
seek to come to the spiritual feeling of God: and that is to know and
experience the wisdom of God, his infinite might and his great goodness, both in himself and in his creatures. For this is contemplation, and
that other is not.

This is what St. Paul said: *In caritate radicati et fundati, ut possitis
comprehendere cum omnibus sanctis quae sit longitudo et latitudo, sublimi-
tas et profundum.*[44] Be rooted and grounded in charity, that you may
know, he says, not a sound in the ear, or sweet taste in the mouth, or any
such bodily thing, but that with the saints you may know and feel what is
the length of the infinite being of God, the breadth of the wonderful
charity and goodness of God, the height of his almighty majesty, and the
bottomless depth of his wisdom.

13.   How a contemplative should be occupied, and with what
      things.

A contemplative should find his occupation in knowing and feeling
these four things, for in them the full knowledge of all spiritual matters
can be understood. This occupation is that same thing St. Paul desired,
saying thus: *Unum vero, quae retro sunt obliviscens, in anteriora me exten-*

dam sequor si quomodo comprehendam supernum bravium.[45] This is as much as to say, One thing is left to me to desire: that I might forget all the things that are behind or backward, always stretching forward with my heart to feel and grasp the supreme reward of eternal glory. Behind are all bodily things, ahead are all spiritual things; and therefore St. Paul wanted to forget all material[46] things, and his own body as well, so that he could see the things of the spirit.

14. How virtues begin in reason and in will, and are ended and made perfect in love and pleasure.

Now I have told you a little about contemplation—what it is or should be—with the intention that you might know it and set it as a beacon before the sight of your soul, desiring all through your life to come to any part of it by the grace of our Lord Jesus Christ. This is the conforming of a soul to be like God, which may be not be achieved unless it is first reformed by the fullness of virtues, turned into affection; and that is when somebody loves a virtue because it is good in itself. There is many a man that has virtues, such as lowliness, patience, charity toward his fellow Christians and so on, only in his reason and will, but without any spiritual delight or love in them. Often he feels grudging, sad and bitter as he practices them, and nevertheless he does it, stirred only by reason and the fear of God. This man has virtues in his reason and will, but not the love of them in affection.[47] But when by the grace of Jesus and by spiritual and bodily exercise the reason is turned into light and the will into love, then he has virtues in affection, for he has so well gnawed the bitter bark of the nut that he has broken it and feeds upon the kernel.[48] That is to say, the virtues which were at first hard to practice are now turned into real delight and savor, as happens when someone enjoys himself in patience, humility, purity, sobriety and charity as much as in any pleasures. Certainly, before[49] virtues are turned like this into affection he can have the second part of contemplation: but in truth he shall not come to the third.

Now, since virtues dispose one to contemplation, you need to use certain means to come to virtues.

15. The means that bring a person to contemplation.

There are three means[50] most commonly used by people who devote themselves to contemplation: the reading of holy scripture and of holy teaching,[51] spiritual meditation, and diligent prayer with devotion. The reading of holy scripture is not practicable for you,[52] and therefore you are the more bound to occupy yourself in prayer and meditation.

By meditation you shall see how far you lack virtues, and by prayer you shall get them. By meditation you shall see your wretchedness, your sins and your wickedness—such as pride, covetousness, gluttony, lechery, wicked stirrings of envy, wrath, hatred, sullenness, angriness, bitterness, sloth and unreasonable worry.[53] You will also find your heart full of vain shames and fears of your flesh and of the world. All these stirrings will always bubble out of your heart as water will run out from the spring of a stinking well,[54] and hinder the sight of your soul from either seeing or feeling purely the love of Jesus Christ. For know well, until your heart is largely cleansed from such sins you cannot have perfectly the spiritual knowledge of God, according to his own witness in the gospel: *Beati mundo corde: quoniam ipsi Deum videbunt.*[55] Blessed be the pure in heart, for they shall see God. In meditation you will also see the virtues that are necessary for you to have, such as humility, mildness, patience, righteousness, strength of spirit, temperance, peace, purity and sobriety, faith, hope and charity.[56] In meditation you will see how good, how fair and how profitable these virtues are, and by prayer you will desire and get them. Without them you cannot be contemplative, for Job speaks thus: *In abundantia ingredieris sepulcrum.*[57] That is to say, In abundant good bodily deeds and spiritual virtues shall you enter your grave, that is, rest in contemplation.

16. What one should use and refuse by virtue of humility.

Now if you are to use these spiritual works wisely and labor in them with confidence, you need to begin at the bottom. To start with you will need three things on which, as on a firm foundation, you will set all your work. These three are humility, sure faith, and a whole intention toward God.

First you must have humility, in this way. You shall regard yourself in your will, and in your feelings if you can, as unfit to live among men or women and unworthy to serve God in the company of his servants; useless to your fellow Christian; lacking both the skill and the strength to perform the good deeds of active life to help your fellow Christians as other men and women do; and therefore as a wretch, cast out and rejected by all men and women, you are shut up in a house alone—so that you should harm neither man nor woman by evil example, since you do not know how to benefit them by good works. Moreover, you ought to look further: that since you are so unfit to serve our Lord outwardly by bodily works, how much more should you regard yourself as unfit and unworthy to serve him spiritually by inward occupation. For our Lord is a spirit, as the prophet says: *Spiritus ante faciem nostram Christus Dominus.*[58] Our Lord Christ is a spirit before our face, and the service proper to him is spiritual, as he says himself: *Veri adoratores adorabunt Patrem in spiritu et veritate.*[59] True servants shall worship the Father in spirit and truth. Then you who are so rough, so ignorant, so carnal, and so blind toward spiritual things and especially in your own soul—which you must know first if you are to come to the knowledge of God—how should you then feel yourself able or worthy to have that state and appearance of contemplative life, which (as I have said) consists mainly in the spiritual knowing and loving of God?

I tell you this, not that you ought to regret your purpose and be dissatisfied with your enclosure, but that you should feel this lowliness genuinely in your heart, if you could, for it is true and not lies. And although you feel like this, you shall still yearn night and day, as far as you are able, to come as near as you can to the state which you have taken, steadfastly believing that by the mercy of God it is the best for you to labor in. And although it may be that you cannot come to its fulfilment here in this life, that you might be at the beginning of it; and firmly trust by the mercy of God to have the fulfilment of it in the glory of heaven.

For truly that is my own life. I feel myself so wretched, so frail and so carnal, and so far in my real feelings from what I speak and have spoken, that I am fit to do nothing but cry for mercy, desiring as I can with hope that by his grace our Lord will bring me to this in the glory of heaven. Do the same yourself, and better, according to the grace God gives you.

The feeling of this lowness will put out of your heart the unwise scrutiny of other people's evil living and the judgment of their works, and it will drive you to behold only yourself, as if there were no one alive but God and you; and you shall judge and regard yourself as viler and more wretched than any other creature that has life, so that you can scarcely endure yourself for the abundance of sin and filth that you will find and feel within. This is how you must feel at times if you want to be truly humble, for I tell you indeed, if true humility is your desire, a venial sin in yourself will seem to you more grievous and painful and will sometimes be greater in your sight than the great mortal sins of other people, and for this reason. The thing that puts your soul off or hinders it most from the feeling and knowing of God ought to be most grievous and painful to you; but a venial sin of your own hinders you more from the feeling and knowledge of God than the sin of others, however great that may be. Therefore it seems that you should arise in your own heart against yourself, to hate and judge in yourself every kind of sin which hinders you from the sight of God more diligently than against the faults of any other people. For if your heart is clean from sins of your own, truly the sins of all others will not harm you, and therefore if you want to find rest here and in the bliss of heaven, follow the advice of one of the holy fathers,[60] saying each day, "What am I?" And do not judge anybody.

17. Who should blame people's faults and censure them, and who should not.

But now you say, "How can this be, since it is a work of charity to rebuke people for their faults, and to censure them with a view to their amendment? It is a work of mercy." To this I reply that in my opinion it is not your duty—or that of anyone else having the state and purpose of contemplative life—to leave off keeping watch on yourself and to rebuke others for their faults, except in very great need when someone would perish without your reproof. It is for those who are active and have authority and charge over others, as have prelates, pastors and people of that kind. They are bound by their office and by way of charity to see, search out and pass righteous judgment on the faults of others: not out of desire and delight in pursuing them but only in need, with fear of God and in his name, for the love and salvation of their souls. Others who are active[61] and have [no][62] charge over others are obliged by charity to rebuke people for their faults only when the sin is mortal, when it cannot well be corrected by anyone else, and when they believe the sinner would be amended by their reproof; otherwise it is better to desist.

This seems to be borne out by St. John, who had the state of contemplative life, and St. Peter, who had the state of active life.[63] At our Lord's last supper with his disciples, when St. Peter secretly prompted St. John, he told St. John how Judas was to betray him; but St. John did not tell St. Peter as he asked. Instead, he turned round and laid his head on Christ's breast and was transported by love into the contemplation of God's mysteries. He was so rewarded that he forgot both Judas and St.

Peter—as token and teaching for others who might want to be contemplative, that they should be ready to do the same.

Therefore you see something here: you must never judge other people or willingly conceive any evil suspicion against them; but you shall love in your heart those who lead an active life in the world,[64] suffering many troubles and great temptations of which you feel nothing as you sit in your house. They have a great deal of labor to support themselves and other people, and if they could, many of them would much rather serve God as you do, in bodily rest: nevertheless in their worldly business they flee many sins which you would fall into if you led their life; and they do many good deeds for which you lack the skill. There is no doubt that many behave thus: who they are, you do not know.

18. Why humble people are to honor others, and in their own hearts lower themselves beneath all others.

Therefore you shall give honor to all and set them above yourself in your heart as your superiors, throwing yourself down under their feet so that in your own sight you are vilest and lowest, since for you there is no fear or danger however much you lower yourself beneath all others, even if it should happen that in God's sight you had more grace than someone else. But there is danger for you in deliberately exalting and lifting yourself in thought above any other person, even if he were the greatest wretch or most sinful villain on earth, for our Lord says: *Qui se humiliat exaltabitur, et qui se exaltat humiliabitur.*[65] Whoever exalts himself shall be humbled and whoever humbles himself shall be exalted.

This part of humility you must have when you begin; by this and by grace you will come to the fullness of it and of all other virtues; for whoever has one virtue, has all.[66] Whatever the amount of humility you have, you will have as much charity, patience and other virtues, though they may not be shown outwardly. Take pains, then, to acquire humility and hold it, for it is the first and last of all virtues. It is the first because it is the foundation, as St. Augustine says:[67] If you think to build a tall house of virtues, first plan for yourself a deep foundation of humility. It is also the last, for it saves and keeps all virtues, as St. Gregory says:[68] He who gathers virtues without humility is like someone preparing and carrying powdered spices in the wind. However many good deeds you may do—fasting, waking, or any other good work—if you have no humility, you do nothing.

19. How people are to behave if they lack the feeling of humility in their affection, without being too fearful about it.

Nevertheless, if you cannot feel this humility in your heart with affection, as you wish, do what you can: humble yourself in your will by your reason, believing that it is as I say even though you do not feel it, and regarding yourself as a worse wretch in that you cannot truly feel what you are; and if you do so, although your flesh rises against it and will not assent to your will, do not be too frightened, but bear and suffer the false feeling of your flesh as a punishment. You shall then despise and reject that feeling and break down that rising of your heart as if it would serve you right to be trodden and spurned under everyone's feet like something thrown away; and so by the grace of Jesus Christ you shall greatly diminish the stirrings of pride, and the virtue of humility that at first existed in the naked will shall be turned into a feeling of affection. Without this virtue, either in a true will or in feeling, anyone who disposes himself to the service of God in contemplative life will stumble like the blind, and shall never come to it. The higher he climbs by means of bodily penance and other virtues, not having this one, the lower he falls. For as St. Gregory says,[69] Anyone who has not learned perfectly to despise himself never yet found the humble wisdom of our Lord Jesus.

20. How for lack of humility heretics and hypocrites exalt themselves in their own hearts above all others.

Hypocrites and heretics[70] do not feel this humility either in good will or in affection, but their hearts and loins are too dry and cold—alien to the soft feeling of this virtue—and inasmuch as they suppose themselves to have it, they are the further from it. They gnaw the dry bark outside, but they cannot come to its sweet kernel[71] and inner savor. They show outward humility in clothing, in holy speech and in lowly bearing, and (as it seems) in many great virtues of body and spirit; but nevertheless in the will and affection of their heart, where humility should be first of all, it is only pretended, for they despise and think nothing of all others, who will not do as they do or teach. They consider them either fools through ignorance or blinded by their carnal way of life, and therefore in their own sight they lift themselves on high above all the rest; they think that they live better than others and that they alone have the truth of good living and the singular grace of God, surpassing other people both in knowledge and in spiritual feeling.

From this view within them arises a great delight in their hearts through which they honor and praise themselves as if there were nobody else. They praise and thank God with their lips, but in their hearts they steal like thieves the honor and thanksgiving from God[72] and set it upon themselves; and so they have no humility either in will or in feeling. A carnal wretch or a sinner who falls every day and is sorry that he does so has no humility in affection, but he has it in a good will; a heretic or hypocrite has neither, for he is in the condition of the Pharisee[73] who with the publican came to the temple to pray, as our Lord says in the gospel. When he came he did not pray or ask anything from God, for he felt he had no need, but he began to thank God, speaking like this: "Lord, I thank you that you give me more grace than anyone else; that I am not like others: robbers, lechers and sinners of that kind." And he looked beside him and saw the publican—whom he knew for a rogue— beating his breast and crying simply for mercy. Then he thanked God that he was not like that: "Lord," he said, "I fast twice a week and pay my tithes honestly." And when he had finished, our Lord says that he went home again without grace as he came, and got nothing at all.

But now you say, "In what way, then, did this Pharisee trespass, since he thanked God and was truthful in what he said?" To this I make the following answer. This Pharisee trespassed inasmuch as he judged and scorned in his heart the publican whom our Lord justified; and he also trespassed in thanking God only with his mouth while choosing to delight in the gifts of God through a secret pride in himself, and stealing the honor and praise from God to set it on himself. Heretics and hypocrites are truly in the same condition as this Pharisee: they will not gladly pray, and if they pray they do not humble themselves in faithful acknowledgment of their wretchedness but make a pretense of thanking and praising God, and speak of him with their mouths; nevertheless their delight is vain and false and not in God; and yet they do not realize it. They do not know how to praise God, for as the wise man says, *Non est speciosa laus in ore peccatoris.*[74] The praise of God is neither beautiful nor seemly in the mouth of a sinner.

Therefore it is profitable for you and me and other wretches like us to avoid the behavior of this Pharisee and the pretended praise of God, and to follow the publican, first asking in lowliness for mercy and the forgiveness of sins, and for the grace of spiritual virtues, so that afterward with a pure heart we can truthfully thank him, praise him, and give him full honor without pretense. For our Lord asks this question by his prophet: *Super quem requiescet Spiritus meus nisi super humilem contritum spiritum et trementem sermones meos?*[75] Upon whom shall my Spirit rest? And he answers himself, saying: Upon none but the humble, poor and contrite in heart who fear my words. Then, if you want the spirit of God to rule your heart, have humility and fear of him.

21.   What things people ought to believe by a firm faith.

The second thing you are obliged to have is a firm belief in all articles of the faith and sacraments of holy church, believing them steadfastly with all the will[76] of your heart. If you should feel any stirring against any of them in your heart through the suggestion of the Enemy, made to put you in doubt and in dread of them, be steadfast and not too badly frightened by the feeling of such stirrings, but forsake your own intellect without disputing or investigating these things, put your faith generally in the faith of holy church, and never mind about that stirring of your heart which you find contrary to it. For the stirring that you feel is not your faith: the faith of holy church is your faith, even though you neither see it nor feel it.[77] Then bear such stirrings patiently as a scourge from our Lord by which he wants to cleanse your heart and make your faith steadfast.

You must also love and honor in your heart the laws and ordinances made by the prelates and rulers of holy church, either in declaring the faith, or in the sacraments,[78] or in the general government of all Christian people. Humbly and faithfully agree to them, even though you do not know the cause of their ordinance; and though some may seem to you unreasonable you shall not judge them or reject them, but accept and honor them even if they concern you little. You shall not receive any opinion, fancy, or peculiar notion under the color of greater holiness, as do some who are not wise—either from your own imagination or by the teaching of anyone else—if it is contrary to the least ordinance or general teaching of all-holy church.

And as well as this you shall steadfastly believe[79] that you are ordained by our Lord to be saved as one of his chosen, by his mercy; and do not budge from this belief whatever you hear or see, whatever temptation you are in. Although you feel that you are so great a wretch that you are worthy to sink into hell, because you do nothing good and do not serve God as you should; yet hold yourself in this faith, and in this hope, and ask mercy: and all shall be very well. Yes—and even if all the devils of hell appeared to you, waking or sleeping, in bodily form, saying that you should not be saved, or all people living on earth, or all the angels of heaven (if that might be) told you the same thing, you should not believe them or be moved much from this faith and hope of salvation.

I say this to you because some are so weak and so simple that when they have given themselves entirely to the service of God, as far as they know, and feel any suggestion—either within, injected by the Enemy, or else from without, by any word of the devil's prophets, which people call soothsayers—that they should not be saved; or that their state or way of living might not be pleasing to God: they are astonished and upset by such words, and so for lack of knowledge they sometimes fall into great sadness and into a kind of despair of salvation. For this reason it seems to me helpful for every creature to have trust in salvation, if by the grace of our Lord Jesus Christ he is fully determined to forsake sin; and if as thoroughly as his conscience tells him he allows no mortal sin to remain in him without soon shriving himself from it, humbling himself before the sacraments of holy church. Much more, then, should those have such trust who give themselves wholly to God and flee venial sins as far as they can. On the other hand, it is equally dangerous for someone who knowingly lies in a deadly sin to have trust in salvation, if through hope from that trust he will not abandon his sin or truly humble himself before God and holy church.

22. How a stable intention is necessary for those who are to please God, and discretion in the works of the body.

The third thing necessary for you to have from the beginning is a whole and stable intention,[80] that is to say, a whole will and desire only to please God: for that is charity, without which everything you do would be nothing.[81] You shall fix your purpose in a continual search and labor to please him, never willingly leaving the good occupation of either body or spirit. You shall not set a time in your heart; for example, you might wish to serve God for so long and then allow your heart to fall willfully into vain thoughts and idle doings, thinking it necessary for the safety of your bodily nature and no longer keeping watch over your heart and your good occupation; seeking rest and comfort outwardly for a time by the bodily senses; or in worldly vanities, as if for recreation of the spirit, so that it should afterward be the sharper for spiritual labor— for I believe that is not true. I do not say that you will be able to put your intention into practice all the time, for often your bodily need to eat, sleep and speak—as well as the frailty of your flesh—will hamper and hinder you, whatever your efforts. Yet I would wish your purpose and your will always to be whole, to work in the spirit and at no time to be idle, but always lifting up your heart by desire for God and for the glory of heaven, whether you are eating or drinking or engaged in any other bodily work, as far as you can. Do not willingly leave it; for if you have this intention it will make you ever lively and sharp in your labor; and if by frailty or negligence you fall into any idle occupation or into vain speech, it will hit your heart sharply like a hammer, making you recoil from all vanities in disgust and turn again hastily to some good occupation.

For with regard to your bodily nature, it is good to use discretion[82] in eating, drinking and sleeping, and in every kind of bodily penance: either in prolonged vocal prayer or in bodily feeling from great fervor of devotion—as in weeping or the like—and in spiritual imagining as well, when one feels no grace. In all these kinds of work it is good to keep discretion, perhaps by breaking off sometimes; for moderation is best. But in the destruction of sin by guarding your heart, and in the perpetual desire for virtues and the glory of heaven and for possession of the spiritual knowledge and love of God—in these hold to no mean,[83] for the more there is of this, the better. For you shall hate sin and all fleshly loves and fears in your heart without ceasing; and you must love virtue and purity and desire them without stint, if you can. I do not say that this intention is necessary for salvation, but I think it profitable, and if you keep it you shall advance more in virtue in one year than you could without it in seven.

23. A short recapitulation of what has been said, and the making of an offering to be given to God.

I have now told you first of the end you shall behold in your desire and move toward as much as you can. I have also spoken of the beginning: what you need to have, such as humility, a sure faith, and a whole intention toward God, on which ground you shall set your spiritual house[84] by prayer and meditation and other spiritual virtues.

Then I speak to you like this. Whether you pray or meditate, or do anything else—good by grace, or bad through your own frailty—or whatever you feel, see or hear, smell or taste, outwardly by your bodily senses or inwardly in the imagination or feeling of your reason or knowledge, bring it all within the faith and rules of holy church. Cast it all in the mortar of humility and pound it small with the pestle of the fear of God, throw the powder of all these things in the fire of desire, and offer it to God. I tell you truthfully that this offering will be very pleasing in the sight of our Lord Jesus, and the smoke of that fire will smell sweet before his face.

That is to say, draw all that you feel within the faith of holy church, / break yourself in humility, and offer the desire of your heart to your Lord Jesus alone, to have him and nothing else but him. If you act in this way I think by the grace of Jesus Christ you will never be overcome by your Enemy. St. Paul taught us so when he said: *Sive manducatis, sive bibitis, sive quicquid aliud facitis: omnia in nomine Domini facite.*[85] Whether you eat or drink, or whatever kind of work you do, do it all in the name of our Lord Jesus Christ, forsaking yourself, and offer it up to him. The means you shall use most are, as I have said before, prayer and meditation. I shall first show you a little about prayer, and then about meditation.

24. How prayer is useful for getting virtues and purity of heart.

Prayer is profitable, and a useful means of getting purity of heart through the destruction of sin and the reception of virtues.[86] Not that you should by your prayer tell our Lord what you desire, for he knows all your needs well enough; but by your prayer make yourself able and ready like a clean vessel to receive the grace that our Lord will freely give you,[87] and this cannot be felt until you are purified by the fire of desire in devout prayer. Although it is true that prayer is not the cause for which our Lord gives grace, nevertheless it is a way by which grace, freely given, comes to a soul.

But now perhaps you want to know how you should pray, and on what you should set the point of your thought[88] in your prayer, and also what prayer would be best for you to use. I would answer the first like this. When you have woken up from your sleep and are ready to pray, you will feel yourself carnal and heavy, slipping down all the time into vain thoughts, either of dreams, or of fancies, or of irrational concerns of the world or your flesh. Then you need to quicken your heart with prayer, and stir it as much as you can to some devotion.[89]

25. How people should pray, and on what the point of the thought shall be set in prayer.

In your prayer you must not aim your heart at a material thing, but your whole effort must be to draw your thoughts inward[90] from any attention to such things, so that your desire might be as it were bare and naked from all that is earthly, always rising upward into God. You cannot see him in the body, or imagine him in a bodily likeness, but you can feel his goodness and his grace when your desire is eased and helped, and as it were strengthened and set free from all carnal thoughts and affections; when it is greatly lifted up by a spiritual power into spiritual savor and delight in God, held still in this for much of your prayer-time, so that you have no great thought of any earthly thing, or else the thought harms you only a little. If you pray like this, then you know how to pray well.

For prayer is nothing but a desire of the heart rising into God[91] by its withdrawal from all earthly thoughts; and so it is compared to a fire, which of its own nature leaves the lowness of the earth and always goes up into the air. Just so, when desire in prayer has been touched and set alight by the spiritual fire which is God, it keeps rising naturally to him from whom it came.[92]

26.   The fire of love.

Not all those who speak of the fire of love really know what it is, for what it is I cannot tell you, except for this. I tell you, it is neither material[93] nor felt in the body. It can be felt in prayer or in devotion by a soul who exists in a body, but he does not feel it by any bodily sense, for although it is true that if it works in a soul the body may pass into a heat—as it were warmed by the pleasant labor of the spirit—nevertheless the fire of love is not in the body, for it is only in the spiritual desire of the soul. There is no doubt of this for any man or woman who feels and knows devotion, but some are simple, supposing that because it is called fire it should be hot like material fire, and therefore I say what I have said.

Now as to that other question as to what prayer would be best to use, I shall speak as it seems to me. You are to understand that there are three kinds of prayer.

27.   That certain spoken prayer ordained by God and by holy church is best for people bound and ordained to it, and for those who have newly given themselves to devotion.

The first is the spoken prayer[94] made specially by God, as is the Our Father, and also made more generally by the ordinance of holy church, like Matins, Evensongs and the Hours; made too by the devout from other special sayings, for example to our Lord and our Lady, and to his saints. Concerning this kind of prayer (which is called vocal), it seems to me that for you who are religious, bound by custom and rule to say Matins and Hours, it is most useful to say these as devoutly as you can. For when you say your Matins you also principally say your Our Father, and to stir you to more devotion it was further laid down that psalms, hymns and other similar pieces made by the Holy Spirit (as is the Our Father) should be said as well. Therefore you shall not say them greedily or carelessly as if you resented being tied to them, but you shall collect your affection and your thought to say them more steadfastly and more devoutly than any other special prayer of devotion, believing indeed that since it is the prayer of holy church there is no vocal prayer so profitable for your ordinary use as that one. And so you shall put away all the heaviness, and by grace you shall turn your necessity into good will, and your bond into great freedom, so that it will be no hindrance to you from spiritual occupation.

After these, if you wish, you may use others, such as your Our Father or anything similar, and I consider the best for you to be those in which you feel most savor and spiritual comfort. This kind of prayer is usually more helpful than any other spiritual occupation for someone to use at the beginning of his conversion.[95] At the outset a person is crude, stupid and carnal (unless he has more grace), and does not know how to think spiritual thoughts in meditation, for his soul is not yet cleansed from old sin. Therefore I think it most helpful to use this kind of prayer (saying his Our Father and Hail Mary, reading his Psalter, and so on): for a person needs a firm staff to hold him up if he cannot run easily by spiritual prayer because his feet[96] of knowing and loving are infirm through sin. This staff is the special spoken prayer ordained by God and holy church to help people's souls: by this prayer the soul of a carnal man who is always falling down into worldly thoughts and affections of the flesh will be lifted up from them and held by them as by a staff. Like a child with milk[97] he will be fed with the sweet words of the prayer, and so ruled by it that he will not fall into errors or fantasies by his vain meditation, since in this kind of prayer there is no deceit, if anyone will steadfastly and humbly labor in it.

28. How perilous it is for those at the start of their turning to God when they leave too soon the common prayer laid down by holy church, and give themselves entirely to meditation.

By this, then, you can see how unwise are those people (if there are any of this kind) who too quickly leave such vocal prayer and other practices of the body, at the beginning of their conversion or soon after, and give themselves entirely to meditation, when they have felt a little spiritual comfort either in devotion or in knowledge, but are not yet stable in it. They are not wise, for often in the quiet of their meditation they imagine and think of spiritual things according to their own wit and follow their bodily feeling before receiving grace for it. Therefore through their indiscretion they often overstrain their wits and break the powers of their body, and so fall into fantasies and singular inventions, or into manifest errors,[98] and by such vanities hinder the grace which God gives them.

The cause of all this is a secret pride and presumption in themselves: for example, having felt a little grace they regard it as so far superior to any other that they fall into vainglory, and in this way they lose it. If they only knew how little it is that they feel in comparison with what God gives or can give, they would be ashamed to say anything about it, except in great necessity. David speaks thus of this kind of spoken prayer in the Psalter: *Voce mea ad Dominum clamavi: voce mea ad Dominum deprecatus sum.*[99] In order to stir other men with both heart and mouth, David the prophet said, "With my voice I cried to God, and with my speech I besought our Lord."

29. The second kind of prayer, which is not fixed in speech but follows the stirrings of those who are in a state of devotion.

The second kind of prayer is spoken, but without any particular set words, and this is when a man or a woman feels the grace of devotion by the gift of God, and in his devotion speaks to him as if he were bodily in his presence. He uses the words that best match his inward stirring for the time and that have come to his mind following the different concerns he feels in his heart, rehearsing either his sins and his wickedness, or the malice and tricks of the Enemy, or else the goodness and mercy of God. And with that he cries to our Lord for succor and help, with the desire of his heart and the words of his mouth, like a man in peril among his enemies, or like someone in sickness showing his sores to God as a doctor,[100] and saying thus: *Eripe me de inimicis meis Deus meus*[101] (Ah, Lord, deliver me from my enemies); or else thus: *Sana, Domine, animam meam, quia peccavi tibi*[102] (Ah, Lord, heal my soul, for I have sinned against you); or anything similar that comes to mind.

And also it seems to him that there is so much goodness, grace and mercy in God that he is glad to praise and thank him with great affection from the heart, using such words and psalms as are fit for the glorifying and praise of God, as David says: *Confitemini Domino, quoniam bonus, quoniam in seculum misericordia eius*[103] (Glorify and praise our Lord, for he is good and merciful); and by other such words as he is stirred to say.

30. How this kind of prayer greatly pleases God, and sometimes makes a person behave in his body as if he were drunk, and makes him wounded in his soul with the sword of love.

This kind of prayer greatly pleases God, for it is only in the affection of the heart, and therefore it never goes away unsatisfied, without some grace. This prayer belongs to the second part of contemplation, as I have said before. Whoever has this gift of God fervently needs to escape for the time from the presence and company of everyone, and to be alone, lest he should be hindered. Whoever has it, let him hold it while he can, for it cannot last long in fervor: if grace comes abundantly it is wonderfully hard work for the spirit, even though it is pleasurable, and it is very wasting[104] for the bodily nature of anyone who uses it much. For if grace comes powerfully, it makes the body stir and turn here and there, like someone mad or drunk[105] who cannot find rest. And this is a point of the passion of love, which by great violence and power breaks down all pleasures and delights in all earthly things; and it wounds the soul[106] with the blissful sword of love so that the body fails and falls down and cannot bear it. This touching is of such great strength that if even the most vicious or carnal person living on earth were once well and mightily touched with this sharp sword, he would be very serious and sober for a great while after, loathing all the delights and pleasures of his flesh and of all earthly things he formerly most enjoyed.

31. How the fire of love lays waste all carnal lusts, as other fire lays waste every material thing.

Jeremiah the prophet speaks thus of this kind of feeling: *Et factus est in corde meo quasi ignis aestuans cl33ususque in ossibus meis, et defeci, ferre non sustinens.*[107] This may be understood so: The love and feeling of God became in my heart not fire, but like glowing fire; for as physical fire burns and lays waste all material things wherever it comes, in just the same way spiritual fire (as is the love of God) burns and lays waste all carnal loves and pleasures in one's soul. And this fire is fixed in my bones, as the prophet said about himself. That is to say, This love fills full the powers of the soul, such as the memory, will and reason,[108] with grace and spiritual sweetness, as marrow entirely fills the bone, and that is within, not outwardly in the senses. Nevertheless, it is so powerful within that it strikes outward in the body, making it all quake and tremble;[109] for it is so far from the bodily nature and so unfamiliar that he sees no reason for it and cannot bear it, but fails and falls down as the prophet said. Therefore our Lord tempers it, withdrawing the fervor and allowing the heart to subside into the sobriety of greater ease. Anyone with the skill to pray often like this is making swift progress in his task. He will acquire more virtues in a little while than someone else as good will get in a long time without this, for all the bodily penance that he could do.[110] And whoever has this does not need to burden his bodily nature with any greater penance than he already bears, if he often prays in this way.

32. The third kind of prayer, in the heart alone and without speaking.

The third kind of prayer is only in the heart, without speaking, and with great rest of body and soul. Anyone who is to pray well in this way needs to have a pure heart, for it belongs to those men and women who by long labor of body and soul—or else by such sharp striking of love as I mentioned—come into rest of spirit, so that their affection is turned into spiritual savor, and so that they can pray in their heart continually, glorifying and praising God, without great hindrance from temptations or vanities, as I have said before in the second part of contemplation.

St. Paul speaks thus of this kind of prayer: *Nam si orem lingua, spiritus meus orat, mens autem sine fructu est. Quid ergo? Orabo spiritu, orabo et mente; psallam spiritu, psallam et mente.*[111] This is as much as to say, If I pray with my tongue alone, by the will of the spirit and with great labor, the prayer is deserving but my soul is not fed; for it does not feel the fruit of spiritual sweetness by understanding. What then shall I do? asks St. Paul, and he answers and says: I shall pray with travail and desire of spirit; and I shall also pray more inwardly in my spirit, without labor, by feeling spiritual savor and sweetness in the love and the sight of God, by which sight and feeling of love my soul shall be fed. So, as I understand, St. Paul knew how to pray. Of this kind of prayer our Lord speaks figuratively in holy scripture: *Ignis in altari meo semper ardebit, et cotidie sacerdos surgens mane subiciet ligna ut ignis non extinguatur.*[112] This is as much as to say, The fire of love shall always be alight in the soul of a devout man or woman, which is the altar of our Lord; and every day in the morning the priest shall lay sticks and nourish the fire. That is to say, This man shall nourish the fire of love in his heart with holy psalms, pure thoughts and fervent desires, so that it never goes out.[113]

33. What people shall do who are troubled with vain thoughts in their prayer.

But now you say that what I tell you of this kind of prayer is too lofty for you: yet it is not hard for me to say this. The difficulty lies in doing it. You say you do not know to pray in your heart as completely or as devoutly as I describe. For when you want to have the intention of your heart held upward to God in prayer, you feel so many vain thoughts of the things you have done or will do, or of other people's actions, with many other such matters hindering and vexing you, that you can feel neither savor nor rest in your prayer nor devotion in what you are saying. And often the more you labor to control your heart, the further it is from you, and sometimes the harder it is from beginning to end, so that you feel that everything you do is merely lost.

As for my talking too loftily to you about prayer, I admit to speaking otherwise than I can or may do. I say it nevertheless with the intention that you should know how we ought to pray if we did well, and since we cannot do so, that we then humbly acknowledge our weakness and call upon God for mercy. Our Lord himself gave this commandment when he said: *Diliges dominum deum tuum ex toto corde tuo, et ex tota anima tua, et ex omnibus viribus tuis.*[114] You shall love God with all your heart, and all your soul, and all your powers. It is impossible for anyone living on earth to fulfil this command as completely as it is said; and yet nevertheless our Lord did tell us to love in this way, with this purpose— as Saint Bernard[115] says—that we should thereby acknowledge our weakness and then humbly call for mercy; and we shall have it.

Nevertheless, I shall tell you how I feel about this question. When you are about to pray, make your intention and your will at the beginning as complete and as pure toward God as you can, briefly in your mind, and then begin and do as you can. And however badly you are hindered from your first resolve, do not be too fearful, or too angry with yourself, or impatient against God for not giving you that savor and spiritual sweetness with devotion which (as it seems to you) he gives to other creatures. Instead, see by it your own weakness and bear it easily, holding your prayer in your own sight (simple as it is) with humbleness of heart, also trusting confidently in the mercy of our Lord that he will make it good—more than you know or feel; and if you do so, all shall be well.

For you must know, you are excused from your debt, and you shall be rewarded for it as for any other good deed done in charity, even though your heart were not in it as you did it. Therefore do your part and allow our Lord to give you what he will, and do not teach him. Although you may seem to yourself heedless and negligent and greatly at fault over such things, nevertheless for this fault and all the other venial sins which cannot be avoided in this wretched life, lift up your heart to God, acknowledging your wretchedness, and cry for mercy with a good trust in forgiveness, and God will forgive you. Do not struggle with it any more or hang on to it any longer, as if you wanted to dispel by force the feeling of such wretchedness: leave off, and go to some good work of body or spirit, and resolve to do better another time. Yet though you fall in the same way another time—yes, a hundred times, a thousand times!—still do as I have said, and all shall be well. For there are many souls who are unable ever to find rest of heart in prayer, but struggle with their thoughts all their lifetime, hindered and troubled by them. If they keep themselves in humility and charity in other respects, they shall have very great reward in heaven for their good labor.

Now I shall tell you a little about meditation, as it seems to me. You shall understand that in meditations no certain rule can be set for someone always to keep, for they are in the free gift of our Lord according to the various dispositions of chosen souls, and according to the state that they are in. Also, according to their progress in virtues and in their state, so he increases their meditations in the spiritual knowing and loving of himself. For if anyone is at a standstill in the knowledge of God and of spiritual things, it seems that he makes little growth in the love of God. That can be shown plainly in the apostles, when on the day of Pentecost they were filled full of burning love by the Holy Spirit; they were not made fools or madmen but wonderfully wise in knowing and speaking of God and spiritual things, as far as anyone could be while living in the body. Holy scripture speaks of them thus: *Repleti sunt omnes spiritu sancto, et ceperit loqui magnalia Dei.*[16] They were filled with the Holy Spirit, and they began to speak of the great marvels of God; and all that knowledge they had from the Holy Spirit by the rapture of love.

34. The meditation of the sinful after they have wholly turned to God.

There are various meditations that our Lord puts into a person's soul, and as I feel I shall tell you some, with this intention: that if you should feel any of them you might work with them the better. At the start of someone's conversion, when he has been much soiled with worldly or fleshly sins, he commonly thinks most about those sins, with great compunction[117] and sorrow of heart, great fits of weeping, and many tears from his eyes as he humbly and diligently asks mercy and forgiveness for them from God. If he is touched sharply (because of our Lord's will to make him clean soon), it will seem to him that his sins are still so foul and so horrible in his sight that he can scarcely bear himself for their weight; and however thoroughly he makes his confession, he yet feels his conscience biting and fretting, so that it seems he is not properly shriven.[118] He will hardly be able to rest, to the point that he could not last in such travail except that our Lord of his mercy comforts him sometimes as he will, with great devotions of his passion or in some other way. In this manner our Lord works in some hearts as he wishes—more or less—and this is the great mercy of our Lord, who wills not only to forgive the sin and the trespass but also to remit both the trespass and its punishment in purgatory for such little pain here as the biting of conscience. And also, if he wants to dispose someone to receive any special gift of his love, that person needs first to be scoured and cleansed by such a fire of compunction for all the great sins he has already committed.

David speaks about this kind of travail in many psalms of the Psalter, and specially in the psalm *Miserere mei Deus, secundum magnam misericordiam tuam*,[119] Then after this travail, and sometimes together with it, our Lord gives to such a person—or else to another who has been kept in innocence by the grace of God—a meditation of his humanity, his birth or his passion, or of the compassion of our Lady, St. Mary.

35. That the meditation of the humanity of Christ, or of his passion, is given by God; and how it shall be recognized when it is given.

When this meditation is made by the Holy Spirit, then it is very profitable and full of grace, and you will know this by the following sign.

Suppose you are stirred to devotion in God, and suddenly your thought is drawn up from all worldly and carnal things, and you feel as if you see in your soul your Lord appear in bodily likeness as he was on earth—how he was taken by the Jews and bound like a thief, beaten and despised, scourged and condemned to death; how humbly he bore the cross upon his back, and how cruelly he was nailed on it; also the crown of thorns upon his head, and the sharp spear that stung him to the heart. As you see this in the spirit, you feel your heart stirred to such great compassion and pity for your Lord Jesus that you mourn and weep and cry with all the powers of your body and of your soul, wondering at the goodness and love, patience and humility of our Lord Jesus, that he would suffer so much pain for such a sinful wretch as you are. And also, above this, you feel so much goodness and mercy in our Lord that your heart rises up into love and gladness for him, with many sweet tears, having great trust in the forgiveness of your sins, and in the salvation of your soul by the power of this precious passion. Then—when the remembrance of Christ's passion or any point of his humanity is thus caused in your heart by such spiritual vision, with devout affection answering to it—then, know well that it is not your own doing, neither the pretense of any wicked spirit, but by the grace of the Holy Spirit. For it is an opening of the eye of the spirit into Christ's humanity, and it may be called the carnal love of God, as St. Bernard calls it,[120] inasmuch as it is set in the human nature of Christ. It is very good, and a great help in destroying great sins, and a way to come to virtues, and so afterward into contemplation of the divine nature. For a person shall not commonly come to spiritual delight in the contemplation of Christ's divinity unless he first comes in imagination[121] by anguish and compassion for his humanity.

This was what St. Paul did, for first he spoke thus: *Nihil indicavi*[122] *me scire inter vos nisi Jesum Christum et hunc crucifixum.*[123] I showed you nothing at all that I knew, except only Jesus Christ, and him crucified; as if he had said, My knowledge and my trust are only in the passion of Christ. Therefore he also said: *Mihi autem absit gloriari nisi in cruce Domini nostri Iesu Christi.*[124] Let every kind of joy and pleasure be forbidden me, except in the cross and passion of our Lord Jesus Christ. And afterward he said this: *Predicamus vobis Christum Dei virtutem, et Dei sapientiam.*[125] As if he said, "First I preached to you of the humanity and of the passion of Christ; now I preach to you of His divinity and power, and of the endless wisdom of God."

36. That the meditation of the passion is often withdrawn from those to whom it is given, for various reasons.

A person does not always have this kind of meditation when he would, but when our Lord wants to give it. He gives it to some men and women throughout their lives, on occasions when he visits them, as some devout men and women are so tender in their affection that when they hear people speak of this precious passion—or when they think about it—their hearts melt in devotion, and they are fed and comforted by its power against all kinds of temptations of the Enemy; and that is a great gift of God. To some he gives it abundantly at first, and later he withdraws it for various reasons: either because a person grows proud of it in his own sight, or for some other sin by which he makes himself unable to receive the grace. Or else our Lord withdraws it[126] and all other devotion sometimes from a man or a woman because he wants to allow him to be tried by the temptations of his Enemy, and in this way he will dispose someone to know and feel him more spiritually. For he said so himself to his disciples: *Expedit vobis ut ego vadam. Si enim non abiero, Paraclitus non veniet ad vos.*[127] It is expedient for you that I go away from you in the body, for if I do not go the Holy Spirit cannot come to you. As long as he was with them they loved him very much, but it was carnally —in the humanity—and therefore it was expedient for them that he should withdraw the bodily form from their sight so that the Holy Spirit could come to them and teach them to love him and know him more spiritually, as he did on the day of Pentecost. In just the same way it is expedient for some that our Lord should withdraw the bodily and carnal likeness from the eye of their soul, so that the heart might be set and fixed more attentively on the spiritual desire and feeling of the divinity.

37. Various temptations of the devil of hell.

Nevertheless a person has first to suffer many temptations, and by the malice of the Enemy these temptations often come to some men and women in various ways after comfort is withdrawn. For instance, when the devil perceives that devotion is greatly removed, so that the soul is left naked,[128] as it were, for a time, then to certain people he sends temptations of lechery and gluttony,[129] so hot and so burning that it will seem to them that they never felt anything as grievous in all their lives before when they gave themselves most to sin: to such a degree that they will think it impossible to stand for long and bear this, but that they must needs fall unless they have help. They therefore feel great sorrow, both through lack of the comfort and devotion that they used to have and through great fear of falling away from God by such manifest sins.

All this is the work of the devil, to make them abandon their good purpose and turn again to sin as they used to do; but for those who will wait a while and suffer a little pain the hand of our Lord is quite near and helps very soon, for he keeps them perfectly safe, and yet they do not know how. As the prophet David said in the person of our Lord: *Cum ipso sum in tribulacione, eripiam eum et glorificabo eum.*[130] I am with him in tribulation, and in temptation I shall deliver him, and I shall make him glorious in my bliss.

Some people he tempts maliciously by sins of the spirit, such as disbelief in articles of the faith, or in the sacrament[131] of God's body; also of despair; or blasphemy[132] toward our Lord or any of his saints;[133] or loathing of their own life; or bitterness and irrational sorrow;[134] or excessive fear for themselves or their own body if they devote themselves entirely to God's service. He also tempts some people—and especially solitary men and women—by means of fear and horrors, quakings and shakings, appearing to them either in bodily form or else in imagination, sleeping and waking; and so vexes them that they can scarcely take any rest; and he tempts them in many other ways as well, more than I can or may say.

38.   Various remedies against the temptations of the devil.[135]

A remedy for such men and women as are troubled in this or any other way may be as follows. First, that they will steadfastly believe that all this sorrow and travail that they suffer in such temptations, which to an ignorant person seems to be desertion by God, is neither rejection by God nor desertion, but trial for their good: either to cleanse the sins already committed, or to give them great increase in their reward,[136] or great disposition to abundant grace, if only they will endure and suffer awhile, and stand fast, so that they do not willfully turn again to sin.

Another remedy is not to fear or take to heart such malicious stirrings of despair or blasphemy, or disbelief in the sacrament,[137] or any similar thing that might be horrible to hear, for the feeling of these temptations defiles the soul no more than if one heard a dog bark or felt a flea bite. They trouble the soul but do not harm it, if a man has the will to despise them and think nothing of them. It is not good to strive with them[138] so as to put them out by force; for the more that people struggle against such thoughts, the more they cling to them; and therefore as far as possible they should withdraw their attention from them as if they cared nothing for them, and direct it to some other occupation. And if they will always hang upon them, then it is good for them not to be angry or despondent when they feel them, but with a good trust in God to bear them like a bodily pain, and as a scourge of our Lord for the cleansing of their sins, as long as he will.

In addition to this, it is good for them to show their hearts to some wise person at the beginning, before these things have taken root in the heart, and that they leave their own judgment to follow his advice: but not to show them lightly to any unlearned or worldly person who has never felt such temptations, for through his own ignorance he might easily bring a simple soul to despair.

To comfort those who are tempted, our Lord speaks thus by his prophet about temptations of this kind, which make someone seem forsaken by God when he is not: *In modico dereliqui te; et in momento indignationis meae percussi te; et in miserationibus meis multis congregabo te.*[139] For a little while I forsook you (that is to say, I allowed you to be troubled a little), and in an instant of my wrath I struck you (that is to say, all the penance and pain that you suffer here is only an instant of my wrath in comparison with the pain of hell or of purgatory), and yet in my manifold mercy I shall gather you together (that is to say, When you feel you are forsaken,[140] then I shall of my great mercy gather you again to me). For when you suppose that you are as it were lost, then our Lord will help you, as Job says: *Cum te consumptum putaveris, orieris ut lucifer et habebis fiduciam.*[141] That is to say, When you are brought so low by laboring in temptation that it seems there is no help or comfort for you but as if you were a man destroyed, yet pray to God, and indeed you shall suddenly spring up as the day star in gladness of heart, and have true faith in God as Job says.

39. How God allows those whom he chooses to be wearied and tempted, and afterward he comforts them and makes them secure in grace.

In the same way, to comfort such people and keep them from despair the wise man speaks thus of our Lord: *In temptatione ambulat cum eo. In primis eligit eum. Timorem et metum et approbationem inducit super illum; et cruciabit illum in tribulatione doctrinae suae, donec temptet*

illum in cogitationibus suis, et credat animae illius. Ad iter directum addu-
cet illum, et firmabit illum, et laetificabit illum, et denudabit abscondita
sua illi, et thesaurizabit super illum scientiam et intellectum justitiae.[142]
This is as much as to say: Because he did not want people to despair in
temptation, the wise man speaks thus to give them comfort. In temptation our Lord does not forsake a person, but he goes with him from the
beginning to the last end; for he says, First he chooses him (and that is
when he draws someone to him by the comfort of devotion); and afterward he brings upon him sorrow and fear and trial (and that is when he
withdraws devotion and allows him to be tempted). Also he says that he
torments him in tribulation until he has tried him well in his thoughts,
and until he will put all his trust fully in our Lord; and then after this our
Lord brings him out into the right way, and fastens the person to him
and gladdens him, and then shows him his secrets and gives him his
treasure of knowing and understanding righteousness.

By these words of holy scripture you can see that these temptations
or any others, however horrible they may be for someone who through
grace is fully determined to forsake sin, are useful and profitable if he
will suffer as he can and await the will of God; not turning again to sins
which he has forsaken for any sorrow or pain or fear of such temptation,
but always standing firm in labor and in prayer. In his endless goodness
our Lord has pity and mercy on all his creatures: when he sees it is time
he lays to his hand, strikes down the devil and all his power and eases
their distress, putting away fears and sorrows and darkness from their
hearts and bringing into their souls the light of grace; and he opens the
sight of their souls, giving them a new spiritual power to withstand all
the temptations of the devil and all mortal sins without great labor; he
leads them into the constancy of good virtuous living, in which he keeps
them (if they are humble) until their last end, and then he takes them
completely to himself.

I tell you this thing in case you are wearied or troubled with any
such kind of temptation: you must not be too frightened, but do as I have
said and better if you can, and I think by the grace of Jesus Christ you
shall never be overcome by your enemy.

40. That a person should not yield to idleness, or carelessly
     abandon the grace given him by God.

After this, when you have escaped such temptations, or our Lord
has so guarded you—as he has done many in his mercy—that you have

not been much troubled by them, then it is good for you not to turn your rest into idleness; for there is many a man that takes rest for himself too soon: but if you will, you shall begin a new game and a new task. That is to enter into your own soul[143] by meditation in order to know what it is, and by the knowledge of it to come to the spiritual knowledge of God. For as St. Augustine says: "By the knowledge of myself I shall get the knowledge of God."[144] I do not say that it is a necessity or duty for you to labor so, or for anyone else unless he should feel himself stirred by grace and as if called to it, for our Lord gives diverse gifts wherever he will—not all to one or one to everybody—apart from charity, which is common to all. Therefore if a man or woman has received a gift from our Lord, such as devotion in prayer or in the passion of Christ, or any other, be it never so small, let him not leave it too soon for anything else unless he truly feels a better one. Nevertheless, if later it is partly withdrawn and he should see something better toward which he feels his heart is stirred, then it seems a call from our Lord to the better, and that is the time for him to follow it and get it.

41. That a person should know the measure of his gift, and always desire more, taking a better one when God wishes to give it.

Our holy fathers[145] in former times taught us to know the measure of our gift and work by that, not making use of pretense to take more upon ourselves than we have felt. We can always desire the best, but we cannot always perform the best, for we have not yet received that grace.

A hound that runs after the hare[146] only because he sees other hounds running will rest when he is tired, and turn back; but if he runs because he sees the hare, he will not flag for weariness until he has it. It is just the same spiritually. If anyone has a grace, however small, and decides to stop working with it and to make himself labor at another that he does not yet have, only because he sees or hears that others are doing so, he may indeed run for a while until he is weary; and then he will turn home again: and if he is not careful he can hurt his feet with some fantasies before he gets there. But when anyone works with such grace as he has while humbly and persistently desiring more, and later feels his heart stirred to follow the grace which he has desired: he can safely run, provided he keeps humility.

And therefore desire from God as much as you can—without moderation or discretion[147]—of all that belongs to his love and the bliss of heaven, for whoever knows how best to desire from God shall have the most feeling of him; but work as you can, and call for his mercy on what you cannot. So it seems St. Paul said: *Unusquisque habet donum suum a Deo, alius autem sic, alius vero sic.*[148] *Item unicuique nostrum data est gratia secundum mensuram donationis Christi.*[149] *Item divisiones gratiarum sunt; alii datur sermo sapientiae; alii sermo scientiae.*[150] *Item ut sciamus quae a Deo donata sunt nobis.*[151] St. Paul says that every man has his gift from God: one this way, and another that, for to every man who is to be saved grace is given according to the measure of Christ's gift; and therefore it is an advantage to know the gifts given us by God, so that we can work by them; for by those we shall be saved. For example, some shall be saved and come to blessedness by bodily actions and by works of mercy; some by great penance; some by sorrow and weeping for their sins all their lifetime; some by preaching and teaching; and some by various graces and gifts of devotion.

42. That a person should labor to know his own soul and its powers, and should break down the ground of sin within it.

Nevertheless, there is one useful and deserving[152] task on which to labor, and (as I think) a plain highway to contemplation, as far as can lie in human effort: and that is for a person to go into himself[153] to know his own soul and its powers, its fairness and its foulness.[154] Through looking inward you will be able to see the honor and dignity it ought to have from the nature of the first making: and you will see too the wretchedness and misery into which you have fallen through sin; and from this sight there will come into your heart a great desire with great longing to recover[155] that dignity and honor which you have lost. You will also feel a loathing and horror of yourself, with a great will to destroy and suppress yourself and everything that hinders you from that dignity and joy. This is a task for the spirit, hard and sharp in the beginning[156] for anyone who will work vigorously in it, for it is a labor in the soul against the ground of all sins,[157] small or great; and this ground is nothing but a false disordered love of a person for himself. Out of this love, as St. Augustine says,[158] springs every kind of sin, mortal and venial; and indeed until this ground is thoroughly ransacked and deeply delved,[159] and as if dried up by casting out all fleshly and worldly loves, a soul can never feel spiritually the burning love of God, or have clear sight of spiritual things by the light of understanding. This is the task that one has to do: to draw up his heart from love and delight in all things physically created, and[160] from the carnal love and feeling of himself, so that the soul can find no rest[161] in any fleshly thought or earthly affection. And if he does so, then inasmuch as the soul cannot promptly find its spiritual rest in the love and sight of God, it must needs feel pain. This task is rather restricted and narrow; nevertheless, it is a way Christ taught in the gospel to those who wanted to be his perfect followers, speaking thus: *Contendite intrare per angustam portam, quoniam arcta est via quae ducit ad vitam et pauci inveniunt eam.*[162] Strive to go in by the strait gate; for the way leading to heaven is narrow, and few people find it. Our Lord tells us in another place how strict this way is: *Si quis vult post me venire, abneget semetipsum, et tollat crucem suam, et sequatur me. Item qui odit animam suam in hoc mundo, in vitam aeternam custodit eam.*[163] That is to say, Whoever wants to come after me, forsake himself and hate his own soul (that is to say, abandon all fleshly love, and hate all his own fleshly life and the feeling of his body through all his senses, for love of me); and take the cross (that is to say, suffer the pain of this a while); and then follow (that is to say, into contemplation of me).

This is a strait and narrow way, so that no bodily thing can pass through it; for it is a slaying of all sins, as St. Paul says: *Mortificate membra vestra quae sunt super terram: immunditiam, libidinem, concupiscentiam malam.*[164] Put to death your limbs on earth: not the parts of your body, but of the soul, such as impurity, lust and unreasonable love for yourself[165] and earthly things. Therefore, as your task hitherto has been to withstand great bodily sins and the open temptations of the Enemy as it were from outside, so now in this inward spiritual work you need to start destroying and breaking down the ground of sin inside yourself as much as you can. And so that you can bring this about quickly, I shall tell you as it seems to me.

43. How a man shall know the dignity and honor due to his soul by nature, and the wretchedness and misery into which it has fallen through sin.

The soul of a man is a life[166] made of three powers—memory, reason and will[167]—in the image and likeness[168] of the blessed Trinity: whole, perfect and righteous. The memory has the likeness of the Father, inasmuch as it was made strong and steadfast by the Father's omnipotence, to hold him without forgetting, distraction, or hindrance from any creature. The reason was made clear and bright,[169] without error or

2 darkness, as perfectly as a soul could have in an unglorified body, and so it has the likeness of the Son, who is infinite wisdom. And the love and the will were made pure, burning toward God without animal pleasure in the flesh or in any creature, by the supreme goodness; and it has the

3 likeness of the Holy Spirit, who is blessed love. So that a man's soul, which may be called a created trinity, was filled with memory, sight and love by the uncreated blessed Trinity, who is our Lord.

This is the dignity, the state and the honor of a man's soul by the nature of the first creation. This is the state you had in Adam before the first sin of man; but when Adam sinned, choosing love and delight in himself and in created things, he lost all this honor and his dignity, and you also lost it in him and fell from that blessed Trinity into a foul, dark, wretched trinity, that is, into forgetfulness of God and ignorance of him, and into bestial pleasure in yourself, and that with good reason, for as David says in the Psalms: *Homo, cum in honore esset, non intellexit; comparatus est iumentis, et similis factus est illis.*[170] When man was in honor, he did not know it, and therefore he lost it and was made like a beast.[171] See now the wretchedness of your soul, for as the memory was at one time stable in God, so now it has forgotten him and looks for its rest in created things—now one, now another—and can never find full rest, because he has lost him in whom there is full rest. It is just the same with the reason and likewise the love, which was pure in spiritual savor and sweetness; now it is turned into a foul bestial pleasure and delight in yourself and created things, and carnal savors, both through the senses (as in gluttony and lechery), and by imagination (as in pride, vainglory and covetousness), insomuch that you can hardly do any good deed without being defiled by vainglory, and you cannot well use any of your five wits purely toward any lovely created thing without your heart being caught and entangled[172] by vain pleasure and delight in it. And this puts out the love of God from the heart, in feeling and spiritual savor, so that it cannot come in. Everyone who lives in the spirit knows all this well.

This is the wretched state of your soul, and the misery for the first sin of man, without all the other wretchedness and sins you have voluntarily added to it. And you must know that even if you had never committed mortal or venial sin with your body, but only this (which is called original because it is the first sin, and that is nothing else but the loss of the righteousness which you were made in), you would never have been saved had not our Lord Jesus Christ delivered you by his precious passion, and restored you again.

→ against Rolle

44. How everyone can be saved by the passion of Christ if he *humanitas Christi* asks, however wretched he may be.

And therefore, if you think I have hitherto spoken too loftily for you, because you cannot take it or fulfil it as I have said or shall say, I am willing to descend to you as low as you wish, as much for my own profit as for yours. Then I speak like this: However great a wretch you may be, and however much sin you have committed, forsake yourself and all your works, good and bad. Cry for mercy, and ask only for salvation by virtue of this precious passion, humbly and with trust, and no doubt you shall have it. You shall be saved from this original sin and every other that you have done: yes, and as an enclosed anchoress you shall be safe. And not only you, but all Christian souls who put their trust in his passion and humble themselves, acknowledging their wickedness, asking for mercy and forgiveness and the fruit of this precious passion alone, and submitting themselves to the sacraments of holy church. Although they may have been encumbered with sin all their lives without ever feeling any spiritual savor or sweetness or spiritual knowledge of God, in this faith and in their good will they shall be saved and come to the bliss of heaven by the power of this precious passion of our Lord Jesus Christ. All this you know well, and yet it pleases me to say it.

See here the infinite mercy of our Lord: how low he descends to you, to me, and to all sinful wretches. Ask for mercy, and have it. So said the prophet in the person of our Lord: *Omnis quicumque invocaverit nomen Domini, salvus erit.*[173] Let everyone, whatever he may be, call on the name of Jesus (that is to say, ask salvation through Jesus), and by his passion he shall be saved. Some people fully accept this courtesy[174] from our Lord and are saved by it; and some in confidence of this mercy and courtesy lie still in their sin and expect to have it when they like: but then they cannot, for they are taken before they know it, and so they damn themselves. But now you say:[175] "If this is true I wonder very much at what I find written among the sayings of certain holy men.[176] Some say, as I understand, that anyone who cannot love this blessed name Jesus, or find or feel in it spiritual joy and delight with wonderful sweetness in this life here, shall be alien to that supreme joy and spiritual

critique of Rolle

sweetness in the bliss of heaven, and he shall never come to it. When I read these words, they truly appall me and make me very frightened, for I consider that by the mercy of our Lord many shall be saved (as you say) through keeping his commandments and through true repentance for their previous evil living who never felt spiritual sweetness, or any inward savor in the name of Jesus or in the love of Jesus. And therefore I am the more surprised at their saying the contrary, as it seems."

As to this, I can give my opinion that what they say is true, if it is rightly understood, and it is not contrary to what I have said: for this name Jesus in English is nothing else but *healer* or *health*. Now, everyone who lives in this wretched life is spiritually sick, for there is no one alive without sin, which is sickness of the spirit, as St. John says of himself and other perfect men: *Si dixerimus quia peccatum non habemus, ipsi nos seducimus, et veritas in nobis non est.*[177] If we say that we have no sin, we deceive ourselves, and there is no truth in us. And therefore a man can never feel or come to the joys of heaven without first being made well from this spiritual illness. But nobody with the use of reason can have this spiritual healing unless he desires it, loves it and takes delight in it, inasmuch as he hopes to get it. Now, the name of Jesus is nothing else but this healing of the spirit; and for this reason it is true what they say, that no one can be saved unless he loves and takes pleasure in the name of Jesus, for no one can be whole in the spirit unless he loves and desires spiritual health. It is just as if someone had a bodily illness: no earthly thing would be so dear or so necessary to him, or so much desired by him, as bodily health, and even though you were willing to give him all the riches and honors of this world without making him whole (if you had that power), you would not please him. And so it is for one who is sick in spirit and feels the pain of spiritual disease; nothing is so dear, so necessary or so much desired by him as spiritual health—and that is Jesus, without whom all the joys of heaven cannot please him. This is the reason, in my opinion, why our Lord in taking our human nature for our salvation did not want to be called by any name that signified his infinite being, or his might, or his wisdom, or his righteousness, but only by the name that showed the cause of his coming: the salvation of man's soul, a salvation most dear and necessary to man. That is the salvation meant by the name Jesus. Then by this it seems true that nobody shall be saved unless he loves this name Jesus, because nobody shall be saved unless he loves[178] salvation, and this love he can have if he lives and dies in the lowest degree of charity.

I can also put it in another way, regarding a person who does not here know how to love this blessed name Jesus with gladness in his spirit, or rejoice in it with heavenly melody: In the bliss of heaven he shall never have or feel such fullness of supreme joy[179] as shall be had and felt by someone who in this life has learned to rejoice in Jesus by abounding in perfect charity. And so their saying can be understood. Nevertheless, he shall be saved and be fully rewarded with the sight of God, provided that in this life he is in the lowest degree of charity by the keeping of God's commandments. For our Lord himself speaks thus: *In domo patris mei mansiones multae sunt.*[180] In my father's house there are many different dwellings. Some are for perfect souls who in this life were filled with the grace of the Holy Spirit and sang praise to God in the contemplation of him, with wonderful sweetness and heavenly savor. Because they had the most charity, these souls shall have the highest reward in the bliss of heaven, for these are called God's darlings. As for other souls, who are imperfect in this life and are not disposed to the contemplation of God, being without the fullness of charity that the apostles and martyrs had when holy church began, they shall have the lower reward in the bliss of heaven, for these are called God's friends. That is what our Lord calls chosen souls in holy scripture, speaking thus: *Comedite amici, et inebriamini carissimi.*[181] Eat, my friends, and drink deep, my darlings, as if he said: "You are my friends—because you kept my commandments and set my love before the love of the world, and loved me more than any earthly thing—you shall be fed with the spiritual food of the bread of life. But you who are my darlings—who not only kept my commandments, but also of your own free will fulfilled my counsels,[182] and beyond that loved me alone and entirely with all the powers of your soul, and burnt in my love with spiritual delight, as did originally the apostles and martyrs and all other souls who were able by grace to come to the gift of perfection—you shall be made drunk with the choicest and freshest wine in my cellar: that is, the supreme joy of love in the bliss of heaven."

45. That a man should try hard to recover his dignity, and reform in himself the image of the Trinity.

Nevertheless, although this may be true of the infinite mercy of God to you and me and all humankind, we must not because of our confidence in this choose to be more careless in the way we live, but more diligent to please him especially now, since we are restored again in hope by this passion of our Lord to the dignity and glory which we had lost by the sin of Adam. Although we could never acquire it here in its fullness, yet we must desire while living here to recover a figure and likeness of that dignity, so that by grace our soul might be reformed[183]— as it were in a shadow—to the image of the Trinity, which we had by nature and afterward shall have fully in glory.[184] For that is the life which is truly contemplative[185] to begin here, in that feeling of love and spiritual knowledge of God, by opening of the spiritual eye; and it shall never be lost or taken away: but the same shall be fulfilled in another way in the bliss of heaven. Our Lord made this promise to Mary Magdalene,[186] who was contemplative, speaking of her like this: *Maria optimam partem elegit, quae non auferetur ab ea.*[187] That Mary had chosen the best part (that is, the love of God in contemplation), for it shall never be taken away from her. I do not say that while living here you can recover such whole or perfect purity, innocence, or knowing and loving of God as you had at first or as you shall have; neither can you escape all the wretchedness and pains of sin, or entirely destroy and quench the false vain love of yourself while living in mortal flesh, or avoid all venial sins. These will always gush out of your heart as water runs[188] from a stinking well, unless they are stopped by great fervor of charity. But if you cannot quench it altogether, I would wish you partly to abate it, and come as close to that purity as you can. For when our Lord led the children of Israel into the promised land, he made them this promise, and through them symbolically to all Christian people: *Omne quod calcauerit pes tuus, tuum erit.*[189] That is to say, As much as you can tread upon here with your foot of true desire, that you shall have in the promised land (that is, in the bliss of heaven) when you get there.

46.   How Jesus shall be sought, desired and found.

Then seek what you have lost, so that you can find it. I well know that if anybody could once have a little inward glimpse of that dignity and spiritual beauty which a soul did have by nature and shall have by grace, he would loathe and despise in his heart all the glory, pleasure and beauty of the whole of this world as the stink of carrion. He would never have the wish to do anything else, night or day (except for the frailty and the bare need of the bodily nature), but desire, mourn, pray, and seek how he could come to it again.

Nevertheless, inasmuch as you have not yet fully seen what it is, because your spiritual eye is still unopened, I shall speak one word for all that you shall seek, desire and find, for in that word is all that you have lost. This word is Jesus. I do not mean this word Jesus painted on the wall, written in letters in the book, formed by the lips with sound from the mouth, or fashioned in the heart by labor of the mind, for this is the way someone out of charity can find him; but I mean Jesus, all goodness, infinite wisdom, love and sweetness;[190] your joy, your worship and your everlasting bliss; your God, your Lord, and your salvation.

So if you should feel great desire in your heart toward Jesus, either by remembrance of this name Jesus, or by the remembrance and saying of any word or prayer, or by anything that you do, and this desire is so great that it puts out as if by force all other thoughts and desires of the world and of your flesh, so that they cannot stay in your heart, then you are doing well in your search for Jesus. And when you feel this desire for God (or for Jesus, both are one) helped and strengthened by spiritual power, so much that it is turned into love and affection, spiritual savor and sweetness, into light and the knowledge of truth—so much that for the time the point of your thought is set on nothing created, and feels no stirring of vainglory or any other evil affection (because they cannot appear at that time) but only is enclosed, rested, softened and anointed in Jesus—then you have found something of Jesus, not yet himself as he is, but a shadow of him. For the better you find him, the more you will desire him. Then by whatever kind of prayer, meditation or occupation you can have the greatest desire for him and the most feeling of him: by that occupation you seek him best, and best find him. Therefore if the question comes to your mind as it were asking what you have lost and what you seek, lift up the desire of your heart to Jesus—even though you are blind and can see nothing of him—and say that he it is whom you have lost, him you want to have, and nothing but him: no other joy, no other bliss, in heaven or on earth, but him. And although it may happen that you feel him in devotion or in knowing, or in any other gift, whatever it may be, do not rest in it as though you had fully found Jesus, but forget what you have found, and always be longing for Jesus more and more, to find him better,[191] as if you had nothing at all. For know well, whatever you feel of him, however much—yes, even if you were ravished[192] into the third heaven with Paul—you have not yet found Jesus as he is. However much you know or feel of him here in this life, he is still above it. And therefore if you want to find him fully as he is in the bliss of loving, never cease from spiritual desire[193] as long as you live.

47. What profit there is in having the desire for Jesus.

Certainly, I would rather feel and have a true desire and a pure longing in my heart for my Lord Jesus, even though I should see nothing of him at all with my spiritual eye, than have without this desire all the bodily penance of all men alive, all visions or revelations of angels appearing, songs and sounds,[194] savors or smells, burnings and delights felt by the body—in short, all the joys of heaven and earth which I could have without this desire toward my Lord Jesus. As I understand, David the prophet felt as I say when he spoke thus: *Quid enim mihi est in caelo, et a te quid volui super terram?*[195] Lord, what is there for me in heaven, or what would I want above the earth, except you? As if he said: Lord Jesus, what heavenly joy is pleasing to me, without desire of you while I am on earth or without love of you when I come to heaven? As one might say, "None at all."

Then if you want to feel anything of him in body or spirit, long to feel a true desire for him, so that it seems your heart can find no other rest in anything but in that desire. David had this longing when he said: *Concupivit anima mea desiderare justificationes tuas in omni tempore.*[196] Lord, my soul longed for the desire of your righteousness at all times. Therefore—as David did—seek desire through desire; and if you can feel it, bind your heart fast to it so that you do not fall away, and so that if you stumble you can soon find it again.

So look for Jesus, whom you have lost. He wants to be sought, and he can partly be found, for he says himself: *Omnis qui quaerit invenit.*[197] Everyone who seeks shall find. The searching is wearisome, but the finding is glorious. Therefore, follow the counsel of the wise man if you want to find him: *Si quaesieris quasi pecuniam sapientiam, et sicut thesaurum effoderis illam, tunc intelliges timorem Domini et scientiam invenies.*[198] If you seek wisdom (which is Jesus) as silver and gold, and delve deep[199] after it, you shall find it. You will have to delve deep in your heart—for there he is hidden—and thoroughly turn out all the loves and pleasures, sorrows and fears of all earthly things: and so you will find wisdom—Jesus.

48. Where and by what means Jesus is to be sought and found.

Therefore be like the woman in the gospel, of whom our Lord said: *Quae mulier habens drachmas decem, et perdiderit unam, nonne accendit lucernam et evertit[200] domum suam et quaerit diligenter donec inveniat eam? Et cum invenerit, convocat amicas suas, dicens: Congratulamini mihi, quia inveni drachmam quam perdideram.*[201] What woman who has lost a coin will not light a lantern, turn her house upside down, and search until she finds it? (As one might say, "None.") And when she has found it, she calls her friends to her and speaks to them like this: "Celebrate with me and make music; for I have found what I had lost—that is, the coin." This coin is Jesus, whom you have lost. If you want to find him, light up a lantern, which is God's word, as David says: *Lucerna pedibus meis verbum tuum.*[202] Lord, thy word is a lantern to my feet. By this lantern you will see where he is and how you are to find him; and with this you can light up another lantern, which is the reason of your soul, for our Lord says: *Lucerna corporis tui est oculus tuus.*[203] The lantern of your body is your bodily eye. In just the same way it can be said that the lantern of your soul is reason, by which the soul can see all spiritual things. By this lantern you can find Jesus; and that is true, if you hold the lantern up from underneath the bushel, as our Lord says: *Nemo accendit lucernam et ponit eam sub modio, sed super candelabrum.*[204] There is no one who lights a lamp in order to set it under a bushel, but on a candlestick. That is to say, the reason shall not be covered up with worldly thoughts and business, or with vain thoughts and carnal affections, but always lifted as high as you can, above all earthly things; and if you do this, you will see all the mess and filth and small specks of dust in your house, that is to say, all the carnal loves and fears in your soul. Not all, as David says: *Delicta quis intelligit?*[205] Who can know all his sins? As one might say, "Nobody." And you shall turn all such sins out of your heart, and sweep your soul clean with the broom of the fear of God, and wash it with the water of your eyes; and so you will find this coin Jesus. He is the coin, he is the penny, and he is your heritage.[206]

This coin shall not be found as easily as it can be said, for this is not the work of one hour,[207] or one day, but of many days and years, with great sweat and toil of the body and labor of the soul. If you do not stop, but search hard, sorrow and sigh deeply, mourn quietly and stoop low, until your eyes water for anguish and pain because you have lost your treasure, Jesus, when he wishes you shall at last truly find your coin, Jesus. And if You find him as I have said—as a shadow or glimmering of him—you can if you will call your friends to you to celebrate together, because you have found your coin, Jesus.

49. Where Jesus is lost, and found through his mercy.

So now see the courtesy and mercy of Jesus. You have lost him, but where? Certainly in your house,[208] that is, in your soul. If you had lost him outside your house, that is to say, if you had lost all the reason of your soul[209] by the first sin, your soul would never have found him again. But he left you your reason, and so he is in your soul and never shall be lost from it. Nevertheless, you are never the nearer to him[210] until you have found him. He is in you, even though he is lost from you, but you are not in him till you have found him. This, then, was his mercy: that he would allow himself to be lost only where he can be found. There is no need to run to Rome or Jerusalem to look for him there,[211] but turn your thought into your own soul where he is hidden (as the prophet says—*Vere tu es Deus absconditus.*[212] Truly, Lord, you are a hidden God) and look for him there.

He himself says so in the gospel: *Simile est regnum caelorum thesauro abscondito in agro; quem qui invenit homo prae gaudio illius vadit et vendit universa quae habet et emit agrum illum.*[213] The kingdom of heaven is like treasure hidden in a field. When a man finds it, for joy of it he goes and sells all that he has and buys that same field. Jesus is treasure hidden in your soul; then if you could find him in your soul and your soul in him, I am sure you would for joy of it want to give up all your pleasure in all earthly things in order to have it.

Jesus sleeps in your heart spiritually as he once slept bodily when he was in the ship[214] with his disciples; but they awoke him for fear of perishing, and at once he saved them from the tempest. Do the same yourself: stir him with prayer and awaken him by crying with desire, and he will soon get up and help you.

50. What hinders a person from hearing and seeing Jesus within himself.

Nevertheless, I suppose that you are asleep to him[215] rather than he to you, for he calls you quite often with his sweet secret voice, very quietly stirring your heart to leave all the jangle[216] of vain things in your soul and give heed only to him, and to hearing him speak. David spoke thus of our Lord: *Audi, filia, et vide, et inclina aurem tuam, et oblivisce populum tuum et domum patris tui.*[217] My daughter, hear and see, and bow your ear to me, and forget the folk of your worldly thoughts and the house of your carnal and natural affections. Look, here you can see how our Lord calls you and all others who are willing to listen to him. What hinders you, then, so that you are unable to see or hear him? Truly, there is in your heart so much din and clamor of vain thoughts and fleshly desires that you can neither hear nor see him; therefore put away unrestful din, break the love of sin and vanity, and bring into your heart the love of virtues, and full charity; and then you shall hear your Lord speak to you. For as long as he does not find his image reformed in you he is a stranger to you, and far away.

51. That humility and charity are the special livery[218] of Jesus, through which man's soul is reformed to his likeness.

For this reason prepare yourself to put on his likeness[219]—that is, the humility and charity[220] which are his livery—and then he will want to know you familiarly and show you his mystery. He said so himself to his disciples: *Qui diligit me diligetur a Patre meo, et manifestabo ei me ipsum.*[221] Whoever loves me shall be loved by my Father, and I shall show myself to him. There is no virtue you can practice—no work you can do—able to make you resemble our Lord without humility and charity, for these especially are the livery of God; and that is clearly seen in the gospel, where our Lord speaks of humility thus: *Discite a me, quia mitis sum et humilis corde.*[222] Learn from me, he says—not to go barefoot, or to travel into the desert and fast forty days, or to choose disciples for yourselves; but from me learn meekness, for I am mild and meek in heart. Also, he speaks like this of charity: *Hoc est praeceptum meum, ut diligatis invicem sicut dilexi vos. Item in hoc cognoscent homines quia discipuli mei estis, si dilectionem habueritis ad invicem.*[223] This is my commandment, that you love one another as I have loved you. For through that people shall know you for my disciples: not because you work miracles, cast out devils, or preach and teach, but if all of you love one another in charity: that is, that you should learn to love your fellow Christian as much as yourself.

52. How a person shall see the ground of sin in himself.

Now you have heard a little of what your soul is, what honor it had, and how it lost it; and I have told you that by grace and constant toil this honor could partly be recovered in respect of feeling. According to my feeble ability, I shall now tell you how you can enter into yourself,[224] to see the ground of sin and destroy as much of it as you can;[225] and so you will be able to recover a part of your dignity.

You must stop all bodily work for a time and all outward activity (as you can well do). Then you must withdraw your thought into yourself and away from your bodily senses, so that you pay no attention to what you hear, see or feel and do not allow the point of your heart[226] to be fixed in them. After this draw your thought inward if you can from all imagination of any material thing, and from all thoughts of your own former bodily actions, and of other people's. It is not difficult to do this when you have devotion, but you shall do as I say when you are without devotion, for then it is much harder. Set your intention and purpose as if you wanted neither to seek, to feel nor to find anything but Jesus alone.[227] This is troublesome,[228] for vain thoughts are always wanting to press thickly into your heart, to draw your thought down to them; but you shall withstand them; and if you do so you shall find something—though not Jesus whom you seek. What, then? Indeed, nothing but a dark and painful image of your own soul,[229] which has neither the light of knowledge nor the feeling of love or pleasure. If you look at it plainly, this image is all wrapped up in black stinking clothes of sin, such as pride, envy, wrath, *accidie*, covetousness, gluttony and lechery.[230]

53. What the image of sin is like, and what it is in itself.

This is not the image of Jesus, but it is an image of sin, as St. Paul calls it: a body of sin and a body of death.[231] This image and this black shadow you carry about with you wherever you go. Many great streams of sin spring out of it, and small ones as well. Just as from the image of Jesus, if it were reformed in you, beams of spiritual light should rise up[232] into heaven—such as burning desires, pure affections, wise thoughts, and virtues in all their honor—so from this image spring[233] stirrings of pride, envy and others like them, which cast you down from the dignity of man into the likeness of a beast.

But perhaps you are beginning to consider what this image could be like, and therefore, to save you from studying it at length, I tell you it is not like any bodily thing. "Then what is it?" you say. Indeed, it is nothing.[234] And that you can find, if you want to try it as I have told you. Draw your thought into yourself, away from all bodily things; and then you shall find nothing at all in which your soul could rest. This nothing is no other than a lack of love and of light, as sin is nothing but an absence of good.[235]

If the ground of sin were greatly diminished and dried up in you, and your soul rightly reformed to the image of Jesus, then if you drew your heart into yourself you would not find nothing, but you would find Jesus. You would find the light of understanding,[236] and no darkness of unknowing;[237] you would find love and pleasure, and no pain of bitterness[238] or remorse. But because you are not yet reformed, when your soul comes in, away from all material things, and finds nothing but darkness and sorrow, it seems like a hundred winters until it is out again by way of some bodily delight or vain thought. No wonder. For anyone who came home to find nothing in his house but stinking smoke and a scolding wife[239] would soon run out of it. Just so, when your soul finds no comfort in yourself, but only the black reek of spiritual blindness and a great scolding from the fleshly thoughts that shout at you and give you no peace, certainly it is soon irked, until it can be out again. This darkness is that same nothing and image of which I have been speaking.

54.   Whoever wants to find Jesus ought to stay[240] and labor in the spiritual darkness of this image of sin.

Nevertheless, in this nothing you need to toil and sweat; that is to say, you should draw your thought into yourself as much as you can, away from all material things, and then—when you find nothing at all but sorrow, pain and blindness—if you wish to find Jesus you should suffer the pain of this nothing, and stay awhile in this darkness, and stand up in your thought against this same nothing by means of diligent prayer to God and fervent desire to him, as if you wanted to overthrow it and go through it. You shall abhor and loathe this same nothing like the devil of hell, and you shall despise it and break it in pieces; for right inside this nothing Jesus is hidden[241] in his joy, and you cannot find him by your seeking unless you pass through the darkness of this nothing. This is the spiritual labor that I spoke of, and this labor is the reason for all this writing: to stir you to it, if you feel grace.

This nothing that I talk about is the image of the first Adam. St. Paul knew it well, for he speaks of it thus: *Sicut portavimus imaginem terreni hominis, ita portemus imaginem iam et caelestis.*[242] As we have formerly borne the image of the earthly man (that is, the first Adam), so we may now bear the image of the heavenly man, who is Jesus, the second Adam. He bore this image, often very heavy, for it was so cumbrous to him that he exclaimed against it in this way: *O quis me liberabit de corpore mortis huius?* Ah, who shall deliver me from this body and this image of death? And then he comforted himself and others in the same way: *Gratia Dei per Jesum Christum.*[243] The grace of God by Jesus Christ.

Now I have told you a little about this image, how it is nothing. Nevertheless, if it should be far from your knowledge, how what I say could be true (that nothing could be an image) since nothing is only nothing, and so you cannot easily understand it, I shall tell you more clearly about this image as it seems to me.

55. What properly the image of sin is, and what comes out of it.

This image is a false disordered love for yourself.[244] Out of this love there come all kinds of sin in seven rivers,[245] which are these: pride, envy, wrath, *accidie*,[246] covetousness, gluttony and lechery. Now, this is something you can feel. Every kind of sin runs out by one of these rivers, driving out charity if it is mortal, or, if it is venial,[247] lessening the fervour of charity. Now you can feel by groping that this image is not nothing, but full of wretchedness, for it is a great spring of love for yourself, with seven rivers of the kind I have mentioned.

But now you say, "How can this be true? I have forsaken the world and I am pushed into a house.[248] I have no dealings with any man; I do not wrangle or fight; I neither buy nor sell; I have no worldly concerns; but by the mercy of God I keep myself chaste and abstain from pleasures. On top of this, I watch and pray, and I labor in body and spirit as well as I can. How should this image be as big in me as you say?"

In reply to this, I grant that in my opinion you do all these works, and more as well; and yet what I say can be true. You are busy stopping the rivers on the outside, as far as you can, but you leave whole the spring within. You are like a man who had a stinking well in his garden, [with[249]] many small streams. He went and stopped the streams and left the spring whole, thinking all was safe, but the water sprang up at the bottom of the well and lay there stagnant in such quantity that it corrupted all the beauty of his garden; and yet no water was running out. It can be just the same with you. If it happens that by grace you have so thoroughly stopped the rivers of this image outside, it is good; but beware of the spring within. Certainly, unless you stop and cleanse that as much as you can, it will corrupt all the flowers in the garden of your soul, however fair they look outwardly in the sight of men.

But now you say, "How shall I know that the bottom is stopped, if I labor at it?" In reply to this, I will tell you how to find out by trial whether this image is in you, and how large it is in you, and by this you will know how much it is stopped in you, and also how little. And inasmuch as pride is the principal river, I shall tell you about it first.

56. What pride is, and when it is sin.

Pride is nothing else (as learned authors say) but love of your own excellence,[250] that is, of your own honor. Then the more you love and enjoy your own honor, the greater is your pride, and so the bigger is this image in you. If you feel in your heart a stirring of pride, that you are holier, wiser, better and more virtuous than someone else; or that God has given you grace to serve him better than others do, and you think all others beneath you, and yourself superior; or you have any other thought about yourself which shows to the sight of your soul an excellence which surpasses other men or women; and from this stirring you feel love, delight and vain pleasure in yourself, that you are like that: this is a sign that you are carrying this black image. Although it may be kept secret from the eye of men, in God's sight it shows itself plainly.

But now you say you cannot escape such stirrings of pride, for often you feel them against your will, and therefore you do not regard them as sin; or, if they are sin, they are no more than venial.

To this I reply thus. As for these impulses of pride, or any others that spring forth—either from the corruption of this foul image or because the Enemy has cast them in—there is no sin in your feeling them. That is a grace and privilege, granted by virtue of the passion of Jesus Christ to all Christian people baptized in water and the Holy Spirit, for certainly to Jews and Saracens[251] not believing in Christ all such stirrings are mortal sins. St. Paul says: *Omne quod non est ex fide peccatum est.*[252] All that is done without faith in Christ is mortal sin. But by his mercy we Christian people have this privilege: that such impulses are not sin, but punishment for the first original sin. However, when by your own negligence and blindness this feeling is received into your thought and turned into love and pleasure, then there is sin—more or less, according to the amount of the love—sometimes venial, and sometimes mortal. When it is venial and when mortal, I do not fully know how to tell you.

57. When pride is mortal sin, and how it is mortal sin for people living carnally.

Nevertheless, I shall say a little, as it seems to me. When the stirring of pride is received and turned into such pleasure that the heart chooses it as its full rest and full delight, and looks for no other end than pleasure in this alone, then this pride is mortal sin,[253] because he makes and chooses this delight as his God, without opposition from his reason or his will. And therefore it is mortal sin.

But now you say, "Who is such a fool as to choose pride as his god?"[254] No one that lives would want to do so." To this I reply that I have neither the knowledge nor the wish to tell in detail who sins mortally in pride, but I shall speak to you in general terms. There are two kinds of pride. One is bodily pride and the other is spiritual.[255] Bodily pride belongs to men living carnally; spiritual pride belongs to hypocrites and heretics. These three sin mortally in pride. I mean such a carnally living person as St. Paul speaks of: *Si secundum carnem vixeritis, moriemini.*[256] If you live according to your flesh, you will die. Then I say this. A secular person who loves and seeks principally his own honor, and chooses pleasure in it as the resting place of his heart and the goal of his joy, he sins mortally.

But now you say, "Who would choose love of his own honor instead of God?" This is my answer, concerning someone who loves his honor in order to seem better and more important than others, and works for this as hard as he can: if he loves it so much that he breaks the commandments of God in order to get it, keep or save it, or breaks love and charity toward his fellow Christian, or is ready wholeheartedly to break this rather than forgo his honor or lose it, either in name or in position or in getting his own way, his sin is indeed mortal, for he loves his honor and chooses it rather than the love of God and his fellow Christian. And nevertheless, this man who sins so mortally would say with his mouth that he did not want to choose pride for his god; but he deceives himself, for he chooses it by his behavior. However, if some other secular man loves his own honor and pursues it, but without loving it so much that he would be ready to commit a mortal sin to get or save it, or break charity toward his fellow Christian, he sins not mortally but venially, more or less, according to the amount of his love and his pleasure, with other circumstances.

58.   How pride is mortal sin in heretics.

A heretic sins mortally in pride,[257] because he chooses his resting place and his delight in his own opinion and in what he says, and he supposes it to be true. That opinion and word is against God and holy church; and therefore he sins mortally in pride, for he loves himself and his own will and wit so much that he will not leave it even though it is plainly against the ordinance of holy church; but he wants to rest in it, as if in the truth, and thus he makes it his god. But he deceives himself, for God and holy church are so united and agreed together that whoever acts against the one is acting against both. Therefore, anyone who says he loves God and keeps his commandments, and yet despises holy church and cares nothing for its laws and ordinances (made by its sovereign head for the government of all Christian people)—he lies. He does not choose God but prefers his own self-love, contrary to the love of God, and where he most thinks to please God, he most displeases him; for he is blind and does not want to see. The wise man speaks thus about this blindness and this false resting of a heretic in his own feeling: *Est via quae videtur homini recta, et novissima eius ducunt ad mortem.*[258] There is a way which seems right to a man, and the last end of it brings him to endless death. The special name for this way is heresy. Those others who commit mortal sins of the flesh and lie in them commonly have misgivings every now and then and feel remorse in their conscience that they are not going the right way, but a heretic supposes he is doing well and teaching well, and nobody as well as he, and so he thinks his way is the right way. Therefore he feels no remorse of conscience or humility in his heart, and unless God in his mercy sends him meekness, he certainly goes to hell in the end. And nevertheless he still supposes himself to have done well, and to be getting himself the bliss of heaven for his teaching.

59. How pride is a mortal sin in hypocrites.

A hypocrite also sins mortally in pride. Anyone is a hypocrite if he chooses vain joy in himself as the resting place and full delight of his heart, like this. When a man does many good works in body and spirit, and then by the suggestion of the Enemy there is put into his mind a view of himself and his good deeds—how good and how holy he is, how honorable in people's esteem, and how high above other people in God's sight—he perceives this stirring and willingly accepts it, because he thinks it to be good and from God, inasmuch as he does all these good deeds better than others; for that is true. And when it is received like this as good with the assent of his will, there arises from it such a love and delight in his heart for himself (that he is so good and so holy and has so much grace) that for the time it ravishes his mind out of all other thoughts, both spiritual and carnal, and sets it on this vain joy in himself as a resting place for his heart. This ravishing in spiritual pride is pleasurable, and therefore he keeps it, holds it and nourishes it as much as he can. For this love and vain delight he prays, he watches, he fasts, he wears the hair shirt and does other kinds of mortification; and this hurts him little. Sometimes he praises and thanks God with his mouth, and sometimes wrings a tear out of his eye, and then he feels all is safe enough, but really all this is for love of himself, which he chooses and receives as if it were love and joy in God; and in that is all the sin. He does not choose sin deliberately as sin, but he chooses this delight and joy that he feels (which is sin) as good and as the resting place of his soul, without any displeasure or opposition from his will, for he takes it for a joy in God; and it is not so. And therefore he commits mortal sin.

Job speaks thus of a hypocrite: *Gaudium hypocritae ad instar puncti. Si accenderit in caelum superbia eius, et caput eius nubes tetigerit, velut sterquilinium in fine perdetur.*[259] The joy of a hypocrite is no more than a point. For if he ascends into heaven with a rising heart and his head touches the skies, at the last end he shall be cast out like a dunghill. A hypocrite's joy is only a point, for however much he worships himself and rejoices in himself all his lifetime, showing himself off with all his good deeds in sight and praise of the world, at last it is nothing at all but sorrow and pain.

But now you say that there are few such people, if any, so blind as to choose and hold vain joy in themselves as if it were joy in God. I do not know how to answer this, and would not want to if I did, but one thing I tell you: that there are many hypocrites, and nevertheless they think they are not. And there are many that fear they are hypocrites, and in fact they are not. Which is one and which the other, God knows, and no one but he. Anyone who will humbly fear shall not be deceived; and whoever thinks he is safe can easily fall. For St. Paul says: *Qui se existimat aliquid esse cum nihil sit, ipse se seducit.*[260] Whoever considers himself to be something when he is nothing at all, deceives himself.

60. How in good people stirrings of pride and vainglory are only venial sins.

Nevertheless, for a man or woman disposed to the contemplative life this pleasure is only venial sin, provided that he voluntarily forsakes himself and offers himself entirely to God,[261] not wanting to sin knowingly in pride or willingly to have vain joy in himself, but only in God, given the power and ability. This is true particularly if after offering this full will to God he feels many stirrings of vainglory, in which he delights for the time because he does not perceive them: this delight is only

venial sin.[262] But on coming to his senses and recognizing the vain pleasure, he rebukes himself, opposes the dissent of his will to this stirring,
and asks God for help and mercy: then our Lord in his mercy soon
forgives the pleasure which was previously sin, and will reward him
further for his good work in withstanding it.

That is a courtesy from our Lord to all who are especially his
servants and more familiar in his court, as are those who for his love
abandon all the sins of the world and the flesh in good faithful resolve to
give themselves entirely, body and soul, to his service, according to their
strength and ability. Enclosed anchorites especially do this, and true
religious who principally for the love of God and the salvation of their
souls enter any religious order approved by holy church, or else if it
happens that they enter religion for a worldly reason at first (such as
their bodily sustenance or the like), provided they repent and turn it into
a spiritual reason such as the service of God. These are true religious, as
long as they keep this resolve and pursue it as they can, according to
their frailty. Likewise any man or woman,[263] whatever degree he occupies in holy church (priest, clerk or layman; widow, maiden or wife),
who for the love of God and salvation of his soul truly and fully forsakes
in his heart all the pleasures and honors of this world that come between
God and him, and all deliberate concern with earthly things, down to the
bare necessity, who offers his will to be wholly his servant, according to
his strength, by devout prayers and holy thoughts and with the good
deeds that he can do in body and spirit, and who keeps his will wholly
and steadfastly set toward God—all these are especially God's servants
in holy church. For this good will and this good purpose that they have
by the gift of God they shall increase in grace and charity while they live
here, and for this special will they shall have a special reward in the bliss
of heaven, before other chosen souls who did not wholly offer their will
and their body to God's service as they did, either openly or in secret.

All these whom I call God's servants, belonging more specially to
his court, do not sin mortally in this enjoyment of vainglory, though by
frailty or ignorance they delight for a time in such stirrings when they
feel them, without perceiving it, for their reason and good sense is
hindered by the pleasure that they feel, so that it cannot see this stirring.
That general will they have already set in their heart—to please God and
forsake every kind of sin, if they recognize it—guards them here amid
such stirrings and in all others that come from frailty, so that they do not
sin mortally. And it shall guard them as long as the ground of that will is
kept intact.

61. How different states in holy church shall have different rewards in the bliss of heaven; and about two rewards, supreme and secondary.

In addition to this, I say more to comfort you and all others having the state of enclosure as anchorites, and also (by the grace of God) to comfort all those who enter any religious order approved in holy church: that all those who are to be saved by the mercy of our Lord shall have a special reward and a singular honor in the bliss of heaven for their state of life, before other souls who did not have that state in holy church, however holy they might be. And this honor is better beyond comparison than all the honors of this world; for if you could see what it is, you would not want to exchange your state, either of anchoress or of religious, for the honor of all this world, even if you could have it without sin; neither would you diminish that singular reward (which is called accidental) in the bliss of heaven.

Nevertheless, so that others do not mistake what I say, I shall put it more plainly. You shall understand that in the bliss of heaven there are two rewards our Lord gives to chosen souls. One is supreme and principal, as is the love and knowledge of God according to the measure of charity given by him[264] to a soul living in mortal flesh. This reward is the best and highest, for it is God himself, and it is common to all the souls that are to be saved, in whatever state or degree they are living in holy church: more or less, according to the quantity and greatness of their charity. For the man that here in this life loves God most in charity shall have the most reward in the bliss of heaven, whatever degree he may be in, whether layman or priest, secular or religious, for he shall most love God and know him, and that is the supreme reward. And as for this reward, it will happen that some secular man or woman[265]—lord or lady, knight or squire, merchant or ploughman, or whatever degree he is in, man or woman—shall have more than some priest or friar, monk or canon, or enclosed anchoress. And why? Indeed, because he loved God more in the charity given by him.

There is another reward, which is secondary, given by our Lord for special good deeds that someone does voluntarily, beyond what he is bound to. The teachers of holy church make mention of three special works: martyrdom, preaching and virginity.[266] Because they surpass all others, these three shall have for their excellence a special reward, which they call an aureole; and that is nothing else but a singular honor and special token ordained by God to reward that special deed, before others who did not do this, and in addition to the supreme reward of love which is common to them and to all others. Other special good works can be described in the same way, which when done faithfully are particularly acceptable in the sight of God and in the judgment of holy church. These are excellent, such as the enclosures of anchorites, done by authority of holy church, and also entries into any approved religious order. And the stricter the order,[267] the more excellent is the reward in the judgment of holy church. Moreover, after these and beneath them, is the taking of priest's orders,[268] either for the cure of people's souls and to administer the sacraments of holy church, or else for private devotion, to please God and to benefit their fellow Christians by the sacrifice of the precious body of our Lord Jesus Christ. Certainly these are special and excellent deeds, plainly shown in the judgment of holy church and in the sight of our Lord, when they are done truly for God, and they shall have a special reward, each man in his degree, in the bliss of heaven. For this accidental reward, the state of a bishop or prelate is above all these works. That this is true appears in holy scripture through the prophet Daniel, where he says: *Tu autem, vade ad tempus praefinitum, et requiesces, et stabis in sorte tua in finem dierum.*[269] This is as much as to say: When the angel had shown Daniel the mysteries of God, he spoke to him thus. "Go to your rest in bodily death; and you shall stand in your calling as a prophet at the last day." And certainly, as Daniel shall stand as a prophet at the last day of judgment and have the honor and excellence of a prophet as well as the supreme blessed reward of the love and sight of God, just so you shall stand as an anchoress (in that calling), and a religious, in the calling of religion; and so with other excellent works. And you shall have a singular honor in that on the day of judgment, surpassing others.

62.   A short exhortation to humility and charity.

Now if you will believe these words, you can from them get consolation for your degree of living, and also material for humility. For although if you are saved you will have such great and special reward for your state of life, nevertheless it may be that many a wife,[270] and many a woman living in the world, shall be nearer God than you are and will love God more and know him better than you do, for all your state. And of that you ought to be ashamed, if you are not busily acquiring love and charity as fully and perfectly as does a man or woman in the world. For if by the gift of God you can have the same amount of charity as a man or woman still engaged in worldly business, you shall have as much of the supreme reward as he; and above that you shall have a singular reward and an honor he shall not have, for the state which you have taken. If you want to do well, make yourself humble and forget your state as if it were nothing at all (for it is true—by itself it is nothing). And let all your desire and your diligence be aimed at destroying sins and getting charity and humility[271] and other spiritual virtues; for everything lies in that.

63. How a person is to know how much pride is in him.

I have nearly forgotten this image, but now I turn to it again. If you want to know how much pride there is inside it, you can further try yourself like this. Now, without flattering yourself, observe wisely whether praise, acclaim, honor or the carnal favor of worldly people or others is pleasing to your heart and turns it to vain gladness and self-satisfaction, so that in your heart you have a quiet feeling that they should praise your life and respect your words more than other people's. Also, on the other hand, if it happens that people reproach you and despise you, regarding you as merely a fool or a hypocrite; or if they slander you or speak evil of you falsely, or molest you without reason in any other way; and you therefore feel anger and resentment against them in your heart, and a great uprising there, with resistance against suffering any shame[272] or disgrace in the sight of the world: if this is how you are, it is a sign that there is a great deal of pride in this dark image, however holy you may seem in the sight of men. Although these stirrings are no more than small and venial, they nevertheless show clearly that there is a lot of pride hidden in the bottom of your heart, like the fox lurking in his den. These stirrings, with many more, spring out of this image so much that you can scarcely do any good work without its being mixed with some pride or vain delight in yourself; so with your pride you defile your good deeds and make them loathsome in the sight of your Lord. I do not say that because they are mixed with this pride they are lost, but I say that they are not as pleasing to our Lord as they would be if they were pure and truly rooted in the virtue of humility.

Therefore, if you want to have purity of heart in order to come to the love of God, not only should you avoid resting your heart in vainglory by deliberately assenting to pride, and deny to your frailty its unthinking pleasure in it (even though that is against your will), but you shall also flee the feeling of pride, and shun it as much as you can. But that you cannot do unless you are very quick and prompt in guarding your heart, as I shall tell you later.

64. Envy and wrath and their branches; and how sometimes a man's person is hated instead of his sin.

Turn this image upside down and look into it well, and you will find limbs of wrath and envy fastened to it, with many branches springing out of them which hinder the love and charity that you ought to have toward your fellow Christians. The branches of wrath and envy are these: hatred, evil suspicion, false and unfounded judgment, sullen resentment rising in your heart, contempt, backbiting, irrational blame, insult, unkindness, displeasure, bitterness and vexation against those that despise you or speak evil of you; with gladness at their distress and harshness against sinful people and others who will not behave as you feel they should; and with great desire in your heart (under the appearance of charity and righteousness) that they should be well-punished and chastised for their sin.

This stirring seems good. Nevertheless, if you look into it well you will sometimes find it more carnal against the person than spiritual against the sin. You are to love the man, however sinful he may be; and you shall hate the sin²⁷³ in every man, whoever he may be. Many are deceived in this, for they set the bitter in place of the sweet and take darkness instead of light, against the saying of the prophet: *Vae vobis qui dicitis malum bonum et bonum malum, ponentes lucem tenebras et amarum in dulce.*²⁷⁴ Woe to those who say that evil is good and good evil, putting light for darkness and bitter for sweet. So do all those who, thinking that they hate the sin, hate the person instead of the sin, when they should hate the sin of their fellow Christian and love the person. Therefore this is a craft in itself, if anyone should know how to do it well.

65. That it is very hard to love people truly in charity, and hate their sin.

There is no difficulty in waking and fasting until your head and body ache, or in going to Rome and Jerusalem on your bare feet, or in rushing about and preaching as if you wanted to convert everybody with your sermons. Neither is it hard to build churches or chapels or to feed poor men and make hospitals. But it is a very difficult thing for someone to love his fellow Christian in charity, and wisely to hate his sin while loving the man. For although it may be true that all the works I have mentioned are good in themselves, nevertheless they are common to good men and to bad, for everyone could do them if he wanted to and had the wherewithal. Therefore I regard it as no great feat to do what everyone can do; but to love one's fellow Christian in charity and hate his sin can be done only by good men, who have it by the gift of God and not by their own labor, as St. Paul says: *Caritas Dei diffusa est in cordibus vestris per Spiritum Sanctum qui datus est vobis.*[275] Love and charity is shed and diffused in your hearts by the Holy Spirit, who is given to you, and therefore it is the more precious, and the rarer to come by.

66. That for the same outward works different people shall have different rewards.

Without this, all other good deeds do not make a person good, or worthy of the bliss of heaven, but this one alone makes him good[276] and all his good deeds worthy of reward. All other gifts of God and works of men are common to good and to bad, to the chosen and to the reprobate, but this gift of charity belongs only to God and to chosen souls.

For the love of God a good man fasts, wakes, goes on pilgrimage and forsakes all the pleasure of this world genuinely in his heart, without pretense; he shall have his reward in the bliss of heaven. A hypocrite does the same works for his own vainglory and receives his reward here. Similarly, a true preacher of God's word, filled with humility and charity, who is sent by God and received by holy church, shall have the aureole as a special reward for his preaching, if he preaches and teaches God's word. A hypocrite or heretic having neither humility nor charity, and not being sent by God or holy church, has his reward here, if he preaches. In the same way, a good man in the secular state builds churches, chapels, abbeys and hospitals, and does other good works of mercy for the love of God. He shall have his reward in the bliss of heaven, not for the good work in itself, but for the good will and the charity that he had by the gift of God in order to do the good works. Another man out of vanity in himself, for worldly honor and praise and for his own name, does the same good works and has his reward here. In all these the reason is that one has charity and the other has none. Which is one and which the other, our Lord knows—and none but he.

67. That everyone's good works that have the appearance of good are to be approved, except those of the open heretic[277] and the man publicly excommunicated.

Therefore we shall love and honor everyone in our hearts, and approve and accept all their works that have the appearance of goodness, even though the doers are bad in God's sight, except those of the open heretic and the person who has been publicly excommunicated. We are to flee and avoid the company of these two especially, and communication with them; and for as long as they rebel against God and holy church we shall reject and reprove their deeds, however good they seem. So if a secular man who is excommunicated builds a church or feeds a poor man, you can safely regard it as nothing, and judge it as it is. Similarly, if an open heretic in rebellion against holy church preaches and teaches, even though he converted a hundred—yes, a thousand—souls, regard the work as nothing at all in his favor, for these men are manifestly out of charity, without which everything one does is nothing. And therefore I say it is a very difficult thing for a person to know how to love his fellow Christian in charity.

All this that I say can be clearly proved by St. Paul's words: *Si linguis hominum loquar et angelorum, caritatem autem non habuero, nihil sum; et si habuero omnem fiduciam ita ut montes transferam, caritatem non habeam, nihil sum; et si noverim mysteria omnia, nihil sum; et si distribuero omnes facultates meas in cibos pauperum, et tradidero corpus meum igni ut ardeam, caritatem autem non habeam, nihil mihi prodest.*[278] St. Paul speaks thus in praise of charity: If I speak the language of all men, and of angels as well, and I have no charity, I am nothing at all; and if I have such great faith that I can overturn mountains and carry them away, and I have no charity, I am still nothing; and also if I had every kind of knowledge of all mysteries, without charity I am yet nothing; and if I give all that I have to poor men, and my body to the fire to be burnt, and I have no charity, it is no profit to me whatsoever. Here by St. Paul's words it appears that one can do every kind of good bodily work without charity; and that charity is nothing else but to love God, and his fellow Christian as himself.

68. That no good work can make one feel safe without charity; and that charity is obtained only by the gift of God to those who are humble; and who is perfectly humble.

Then how should any poor wretch living on earth, whatever he may be, have delight, trust or confidence in himself, for anything he has the strength or knowledge to do with all his bodily powers and all his natural reason, since all this is worth nothing without love and charity to his fellow Christian? And this charity cannot be acquired[279] by any effort of his own, for it is a free gift of God, sent into a humble soul, as St. Paul says. Then who dares boldly say,[280] "I have charity," or, "I am in charity"? Indeed, nobody can say it but one who is perfectly and truly humble. Others can believe and hope of themselves that they are in charity by the tokens of charity; but someone who is perfectly humble feels it, and therefore he could safely say it. St. Paul was humble in this way, and therefore spoke thus of himself: *Quis nos separabit a caritate Dei? Tribulatio an angustia?* etc.[281] Who shall part me from the charity of God? Tribulation or anguish? And he answers himself, and says that no created thing shall put me away from the charity of God which I have in Christ Jesus.

Many a man does works of charity and has no charity, as I have said. To reprove a sinner for his sin at the proper time in order to amend him is a work of charity; but to hate[282] the sinner instead of the sin is against charity. A truly humble person knows how to distinguish[283] one from the other, and no one but he. For if someone had all the moral virtues of all the philosophers, he would not be able to do this: he would know how to hate the sin of all other men, because he hates it in himself, but he could not love the man in charity for all his philosophy. In the same way, if a man with knowledge of all science and divinity is not truly humble, he will easily err and stumble, mistaking the one for the other; but humility is worthy to receive from God a gift which cannot be learned by human teaching. Therefore he that is humble knows how to hate the sin and truly love the man.

But now perhaps you are beginning to be afraid, because I said that charity cannot be acquired[284] by any work that you can do. How, then, are you to behave? To this I say that there is nothing so hard to acquire as charity. This is true as regards your own efforts, but on the other hand I say there is no gift of God that can be had as easily as charity, for our Lord gives no gift as freely, as gladly or as widely as he does charity. How shall you have it, then? you say. Be meek and lowly in spirit, and you shall have it; and what is easier to do than to be meek? Indeed, nothing. Then it seems that nothing is so easily to be had as charity; and therefore do not be too afraid of that. Be humble, and have it.

St. James the Apostle speaks thus: *Deus superbis resistit; humilibus autem dat gratiam.*[285] Our Lord, he says, resists the proud, but to the humble he gives grace; and this grace is properly charity.[286] For you shall have charity according to the measure of your humility; if you have humility imperfectly[287]—only in will and not in affection—then you shall have imperfect charity. This is good, for it is sufficient for salvation, as David says, *Imperfectum meum viderunt oculi tui.*[288] Lord, with your eyes of mercy you see my imperfection. But if you have humility perfectly, then you shall have perfect charity, and that is best. We need to have the other if we want to be saved, but this we shall desire. Then if you ask me who is perfectly humble, you shall at this time have no more from me about humility than this: that man is humble[289] who has true knowledge and feeling of himself as he is.

69. How a person is to know how much wrath and envy is hidden in the bottom of his heart.

Now turn yet again to this image. If you want to try how much wrath and envy is hidden in the bottom of your heart, unfelt by you, look well and consider yourself carefully when such stirrings of wrath and envy against your fellow Christian spring out of your heart. The greater the uprising that you have, and the more stirred you are against him by sullenness, bitterness or ill-will, the greater is this image in you, for the more impatiently you grumble—either against God, for any tribulation or sickness, or other bodily trouble sent by him, or against your fellow Christian, for anything he does against you—the less is the image of Jesus reformed in you.

70. By what signs you are to know whether you love your enemy, and what example you shall take from Christ in order to love him in the same way.

I do not say that such complaints and carnal bitterness are mortal sins; but I say that they hinder purity of heart and peace of conscience, so that you cannot have the full charity by which you should come to the contemplative life. For that end is the purpose of all that I say about your need to cleanse your heart, not only from mortal sins but also from venial ones as much as you can, so that the ground of sin might by the grace of Jesus Christ be somewhat abated in you. For although it may be that for a time you feel no ill-will against your fellow Christian, you are still not sure that the ground of wrath is extinct in you; and you are not yet lord of the virtue of charity. Let him touch you a little with an angry or malicious word, and you will feel at once whether your heart is yet healed by the fullness of charity. The more you are stirred against the person and the greater your ill-will,[290] the further you are from perfect charity toward your fellow Christian; the less you are stirred, the nearer you are to charity.

cf. Julian on love and charity

If you are not stirred against the person—either outwardly by an angry face, or in your own heart by any secret hatred, to despise or judge him or set him at nought—but the more shame and disgrace he causes you in word or deed, the more pity and compassion you have for him, as you would for a man out of his mind; and if you feel you cannot find it in your heart to hate him (because love is so good in itself), but you pray for him, help him, and desire his amendment—not only with your mouth as hypocrites know how to do, but with the affection of love in your heart—then you have perfect charity toward your fellow Christian. St. Stephen had this charity perfectly when he prayed for those that stoned him to death, and Christ counselled it for all who wanted to be his perfect followers when he said: *Diligite inimicos vestros, benefacite his qui oderunt vos, orate pro persequentibus et calumniantibus vos.*[291] Love your enemies and do good to them that hate you; pray for those who persecute and slander you. And therefore if you want to follow Christ, be like him in this craft: learn to love your enemies and sinful men, for all these are your fellow Christians.

Look and consider how Christ loved Judas, who was both his deadly enemy and a sinful wretch. How gracious and kindly Christ was to him, how courteous and how lowly to one that he knew deserved damnation; and nevertheless he chose him as his apostle; he sent him to preach with other apostles and gave him power to work miracles. He showed him the same friendliness in word and deed as he did the other apostles; he washed his feet and fed him with his precious body and preached to him, as he did for the others. He did not accuse him openly (for it was a secret), and neither did he revile him, despise him or ever speak evil of him; and yet if he had done all this he would have spoken only the truth. Furthermore, when Judas captured him, he kissed him and called him his friend. All this charity was shown by Christ to Judas, whom he knew to be worthy of damnation, not in any way pretending or flattering, but in the truthfulness of good love and pure charity. For though it was true that Judas was unworthy to have any gift of God, or any token of love, because of his wickedness, nevertheless it was right and fitting that our Lord should appear as he is. He is love and goodness, and therefore it is proper for him to show love and goodness to all his creatures, as he did to Judas. I do not say that Christ loved him for his sin, or that he loved him as one of his chosen, as he did St. Peter; but he loved him inasmuch as Judas was created by him, and he showed him tokens of love—if only he had wished to be amended by them.

If you can, follow this in some measure; for although your body is shut in a house, nevertheless in your heart (which is the place of love) you should be able to have some of such love as I speak of for your fellow Christian.

Whoever considers himself to be a perfect follower of Christ's teaching and living—as somebody may think he is for his preaching and teaching, and his Christlike poverty in worldly goods—certainly deceives himself if he does not know how to follow Christ in this love and charity: to love every one of his fellow Christians—good and bad, friends and foes—without pretense or flattery, contempt in his heart against the man, bitterness or spiteful fault-finding. The nearer he supposes himself to be, the further he is away. For Christ spoke like this to those who wanted to be his disciples: *Hoc est praeceptum meum, ut diligatis invicem sicut dilexi vos.*[292] This is my commandment, that you love one another as I have loved you. For if you love as I have loved, then you are my disciples.

But now you say,[293] "How am I to love a bad man as well as one that is good?" In reply to this I say that you are to love both in charity, but not for the same reason, as I shall explain. You shall love your fellow Christian as yourself. Now, you are to love yourself only in God, or else for the sake of God. In God you love yourself when you are righteous by grace and virtues; and you are not loving yourself except for that righteousness and virtue that God gives you: then you love yourself in God, for you are loving nothing in yourself but God. Also you love yourself for God's sake: so if you were in mortal sin and wanted to be made righteous and virtuous, then you love yourself, not as you are—for you are unrighteous—but as you want to be. You are to love your fellow Christians in just the same way. If they are good and righteous, you shall love them by charity in God only because they are good and righteous, for then you are loving God in them (as goodness and righteousness) more than themselves. If they are bad through mortal sin, as are your enemies who hate you, or others of whose lack of grace you have full evidence, you are still to love them: not as they are, and not as good and righteous men, for they are bad and unrighteous; but you shall love them for the sake of God, in that they could be good and righteous. And so you shall hate nothing in them but the thing which is contrary to righteousness, and that is sin. This is the teaching of St. Augustine,[294] as I understand, to distinguish the love of the man from the hatred of the sin, in loving your fellow Christian. Someone who is humble—or truly wants to be—knows how to love his fellow Christian in this way, and none but he.

71. How a person is to know how much <u>covetousness</u> is hidden in his heart.

Lift up this image, look it over well, and you will be able to see that covetousness and the love of earthly things occupy a great part of it, even though it may seem little. You have forsaken the riches and great possessions of this world and are shut in a dungeon, but have you quite forsaken the love of all these? Not yet, I think. There is less difficulty in forsaking worldly goods[295] than in forsaking the love [of] them: perhaps you have not forsaken your covetousness but have changed it from great things into small,[296] as from a pound into a penny, and from a silver piece into the disk of a halfpenny. This is a poor exchange, and you are not a good merchant![297] These examples are childish; nevertheless they are tokens of greater things. If you do not believe me, test yourself. If you have love and delight in the having and holding of anything that you own, such as it is, and feed your heart with this love for a time; or if you have a desire and yearning to possess something that you do not have, and through this desire your heart is troubled and vexed with undue concern, so that the pure desire of virtues and of God cannot rest within it: this is a sign that there is covetousness in this image. And if you want to make a better proof, notice if anything that you have is taken away from you by force, by borrowing, or in any other way, so that you cannot get it again, and you are distressed, angered and troubled over it in your heart, both because you lack that thing which you want to have and cannot, and also because you are moved against the person who has it, to contend and quarrel with him over his unwillingness to restore it again when he could. This is a sign that you love worldly goods, for this is how worldly people behave when their goods and their riches are taken from them. They are gloomy, sorrowful and angry, and contend and quarrel openly in word and deed with those that have them. You do all this secretly in your heart where God sees; and yet you are more at fault than a secular person; for you have seemingly forsaken the love of all worldly things, but he has not. Therefore he is excused, even though he contends and sues for his goods in order to have them again by lawful means.

But now you say that you ought to have what you need of such things as befit you, in the same way as a secular person. I quite agree with this; but you should not love the thing in itself, or take any pleasure in the holding or keeping of it, or feel sorrow or rancor in its loss or withdrawal. For as St. Gregory says: "The sorrow that you have in the loss of a thing is the measure of the love that you had in keeping it."[298] And therefore if your heart were made holy and you had really felt a desire for spiritual things, and if you also had a sight of the smallest spiritual thing there is, you would think nothing of all the love and pleasure of anything in the world: it should not cling to you. For to love and possess more than you reasonably need,[299] only for delight and pleasure, is a great fault. In the same way, to fix your love upon some necessary thing for its own sake, that is a fault, but not so great; but to have and use[300] something that you need, and not love it more than nature or need demands (without which the thing cannot be used), that is not a fault.

Certainly on this point, as I believe, many who have the state of poverty are greatly hampered and hindered from the love of God. I accuse no one, neither do I condemn any state, for in every state some are good and some are otherwise; but one thing I say to every man or woman who has taken the state of voluntary poverty, whether he is religious or secular, or whatever degree he is in: so long as his love and affection are bound, fastened and as it were entangled[301] with the coveting of earthly goods that he has or would like to have, he cannot truly have or feel the pure love and clear sight of spiritual things. For St. Augustine speaks thus to our Lord: "Lord, the man who loves anything beside you that he does not love for your sake loves you only a little."[302] The more love and yearning that is in you for any earthly thing, the less is the love of God in your heart, for although it may be that this love of earthly things does not put people out of charity (unless it is so great that it stifles the love of God and of their fellow Christians), it certainly hinders and impedes them from the fervor of charity, and also from that special reward which in the bliss of heaven they should have for perfect poverty; and that is a great loss, if they could see it. For if anyone could know spiritual reward—how good, how precious and how valuable it is, because it is everlasting—he would not want to hinder or lessen the smallest reward of that heavenly bliss (which he could have if he wished) for the love of all earthly joy or the possession of all earthly things, even though he could have them without sin.

I speak further than I do, but I pray you or anyone else, whoever is willing, to do as I say if you can, by the grace of God. For that would be a comfort to my heart: that though I cannot have it in myself as I say, I could have it in you, or in another creature who has received more plentiful grace from our Lord than I.

But now see: since covetousness in the bare ground hinders a man or woman so much from the spiritual feeling of the love of God, how much more it hinders and encumbers men and women in the world, who with all their senses and their practical efforts set themselves to toil night and day to get riches and an abundance of worldly goods. They do not know how to take any delight except in the things of the world; neither do they want to, for they do not seek it. I say no more of them at this time, for in this writing I am not speaking to them. But this I do say: if they could and would see what they are doing, they would not behave in this way.

72.   How a person shall know when he does not sin in eating and drinking; and when he sins mortally, and when venially.

You can see yet more in this image, although it is dark, and that is fleshly love for yourself in gluttony, *accidie*[303] and lechery. These carnal appetites make a person quite bestial,[304] far from the inward savor of the love of God and from the clear sight of spiritual things.

But now you say that since you must needs eat, drink and sleep, and cannot do that without pleasure, it seems to you that this pleasure is no sin. To this I reply that if in eating and drinking and other things needed by the body you keep moderation according to your need, as reason requires, and receive no more pleasure than nature requires, and you do all this for the spiritual delight you feel in your soul, certainly I grant that you do not sin at all in this, for then you know well how to eat and sleep. Truly and undoubtedly I am very far from that knowledge, and further from the practice of it: eating is mine by nature, but I cannot know how I should eat except by grace. St. Paul had this skill by grace, as he says himself: *Ubique et in omnibus institutus sum; et satiari, et esurire, abundare, et penuriam pati. Omnia possum in eo qui me confortat.*[305] I am informed and taught in all things; for I know how to hunger, and how to eat; what to do with plenty, and with poverty; I can do everything in him who strengthens me. St. Augustine also spoke to our Lord: "You have taught me that I should take food as medicine."[306] Hunger is a sickness of nature, and food is the medicine for it. Therefore the pleasure that comes with it is not a sin, insofar as it is natural and needful; but when it passes into lust and the wish for pleasure, then it is sin. And so it is there that all the difficulty lies, in knowing how to distinguish wisely the need from the lust and from the will for pleasure. They are so knitted together, and the one comes so much with the other, that it is hard to receive one as the need and reject the other as willful lust, which often comes disguised as need.

Nevertheless, since it is the case that need is the ground of this sin, and that need is no sin—for a man ought to eat and drink and sleep however holy he is—therefore the delight and pleasure that come in the guise of this need and go beyond it are the less sinful. For it is not common for anyone to sin mortally through gluttony[307] unless he is encumbered with other mortal sins that he has already committed: then he may the more easily sin mortally in this. For this is true: somebody who chooses delight and pleasure for his flesh in the delicious abundance of food and drink, and makes it the complete resting place of his heart, so that in his heart he never wants to have any other life or any other joy but to live forever in such pleasures of his flesh, if he could, there is no doubt that he sins mortally, for he loves his flesh more than God; but someone who lies in a mortal sin of pride, envy or suchlike is blinded and so bound by the devil that for the time he does not have the full power of his free will, and therefore he cannot well withstand fleshly pleasures when they come, but willingly falls upon them as a beast does upon carrion. And inasmuch as he has no general will already set principally toward God (because he is in mortal sin), the lust of gluttony into which he falls is easily a mortal sin for him, because he makes no resistance, either in general or in particular.

But another man or woman who is in grace and charity has always a good general will toward God in his soul—whether asleep or awake, eating or drinking, or whatever good deed he is doing—by which will he desires and chooses God above everything; and he would rather forbear from all the pleasure of this world than from his God, for love of him. Although this will is only general, it is of such great power by the grace of our Lord Jesus that it saves and keeps him from mortal sin, even though he falls by frailty into pleasure or delight in food or drink, or other such sickness, in the excess of eating either too much, or too often, or too greedily, or too lustily and luxuriously, and too soon and at the wrong time. This is true so long as he is in charity by other good works[308] and keeps this general good will in all that he does, and especially too if he acknowledges his own wretchedness between whiles, and above all cries for mercy, resolving to withstand such fleshly appetites. Our Lord is good and merciful, and to a humble soul he very soon forgives these venial sins of gluttony. For the stirrings and pleasures of gluttony are the most excusable and least perilous of all sins, inasmuch as they are the hardest to escape because of the need of the bodily nature. Therefore you are not to arise against the ground of this sin as you shall against all other sins, for the ground of this sin is only need, which cannot be escaped—unless you want to do worse and slay the need, as many fools do, who ought to slay the thief and spare the true man. That is to say, they should slay the unreasonable lust and the willful pleasure, and spare and keep the bodily nature; and that is not what they do.

But against all other sins you are to arise, to destroy not only the mortal sins and the great venial ones but also the ground of them, as much as you can. See by this reasoning. You cannot live without food and drink; but you can live without lechery if you will, and always be the better; and therefore not only shall you flee the act of lechery (which is mortal sin) and also the willful delight in it in your heart without the act (which is venial sin—and sometimes deadly); but you shall also labor against the ground of it, to destroy the feeling and the uprising of carnal impulses.

73. That the ground of lechery should be destroyed with the labor of the soul, not of the body.

But this labor against the ground of lechery is to be spiritual, with prayers and virtues of the spirit, and not bodily, by means of bodily penance, for you must know that though you watch and fast, scourge yourself and do all that you know, you shall never have that cleanness and chastity without the gift and the grace of lowliness. It would be easier to kill yourself than to flee the stirrings and feelings of the lusts of lechery, either in your heart or in your flesh, with any bodily penance; but by the grace of Jesus in a humble soul the ground can be largely blocked and destroyed, and the spring[309] can be dried up; and that is true chastity in body and soul. One can speak in the same way of pride, covetousness and suchlike—for you could live without being either proud or covetous—and therefore you are to destroy all the feelings of them, as much as you can; but in gluttony you shall rise and strike away the unreasonable stirrings and keep the ground whole. Therefore, some-

146

one who rises up against the feeling of carnal pleasure in food and drink more severely and sharply than against the feelings and stirrings of pride (which, because they seem fair, are not easily rejected), or of envy, wrath, covetousness or lechery, I say he is half blind; for he does not yet see how foul in God's sight is spiritual uncleanness such as pride and envy. I think if a man could see with the eye of his spirit how foul pride and covetousness are in the sight of God, and how contrary to him, he would have more abhorrence for a stirring of pride and the vain pleasure of it; and in the same way he would loathe and rise up against an evil intention of envy or wrath toward his fellow Christian more than against many a stirring and delight in gluttony or lechery.

Nevertheless not everyone thinks so, for people are usually more frightened to feel the stirring of a carnal sin, and are more sorrowful and anxious about it, than over great pleasures in vainglory or in other sins of the spirit; but they are not wise. For if they would only understand holy scripture and the commentaries of learned men upon it,[310] they would find it as I say; but I neither can nor will go over these now.

74.   That people should be careful to put away all stirrings of sin, but more careful over sins of the spirit than of the body.

I do not want to excuse those who fall into the pleasures of gluttony and lechery, and say that they do not sin, for I know well that all species of these are sin, more or less, in proportion to the lust and willful pleasure, with other circumstances; but I would wish you to know and weigh each sin as it is: the greater the more, as are all spiritual sins, and the smaller the less, as are the carnal ones; and yet you are nevertheless to hate and flee all of them—both carnal and spiritual—as you are able. For you must know that the desires of the flesh and irrational pleasure in food and drink, or any pleasure that belongs to the body, beyond reasonable need, are very heavy, painful and bitter, and much to be avoided by a soul that desires purity and the spiritual feeling of God, even though they are not always great sins for someone that is in charity. For until the flesh has lost much of its outward bestial savor, the spirit cannot feel the inward savor that is natural to it; and therefore if you want to come to purity of heart you ought to withstand the unreasonable stirrings of fleshly desires. But you shall not rise up against the ground, as I have said before; for the ground of it is need (such as natural hunger), which you must needs feel and attend to at the right time, helping yourself against it with the medicine of food in your wish to guard yourself rationally against a bodily sickness, in order to serve God the more freely in body and soul.

75. That hunger and other pains of the body greatly hinder the work of the spirit.

You must know that any man or woman who is to be spiritually occupied in meditation will be greatly hampered in spirit and hindered from the knowing and beholding of spiritual things (unless he has more grace) if he willfully takes on some undue pain of hunger, or bodily sickness in the stomach, the head, or another part, for lack of good self-rule, through too much fasting, or in any other way. For though it may be that bodily pain (either of penance or of sickness), or else bodily occupation, is at times no hindrance to the fervor of love to God in devotion, but often increases it; nevertheless, I consider that it hinders the fervor of love in contemplation,[311] which may not be had or felt soberly except in great rest of body and soul. Therefore do fairly what concerns you, look after your bodily nature according to reason, and then suffer God to send what he will, whether it be health or sickness; take it gladly, and do not willfully complain against him.

76. What remedy is to be used against one's errors in eating and drinking.

Do then as I say: take your food as it comes, and make reasonable provision for it if necessary. Take it gladly as you need it, but be careful of the pleasure that comes with need. Eschew too much as well as too little, and when you have finished and there comes to your mind some remorse of conscience—that you have eaten either too much or too little—and it begins to weary you and distract you to overmuch bitterness, lift up the desire of your heart to your good Lord Jesus and acknowledge yourself as a wretch and a beast. Ask him for forgiveness and say you want to amend it, and trust in forgiveness by his mercy. And when you have done so—the shorter the better—then leave off and spend no longer with it. Do not strive too hard, as if you wanted to destroy it utterly, for it is not worthwhile to do so and you shall never bring it about in this way; but promptly assign yourself to some other occupation of body or spirit for which you feel you are ready, so that you can advance more in other virtues such as humility and charity.[312]

For you must know that someone who has no regard in his desire and his labor for anything other than humility and charity—always craving for them and the way to get them—in that desire, and with the work that follows, in one year he shall progress and grow more in all other virtues (such as chastity, abstinence and the like, and with little regard to them) than he would without this desire progress in seven, even though he struggled continually against gluttony, lechery and so on, beating himself with scourges every day from morning to the time of evensong.

77. That through diligent desire and labor in humility and charity one comes the sooner to other virtues, to labor in them.

Then acquire for yourself humility and charity, and if you are willing to toil and labor diligently for them you shall have enough to do in getting them; and if you can get them they will rule and measure[313]—in complete secrecy—how you are to eat and how you shall drink, and succor every need of your body, so that nobody shall know unless you wish. And that will not be in perplexity, doubt, trouble or sadness, or in pleasure or frivolity, but in the peace of a glad conscience, with a sober restfulness.

I am speaking more than I intended on this matter, but nevertheless do as I say if you can, and I expect God will make all well.

By this, then, that I have said, you can look some way into this image of sin and see how much it hinders you. The gospel says how Abraham spoke in this way to the rich man that was buried in hell: *Chaos magnum inter nos et vos firmatum est ut hi qui volunt transire ad vos non possint, nec huc transmeare.*[314] There is a great chaos, that is to say, a thick darkness, between us and you, so that we cannot come to you, nor you to us. This dark image in your soul and in mine can also be called a great chaos, a great darkness, for it hinders us so that we cannot come to Abraham, who is Jesus, and it hinders him, so that he will not come to us.

78. What comes out of the darkness of the image of sin, and what comes through its windows.

Light up your lantern,[315] and see in this image five windows by which sin comes into your soul, as the prophet says: *Mors ingreditur per fenestras nostras.*[316] Death comes in by our windows. These windows are your five senses, by which your soul goes out from itself to seek its delight and its nourishment in earthly things, against its own nature: for example, by the eye, to see fair and curious things; by the ear, to hear wonders and new things; and so with the other senses. By the improper use of these senses for willful vanity the soul is much hindered from the spiritual senses within; therefore you ought to block these windows or shut them except when need demands their opening. You would not find that hard if you could once see your soul by clear understanding: what it is, and how fair it is in its own nature, were it not so overlaid with a black mantle[317] from this foul image.

79. That for lack of self-knowledge a soul journeys out by the five senses in search of pleasure.

But because you do not know it, you leave the inward sight of yourself and look for food outside, like a beast without reason.[318] So says our Lord, threatening a chosen soul in holy scripture: *Si ignoras te, O pulcra inter mulieres, egredere et abi post vestigia gregum sodalium tuorum, et pasce hoedos tuos.*[319] O fair among women, if you do not know yourself go out and follow the steps of the flock of your fellows, and feed your goats. And this is as much as to say: O soul, fair by nature, made to the likeness of God,[320] in your body as frail as a woman by reason of the first sin, because you do not know yourself that angels' food should be your delicacies within, you go out by way of your bodily senses to seek your food and your pleasure like a beast of the flock, that is, like one of the reprobate, and with it you feed your thoughts and your affections, which are as unclean as goats.

80. That a soul should not search outside but ask Jesus within for all that it needs.

It is shameful for you to do this, and therefore turn again home into yourself[321] to stay indoors; and beg no more outside, especially for pig-food.[322] If you still want to be a beggar, ask and crave within from your Lord Jesus, for he is rich enough, and more glad to give than you are willing to ask. And do not run out any more[323] like a beast of the flock, and like a worldly man or woman with no other delight than in his bodily senses. If you do so, your Lord Jesus is willing to give you all that you need. He can lead you into his wine cellar and make you try which of his wines pleases you best, for he has many casks. A chosen soul rejoicing in holy scripture speaks like this of our Lord: *Introduxit me rex in cellam vinariam.*[324] A king led me into a wine cellar; and that is to say, Inasmuch as I forsook the drinks of carnal pleasures and worldly delights (which are bitter as wormwood) for the delight of glory, therefore the king[325] of glory, our Lord Jesus, led me in, that is to say, first into myself, to behold and know myself, and afterwards he led me into his cellar, that is to say, above myself by ascending[326] into him alone; and gave me some of his wine to try, that is, to taste a sample of spiritual sweetness and heavenly joy.

These words are not from me, a miserable wretch living in sin, but they are the words of the spouse of our Lord in holy scripture; and I say them to you so that you can draw in your soul from outside, and follow as far as you can.

81. That the hole of the imagination needs to be stopped as well as the windows of the senses.

But now you say[327] that you are doing this. You neither see nor hear worldly things, and make no more use of your bodily senses than need demands, and that is why you are enclosed. To this I say: If you behave thus (as I expect you do), then you have blocked a great window[328] of this image; but still you are not secure[329] because you have not stopped the secret holes of imagination in your heart, for though you do not see me with your bodily eye, you can see me in your soul by imagination,[330] and you can do the same with all other bodily things. Then if your soul is willingly fed with the vanities of the world by imagination—in desiring such worldly things as self-willed comfort and ease—in fact, though your soul is indoors as regards your bodily senses, nevertheless by such vain imagining it is a long way outside.

But now you ask whether it is any great sin for a soul to occupy itself in such vanities, either in the senses or in imagination. To this I say: I would not wish you ever to ask this question of anybody, for someone who wants truly to love God does not commonly ask whether this sin or another is the greater. He shall feel that whatever hinders him from the love of God is a great sin, and it shall seem to him that there is no sin but a thing that is not good and hinders him from the love of God. What is sin but a lack and a shunning of good?[331] I do not say that it shall be as painful to him as a mortal sin or a venial one would be, and I do not deny that he may know a mortal from a venial sin and avoid it more.

82. When the use of the senses and the imagination is mortal sin, and when venial.

Nevertheless, I shall say something in reply to your question, as it seems to me, for your desire draws more out of my heart than I thought to have said in the beginning. Our Lord says in the gospel: *Homo quidam*

fecit cenam magnam et vocavit multos. Et misit servum suum dicere invi-
tatis ut venirent. Primus dixit: "Villam emi; rogo te, habe me excusatum."
Secundus dixit: "Juga boum emi quinque, et eo probare illa." Et tertius
dixit: "Uxorem duxi, et ideo non possum venire."[332] A man made a great
supper and called many to it, and at suppertime he sent his servant after
those who were invited. The first made an excuse for not being able to
come, because he had bought a farm. In the same way the next excused
himself because he had bought five yoke of oxen and was going to try
them out, and the third because he had married a wife. I leave out any
talk of the first and the last and tell you about the middle one who bought
the oxen, for he has to do with this theme.

These five yoke of oxen signify the five senses, which are animal,
like an ox. Now, this man who was called to the supper was not rejected
for buying these oxen but for going to try them out, and so being unwilling to come. In just the same way I say to you: It is no sin to have your
senses and to use them in need,[333] but if you purposely go to try them
with vain delight in created things, then it is sin. For if you choose that
delight as the final resting place of your soul and as all you want, so that
you do not care to have any other glory than such worldly vanity: then it
is mortal, for you choose it as your God, and so you shall be put out from
the supper. For St. Paul forbade us to make such a trial of our senses
when he said: *Non eas post concupiscentias tuas.*[334] You shall not go after
your lusts or purposely put your appetites to the test. A man or woman
encumbered with mortal sins shall not easily escape mortal sin in this,
even if he does not see it. But I do not think this concerns you. Nevertheless, if through frailty you take delight in your senses and in such vanity,
but with that you keep yourself in charity in other respects and do not
choose this delight as the full resting place of your soul, but always set
God in your desire before all other things, this sin is only venial—more
or less, according to the circumstances. And for these venial sins you
shall not be put out from the supper in the glory of heaven, but while you
live on earth you shall lack the tasting and sampling of that delicious
supper unless you diligently use all your powers to withstand such venial
sins. For although it is true that venial sins do not break charity,[335] they
certainly impede the fervor and spiritual feeling of it.

83. How an anchoress is to behave toward people that come
to her.

But now you say that you cannot keep yourself from hearing vain
things, because various people, both secular and otherwise, often

come[336] to speak with you and sometimes tell you tales of vanity. To this I reply that talking with your fellow Christians is not much against you but sometimes helps you, if you will work wisely. By it you can test the charity you have toward your fellow Christian, whether it is great or little. Like every man and woman you are bound to love your fellow Christian, first of all in your heart and also in deed, to show him tokens of charity as reason requires, according to your power and your knowledge. Now it is not your duty to go out of your house looking for an opportunity to benefit your fellow Christian through works of mercy, because you are enclosed; nevertheless you are bound to love[337] them all in your heart, and truly to show tokens of love to those that come to you. Therefore, if anyone wants to speak with you, whatever he is and of whatever rank, and if you do not know who he is or why he comes, be ready quickly with a good will to know what he wants. Do not be haughty or keep him waiting for long, but look how willing and glad you would be if an angel from heaven wanted to come and speak with you! Be just as ready and obliging in your willingness to speak with your fellow Christian when he comes to you, for you do not know who he is, why he comes or what need he has of you, or you of him, until you have tried; and although you may be in prayer or devotion, so that you grudge breaking off (because you feel you should not leave God for any man's talk), in this case I feel it is not so, for if you are wise you shall not leave God, but you shall find him, have him and see him in your fellow Christian[338] just as well as in your prayer. If you well knew how to love your fellow Christian, speaking to him discreetly should be no hindrance to you.

Discretion you shall have in this way, as it seems to me. Whoever comes to you, ask him humbly what he wants, and if he comes to tell of his trouble and to be comforted by what you say, hear him gladly and let him say what he wants, to ease his own heart; and when he has finished, comfort him if you know how, kindly and charitably, and soon break off. Then after that, if he falls into idle tales or vanities of the world or of other people's doings, say little in reply and do not feed his talk, and he will soon feel bored and soon take his leave. If another man comes to instruct you, as a man of holy church, hear him humbly, with reverence for his order; and if what he says comforts you, question him, and do not presume to teach him, for it is not your place to instruct a priest except in necessity.[339] If his talk does not comfort you, say little in reply and he will soon take his leave. If it happens that others come to give you alms, or else to hear you speak, or to be taught by you, speak kindly and humbly to them all. Do not reprove anyone for his faults—it is not your concern—unless he is so friendly with you that you are sure he will take it from you. In short, you may say as much as you conceive should profit your fellow Christian (especially in the spirit), if you have the knowledge and he is willing to accept it. And keep silent about all other things as far as you can, and in a short time you will have only a small crowd to hinder you. So it seems to me: do better if you can.

84. The dark image of sin, and its clothing.

From what I have said you can see a little of the darkness of this image; not that I have described it fully as it is, for I do not know how; nevertheless, by means of this little you can see more if you look thoroughly.

But now you say: "How can you tell that I carry about such an image as you describe?" To this I know an answer. I can take for myself a word said by the prophet, and it is this: *Inveni idolum mihi.*[340] That is to say, I have found a false image in myself that men call an idol, very foully disfigured and deformed with the wretchedness of all these sins that I have spoken of, by which I am cast down into many carnal pleasures and worldly vanities, from cleanness of heart and from the feeling of spiritual virtues, more than I can or may say; and for this I repent and cry for mercy. By this wretchedness that I feel in myself—much more than I know how to say—I am the more able to tell you of your own image, for we all come of Adam and Eve, clad in clothes of beasts' hide, as holy scripture says of our Lord: *Fecit Deus Adae et uxori ejus tunicas pelliceas.*[341] Our Lord made clothes of beasts' hide for Adam and his wife as a sign that for his sin he was misshapen like a beast. With these bestial clothes we are all born, wrapped up and disfigured from our natural shape.[342]

85. Which are the limbs of the image of sin.

This, then, is an ugly image to look at. The head is pride, for pride is the first and principal sin, as the wise man says: *Initium omnis peccati superbia.*[343] Pride is the beginning of every kind of sin. The back and the hind part of it is covetousness, as St. Paul says: *Quae retro sunt obliviscens in anteriora me extendo.*[344] I shall forget all earthly things, which are behind, and I shall reach forward to things eternal. The breast in which the heart is placed is envy, for that is no carnal sin but a sin of the devil, as the wise man says: *Invidia diaboli mors intravit in orbem terrarum. Imitantur illum omnes qui ex parte eius sunt.*[345] By the envy of the devil death came into the whole world, therefore all those who are on his side follow him in this. Its arms are wrath, inasmuch as a man avenges himself in his wrath with his arms, against the forbidding of Christ in the gospel: *Se quis percusserit te in unam maxillam, praebe ei et alteram.*[346] If someone strikes you on one cheek, you are not to hit back, but offer him the other cheek. The belly of this image is gluttony, as St. Paul says: *Esca ventri, et venter escis; Deus hunc et has destruet.*[347] Food serves the belly, and the belly serves to get food; but God shall destroy both belly and food. That shall be at the last end, in the full reforming of his chosen and in the judgment of the reprobate. Its members are lechery, of which St. Paul speaks like this: *Non exhibeatis membra vestra arma iniquitatis ad peccatum.*[348] You are not to give your members—especially your privy members—to be the weapons of sin. The feet of this image are *accidie,*[349] and therefore the wise man speaks to the sluggard, to stir him to good works: *Discurre, festina, suscita amicum tuum.*[350] That is to say, Run about quickly to do good works, and make great haste, for time is passing, and arouse your friend, who is Jesus, by devout prayer and meditation.

You have heard here about the members of this image.

86. What the image of Jesus is made of, and the image of sin; and how we are going about in the image of sin.

This is not the image of Jesus, but it is more like an image of the devil, for the image of Jesus is made of virtues, with humility and perfect love and charity;[351] but this is made of false carnal love for yourself, with all these members fastened to it. This image is borne by you and every man, whoever he may be, until by the grace of Jesus it is to some extent destroyed and broken down. So it seems that David says in the book of Psalms: *Verumtamen in imagine pertransit homo; sed et frustra conturbatur.*[352] This is to say, Although in the beginning a man was made stable and steadfast in the image of God, yet because of sin, living in this world he proceeds in this image of sin, by which he is made unstable and troubled in vain. St. Paul also speaks of this image: *Sicut portavimus imaginem terreni hominis, sic portemus imaginem caelestis.*[353] That is to say, If we want to come to the love of God, as we have hitherto borne the image of the earthly man, the first Adam (that is, the image of sin), so let us now bear the image of the heavenly man Jesus, which is the image of virtues. Then what are you to do with this image? I answer you with a word that the Jews spoke to Pilate about Christ: *Tolle, Tolle, crucifige eum!*[354] Take this body of sin and put it upon the cross. That is to say, Break down this image and slay the false love of sin in yourself. As Christ's body was slain for our trespasses, so, if you want to be like Christ you should slay your carnal appetite and the fleshly lust in yourself. So said St. Paul: *Qui autem Christi sunt, carnem suam crucifixerunt cum vitiis et concupiscentiis.*[355] Those who are Christ's followers have crucified and slain their flesh (that is, the image of sin), with all the lusts and unreasoning appetites of it. Then slay and break down pride, and set up humility; also, break down wrath and envy, and raise up love and charity to your fellow Christian; instead of covetousness, poverty of spirit; in place of *accidie*,[356] fervor of devotion, with a glad readiness for all good works; and instead of gluttony and lechery, sobriety and chastity in body and in soul. So counselled St. Paul when he said: *Deponentes veterem hominem cum actibus suis qui corrumpitur secundum desideria erroris; et induite novum hominem, qui secundum Deum creatus est in sanctitate et iustitia.*[357] You are to put down the old man (that is, the image of sin and the old Adam) with all his members, for he is rotten with the desires of error, and you shall dress and clothe yourself in a new man, who is the image of God, through holiness, righteousness and the fullness of virtues. Who shall help you to break down this image? Certainly, your Lord Jesus. In his strength and in his name you shall break down this idol of sin. Pray to him diligently and with desire, and he shall help you.

87. What profit comes from keeping the heart, and how much the soul is in what it loves.[358]

Then gather your heart together and follow the counsel of the wise man when he says thus: *Omni custodia serva cor tuum, quoniam ex ipso vita procedit.*[359] Guard your heart with all your care, for out of it comes life. And that is true, when it is kept well, for then there come out of it wise thoughts, pure affections, and burning desires for virtues, charity and the bliss of heaven, making the soul live a blessed life. Also the opposite way if it is not kept; then, as our Lord says in the gospel: *De corde exeunt cogitationes malae quae coinquinant hominem.*[360] Bad thoughts and impure affections spring out of the heart, which defile a man, as our Lord says. They either take away[361] the life of the soul by mortal sin, or else they enfeeble the soul and make it sick, if they are venial. For what is a man but his thoughts and his loves?[362] These alone make him good or bad. As much as you love God and know him,[363] so large is your soul; and if you love him little, little is your soul; and if you have no love for him, your soul is nothing: it is nothing toward God, but it is large in sin. If you want to know what you love, look at what you think about; for where the love is, there is the eye, and where the pleasure is, there is the heart thinking most. If you love God greatly, you will like to think about him a great deal; and if you love him little, then you will give him little thought. Rule your thoughts well,[364] and your affections, and then you are virtuous.

88. How the image of sin shall be broken down.

Then begin, and break this image. When you have inwardly considered yourself and your wretchedness as I have said—how proud, how envious and resentful, how covetous, how carnal and how full of corruption you are; also how little knowledge, feeling or savor you have of God, and how wise and lively you are in your savor of earthly things, so that in short you feel yourself to be as full of sin as the skin is full of flesh—although you think of yourself in this way, do not be too frightened. When you have done this, lift up the desire of your heart to your Lord Jesus and pray to him for help;[365] cry to him with great desires and sighings, that he will help you to bear the heavy burden of this image,[366] or else that he will break it. Think too how shameful it is for you to be fed with the pigfood[367] of fleshly savors when you should feel the spiritual savors of heavenly joy. If you do so, you are then beginning to rise against the whole ground of sin in yourself as I have said; and it may so be that you will feel pain and sorrow: I expect you never felt greater. For you are to understand that no soul can live without great pain[368] unless he has rest and delight either in his Creator or in a creature. Then when you rise against yourself by fervent desire to have some feeling of your Lord Jesus, to draw out your love from all material things and from rest in your own bodily feeling inasmuch as you are encumbered with yourself, and it seems that all creatures rise against you, and everything in which you formerly delighted turns you to pain, and when you thus forsake yourself and cannot easily find comfort in God, your soul must needs suffer pain. Nevertheless, I think that if anyone is willing to suffer this pain a while, steadfastly clinging to that desire (that he wants nothing but his Lord)[369] and would not easily fall from it or seek any outward comfort for a time (for it does not last long), our Lord is near and will soon ease the heart. He will help you to bear your body, full of corruption, and he wants to break down this false image of love in yourself—not all at once, but little by little—until you are in some measure reformed to his likeness.

89.   How one is to behave toward the stirrings of pride and all other vices.

After such a thorough rising against yourself, you shall when it is past rule yourself more soberly and calmly, and set yourself to guard your thoughts and affections more firmly, in order to know whether they are good or bad. And then if you feel any stirring of pride in any of its varieties, look to it quickly if you can; do not let it escape easily, but take it into your mind and rend it, break it, despise it, and do it all the injury you can. Be sure you do not spare it, or believe it, however fairly it may speak, for it is false even though it seems true, as the prophet says: *Popule meus, qui te beatum dicunt ipsi te decipiunt, et in errorem mittunt.*[370] That is to say: You man of my people, those that say you are blessed and holy beguile you and bring you into error. And if you do this diligently and often, you shall by the grace of Jesus stop much of the spring of pride[371] within a short time, and so much abate the vain delight of it that you shall scarcely feel it; and if you do feel it, it will be weak and as it were half-dead, so that it shall not harm you much. And then you will be able to have a spiritual sight of humility,[372] how good and fair it is; and you will desire and love it for its own goodness, so that it shall please you to be regarded as you are, and if necessary to suffer contempt and scorn gladly for the love of righteousness.

In the same way, when you feel stirrings of wrath and a resentful rising of the heart, or any ill-will against your fellow Christian for any kind of cause, even though it may seem reasonable and in the cause of charity, be careful of it, and with your thought be ready to restrain it, so that it does not turn into fleshly appetite. Withstand it, and as far as you can do not pursue it either in word or in deed, but as he rises strike him down again; and so you shall slay it with the sword of the fear of God, that it shall not harm you. For in all these stirrings of pride, vainglory, envy or anything else, you must know that as fast as you perceive it and resist it with the displeasure of your will and reason, you slay it, even though it may still cling to your heart against your will and does not want to pass away easily: do not fear it, for it hinders your soul from peace but it does not defile your soul.

You are to behave in just the same way against all evil stirrings of covetousness, *accidie*,[373] gluttony and lechery, that you may always be ready with your reason and will[374] to reject and despise them.

↳ pedes mentis

90. What most helps a person's knowledge, and gets for him what he lacks, and most destroys sin in him.

You can do this better and more promptly if you take pains to set your heart most upon one thing. That thing is nothing other than a spiritual desire toward God—to please him, love him, know him, see him and have him, here by grace in a little feeling, and in the glory of heaven with a full being. If you keep this desire, it will teach you well which is sin and which is not, and which is good, and which is the better good. And if you are willing to fasten your thought to it, it will teach you all you need and get you all that you lack. And therefore, when you arise against the ground of sin in general, or else against any special sin, hang fast on to this desire and set the point of your thought more upon God whom you desire than on the sin which you reject, for if you do so, then God fights for you and he shall destroy sin in you. You shall much sooner come to your purpose if you do this than if you leave the humble desire that looks principally to God and resolve to set your heart only against the stirring of sin, as if you wanted to destroy it by your own strength: in that way you shall never bring it about.

91. How a person shall be shaped to the image of Jesus, and Jesus shaped in him.

Do as I have said, and better if you can, and by the grace of Jesus I think you will make the devil ashamed,[375] and so break away these wicked stirrings that they shall not do you much harm; and in this manner that image of sin can be broken down in you and destroyed, by which you are deformed from the natural shape of the image of Christ. You shall be formed again to the image of the man Jesus by humility and charity, and then you shall be fully shaped to the image of Jesus God, living here in a shadow by contemplation, and in the glory of heaven by the fullness of truth. St. Paul speaks thus of this shaping to the likeness of Christ: *Filioli, quos iterum parturio, donec Christus formetur in vobis.*[376] My dear children, whom I bear as a woman bears a child until Christ is again shaped in you. You have conceived Christ through faith,[377] and he has life in you inasmuch as you have a good will and a desire to serve and

enclosure

159

please him; but he is not yet fully formed in you, nor you in him, by the fullness of charity. And therefore St. Paul bore you and me and others in the same way with travail, as a woman bears a child, until the time that Christ has his full shape in us, and we in him.

Anyone who thinks to come to the practice and the full use of contemplation except by this way[378]—that is to say, by the fullness of virtues—he does not come by the door; and therefore he shall be cast out as a thief. I do not deny that by the gift of God a person may at times have a tasting and a glimmering of the contemplative life, some at the beginning, but the steadfast feeling of it he shall not have. For Christ is the door, and he is the porter; and without his leave and his livery[379] no one can come in there, as he says Himself: *Nemo venit ad Patrem nisi per me*.[380] No one comes to the Father but by me. That is to say, Nobody can come to the contemplation of the Deity unless by the fullness of humility and charity he is first reformed to the likeness of Jesus in his manhood.

92. The reason for writing this book, and what the lady for whom it was made is to do when she reads it.

See, I have told you a little as it seems to me, first, of what contemplative life is, and afterward about the ways which by grace lead you to it. Not that I have in feeling and in working[381] what I have in saying: nevertheless by these words (such as they are), first, I want to stir my own negligence in order to do better than I have done, and also my purpose is to stir you (or any other man or woman who has taken the state of contemplative life) to toil more humbly and diligently in that kind of [life] by such simple words as God gives me grace to say.

And so if there is any word in it that stirs or encourages you the more to the love of God, thank God, for it is his gift and not from the word. If it happens not to comfort you, or else you do not readily take it in, do not ponder it too much, but lay it aside for another time and give yourself to your prayer or to another occupation. Take it as it will come, and not all at once. So with these words that I write: do not take them too strictly, but where, after thinking them over well, you feel that I speak too shortly—either for lack of English or for want of reason—I beg you to amend it, only where it is necessary. Also, not all these words that I write to you concern a person in active life, but they are for you or someone else who has the state of contemplative life.

The grace of our Lord Jesus Christ be with you, and with him who writes this book.

Notes

1. *called you:* Cf. Ephesians 4.1.
2. *dead man:* The vowed religious life is a radical expression of the Christian's death to sin and new life to God which is expressed in baptism. Pauline texts that are relevant here include Romans 6.2, 6.7, 6.8; Colossians 2.20, 3.3, etc. At the enclosure of an anchoress a Requiem Eucharist might be sung. Cf. *The Ancrene Riwle,* ed. M. B. Salu (London, 1955), p. 47: "What is her anchor-house but her grave?"
3. *semblance* (likeness) *of holiness:* Cf. William of St. Thierry, in Déchanet, p. 166: "It is not only the form of piety, but in all and above all the reality that your state promises."
4. *St. Gregory:* The classic treatment of the lives of action and contemplation in the tradition of Augustine, Gregory and Bernard is in Butler's *Western Mysticism.* The passage that Hilton gives here on Gregory's authority might seem to be recalling *Homilia in Ezekiel* 2, 2.8, cited by Butler, 171f. But there are other elements too. Cf. Bede, *Homilia,* 1.9 (CCh 122, 64f.), which goes beyond Gregory's teaching in its equation of the contemplative life with the vowed religious life. For the active life in its secondary sense, as the ascetic preparation for the contemplative, and for the emphasis on discretion, cf. William of St. Thierry, in Déchanet, p. 242.
5. *and spiritual:* The seven corporal works of mercy are to feed the hungry, to give drink to the thirsty, to clothe the naked, to harbor the stranger, to visit the sick, to minister to prisoners, to bury the dead. The seven spiritual works of mercy are to convert the sinner, to instruct the ignorant, to counsel the doubtful, to comfort the sorrowful, to bear wrongs patiently, to forgive injuries, to pray for the living and the dead.
6. *discretion:* There is a long antecedent tradition. Cassian refers to discretion as "parent, guardian and moderator of all virtues" (*omnium ... virtutum generatrix, custos, moderatrixque*" (*Collationes* 2.4) and speaks of its importance in regulating ascetic discipline. Cassian's definition is restated by Bernard (*In Cant.* 49.2.5) in a context dealing with the proper ordering of charity—a context with which Hilton was demonstrably familiar. (Cf. *Mixed Life,* Ogilvie-Thomson, p. 8, with notes.)
7. *and charity:* Cf. ST 2-2, q. 184, a. 1.
8. *three parts:* The threefold division of the spiritual life is conventional, e.g., ST, 2-2, q. 24, a. 9. But in *Scale* 1, in contrast to *Scale* 2, the division does not answer precisely to that of beginners, proficients, perfect souls. Rather, it answers to an ascending scale of progress: rational knowledge alone: affection; knowledge and love.
9. *acquired:* MS C *geten,* MS Y *adquisitam.* See p. 58 for *sigla.*
10. *no stranger comes:* The reference is to the "sealed well" (*fons signatus*) of Song of Songs 4, 12. Cf. Bernard, *In Cant.* 3.1.1 (Leclerq, p. 14), but more particularly Hugh of St. Victor, *De Laude Caritatis* (PL 176.975), referring this text to charity.

11. *nihil sum:* Cf. 1 Corinthians 13.2—not an exact quotation.

12. *aedificat:* 1 Corinthians 8.1. Cf. Augustine, *De Trinitate* 12.11.16: "For when by the neglect of the love of that wisdom [*sapientia*] which always abides constantly, knowledge [*scientia*] is desired from the experience of changeable and temporal things, it puffs up, it does not build up."

13. *wine:* John 2.1–11. For the "wine" as a symbol of the sweetness of God's love, cf. e.g. Hugh of St. Victor, *De Arca Noe Morali (Noah's Ark,* morally interpreted) 1.1 (PL 176, 619): "Our bridegroom . . . offers the good wine last, when he allows the mind [*mentem*] which he prepares to fill with the sweetness [*dulcedine*] of his love, first to experience the bitterness of the sting of tribulations, so that after tasting bitterness it may more eagerly drink the sweetest cup of charity. *The Book of Vices and Virtues,* one of the Middle English versions of the *Somme le Roy,* similarly compares the wine of John 2 to wisdom, and contrasts it with the arid knowledge of clerks (Francis, EETS OS 217, pp. 104–5, 272).

14. *Architriclin:* after John 2.9 (Vulgate): architriclinus, a translation of the Greek word for "ruler of the feast," but taken here to be a personal name.

15. *devotion:* St. Thomas (ST 2-2, q. 82, a. 1) defines devotion as "a certain will to give oneself promptly to the service of God." Hugh of St. Victor (*De Arca Noe Morali* 3.5, PL 176.651) defines it as "the fervor of a good will, which the mind is unable to confine, so that it shows itself by certain signs."

16. *but:* Om. C; supplied from MS. H (Harley 6579).

17. *est dominus:* Psalm 33.9. See ch. 30, p. 101, with note 105.

18. *bodily rest:* St. John of the Cross (*Ascent* 2.13.4) lists desire for silence, solitude and recollection as one of the marks of entering on the illuminative way. See further on 1.36, p. 107, with note 126.

19. *meditate: thynk on* (C); *meditari* (Y). Middle English has the noun *meditacion,* but OED does not record any use of the verb "to meditate" before 1560.

20. *name of Jesus:* All this and what follows may be compared with that devotion to the name of Jesus, which found a particular expression in Richard Rolle and his followers. For Hilton's criticism of some aspects of this devotion, see chs. 10–11 and ch. 44.

21. *vestris Domino:* Ephesians 5.18f.

22. *affection:* Cf. Augustine, *Enarrationes in Psalmos 135.8:* "We understand wisdom to be in the knowledge and love of that which always is, and abides unchangeably, that is God." This passage is familiar through Peter Lombard's discussion of the Gift of Wisdom in his *Sentences,* which were prescribed for study at the Universities. See his *Sententiae in IV Libris Distinctae (Spicilegium Bonaventurianum,* Grottaferrata, 1971, 1981), Liber 3, dist. 35, c. 1, n. 4 (vol. 2, p. 199).

23. *ravished:* Cf. 2 Corinthians 12.2, *raptum . . . ad tertium caelum. Raptus* is a commonplace term in Latin theology for the contemplative experience.

24. *intellectually* translates *by vnderstondyng.*

25. *cum illo:* 1 Corinthians 6.17. For *unitas spiritus* in Bernard, see especially Gilson, ch. 5. On the history of this theme, see Bernard McGinn, "Love, Knowledge and *Unio Mystica* in the Western Christian Tradition," in *Mystical Union and Monotheistic Faith*, ed. Moshe Idel and Bernard McGinn (New York: Macmillan, 1989), pp. 59–86.

26. *facie ad faciem:* 1 Corinthians 13.12.

27. *deliciis meis:* Psalm 138.11. A very commonplace text in the contemplative tradition. Cf. for instance, Augustine, *Enarrationes in Psalmos* 138.14, on the recovery of the "likeness of God," referring also to Luke 15.8, which Hilton uses in *Scale* 1.48; Gregory, *Moralia in Job* 16.19.24, referring to the illumination of the mind to understand scripture as purity of heart is recovered.

28. *boni et mali:* Hebrews 5.14. The contrast between milk for beginners and solid food for more mature souls is taken up elsewhere by Hilton, e.g., *Scale* 2.10, pp. 206–207; 2.31, p. 258.

29. *holy men.* Hilton disclaims personal experience.

30. *urget nos:* 2 Corinthians 5.13f.

31. *a Domini spiritu:* 2 Corinthians 3.18.

32. *blessed love:* This is much more than a simple translation of St. Paul's text; Hilton introduces some of his characteristic theological themes. In Augustinian theology, understanding (*intellectus, intelligentia*) is the middle term between faith (*fides*) and the open vision of God in heaven (*species*). Likewise, the desire for God (*desiderium Dei*) is contrasted with the love of God (*amor Dei*), which is fully realized only in the life to come. See Introduction, pp. 43–44.

33. *occupied in prelacy:* Insofar as this refers to women, it must refer to superiors of religious communities.

34. *revelations:* Hilton is making the same distinction as St. Thomas Aquinas between *gratiae gratis datae*, graces given occasionally for the edification of the recipient or of the church, and *gratia gratum faciens*, sanctifying grace. Cf. St. Thomas, ST 1–2, q. 111, a. 1. The substance of this and the two following chapters is to be found in *Of Angels' Song*.

35. *in the body or in the imagination:* Following St. Augustine, visions are commonly classified as intellectual (representing spiritual reality to the intellect), imaginary (representing spiritual reality in quasi-physical form by means of the imagination), and corporal (representing physical reality in quasi-physical form). Cf. Augustine, *De Genesi ad Litteram*, 12.6.15.

36. *heat that can be felt:* See further *Scale* 1.26. Although Hilton does not name names here, his criticism of attachment to imaginary visions, and to sensible experience of sounds and heat from a purportedly spiritual source must have in mind the enthusiasts who on the basis of certain elements in Richard Rolle's teaching attached undue importance to just such phenomena. Among the many places where Rolle refers to "heat, sweetness and song" (*fervor, dulcor, canor*) the *Incendium Amoris* is famous. See *Fire of Love*, ed. Margaret Deanesly (Manches-

ter, 1915), ch. 15, pp. 187ff. For Hilton's critique of other aspects developed from Rolle's teaching, see ch. 44, pp. 115–117.

37. *a good angel:* Since angels are creatures and yet pure spirit, they are seen as mediating between the worlds of sense and spirit, and interpreting that which is spiritual to creatures who in their present state rely on the bodily senses and imagination for perception and conceptualization.

38. *an angel of light:* 2 Corinthians 11.14.

39. *ex Deo sit:* 1 John 4.1. Cassian quotes this text in his discussion of "discretion" in *Collationes* (*Conferences*) 1.20. Hilton is here taking up what he has himself said earlier in his *Epistola de Lectione.* See Clark and Taylor, pp. 230–31.

40. *body of sin:* See below, note 231.

41. *Mary Magdalene:* A legend has it that Mary Magdalene came to Provence and spent the last thirty years of her life there in a cave. In the Middle Ages she was commonly identified with Mary the sister of Martha, and so became the type of both the penitent and the contemplative. See *The Oxford Dictionary of the Christian Church*, ed. F. L. Cross (Oxford, 1957), s.v. Mary Magdalene.

42. *hic non est a Deo:* 1 John 4.3.

43. *person's soul:* Cf. ST 2–2 q. 44, a. 1: The end of the spiritual life is that a person should be united to God, which is done through charity.

44. *profundum:* Ephesians 3.17–18. Cf. St. Bernard, *De Consideratione* 5.14.32, referring to Ephesians 3.18. He takes the length to refer to meditation on God's promises, the breadth to refer to the recollection of his benefits, the height to the contemplation of his majesty, the depth to the searching out of his judgments.

45. *bravium:* Philippians 3.13f. The form of the quotation differs from the standard Vulgate.

46. *material:* MS C *bodily.*

47. *in affection:* Cf. William of St. Thierry, in Déchanet n. 43, p. 178: "There are 'animal' men who in themselves are neither led by reason, nor drawn by affection. Yet, set in motion by the authority of others, or roused by the teaching of others, or urged on by the example of others, they approve the good where they find it. Yet they do this like blind men who are led by the hand; their role is to imitate others. There are 'rational' men, who through the judgment of reason and the discernment [*discretio*] of natural knowledge, have knowledge of the good and the appetite for it, but do not yet have any affection for it. There are 'perfect' men, who are led by the Spirit [cf. Romans 8.14], who are more fully illuminated by the Holy Spirit; and because they receive the savor of that good by the love of which they are drawn, they are called wise.

48. *kernel:* Cf. Guigo II, *Scala Claustralium* (*The Ladder of Monks*), ed. E. Colledge and J. Walsh, SC 163, 1970, pp. 84–86: "Reading presents as it were solid food to the mouth, meditation chews and breaks it, prayer acquires a savor, contemplation is that very sweetness which

gladdens and renews. Reading is in the bark, meditation is in the sap, prayer is in the asking for what one desires, contemplation is in the delight of a sweetness that has been attained. The image of the bark and the kernel recurs in *Scale* 1.20, p. 92; *Scale* 2.43, p. 294. It is something of a commonplace, and is found also in *The Epistle of Prayer* by the author of *The Cloud of Unknowing* (see Hodgson, p. 57), as well as in *Cloud* itself (Hodgson, p. 107), and in a gloss attached to the Middle English version of *The Mirror of Simple Souls* (See Doiron, p. 255).

49. *before:* Emended from MSS. Y and H. C has *when.*

50. *three means:* The triad of *lectio, meditatio, oratio* is commonplace. Cf. Guigo II, loc. cit.

51. *holy teaching: Lectio* includes not only the reading of scripture, but also that of recognized ecclesiastical writers who expound scripture; cf. B. Smalley, *The Study of the Bible in the Middle Ages,* 2d ed. (Oxford, 1952), p. 12.

52. *for you:* Presumably Hilton's reader could not read Latin. *Scale* 2.43, p. 295 assumes that *lectio,* or at any rate the meaning of scripture, is accessible to everyone, although there is no indication there that Hilton is concerned about English as distinct from Latin bibles.

53. *unreasonable worry:* This list is loosely based on the seven traditional capital sins, as listed in, for instance, St. Thomas ST 1–2, q. 84, a. 4, on the basis of Gregory, *Moralia* 31.45.87. The normal list is pride (with vainglory), envy, anger, accidie (*accedia, tristitia*), avarice, gluttony, lust. The roots of this classification may be traced further back to Evagrius Ponticus, *Praktikos,* and Cassian, *Collationes* 5, *Institutiones passim;* Evagrius and Cassian list eight principal temptations or vices.

54. *a stinking well:* An illustration commonly used by Hilton in both his English and Latin writings. A possible source is Pseudo-Anselm, *Similitudines* 6–10 (PL 159.607–8). But other sources are possible too; for instance, Hugh of St. Victor. See *De quinque Septenis,* in *Six Opuscules Spirituels,* ed. R. Baron, SC 155, 1969, c. 2, p. 102, referring to the seven capital sins as seven springs.

55. *videbunt:* Matthew 5.8.

56. *charity:* Hilton is given to making such lists of virtues, including echoes of the fruits of the Spirit listed by St. Paul (Galatians 5.22–23) and the three theological or infused virtues.

57. *sepulcrum:* Job 5.26. Similarly expounded in Gregory, *Moralia* 6.37.56.

58. *Dominus:* Lamentations 4.20. Cited in the form familiar through the Latin rendering of Origen's biblical commentaries, and used by Bernard. This text is important in Bernard's doctrine of the "carnal" knowledge and love of God in Christ, which Hilton follows. See on *Scale* 2.30, p. 255.

59. *veritate:* John 4.23.

60. *fathers: Vitae Patrum* 5.9.5 (PL 73.910).

61. *active:* MS Y has marginal emendation *contemplatiuus* but our reading

is supported by C and H and is to be preferred as the *lectio difficilior*.

62. *no:* omitted by C; supplied from H and Y.

63. *state of active life:* For Peter and John as types of the active and contemplative lives respectively, see Augustine, *Tractatus in Ioannis Evangelium* 124.5. The same illustration is repeated in Bede, *Homilia* 1.9; see ch. 2, p. 78, with note 4 on Ch. 1.

64. *active life in the world:* There is a similar injunction in *The Prickynge of Love* (closely following the Latin), for contemplatives to respect those of active state. See H. Kane, ed. (Salzburg, 1983), ch. 28, p. 142.

65. *humiliabitur:* Luke 14.11.

66. *has all:* After Augustine, *Epistola* 167.4.14. This was a common adage. See Peter Lombard, *Sententiae in IV Libris Distinctae* (*Spicilegium Bonaventurianum*, Grottaferrata, 1971, 1981), *Lib.* 3, *dist.* 36, cap. 2, n.5.

67. *Augustine says: Sermo* 69.1.2.

68. *Gregory says: Homilia in Evangelia* 7.4 (PL 76.1103). Cf. also Pseudo-Gregory, *Expositio in Psalmos Poenitantiales*, psalm 37 n. 3 (PL 79.569). This is probably to be ascribed to Eribert, Bishop of Reggio in the eleventh century. See G. Mercati, *Revue Bénédictine* 31, pp. 250–57.

69. *Gregory says: Moralia* 34.32.43.

70. *and heretics:* Cf. chs. 58–59.

71. *kernel:* Cf. note 48 above.

72. *from God:* Cf. Bernard, *De Diligendo Deo* (*On the Love of God*) 2.3–4 (Leclerq, vol. 3, pp. 121–23).

73. *Pharisee:* Luke 18.10ff.

74. *peccatoris:* Ecclesiasticus 15.9.

75. *sermones meos:* Isaiah 66.2.

76. *all the will:* St. Paul says (Galatians 5.6) that faith works by love. But in the background here is also William Flete, *De Remediis Contra Tentationes*, MS Bodleian Library Oxford, Bodley 43 (=B), p. 141, referring to faith as a habit of the will (*habitus voluntatis*).

77. *nor feel it:* Because faith is a supernatural and "infused" virtue, it is not accessible to the bodily senses.

78. *sacraments:* For Hilton's defence of orthodox doctrine on the Eucharist, see *Scale* 1.37, p. 108; on confession, see *Scale* 2.7, pp. 201–203.

79. *believe:* C has *trowe*, and we have followed this reading. Fishlake (Y) has *sperare*, and twice later in the same chapter gives *spe* for C's *trowthe*; on a further occasion he represents C's *trowthe* and hope simply by *spes*. In each case H reads *hope*.

80. *intention:* The subject matter of this chapter is closely related to *Epistola de Lectione*, in Clark and Taylor, pp. 233–34. What Hilton is describing is known as the "virtual intention"—the intention that may not always be consciously present to the mind, but which is implied by the previous conscious willing of a particular end. Cf. ST 1–2, q. 1, a. 6, ad 3.

81. *nothing:* Cf. 1 Corinthians 13.1–3.

82. *discretion:* Cf. note 6 above.

83. *hold to no mean:* Cf. Bernard, *De Diligendo Deo* 1.1: "The reason for

loving God is God; the measure is, to love him without measure (*sine modo*)."

84. *your spiritual house: House* has the double meaning of (1) the cell; (2) the house of the soul. Similarly in William of St. Thierry, Déchanet, p. 250. For echoes of this context, see *Scale* 1.53, p. 125, note 239.

85. *facite:* 1 Corinthians 10.31.

86. *virtues.* Cf. in Guigo II in Colledge and Walsh, p. 84; "Prayer is a devout intention to God, to remove evil things and obtain good things."

87. *freely give you.* This is common teaching in the Augustinian tradition. Cf. Augustine, *Ep.* 130.8.17: "Our Lord and God does not wish that our will should tell him what it is impossible for him not to know; but he wishes our desire to be exercised in prayers, whereby we may be able to receive what he is preparing to give." Similarly Gregory, *Dialogi* 1.8; ST 2–2, q. 83, a 2.

88. *point of your thought.* Equivalent to Augustine's *acies mentis;* cf. E. Gilson, *The Christian Theology of St. Augustine,* (English translation, London, 1961) p. 352, note 28.

89. *to some devotion.* Cf. *Mixed Life,* Ogilvie-Thomson, pp. 50–51.

90. *thoughts inward.* The process of introversion and recollection is commonplace within the Augustinian tradition. But particularly close to Hilton is Gregory, *Homilia in Ezekiel* 2.5.9, cited by Butler, p. 70.

91. *rising into God.* St. Thomas, following St. John of Damascus, defines prayer as "an ascent of the mind to God" (*ascensus intellectus in Deum*) ST 2–2, q. 83, a. 13. Hilton's approach is more affective; cf. rather Guigo II, note 86 above.

92. *it came.* Cf. William of St. Thierry, Déchanet p. 332; "The will, when it rises up, like a fire rising to its own place, when it joins itself to the truth, and climbs to the heights, it is love (*amor*). When it receives the milk of grace to help it forward, it is love (*dilectio*). When it seizes, when it holds, when it enjoys, it is charity (*caritas*), it is unity of spirit."

93. *material.* MS. C: *bodily.* Cf. ch. 10 above. Hilton's careful explanation of the properly supernatural and interior character of the "fire of love" is intended as a corrective to those who leaned heavily on some aspects of Richard Rolle's teaching. In the *Incendium Amoris* and elsewhere Rolle lays heavy emphasis on the sensible character of the "heat" which, with "sweetness" and "song," he takes to be the expression of the love of God. See Deanesly, pp. 184f. This "heat" is not felt simply in the mind, but in reality—*non estimative sed realiter.*

94. *spoken prayer.* Hilton's teaching on the importance of vocal prayer with special reference to those whose state in the church binds them to the recitation of the Hours takes up points made in *Epistola de Lectione,* in Clark and Taylor pp. 234–38.

95. *conversion.* The Latin word *conversio* was habitually used especially to describe the orientation of life to God that marks the beginning of the religious life.

96. *feet.* The "foot of love" (*pes amoris*) is familiar in the tradition deriving from Augustine. Cf. for instance Augustine, *Enarrationes in Psalmos*, 9.15: "The foot of the soul is rightly understood as the love (*amor*); when it is crooked, it is called cupidity (*cupiditas*) or wantonness (*libido*); but when it is upright (*rectus*), it is called love or charity (*dilectio vel caritas*)."

97. *milk.* Cf. Ch. 9, p. 83, with note 28 above.

98. *manifest errors.* The warning against giving up too soon the practice of vocal prayer, and the liability to error that this entails, is matched in *Of Angels' Song,* in Takamiya, p. 13 or in modern English, in Dorward, p. 19.

99. *deprecatus sum.* Psalm 141.2.

100. *a doctor.* The image of God, or Christ, as a doctor, is a familiar one. See R. A. Arbesmann, "The Concept of 'Christus Medicus' in St. Augustine," *Traditio* 10 (1954), pp. 1ff.

101. *Deus meus.* Psalm 58.2.

102. *peccavi tibi.* Psalm 40.5.

103. *misericordia eius.* Psalm 135.1.

104. *very wasting.* Cf. the *ignis aestuans* of Jeremiah 20.9, cited in ch. 31.

105. *mad or drunk.* Richard of St. Victor, *Benjamin Minor,* c. 37 (PL 196.26–27), refers to an interior sweetness (*dulcedo*) in the soul which in scripture is variously termed taste (*gustus*) or intoxication (*ebrietas*). Richard cites Psalm 33.9, *Gustate et videte quoniam suavis est Dominus.* Cf. *Scale* 1.6, Hilton's second part of contemplation. There is similar teaching in *The Prickynge of Love,* based closely on the Latin *Stimulus Amoris.* See Kane, p. 20, pp. 134–35.

106. *wounds the soul.* Similarly, this recalls the first of Richard of St. Victor's four degrees of love in *De IV Gradibus Violentae Caritatis—Amor Vulnerans.* The term derives from Canticle 5.8. See especially PL 196.1209: "Does not the heart seem struck, when that fiery arrow of love pierces the human soul right through, and transfixes the affection, so that it cannot contain or conceal the heat of its desire?"

107. *non sustinens.* Jeremiah 20.9. This text is cited by Gregory, *Moralia* 23.11.18, with reference to the compulsion felt by the just to speak against the faults of evil livers, lest by passing these over they seem to acquiesce in them.

108. *memory, will and reason.* Augustine speaks of a triad of *memoria, intelligentia, voluntas* in the human soul, a created trinity that constitutes the image or reflection of the uncreated Trinity: *De Trinitate* 10.11.17–12.19. Augustine finds various "created trinities" in man, but it is this particular one which became normative for medieval thought and is recalled in Peter Lombard, *Sentences* 1, d. 3, c. 2. The standard work on this whole area of Augustine's theology is Michael Schmaus, *Die Psychologische Trinitätslehre des heiligen Augustinus,* (Münster/Westfalen, 1927), not available in English. *Memoria* in this context does not refer simply to the recollection of things past, but includes the awareness of present—and future—things. Where Augustine has *intelligentia*, Hilton has "reason," which Fishlake here and elsewhere renders by *ratio*.

109. *quake and tremble.* Cf. notes 105, 106.
110. *could do.* This sentence, obscure in C and H, has been slightly amended from Y.
111. *et mente.* 1 Corinthians 14.14f.
112. *extinguatur.* Leviticus 6.12. For the background, cf. Gregory, *Moralia* 25.7.15. Cf. also *Mixed Life*, Ogilvie-Thomson p. 37; *Scale* 2.21, p. 230, *Scale* 2.42, p. 290.
113. *goes out.* MS. H adds: "Our Lord gives this rest to some of his servants, as it were for a reward of their labor and a shadow of the love which they shall have in the joy of heaven"; this is not in C but is matched in Fishlake's version (MS. Y).
114. *viribus tuis.* Luke 10.27.
115. *Saint Bernard:* St. Bernard, *In Cant.* 50.1.2. For Hilton's knowledge of this area of St. Bernard's sermons on the Song of Songs, cf. *Mixed Life*, Ogilvie-Thomson, p. 8, notes.
116. *magnalia Dei.* Acts 2.4;11.
117. *compunction.* Commonly associated with tears in the ecclesiastical tradition, e.g. Isidore, *Sententiae* 2.12 (PL 83.613): "Compunction of heart is humility of mind with tears."
118. *not properly shriven.* Hilton touches on this problem at various places. Cf. *Scale* 1.21, p. 94, on resisting doubts as to one's salvation; 2.21, p. 228; 2.22, p. 231. The matter is referred to by William Flete, *De Remediis*, who speaks of the temptation to doubt regarding one's salvation —MS. Bodley 43, p. 141: *diffidentia, hesitatio;* or else to doubt the reality of one's absolution for past sins (p. 145).
119. *misericordiam tuam.* Psalm 50.3 (50.1 in Psalter).
120. *Bernard calls it.* St. Bernard's doctrine on the progression from the love of Christ "according to the flesh" to a more directly spiritual love, which corresponds to the recovery of purity of heart and is less self-regarding, is stated at various places. See especially *In Cant.* 20.2.3–5.9, including reference to the characteristic texts John 16.7 and Lamentations 4.20. See further *Scale* 2.30, p. 255.
121. *imagination.* On the role of the imagination, see especially *Scale* 2.31, p. 258, with note 210.
122. *indicavi.* The word in C could be read *iudicavi* or *indicavi;* the standard Vulgate text is *iudicavi.* But Hilton's "showed" indicates that he read *indicavi.*
123. *crucifixum.* 1 Corinthians 2.2. Cf. Gregory, *Homilia in Ezekiel* 1.9.31.
124. *Christi.* Galatians 6.14.
125. *sapientiam.* 1 Corinthians 1.23–24; Cf. Augustine, *Tractatus in Ioannis Evangelium* 98.2–3.
126. *withdraws it.* William Flete writes in the *De Remediis* (p. 144): "God in his kindness gives some people the devotion of sweetness at the beginning of their conversion . . . and afterwards withdraws it so that they may gain in merit, and in doing so may attain a higher crown." Flete goes on to cite Christ's words to Peter in John 21.18, and cites also 1 Corinthians 3.2 on the transition from milk for babes to whole

food for the mature. The process Hilton is describing here may also be compared to St. John of the Cross's account of the "passive night of the senses"—sometimes called by modern writers the "ligature"—in which the capacity to meditate is withdrawn as God begins to pour a more direct and spiritual contemplation of himself into the soul, with the call to engage more directly against the roots of sin in what on the basis of his terminology is called the "active night of the spirit." See, e.g., St. John of the Cross, *Ascent*, Book 2, ch. 12–15. See further the Introduction, pp. 48–49.

127. *non veniet ad vos*. John 16.7. Cf. above, note 120.

128. *naked*. That is, arid and bereft of sensible devotion. This is not the same thing as the apophatic "nakedness" of *The Cloud of Unknowing*, where the stripping away of distinct images of God, or of desire for anything less than God, is a deliberate activity of the soul.

129. *lechery and gluttony*. St. John of the Cross likewise notes that temptation to violent carnal sin—or to blasphemy—attends the withdrawal of ability to meditate. *Dark Night*, 1.14.1–2.

130. *glorificabo eum*. Psalm 90.15.

131. *sacrament*. Professor Bliss advised that MS. C's plural reading, *sacramentz*, was unique. Fishlake in MS. Y has *de sacramento altaris*. The reference must be to the Eucharist, and reflects the effects of the Wycliffite controversy. Although Hilton generally owes much to Flete in this area of his book, doubt about the Eucharist is not mentioned in Flete's book, which of course long antedates the Wycliffite disputes.

132. *despair or blasphemy*. Flete, *De Remediis*, p. 139, refers to "fantastic imaginary concepts, erroneous or foul (*foeda*), and blasphemies." Blasphemy is another of the temptations mentioned by St. John of the Cross in connection with the passive night of sense.

133. *his saints*. Lollards came to object to prayers to the saints as detracting from the worship due to God. For this point, and the orthodox answer to this objection, see *Selections from English Wycliffite Writings*, ed. A. M. Hudson (Cambridge, 1978), pp. 19, 23.

134. *bitterness and irrational sorrow*. The word rendered "sorrow" is *heuynes* in MS. C, *tristitia* in Fishlake's translation. This is not precisely the same as "depression" with its modern connotation of a morbid psychological condition. *Tristitia* is one of the synonyms for *accidie* in some classifications of the seven capital sins. It is taken for granted that however disabling this condition may be, it is something for which a person remains responsible, and it should not be indulged. Flete writes in the *De Remediis* (p. 142): "Often he (i.e., the devil) sends such bitterness [*amaritudo*] into the minds of the faithful, causing agitation to their complexion and striking fear into them, that life seems to them a punishment and death a remedy."

135. (Title). This is the title of Flete's book.

136. *reward*. Cf. note 126 above.

137. *sacrament.* See note 131 above. Here too MS. C's plural reading, *sacramentz,* is unique. Fishlake in MS. Y has *de sacramento.* Once again the reference is to the Eucharist.

138. *strive with them.* Cf. Flete, *De Remediis,* p. 140: "A man must not wonder or dally with these, nor follow them up, nor probe into them, nor investigate their causes to any extent."

139. *congregabo te.* Isaiah 54.7. This text is cited in a similar context by William Flete, *De Remediis,* p. 143. But Hilton seems to have known the use of this text by Gregory. See on ch. 39.

140. *forsaken.* William Flete speaks of a sense of forsakenness by God: "Credunt enim se a Deo esse derelictos" (*De Remediis,* p. 142). He goes on to insist that as long as the will remains directed to God in the face of temptation, the soul remains united to God by faith, hope and charity, the supernatural and "infused" virtues (p. 143). Hilton gives similar teaching, still recalling something of William Flete, in *Scale* 2.28. See *Scale* 2, note 185.

141. *habebis fiduciam.* Job 11.17. Applied in a related sense by Gregory, *Moralia* 10.18.34–35.

142. *intellectum justitiae.* Ecclesiasticus 4.18–21. Gregory, *Moralia* 20.24.51, cites Ecclesiasticus 4.18–19a, together with Isaiah 54.7. Cf. note 139 above.

143. *into your own soul.* For the process of introversion and recollection, cf. for instance Gregory, *Homilia in Ezekiel* 2.5.9, indicated at note 90 above. This method is a commonplace in the tradition of Augustine and Gregory.

144. *of God.* The reference may be either to Augustine, *Soliloquia* 2.1.1.: "By knowing myself I shall know you (*Noverim me, noverim te*)," or perhaps to the Pseudo-Augustinian *De Spiritu et Anima,* c. 52 (PL 40.818): "And so by knowing ourselves to come to the knowledge of God." This treatise is translated by Erasmo Leiva and Sr. Benedicta Ward in *Three Treatises on Man: A Cistercian Anthropology,* ed. Bernard McGinn (Kalamazoo, MI, 1977), pp. 181–288. It has been suggested that *De Spiritu et Anima* may be by Ralph of Flaix (*fl.* 1157). See B. Smalley, *Studies in Mediaeval Thought and Learning* (London, 1981), pp. 91ff.

145. *Our holy fathers:* Cf. Cassian, *Collationes* 14.5, citing Romans 12.6–8.

146. *A hound that runs after the hare:* The *exemplum* is a standard one, derived from *Vitae Patrum* 5.7.35 (PL 73.901).

147. *without moderation or discretion:* Cf. ch. 22, with note 83 above.

148. *vero sic:* 1 Corinthians 7.7.

149. *donationis Christi:* Ephesians 4.7.

150. *scientiae* 1 Corinthians 12.4; 8.

151. *sunt nobis:* 1 Corinthians 2.12.

152. *deserving:* Emended from H and Y. C reads *nedeful.*

153. *to go into himself:* Cf. chs. 40–41. The teaching that follows is matched in Hilton, *Epistola de Leccione,* in Clark and Taylor, pp. 221–22.

154. *its fairness and its foulness:* Cf. *Scale* 2.12, p. 211.

155. *recover:* Emended from H and Y. C reads *receyve.*

156. *hard and sharp in the beginning:* Cf. Benedict, *Regula*, c. 58: *Praedicentur ei omnia dura et aspera per quae itur ad Deum,* "Let him be told of all the hard and sharp things on the road to God." After Cassian, *Collationes* 24.25.

157. *the ground of all sins:* Inordinate self-love, bound up with pride, is the ground (foundation) of all sins, as humility is the ground (foundation) of virtues. Cf. ch. 18 above, with note 67. On pride, see especially chs. 55–56, 85.

158. *as St. Augustine says:* The reference may very well be to *De Civitate Dei* 14.28, referring to the two cities, the earthly and the heavenly: the earthly, self-love to the point of contempt of God; the heavenly, love of God to the point of contempt of oneself. This passage is recalled in *De Imagine Peccati*, in Clark and Taylor, p. 74. Cf. also *Sermo* 96.2 (PL 38.585); 330.3 (PL 38.1457); *Tractatus in Ioannis Evangelium* 25.16: "The head of all sicknesses is pride, because pride is the head of all sins."

159. *deeply delved:* Cf. *Scale* 1.47, p. 120.

160. *physically created and:* Emended from Y, which reads *ab amore et delectatione omnium creaturarum corporalium et ab amore.* C omits all between "love" and "love," while H has a greatly expanded version which presupposes the Y reading.

161. *find no rest:* Cf. Augustine, *Confessiones* 1.1.1: *Inquietum est cor nostrum, donec requiescat in te.*

162. *inveniunt eam:* Luke 13.24; Matthew 7.13–14.

163. *custodit eam:* Matthew 16.24, John 12.25.

164. *malam:* Colossians 3.5.

165. *unreasonable love for yourself:* This assumes the Augustinian doctrine of the "order of love" (*ordo caritatis*). God alone is to be "enjoyed" (*frui*); created things are to be used (*uti*) in relation to God. God is to be loved for himself (*propter seipsum*); oneself, and other people, are to be loved "in God" or else "for God"—all good and attractive qualities in them being referred to the Creator, so that it is God who is loved in them. See Augustine, *De Doctrina Christiana* 1.4.4; 1.22.20–27.28. See further ch. 70, p. 142, with note 294.

166. *The soul ... is a life:* See below, *Scale* 2.30, p. 252, with note 194 for *Scale* 2.

167. *memory, reason and will:* See note 108 above. Power, Wisdom, and Love (or Goodness) are commonly appropriated to the three Persons of the Trinity on the basis of Augustine's theology. These attributes are not of course peculiar to any one Person of the Trinity, but they reflect the mode of disclosure of the three Persons. The Father's power is shown in creation; Christ is the wisdom of God (1 Corinthians 1), while the love of God is shed abroad in our hearts through the gift of the Holy Spirit (Romans 5.5). See, for instance, Augustine *De Trinitate* 7.1.2–4; 15.17.29–31; ST 1, q. 39, a. 8 (including orientation on the medieval developments).

168. *the image and likeness:* Cf. Genesis 1.26. For Hilton's distinction between image and likeness, see Introduction, pp. 35–36.

169. *the reason was made clear and bright:* The contrast between the intuitive awareness of God before the fall and the instability and restlessness of human beings after the fall is another commonplace of theology, especially of Augustinian theology. See, for instance, Augustine, *De Civitate Dei* 14.10; Hugh of St. Victor, *De Arca Noe Morali,* Prologue.

170. *factus est illis:* Psalm 48.13/21. This use of the text was a commonplace, deriving from especially Augustine, *De Trinitate* 12.11.16.

171. *like a beast:* This does not have quite the pejorative sense in Hilton's thought that it would in the twentieth-century, but presupposes the psychology (derived from Augustine) Hilton sets out in *Scale* 2.13 (q.v.). Because the rational element is no longer turned toward God, it is no longer in control of bodily senses and emotions.

172. *caught and entangled:* Perhaps a reference to the trapping of birds. C reads *taken and gleymed,* Y *illaqueatum ... et inviscatum.* Bird lime was made from the berries of mistletoe (*viscum*).

173. *salvus erit:* Joel 2.32.

174. *courtesy:* Julian of Norwich speaks often of the "courtesy" of God toward humankind. "The greatest fulness of joy that we shall have ... is the marvellous courtesy and homeliness of our Father, that is our maker, in our Lord Jesus Christ, that is our brother and our saviour" (*Revelations of Divine Love,* long text, ch. 7). St. Francis of Assisi stressed *cortesia* as a divine attribute. See *Fioretti,* ch. 37. See further, W. Riehle, *The Middle English Mystics* (London, 1981), pp. 53–54.

175. *But now you say:* An answer to a real or purported question is a common device of Hilton. The passage that follows, to the end of the chapter, is missing from many MSS. and added to H on an inserted leaf, but is considered to be an authorial addition. See Introduction, p. 54.

176. *sayings of certain holy men:* The reference must be especially to Richard Rolle, who gave particular point to the common devotion to the name of Jesus. The kind of thing that Hilton has in mind is found in, e.g., Rolle, *In Aliquot Versus Cantici Canticorum,* a wide-ranging tract based on the first few verses of the Song of Songs. Part of this, commenting on Canticle 1.3, *Oleum effusum nomen tuum,* circulated widely as a tract in its own right, under the name of *Encomium Nominis Jesu.* See Allen, pp. 62–83. A typical passage runs: "Therefore whoever you are who prepare yourself to love God, if you do not wish to be deceived nor to deceive ... keep this name of Jesus always in your memory (*memoria*). ... Whatever you do, even if you give away everything that you have, unless you love the name of Jesus you labor in vain. ... For only those who have loved Jesus in this present life will be able to rejoice in Jesus [i.e., in the life to come]" (MS. Trinity Coll. Dublin, 153, pp. 158ff.).

177. *nobis non est:* 1 John 1.8.

178. *unless he loves:* "this name ... he loves" om. C; supplied from readings of H and Y.

173

179. *fullness of supreme joy:* The reward in heaven is the vision of God according to the degree of one's love for God on earth. Cf. *Scale* 1.61. p. 132, with note 264.
180. *mansiones multae sunt:* John 14.2. This exegesis is commonplace. Cf. Gregory, *Moralia* 35.19.46.
181. *carissimi:* Canticle 5.1. This exegesis again is commonplace; e.g. Richard of St. Victor, *Benjamin Major* 4.16 (PL 196.155).
182. *commandments . . . counsels:* The counsels refer to the vowed religious life, but Hilton sees the highest gift of charity as something over and above the vowed offering of oneself to God. Cf. ch. 61, p. 132, with note 265.
183. *reformed:* The term is derived from Romans 12.2—*reformamini in novitate sensus vestri.* Cf. *Scale* 2.31, p. 257, with note 205.
184. *grace . . . glory:* According to St. Thomas, ST 2–2, q. 24, a. 3, ad 2, grace is a certain beginning of glory in us (*quaedam inchoatio gloriae*).
185. *that is the life which is truly contemplative:* Cf. chs. 8–9.
186. *Mary Magdalene:* Cf. note 41 above.
187. *auferetur ab ea:* Luke 10.42. On the sisters Martha and Mary as types of the active and contemplative lives, see Butler, pp. 160ff. (Augustine); 172 (Gregory); 191 (Bernard).
188. *as water runs:* Cf. Ch. 15, p. 88.
189. *tuum erit:* Deuteronomy 11.24.
190. *Jesus: all goodness, infinite wisdom, love and sweetness:* The rhetorical accumulation of epithets for Jesus, or God, is characteristic of Hilton. Strictly, wisdom and love are appropriated to the Son and the Holy Spirit in Augustinian theology, yet they are common to all three Persons of the Trinity. Cf. ch. 43, p. 113, with note 167.
191. *more and more, to find him better:* Cf. Philippians 3.13–14, cited ch. 13, pp. 86–87 above.
192. *ravished:* Cf. 2 Corinthians 12.2.
193. *loving . . . desire:* For the tension between desire and love in Augustinian theology, cf. ch. 9, p. 83, with note 32.
194. *songs and sounds:* Cf. chs. 10–11.
195. *super terram:* Psalm 72.25.
196. *omni tempore:* Psalm 118.20.
197. *Omnis qui quaerit, invenit:* Matthew 7.8.
198. *invenies:* Proverbs 2.4–5. After Gregory, *Moralia* 5.5.8.
199. *delve deep:* Cf. ch. 42 above, p. 112.
200. *evertit:* The standard Vulgate text has *everrit.*
201. *quam perdideram:* Luke 15.8–9. As the drachma bears the image of the emperor, so the human soul bears the image of God or of Christ. This interpretation of the parable was a commonplace, traceable ultimately to Origen, *Hom. in Genesim* 13.4 (PG 12.234f). It is repeated in Augustine, Gregory, and the subsequent tradition.
202. *verbum tuum:* Psalm 118.105. For the *lucerna* as scripture, cf. Gregory, *Moralia* 19.11.18.

203. *oculus tuus:* Matthew 6.22.
204. *candelabrum:* Matthew 5.15.
205. *Delicta quis intelligit?* Psalm 18.13.
206. *your heritage:* Cf. Romans 8.17.
207. *this is not the work of one hour:* Cf. William of St. Thierry, Déchanet, p. 216: "But this work is not achieved in one moment of conversion, nor is it of one day, but it is of a long time, of much work, of much sweat."
208. *in your house:* For the soul as a house, cf. for instance Augustine *Confessiones* 1.5.6.; the image is commonplace.
209. *the reason of your soul:* For the reason in humankind as constituting the *imago Dei,* cf. for instance Augustine, *De Trinitate* 14.4.6; Hugh of St. Victor, *De Sacramentis* 1.6.2 (PL 176.264); St. Thomas ST 1, q. 93, a. 6.
210. *you are never the nearer to him:* Very many parallels in Augustine may be cited; e.g., *Confessiones* 4.12.18: "He is within the heart, but the heart has wandered from him." Cf. also *Confessiones* 2.2.3; 7.7.11; *Enarrationes in Psalmos* 99.5.
211. *There is no need . . . to look for him there:* For a similar thought, cf. Bernard, *Sermo de Adventu Domini* 1.10: "Man, you need not cross the sea, nor enter the clouds, nor climb over the Alps. . . . For the Word is near, in your mouth and in your heart" (Deuteronomy 30.14).
212. *Deus absconditus:* Isaiah 45.15. There is similar use of the text in Eckhart, *Deutsche Werke* 1, p. 253; but Eckhart and Hilton are presumably drawing on a common tradition.
213. *agrum illum:* Matthew 13.44. Similarly already in Hugh of St. Victor, *De Arca Noe Morali* 3.6.
214. *when he was in the ship:* This illustration, based on Matthew 8.23–27, is a favorite one with Augustine. See the indices to the C Ch editions of his *Enarrationes in Psalmos* and *Sermo.* Cf. also his *Tractatus in Ioannis Evangelium* 49.19.
215. *you are asleep to him:* Among the very many uses of Matthew 8.23–27 in Augustine, see especially *Enarrationes in Psalmos* 34.1.3: "When he is said to be asleep, it is we who are asleep; and when he is said to arise, it is we who are aroused [*excitamur*]."
216. *jangle:* Elsewhere (e.g., below in this chapter) Hilton speaks of "din." This is equivalent to the *tumultus* or *strepitus* of which Augustine and Gregory speak in very many places; e.g., Augustine, *Confessiones* 4.11.16; 10.2.2; Gregory, *Moralia* 4.30.57f; 4.34.68.
217. *patris tui:* Psalm 44.11. This is a commonplace text in reference to the baptismal life (Origen, *Homilia in Exodum* 3.4, PG 12.309), and more specifically to the religious life, which is a radical working out of the baptismal life. See especially Cassian, *Collationes* 3.6, with reference to the "three renunciations," and citing also Genesis 12.1. Hilton uses Genesis 12.1 in the same sense as Cassian of the vowed religious life in *Epistola de Utilitate,* in Clark and Taylor, p. 152.
218. (Heading) *livery:* Emended from H *liuere,* Y *librata;* C reads *louers.* Similar emendations are made at lines 8 and 14. Hilton is assuming the Pauline idea of "putting on" Christ; cf. Romans 13.14, Galatians 3.27, etc.

219. *his likeness:* Cf. Genesis 1.26, and Introduction, pp. 35–36.

220. *humility and charity:* the life of conformity to Christ is summed up in these "inclusive" virtues. Cf. ch. 18, p. 91.

221. *ei me ipsum:* John 14.21.

222. *humilis corde:* Matthew 11.29.

223. *ad invicem:* John 13.34f.

224. *to enter into yourself:* Cf. ch. 42, pp. 112–113.

225. *to see the ground of sin . . . as you can:* This is equivalent to what in the terminology derived from St. John of the Cross would be called the "active night of the spirit." See Introduction, pp. 48–49.

226. *the point of your heart.* In so far as "heart" and "mind" are synonymous in Hilton, this may be equated with the *acies mentis.* Cf. ch. 24, p. 97, with note 88.

227. *as if you wanted . . . but Jesus alone:* This is taken up again in *Scale* 2, chs. 21–22, pp. 226–232.

228. *This is troublesome:* Here and in what follows, Hilton is building on what he has earlier implied in *Epistola de Lectione,* in Clark and Taylor, p. 222.

229. *a dark and painful image of your own soul:* The "image of sin" is a travesty of the proper humanity, which is the image of God. In *De Imagine Peccati* Hilton brings out this contrast by means of the distinction between *imago* and *simulacrum* (Clark and Taylor, p. 99).

230. *such as . . . gluttony and lechery:* The traditional list of seven capital sins, as listed in Peter Lombard, *Sentences,* Book 2, dist. 42, c. 6, on the basis of Gregory, *Moralia* 31.45.87. The classification of seven (or eight) capital sins may be traced further back, to Evagrius Ponticus, *Praktikos;* and Cassian, *Collationes,* Book 5. *Accidie* derives from the Greek *akēdia* and is a technical term referring to a disinclination to any spiritual activity. Evagrius and Cassian make a distinction between *tristitia* (Greek *lupē*) and *accidie.* Medieval Latin writers often represent *accidie* simply by *tristitia.* In English it is sometimes represented by "sloth."

231. *a body of sin and a body of death:* Cf. Romans 6.6. Hilton is here building on what he has written earlier in *De Imagine Peccati,* in Clark and Taylor, p. 73.

232. *rise up:* Cf. *steien* (H) and *orirentur* (Y). C reads *steine,* or possibly *steme.*

233. *from this image spring:* Cf. ch. 15., p. 88.

234. *it is nothing:* "nothing" for Hilton refers to a state of darkness and emptiness within a human being; this in partial contrast to the position taken up in *The Cloud of Unknowing* (ch. 68), where "nothing" refers in part at least to the "otherness" of God in terms of Dionysian apophaticism—though it should be added that the *Cloud* also incorporates elements drawn from Augustine and Gregory the Great.

235. *an absence of good:* Evelyn Underhill's pioneer edition, based on MS. H, has "wanting of God." This is due to ambiguity in the Middle

English form *gode*. MS. C reads *wantynge of gode*, and Fishlake (Y) has *priuacio boni*? That evil, or sin, is a *privatio boni*, a commonplace of Augustinian theology: e.g., Augustine, *Confessiones* 3.7.12; *Enchiridion*, c. 11.

236. *light of understanding:* Cf. ch. 9, p. 83, with note 32.
237. *no darkness of unknowing:* "Darkness" for Hilton reflects a condition within mankind itself. It is bound up with the "darkness" of sin, as exemplified especially in the tradition of Gregory the Great; e.g., *Moralia* 5.7.12; 27.26.49. So, for Hilton, "darkness of unknowing" has a pejorative sense; it is not the same as the "cloud of unknowing" in the book of that name, which is bound up with Dionysian apophatic theology.
238. *bitterness:* This term has a rich background in Gregory too. Commenting on Job 3.5, *Involvatur amaritudine*, Gregory speaks of the "bitterness" of penitence (*Moralia* 4.18.33). For Hilton's familiarity with this area of Gregory's writing, see on *Scale* 2.24, p. 235, with note 129 for *Scale* 2.
239. *a scolding wife:* There is an allusion here to Proverbs 21.9; 25.24. Cf. William of St. Thierry, in Déchanet, p. 250: "Let it [i.e., the soul] not have in its house, as Solomon says, a quarrelsome wife, its flesh . . ."
240. (Heading and line 17 below) *stay:* This will be taken up again in *Scale* 2.24, p. 236.
241. *Jesus is hidden:* Cf. ch. 49 above, p. 122.
242. *et caelestis:* 1 Corinthians 15.49. Cf. ch. 86, p. 155.
243. *O quis . . . per Jesum Christum:* Romans 7.24f.
244. *a false disordered love for yourself:* Cf. above, ch. 42, p. 112.
245. *seven rivers:* Cf. ch. 15, p. 88; ch. 55, p. 126.
246. *accidie:* See above, on ch. 52, p. 124, with note 230.
247. *mortal . . . venial:* On the distinction between mortal and venial sins, cf. below, ch. 87, pp. 156–157. The distinction between mortal sin and venial sin derives from 1 John 5.16–17, where a sin "unto death" is contrasted with one that is not "unto death." According to St. Thomas, ST 1–2, q. 88, a. 1., mortal sin represents a sickness of the soul that is irreparable by any intrinsic principle, and which requires a fresh infusion of grace to be cured, while venial sin does not break a person's direction to his last end in God. On Hilton's identification of grace with charity, see below, ch. 68, p. 138, with note 286.
248. *pushed into a house:* William of St. Thierry, Déchanet, p. 226, speaks of the two cells (*cellae*) of the monk: one exterior, the physical cell enclosing soul and body together; the other interior, the conscience.
249. *with:* om, C; supplied from H.
250. *love of your own excellence:* A standard definition derived from Augustine, *De Genesi ad Litteram* 11.14.18. It is repeated by, for instance, St. Bernard, *De Gradibus Humilitatis* 4.14. Hilton cites it in *De Imagine Peccati* (Clark and Taylor, p. 75). His analysis of the seven capital sins in *Scale* 1 is based on what he has written in this earlier work.

251. *to Jews and Saracens:* Hilton holds a severely ultra-Augustinian view of the status of the unbaptized, cf. *Scale* 2.3, p. 197. He might have found support for the opinion he states here in St. Anselm, *Tractatus de Concordantia Praescientiae Dei cum Libero Arbitrio,* q. 3, c. 7; or in Augustine, *De Nuptiis et Concupiscentia,* 1, 25–26; or *Contra duas Epistolas Pelagianorum* 1.13.27. St. Thomas, ST 1–2, q. 89, a. 5, explicitly rejects this view, referring to Anselm, and remarks that the sins of unbelievers are less culpable than those of believers, because the latter have received a greater gift from God.

252. *peccatum est:* Romans 14.23.

253. *then this pride is mortal sin:* St. Thomas says (ST 2–2, q. 162, a. 5) that because pride is a turning away from God, it is according to its *genus* a mortal sin; yet in fact, because it is not always the subject of full consent, it is not mortal sin in every case, and indeed is probably rarely mortal sin in individual cases.

254. *as to choose pride as his god?* Pride is here taken as the exaltation of one's own will in the place of God's.

255. *bodily pride . . . spiritual:* The distinction between bodily and spiritual pride is traditional; cf. Cassian, *Institutiones* 12.2; Gregory, *Moralia* 34.23.49. Hilton's application of spiritual pride to hypocrites and more particularly to heretics reflects his own topical concerns.

256. *moriemini:* Romans 8.13.

257. *A heretic sins mortally in pride:* Heresy was becoming a live issue at the time when Hilton wrote *Scale* 1. His severe attitude arises because he sees heresy as an act of self-will and divisiveness. Cf. *Scale* 2.26, pp. 240–241.

258. *ad mortem:* Proverbs 14.12.

259. *in fine perdetur:* Job 20.5–7. Hilton is here in line with Gregory, *Moralia* 15.3.4–4.5.

260. *ipse se seducit:* Galatians 6.3.

261. *offers himself entirely to God:* Cf. *Scale* 1.22, p. 95, with note 80 on the value of the general intention directed to God.

262. *venial sin:* Cf. St. Thomas, ST 1–2, q. 88, a. 1, ad 2: "Venial sin does not exclude the habitual ordination of the human act to the glory of God, but only excludes the actual ordination of such acts, because it does not exclude charity, which habitually ordains to God."

263. *any man or woman:* Hilton is at pains to emphasize that vowed religious have no exclusive prerogative of holiness. He is quite compatible with traditional teaching here (cf. notes on ch. 61), but his emphasis on the positive value of the Christian life offered to God in the world as well as in the cloister is an important aspect of his teaching. This converges with the outlook of *Mixed Life* (see Introduction, pp. 41–42), and in some measure opens the way to the wider perception in *Scale* 2, as to who may be called to contemplation.

264. *the love and knowledge . . . charity given by him:* Cf. ST 1, q. 12, a. 6: "He will participate more greatly in the light of glory, who has more charity . . . and he will be more blessed." Similarly ST, 1–2, q. 114, a. 4. A

greater or less degree of charity may be given according to God's will, "at the will of the Holy Spirit who distributes his gifts as he will" (ST, 2–2, q. 24, a. 3).

265. *it will happen that some secular man or woman:* Cf. ST 2–2, q. 182, a. 2: "It can happen that someone may merit more in the works of the active life than another in the works of the contemplative life, that is, if on account of the abundance of the divine love, so that God's will may be fulfilled for his glory, he bears for a while with being separated from the sweetness of divine contemplation."

"The exterior work serves to increase the accidental reward, but the increase of merit in respect of the essential reward consists principally in charity" (*ad* 1).

266. *martyrdom, preaching and virginity:* On the aureole as a secondary reward for these works, see e.g., ST Suppl, q. 96, a. 1, 5–7.

267. *the stricter the order:* A popular view, expressed for instance in the *Epistle* of Abbot Robert in the early twelfth century—PL 170.665: "In holy church, the stricter the Order, the higher it is." St. Thomas gives a more balanced view: "A religion is not to be preferred because it has stricter observances, but because its observances are ordained with greater discretion to the end of the religious life [i.e. charity]" (ST 2–2, a. 188 a. 6, ad 3).

268. *the taking of priest's orders:* This is not listed by St. Thomas among the works which attain an aureole, but the addition reflects Hilton's pastoral interest.

269. *in finem dierum:* Daniel 12.13.

270. *many a wife:* Cf. ch. 61 above, p. 132.

271. *charity and humility:* Cf. chs. 20; 22; 51, pp. 93–94, 95–96, 123.

272. *resistance against bearing any shame:* Cf. *De Imagine Peccati*, in Clark and Taylor, p. 89: "You want to be humble without being despised"; earlier, Gregory, *Homilia in Ezekiel* 2.8.15: "He wishes indeed to be in a humble place, but he does not want to be regarded as contemptible."

273. *You are to love the man ... and hate the sin:* Cf. ch. 65; 68; 70; pp. 135–136, 138, 141–142, with note 294.

274. *in dulce:* Isaiah 5.20 (differs slightly from the standard text).

275. *est vobis:* Cf. Romans 5.5. On charity as an "infused" virtue, beyond the reach of our natural powers, see e.g., ST 2–2, q. 24, a. 2.

276. *this one alone makes him good:* Cf. 1 Corinthians 13.1ff. See further *Scale* 2.34; 36; pp. 266, 269–270, with note 265 for *Scale* 2.

277. *open heretic:* Cf. ch. 58, pp. 128–129.

278. *nihil mihi prodest:* 1 Corinthians 13.1–3.

279. *acquired:* geten (C); adquiri (Y). Cf. note 284 below.

280. *Then who dares boldly say:* The question of whether a man could know that he was in a state of grace was commonly debated; cf. ST 1–2, q. 112, a. 5. St. Thomas allows that a man may know that he is in grace by special revelation, or else "conjecturally by some signs"—such as delighting in God and despising worldly things, and in not being

conscious of any mortal sin. Hilton's teaching does not depend on St. Thomas here, although his teaching in *Scale* 2 on contemplation as an awareness of the life of grace will converge with that of St. Thomas in other respects.

281. *angustia? etc.* Romans 8.35.

282. *To reprove . . . to hate:* Cf. *Scale* 1.70, pp. 141–142, with note 294.

283. *knows how to distinguish:* Cf. ch. 70, p. 142.

284. *acquired: geten* (C); *adquiri* (Y). Hilton is again deliberately contrasting charity as an "infused" virtue, a sheer gift of God, with virtues that may be "acquired" by human effort—cf. ch. 65, p. 136, with note 275.

285. *dat gratiam:* James 4.6.

286. *this grace is properly charity:* St. Thomas says (ST 1-2, q. 110, a. 3) that the infusion of [sanctifying] grace is logically distinct from charity. Hilton's viewpoint stands here closer to the Franciscan tradition, represented by, for instance, Duns Scotus. For Duns, grace and charity may be identified insofar as grace is a participation in the divine nature, and God is love or charity. At the same time, while all grace is charity, not all charity is grace. Grace is the created gift; charity can be both the created gift, and the uncreated Gift, which is God himself. See Duns Scotus, *In Sententias* 2, d. 27, q. un., n. 4; *Reportatio Parisiensis* 2, d. 27, q. un, n. 3–4.

287. *humility imperfectly:* The contrast between "perfect" and "imperfect" humility will be developed further in *Scale* 2.20, pp. 225–226; 2.37, pp. 271–272. See Introduction, p. 50.

288. *oculi tui:* Psalm 138.16.

289. *that man is humble:* After Bernard, *De Gradibus Humilitatis* 1.2: "*Humilitas est virtus, qua homo verissima sui cognitione sibi ipse vilescit.*"

290. *the more you are stirred . . . greater your ill-will:* See Ch. 89, p. 158.

291. *calumniantibus vos:* Matthew 5.44.

292. *dilexi vos:* John 13.34.

293. *But now you say:* From here to the end of the chapter is probably an authorial addition to the *Scale*. See Introduction, p. 54.

294. *the teaching of St. Augustine:* See Augustine, *De Doctrina Christiana* 1.27, 28: "Every sinner insofar as he is a sinner is not to be loved; and every man insofar as he is a man, is to be loved on account of [*propter*] God; God truly is to be loved for himself [*propter seipsum*]." Cf. *Tractatus in Ioannis Epistolam* 8.10: "For you do not love in him what he is, but what you wish that he should be"; *Confessiones* 4.9.14: "He loves you, and his friend in you [*in te*] and his enemy on account of you [*propter te*]"; *Sermo* 4.19 (PL 38.43); *Enarrationes in Psalmos* 138.28.

295. *There is less difficulty in forsaking worldly goods:* After *De Imagine Peccati*, in Clark and Taylor, pp. 88–89.

296. *you . . . have changed it from great things into small:* Cf. Cassian, *Collationes* 4.21: "For they show that they have not cut out the vice of cupidity and avarice, which they cannot practice in relation to

precious objects, but they show that they have changed the former passion (to small objects)." Ailred, *De Institutione Inclusarum*, c. 3 (C Ch CM I, p. 639), deals with the problem of avaricious religious.

297. *you are not a good merchant!* Cf. *De Imagine Peccati*, in Clark and Taylor, p. 97.

298. *As St. Gregory says ... in keeping it:* After *Moralia* 1.5.7 or 31.13.21.

299. *to love and possess ... need:* Cf. on ch. 72, pp. 144–145, with note 306.

300. *to have and to use:* See Augustine, *De Doctrina Christiana* 1.4.4. To enjoy (*frui*) means to cleave to something in love for its own sake (*propter seipsam*). To use (*uti*) means that the use of a thing is referred to the obtaining of the object of love. Augustine will go on to say that it is only God who is to be enjoyed, that is, loved for his own sake (1.22.20–21).

301. *entangled:* Cf. ch. 43, p. 114, and note 172.

302. *St. Augustine ... only a little: Confessiones* 10.29.40.

303. *accidie:* Cf. ch. 52, p. 124, with note 230.

304. *bestial:* Cf. ch. 43, p. 114, with note 171.

305. *me confortat:* Philippians 4.12–13.

306. *St. Augustine ... as medicine: Confessiones* 10.31.44. Augustine refers to the delicate balance between the proper satisfaction of bodily need (*necessitas*), and self-indulgence through concupiscence (*concupiscentia*). In *Scale* I Hilton is following Augustine closely. A related passage in Hilton's earlier *De Imagine Peccati* (Clark and Taylor, p. 92) refers severely to hunger as a punishment justly inflicted for original sin, and refers in lurid terms to the reader's ravenous appetite. *Scale* I here, as elsewhere, has removed the rough edges from the earlier Hilton.

307. *it is not common ... mortally through gluttony:* Hilton sees spiritual sins as more serious than carnal ones (see ch. 73). Mortal sin in gluttony discloses a state of mortal sin on other fronts.

308. *as long as he is in charity by other good works:* Cf. ch. 60, pp. 130–131, with note 262.

309. *the spring:* Cf. ch. 15; ch. 55; pp. 88, 126.

310. *holy scripture and the commentaries of learned men upon it:* The distinction between spiritual and carnal sins is made by Cassian, *Collationes* 5.3–4. Hilton's insistence that spiritual sins are in principle graver than carnal sins is the common view of theologians. See ST 1–2, q. 73, a. 5.

311. *devotion ... contemplation:* For the distinction, cf. ch. 9, p. 82; on devotion as contrasted with contemplation, cf. Introduction, p. 37.

312. *humility and charity:* Cf. chs. 20; 51; pp. 93–94, 123, etc.

313. *rule and measure:* There is similar teaching in the *Cloud*, ch. 12. Cf. Richard of St. Victor, *Benjamin Minor*, ch. 7 (PL 196.6): "Virtue is nothing other than an ordered and moderate affection of the mind [*animi affectus ordinatus et moderatus*]."

314. *huc transmeare:* Luke 16.26. Similarly in *Epistola de Lectione*, in Clark and Taylor, p. 222. After Bernard, *Sermo de Voluntate Divina*, in Leclerq, pp. 37f. (= *Sermo in Quadragesima* 6.1, PL 183.182).

315. *your lantern:* Cf. ch. 48, p. 121.
316. *per fenestras nostras:* Jeremiah 9.21. This interpretation of the text is commonplace: cf. Gregory, *Moralia* 21.2.4. The text is used in the same sense in Bernard, *De Gradibus Humilitatis* 10.28. For other indications of Hilton's familiarity with *De Gradibus Humilitatis,* see below on chs. 79, 80, 87 (pp. 150, 156, notes 319, 323–324, 359). Hilton describes the disorder of the bodily senses in consequence of the Fall at some length in *De Imagine Peccati* (Clark and Taylor, pp. 93–96).
317. *a black mantle:* Cf. ch. 52, p. 124, "black stinking clothes of sin."
318. *like a beast without reason:* Cf. ch. 43, p. 114, with note 171.
319. *hoedos tuos:* Canticle 1.7. The use of this text in such a sense is commonplace. Among the places where St. Bernard uses it in this sense are *De Gradibus Humilitatis* 7.21; 10.28; *In Cant.* 35.1.1–2.3. William of St. Thierry uses the text in a like sense in his *Expositio in Cant.* (PL 180.493–4). But it is Bernard's writings with which Hilton shows specific familiarity. On self-knowledge, cf. ch. 42, p. 112. Hilton uses Canticle 1.7 in the same sense in *Epistola de Lectione* (Clark and Taylor, p. 222).
320. *made to the likeness of God:* Cf. Genesis 1.26. On the distinction between image and likeness, see ch. 43, p. 113, with note 168.
321. *turn again home into yourself:* The recovery of the *similitudo Dei* by introversion is a commonplace in the Augustinian tradition. Cf. for instance Augustine, *De Vera Religione* c. 39: "Do not go outside, return into yourself; God lives in the inner man—the Truth whom those who seek him without in no way reach."
322. *beg no more outside, especially for pigfood:* Cf. Luke 15.16. The notion that the journey of the prodigal son into a "far country" represents a loss of the *similitudo Dei* is traditional. For the "region of unlikeness" (*regio dissimilitudinis*) see Augustine, *Confessiones* 7.10.16. On this, see P. Courcelle, "Tradition Néo-platonicienne et Traditions Chrétiennes de la Région de Dissemblance," *Archives d'Histoire Doctrinale et Littéraire du Moyen Âge* 24 (1957), pp. 5–33.
323. *do not run out any more:* Cf. Canticle 1.7, cited in ch. 79, p. 150.
324. *vinariam:* Canticle 2.4. Similar use of the text in Bernard, *De Gradibus Humilitatis* 7.21.
325. *king:* Emended from *kyng* (H) and *rex* (Y), C reads *likyng.*
326. *ascending:* C's *ouerpassyng* strictly corresponds to the Latin *excessus* (cf. *Scale* 1.9, p. 83, citing 2 Corinthians 5.13). Fishlake in his Latin version (Y) paraphrases: *supra meipsum per ascensum in ipsum solum.*
327. *But now you say:* The construction is a common one in Hilton, where he is stating (and answering) a real or purported objection. In this instance he is following closely what he has already written in *De Imagine Peccati* (Clark and Taylor, p. 97): *Forsitan mihi dicis quod multum solitarius es et quasi abstractus a mundiali conversatione.*
328. *a great window:* Cf. Jeremiah 9.21.
329. *but still you are not secure:* For the sense, cf. *Scale* 1.55, p. 126. Ailred, *De Institutione Inclusarum,* c. 2, makes a like point.

330. *imagination:* The imagination mediates between spirit and bodily sense, enabling the soul to picture spiritual things in terms derived from the world of bodily sense. Cf. *Scale* 2.31, pp. 258–259.
331. *What is sin . . . good?* Cf. ch. 53, p. 124, with note 235.
332. *non possum venire:* Luke 14.16–20. This application is commonplace and is found already in Augustine, *Sermo* 112.2–3. Hilton applies the text similarly in *De Imagine Peccati* (Clark and Taylor, pp. 96–97).
333. *in need:* Cf. ch. 72, p. 145.
334. *concupiscentias tuas:* Although Hilton refers to St. Paul, and the thought is close to Romans 6.12, the text is actually Ecclesiasticus 18.30, cited in the old Latin form familiar through the writings of St. Augustine and repeated, for example, in St. Benedict's *Rule*, ch. 7, ed. McCann (London, 1952), p. 40.
335. *venial sins do not break charity:* Cf. ch. 55, p. 126; ch. 87, pp. 156–157.
336. *various people . . . often come:* Ailred, *De Institutione Inclusarum*, c. 7 deals with how the recluse should receive visitors. The matter is a traditional concern, and Hilton seems independent of Ailred.
337. *love:* omitted by C; emended from H and Y.
338. *you shall find him . . . in your fellow Christian:* This point derives from St. Paul's insistence that we are members of Christ in his body (cf. Romans 12.4f). Hilton makes a like point in *Mixed Life*, Ogilvie-Thomson pp. 25–26.
339. *it is not your place to teach a priest except in necessity:* Contemplatives should not correct others except in case of necessity. Cf. ch. 17, pp. 90–91.
340. *Inveni idolum mihi:* Hosea 12.8. Similarly in *De Imagine Peccati* (Clark and Taylor, p. 73).
341. *tunicas pelliceas:* Genesis 3.21. This use of the text is commonplace. Cf. Augustine, *De Trinitate* 12.11.16: "Stripped of their first garment, they deserved clothes of skins (*pelliceas tunicas*) in their mortality."
342. *shape:* Latin *forma,* as in Fishlake's translation here. Augustine, *De Trinitate* 14.16.22, refers to the image of God in man after the Fall as "deformed and discolored" (*deformis et decolor*).
343. *Initium omnis peccati superbia:* Ecclesiasticus 10.15. Commonplace. Augustine, *Enarrationes in Psalmos* 73.16, refers to pride as the "head of the dragon," citing Ecclesiasticus 10.15.
344. *me extendo:* Philippians 3.13.
345. *ex parte eius sunt:* Wisdom 2.24f.
346. *et alteram:* Matthew 5.39.
347. *has destruet:* 1 Corinthians 6.13.
348. *ad peccatum:* Romans 6.13.
349. *accidie:* Cf. ch. 52 above, with note 230.
350. *amicum tuum:* Proverbs 6.3.
351. *humility and perfect love and charity:* Cf. ch. 51, p. 123.
352. *conturbatur:* Psalm 38.7. Cited to the same purpose in Augustine, *De Trinitate* 14.4.6; 14.14.19.
353. *caelestis:* 1 Corinthians 15.49. Cf. ch. 54, p. 125. *De Imagine Peccati* (Clark and Taylor, p. 98).

354. *crucifige eum:* John 19.15. *De Imagine Peccati* (Clark and Taylor, p. 98), says simply, "Let the body of sin be destroyed" (cf. Romans 6.6), and urges that this idol be broken down by the power of the name of Jesus, just as the images of the Gentiles were once destroyed.

355. *concupiscentiis:* Galatians 5.24.

356. *accidie:* Cf. ch. 52, with note 230.

357. *et iustitia:* Ephesians 4.22; 24. Similarly in Hilton, e.g., *Scale* 2.31, p. 258, citing Ephesians 4.23–24. Similarly Ephesians 4.23f, in Augustine, *De Trinitate* 12.7.12; 14.16.22.

358. (Heading) *in what it loves:* Supplied from H; omitted by C and Y. Cf. p. 157, lines 5 to 9.

359. *vita procedit:* Proverbs 4.23. A commonplace text. Used by Bernard, *De Gradibus Humilitatis* 10.28 of cutting out curiosity. Gregory, *Moralia* 25.8.20, links the text with Matthew 15.19, but it is not certain that this is a specific source.

360. *hominem:* Matthew 15.19–20.

361. *they either take away:* Cf. ch. 55, with note 247.

362. *What is a man . . . and his loves?* Cf. perhaps Augustine, *Soliloquiae* 1.1.5: "I have nothing but my will [*Nihil aliud habeo quam voluntatem*]."

363. *As much as you love God and know him:* Cf. Richard Rolle, *Incendium Amoris*, in Deanesly, p. 164: "He who loves much is great, he who loves less is less; because according to the greatness of the love that we have in us, we are valued by God." But this is not an exact parallel, and in any case Rolle and Hilton are drawing on a common tradition, which they expound a little differently.

364. *Rule your thoughts well:* Cf. ch. 87, p. 156.

365. *to your Lord Jesus, and pray to him for help:* Cf. ch. 86, p. 156.

366. *the heavy burden of this image:* St. Bernard, *De Diligendo Deo* 13.36, refers to the "heavy and unbearable yoke laid upon all the sons of Adam," recalling Ecclesiasticus 40.1. This area of Bernard's writing was well-known to Hilton—see Clark and Taylor, p. 465 (sources) *Scale* 2.40, p. 281.

367. *pigfood:* See ch. 80, p. 150.

368. *no soul can live without great pain:* After Gregory, *Moralia* 18.9.16. This is a commonplace; for example, it is echoed in Rolle, *Incendium Amoris*, in Deanesly, p. 210.

369. *that he wants nothing but his Lord:* Cf. ch. 52, p. 124; taken up again in *Scale* 2.21–22; pp. 228, 230–231.

370. *errorem mittunt:* Isaiah 3.12. The text differs from the standard Vulgate.

371. *the spring of pride:* Cf. ch. 55, p. 126.

372. *a spiritual sight of humility:* Cf. *Mixed Life*, in Ogilvie-Thomson, pp. 53–54.

373. *accidie:* Cf. ch. 52, with note 230.

374. *with your reason and will:* Cf. ch. 14, p. 87.

375. *make the devil ashamed:* Cf. *Scale* 2.45, pp. 229–300.

376. *formetur in vobis:* Galatians 4.19. The birth of Christ in the soul is a familiar theme since the Church Fathers, indeed, since the time of St. Paul, as the text indicates. See H. Rahner, "Die Gottesgeburt: die Lehre der Kirchenväter von der Geburt Christi im Herzen des Gläubigen," *Zeitschrift für Katholische Theologie* 59 (1935), pp. 333–418. The theme is familiar in the early Cistercians; see, e.g., St. Bernard, *Sermo in Vigilia Nativitatis Domini* 6.7–8; Gilbert of Hoyland, *In Cant.* 10.3. Hilton did not depend on the Rhineland writers here.

377. *You have conceived Christ through faith:* Cf. already *Epistola de Lectione* (Clark and Taylor, p. 242). These passages have an eye to the familiar contrast between faith and feeling (or understanding). Cf. ch. 9, p. 83, with note 32.

378. *Whoever thinks to come . . . except by this way:* This passage stands close to two passages in *The Prickynge of Love*, in Kane, pp. 73, 124, which are perhaps recalling St. Bonaventure, *Itinerarium Mentis in Deum*, Prol. 3. What Hilton says in *Scale* 1 at this point is taken up again and recast in *Scale* 2.27, p. 245. The same teaching is reflected in *The Book of Privy Counselling*, in *The Cloud of Unknowing* (Hodgson, p. 159).

379. *his leave and his livery:* Cf. ch. 51, p. 123, note 218 on Pauline overtones.

380. *nisi per me:* John 14.6. This text is cited in *The Prickynge of Love*, p. 73 (peculiar to the English version).

381. *Not that I have it in feeling or in working:* A characteristic disclaimer. Cf. ch. 9, p. 83; ch. 71, p. 144.

Book Two

Book Two

Table of Contents

As first written, MS. H (B. L. Harley 6579) contained no chapter headings, though a few were later added by another hand. In the present edition we have disregarded the incomplete headings inserted in Book 2 and have used instead, both here and in the text, the titles given in the complete *tabula*, which appears at the end of the work (ff. 141r–143v). These agree broadly with the Latin chapter headings in MS. Y (York Cathedral Chapter Library XVI K 5).

Book Two

likeness of God and the likeness of sin

1. That a man is the image of God according to the soul and not the body.

Because you have a strong desire to hear more of an image that I have partly described to you before, and ask it by charity, I will gladly yet fearfully bow to your wish, and with the help of our Lord Jesus Christ (in whom I place all my trust) I shall disclose to you a little more about this image. To begin with, if you want to know plainly what I mean by it, I tell you truthfully that I understand nothing else but your own soul, for your soul, my soul, and every rational soul is an image, and an honorable one at that, since it is the image of God, as the apostle said: *Vir est imago Dei.*[1] That is, man is the image of God, and made to his image and likeness, not outwardly in bodily shape but in the powers of it within, as holy scripture says: *Formavit Deus hominem ad imaginem et similitudinem suam.*[2] That is, our Lord God shaped man in soul to his own image and likeness.

This is the image that I have spoken of. This—made to the image of God in the first creation—was wonderfully bright and fair, full of burning love and spiritual light, but through the sin of the first man, Adam, it was deformed and changed into another likeness, as I have said before. For it fell from that spiritual light and that heavenly food into the painful darkness and lust of this wretched life, exiled and cast out from the heritage of heaven (which it should have had if it had stood still) into the wretchedness of this earth, and afterward into the prison of hell, there to stay eternally; and from this prison it could never have come again to

193

that heavenly heritage without being reformed to the first shape and the first likeness. But that reforming could not be carried out by any earthly man, since every man was in the same plight, and none was capable of helping himself, much less any other man. It therefore had to be done by him who is more than a man, and that is God alone; and that was reasonable: that the one who should reform man and restore him to bliss (if he was to be saved) was he who of his infinite goodness first created him for it. How then this image could be reformed, and how it is reformed to the first likeness by him who first formed it I shall tell you by the grace of God, for that is the purpose of this writing.

2. How it was necessary that only through the passion of Christ could there be restoration and reformation for mankind, which was deformed by the first sin.

Now I shall tell you how the justice of God[3] requires that a trespass once done shall not be forgiven unless amends are made for it, if that is possible. Now it is true that mankind, which was whole in Adam (the first man), trespassed against God so very grievously when it violated his special command and yielded to the false counsel of the devil, that it justly deserved to be parted from him and condemned to hell without end: so far, that if the justice of God was to stand it could not be forgiven unless amends and full satisfaction were first made for it. But this could be done by no man who was man alone and had come from Adam by natural generation, for the reason that this trespass and dishonor was infinitely great, and therefore it surpassed the power of man to make amends for it; and also for this reason: he who has trespassed and is to make amends ought to give to him against whom he has trespassed all that he owes even without the trespass, and in addition he ought to give something that he does not owe, only because he has trespassed. But mankind had nothing with which to pay God for his trespass beyond what he owed him, because whatever good deed man could do in body or in soul it was no more than his debt, since (as the gospel says) everyone ought to love God with all his heart and all his soul and all his powers. He could not do better than this; and nevertheless this deed was not sufficient for the reforming of mankind, nor could he do it without first being reformed. So it was necessary—if man's soul was to be reformed and the trespass made good—that our Lord God himself should reform this image and make amends for this trespass, since no man could. But that was impossible for him in his divinity; for he could not and ought not to make amends by suffering punishment in his own nature. He therefore had to take the same human nature that had trespassed, and become man; and this he could not do by the common law of generation, for it was impossible for God's Son to be born of a woman touched by man, so he must become man through a generation made by grace through the working of the Holy Spirit, from a pure gracious maiden, our Lady, St. Mary. And so it was done: for our Lord Jesus, God's Son, became man, and through his precious death that he suffered made amends to the Father of heaven for man's guilt; and that he could well do, because he was God, owing nothing for himself except inasmuch as he was man, born of the same nature as Adam who first trespassed. And so although he did not owe it for his own person—because he himself could not sin—nevertheless he owed it by his free will for the trespass of human nature, which nature he took by his infinite mercy for the salvation of man. For it is true that there never was a man who could yield anything of his own to God that he did not owe, except this blessed Jesus, for he could pay God one thing that he in himself did not owe, and that was one thing alone—to give his precious life for love of justice by the voluntary taking of death. This he did not owe. All the good he could do in his life for the honor of God, that was only due; but to take death for love of justice was something to which he was not bound.

He was bound to justice, but he was not bound to die, for death is only a punishment ordained for man because of his own sin; but our Lord Jesus never sinned and could not sin, and therefore he was not obliged to die. Then, since he had no duty to die and yet died by his own will, he paid God more than he owed; and since that was the deed of the best man, and the most honorable [deed][4] that ever was done, it was reasonable that the sin of mankind should be forgiven, inasmuch as mankind had found a man of the same nature without stain of sin (that is, Jesus) able to make amends for the trespass committed and to pay our Lord God all that he owed, and furthermore something that he did not owe. Then since our Lord Jesus—God and man—died thus for the salvation of man's soul, it was just that sin should be forgiven, and that man's soul (which was his image) should become capable of reformation and restoration to the first likeness, and to the bliss of heaven.

This passion of our Lord and this precious death are the ground of all the reforming of man's soul, without which it could never have been reformed to his likeness or come to the glory of heaven. But blessed may he be in all his work! Now it is true that by virtue of this precious passion the burning sword of the cherub that drove Adam out of Paradise is now put away, and the eternal gates of heaven are open to every man who wants to enter there, for the person of Jesus is both God and king of heaven, equal in glory to the Father, and as a man he is porter at the gate, ready to receive every soul that wishes to be reformed to his likeness here in this life. For now every soul may be reformed to the likeness of God if he will, since the trespass is forgiven and amends made through Jesus for the first guilt. Nevertheless, though this is true, not all souls have the profit or the fruit of this precious passion, neither are they reformed to his likeness.

3. That by their own fault Jews and infidels, and also false Christian men, are not reformed effectually through the virtue of the passion.

Two kinds of people are not reformed by virtue of this passion. Those who do not believe in it are one kind; those who do not love it are the other. Jews and infidels do not have the benefit of this passion, because they do not believe in it. Jews do not believe that Jesus, the son of the Virgin Mary, is the Son of the God of heaven. Also, the infidels do not believe that the supreme Wisdom of God was willing to become son of man, and in humanity suffer the pains of death; and therefore the Jews held the preaching of the cross and of the passion of Christ as nothing but slander and blasphemy, and the infidels hold it as nothing but illusion and folly. But faithful Christians have held it to be the supreme Wisdom of God, and his great might. So said St. Paul: *Praedicamus vobis Christum crucifixum, Iudaeis quidem scandalum, gentibus autem stultitiam: ipsis autem vocatis Iudaeis, et Graecis, Christum Dei virtutem, etc.*[5] That is, We preach to you that you may believe that Jesus Christ crucified, the son of Mary, is God's Son, the supreme Virtue and Wisdom of God; that same Jesus is only a stumbling-block and folly to Jews and infidels who do not believe in him. And therefore these people by their disbelief exclude themselves from the reforming of their own souls, and if their unbelief stands they shall never be saved or come to the bliss of heaven. For it is true that from the beginning of the world to the last end, no one was ever saved or shall be saved without having faith—either general or special[6]—in Jesus Christ, coming or already come. For just as all chosen souls that were before the incarnation under the Old Testament had faith in Christ—that he should come and reform man's soul—either openly, as patriarchs and prophets and other holy men had, or else secretly and generally as children and other simple and imperfect souls had who lacked any special knowledge of the mystery of the incarnation, in the same way all chosen souls under the New Testament have faith in Christ, that he has come—either openly and consciously as spiritual men and wise men have, or else generally, as have children who die baptized, and other simple and unlearned souls who are nourished in the bosom of holy church. Since this is true, then it seems to me that these men are greatly and grievously in error[7] who say that Jews and Saracens can be saved by keeping their own law, although they do not believe in Jesus Christ as holy church believes, inasmuch as they think their own faith is good and sure, sufficient for their salvation, and in that faith they do, as it seems, many good works of righteousness. And perhaps if they knew that Christian faith was better than theirs, they would leave their own and take it: therefore they should be saved. No, this is not enough, for Christ, God and man, is both the way and the end, and he is mediator between God and man. Without him no soul can be reconciled or come to the bliss of heaven. And therefore those who do not believe in him, that he is both God and man, can never be saved or come to glory.

Other people also who do not love Christ or his passion are not reformed in their soul to his likeness, and these are false Christians who are out of charity and live and die in mortal sin. They well believe (as it seems) that Jesus is God's Son, and that his passion is sufficient for the salvation of man's soul, and they also believe all the other articles of the faith, but it is an unformed and dead faith, for they do not love him, neither do they choose the fruit of his passion, but they lie still in their sin and in the false love of this world up to their last end. And so they are not reformed to the likeness of God, but go to the pains of hell eternally, as Jews and Saracens do[8]—and into much more pain than they do, in that they had the faith and did not keep it.[9] For that was a greater trespass than if they had never had it.

Then, if you want to know which souls are reformed here in this life to the image of God by virtue of his passion, certainly only those that believe in him and love him. In those souls the image of God, which through sin was deformed as if into the likeness of an ugly beast, is restored and reformed to the first shape, and to the honor and excellence that it had in the beginning. Without such restoring and reforming no soul shall be saved or come to glory.

4. Two ways of reforming this image: in part and in fullness.

Now you say, "How can this be true: that the image of God, which is man's soul, could here in this life be reformed to his likeness in any creature?" It seems not—that it could not be—for if it were reformed, then it should have a stable memory, clear sight and pure burning love of God and spiritual things everlastingly, as it had in the beginning; but that exists in no creature (as you believe), living here in this life. For as regards yourself, you can well say you seem very far from it. Your memory, your reason and the love of your soul are set so much on the consideration and love of earthly things that you have very little feeling of the things of the spirit. You feel no reforming in yourself, but despite anything you can do, you are so wrapped round with this black image of sin that whichever way you turn you feel yourself defiled and spotted with the fleshly impulses of this foul image. You feel no other change from fleshliness into spirituality, either in the secret powers of your soul within or in outward bodily feeling. For this reason it seems to you impossible that this image could be reformed; or else, if it could be reformed, you then ask how this might be done.

To this I answer and say thus. There are two ways to reform the image of God that is man's soul: one is in fullness; the other is in part. Reforming in fullness cannot be had in this life, but it is postponed after this life to the glory of heaven, where man's soul shall be fully reformed: not to that state that it had by nature at the first beginning or could have had through grace if it had stayed whole, but through the great mercy and the infinite goodness of God it shall be restored to much greater glory and much higher joy than it should have had if it had never fallen. For then the soul shall receive the full feeling of God[10] in all its powers, without admixture of any other affection,[11] and it shall see human nature in the person of Jesus above the nature of angels, united to the Godhead. For then Jesus—both God and man—shall be all in all, and he alone, and none but he, as the prophet says: *Dominus solus exaltabitur in illa die*.[12] That is, Our Lord Jesus in that day—meaning the everlasting day— alone shall be exalted, and none but he. And in the same way the body of man shall then be glorified, for it shall fully receive the rich dowry of immortality, with all that belongs to it. A soul shall have this with the body, and much more than I can say, but that shall be in the bliss of heaven and not in this life; for although it happens that the passion of our Lord is the cause of this full reforming of man's soul, nevertheless it was not his will to grant this full reforming directly after his passion to all chosen souls that were living at that time; but he delayed it until the last day, for this reason.

It is true[13] that our Lord Jesus of his mercy has ordained a certain number of souls to salvation. This number was not fulfilled in the time of his passion, and therefore it had to be fulfilled in the length of time, through the natural generation of men. Then if it had so been that directly after the death of our Lord every soul who had believed in him should at once have been blessed and fully reformed without any further waiting, there would have been no creature then alive who did not want to receive the faith, in order to be blessed; and then procreation would have ceased, and so we (the chosen souls now living) and other souls coming after us would not have been born, and thus our Lord would have failed to complete his number. But that cannot be, and therefore our Lord provided much better for us in that he delayed the full reforming of man's soul to the last end, as St. Paul says: *Deo pro nobis melius providente, ne sine nobis consummarentur.*[14] That is, our Lord provided better for us in putting off the reforming than if he had granted it then, for this reason: that the chosen souls before this time should not make a complete end without us who come after. Another reason is this: because man in his first creation by God was set in his free will and had free choice as to whether he would fully possess God or not, it was therefore right, since he would not choose God then, but wretchedly fell from Him, that if he were afterward to be reformed he should again be placed with the same free choice that he had at first, as to whether he would have the profit of his reforming or not. And this may be a reason why man's soul was not fully reformed at once after the passion of our Lord Jesus Christ.

5. That reforming in part is of two kinds: one in faith and the other in feeling.

The other reforming of this image is in part, and this reforming may be had in this life; and unless it is gained in this life it never can be had, and the soul shall never be saved. But this reforming is of two kinds: one is in faith alone, and the other is in faith and in feeling.[15]

The first, which is reforming in faith alone, is sufficient for salvation; the second is worthy of surpassing reward in the bliss of heaven. The first may be gained easily and in a short time; the second not so, but through length of time and great spiritual labor. The first can be had together with the feeling of the image of sin, for though a man feels nothing in himself, but all stirrings of sin and fleshly desires, notwith-standing that feeling, if he does not deliberately assent to it[16] he may be reformed in faith to the likeness of God. But the second reforming drives out the enjoyment and feeling of fleshly stirrings and worldly desires and allows no such spots to remain in this image. The first reforming is only for souls beginning and proficient,[17] and for people in active life;[18] the second is for perfect souls and contemplatives. By the first reforming the image of sin is not destroyed, but it is left as if all whole in feeling; but the second reforming destroys the old feelings of this image of sin and brings into the soul new gracious feelings through the working of the Holy Spirit. The first is good; the second is better, but the third, which is in the bliss of heaven, is best of all. Let us first begin to speak of the one, and afterward of the other, and so we shall come to the third.

6. That through the sacrament of baptism, which is grounded in the passion of Christ, this image is reformed from original sin.

Two kinds of sins make a soul lose the shape and the likeness of God. One is called original, which is the first sin, and the other is called actual, which is sin willfully committed. These two sins put a soul out of the bliss of heaven and condemn it to the endless pain of hell, unless it is reformed to the likeness of God through his grace before it passes hence out of this life. Nevertheless, against these two sins there are two reme-dies by which a deformed soul may be restored again. One is the sacra-ment of baptism against original sin; the other is the sacrament of pen-ance against actual sin. Because of original sin, the soul of a child born and unchristened has no likeness of God: he is nothing but an image of the devil and a brand of hell;[19] but as soon as it is christened it is reformed to the image of God,[20] and by virtue of the faith of holy church is suddenly turned[21] from the likeness of the devil to become like an angel of heaven. The same also happens in a Jew or a Saracen. Before they are christened these are nothing but bondslaves of hell, but when they for-sake their error, submit humbly to faith in Christ and receive the bap-tism of water in the Holy Spirit, certainly without any further delay they are reformed to the likeness of God: so fully, as holy church believes, that if they could pass out of this world directly after baptism they should fly straight to heaven without any more hindrance, however much sin they had committed in the time of their unbelief, and they should never feel the pain of hell or of purgatory. And that privilege would be theirs by the merit of the passion of Christ.

7. That this image is reformed from actual sins through the sacrament of penance, which consists of contrition,[22] confession and satisfaction.

In the same way, I say this truly of any Christian man or woman who has lost the likeness of God through mortal sin, breaking God's commandments: if through the touch of grace he indeed forsakes his sin with sorrow and contrition of heart, and fully intends to amend and turn to God and to good living, and with this intention receives the sacrament of penance if he can—or if he cannot, he has the will to do it—then the soul of this man or woman, deformed as it was before to the likeness of the devil through mortal sin, is now by the sacrament of penance restored and shaped again to the image of our Lord God. This is a great courtesy of our Lord's, and an infinite mercy, who so easily forgives all kinds of sin and so promptly gives abundant grace to a sinful soul that asks him for mercy. He does not wait for great penance to be done[23] or for painful bodily suffering before he forgives it, but he asks for a loathing of sin and a full forsaking[24] by the will of the soul, for love of him, and a turning to him of the heart: this he asks, because this he gives. And then, when he sees this, without any delay he forgives the sin and reforms the soul to his likeness. The sin is forgiven, so that the soul shall not be damned. Nevertheless, the punishment due for the sin is not yet fully forgiven unless contrition and love are the greater; and therefore he is to go and show himself and make confession to his spiritual father, and receive the penance enjoined for his trespass, and gladly fulfil it, so that both the sin and the punishment may be done away with before he passes hence.

This is the just ordinance of holy church for the great profit of man's soul: that though the sin may be forgiven by virtue of contrition, nevertheless, in fulfilment of humility and to make complete satisfaction, he shall if he can make plenary confession to his priest, for that is his token and his warrant of forgiveness against all his enemies, and this it is necessary to have. For if a man had forfeited his life to a king of this world, there would not be full security for him in getting only forgiveness from the king, unless he had a charter to be his token and his warrant against all other men. Just so it can be put spiritually: if through mortal sin a man has forfeited his life to the king of heaven, it is not enough for his full security to have God's forgiveness only by contrition, between God and himself, unless he has a charter made by holy church, if he can come by it: and that is the sacrament of penance, which is his charter and his token of forgiveness. For since he has forfeited both to God and to holy church, it is proper for him to have forgiveness from the one and a warrant from the other. This is one reason why confession is necessary.

Another reason is this. Since this reforming of the soul stands in faith alone and not in feeling, a carnal man who is rough and untaught, and cannot make judgments with ease (except outwardly upon material things), might not be convinced that his sins had been forgiven him without some bodily token: and that is confession, through which token he is made quite sure of forgiveness if he does what is in him. This is the faith of holy church, as I understand.

Still another reason is this. Although the ground of forgiveness does not stand primarily in confession, but in contrition of the heart and in repentance for sin, nevertheless I suppose there is many a soul that would never have felt true contrition or fully forsaken its sin if there were no confession, for it often happens that at the time of confession the grace of compunction[25] comes to a soul that never before felt grace, but was always cold and dry, and far from the feeling of grace. Therefore, since confession was so profitable to the larger part of Christian people, holy church for greater assurance ordained it generally for all: that every man and woman should at least once a year confess to their spiritual father all their sins that come to mind, however much contrition they have had before.

Nevertheless, I am sure that if all had been so busy keeping themselves away from every kind of sin, and had come to as great knowledge and feeling of God as some men have, holy church would not have ordained the token of confession as a necessary bond, for there would have been no need; but because all men are not so perfect—and perhaps the great majority of Christian people are imperfect—holy church ordained[26] confession by way of general obligation to all Christians who wish to own holy church as their mother and want to be obedient to her bidding. If this is true, as I think it is, then anyone is greatly mistaken[27] if he says generally that the confession of sins to a priest is neither necessary to a sinner nor expedient, and that nobody is bound to it, for from what I have said it is both necessary and useful to all souls who in this wretched life are defiled with sin, and especially to those who through

mortal sin are deformed from the likeness of God and cannot be reformed to his likeness except by the sacrament of penance. And this
consists in the first place of contrition and sorrow of heart; and in the
second, of oral confession following afterward, if possible. In this manner—by the sacrament of penance—a sinful soul is reformed to the
image of God, and to his likeness.

8. How in the sacraments of baptism and penance this
   image[28] is reformed through a hidden imperceptible
   working of the Holy Spirit, even though it is not seen
   or felt.

But this reforming stands in faith and not in feeling, for just as the
property of faith is to believe what you do not see,[29] so it is to believe
what you do not feel. But someone who is reformed to the image of God
in his soul by the sacrament of penance feels no change taking place in
himself other than he did, either outwardly in his bodily nature or
within, in the hidden substance of his soul. In his feeling, he is as he was;
and he feels the same stirrings of sin and the same corruption of his flesh
in passions and worldly desires rising in his heart as he did before. Yet
he is nonetheless to believe that through grace he is reformed to the
likeness of God, even though he may neither feel it nor see it.[30] He may
well feel sorrow for his sin, and a turning of his will from sin to purity of
living, if he has grace and keeps a good watch on himself; but he can
neither see nor feel the reforming of his soul: how it is wonderfully and
imperceptibly changed from the filth of a devil to the fairness of an angel
through a secret gracious work of our Lord God. He cannot see it, but
he shall believe it; and if he believes it, his soul is then reformed in faith.

For just as holy church believes that by the sacrament of baptism
truly received a Jew, a Saracen or a newborn child is reformed in soul to
the likeness of God through a secret imperceptible working of the Holy
Spirit, notwithstanding all the carnal stirrings of his body of sin, which
he shall feel after his baptism just as he did before, so by the sacrament of
penance, humbly and truly received, a false Christian encumbered with
mortal sin all his lifetime is reformed in his soul within—imperceptibly,
except for the conversion of his will through a secret power and a
gracious action of the Holy Spirit. This suddenly takes effect, and in the
passing of a moment or the twinkling of an eye sets right a froward soul,
turning it from spiritual filth to invisible beauty. From a servant of the

devil is made a son of joy, and from a prisoner of hell a partner in the heritage of heaven, notwithstanding all the fleshly feeling of this sinful image that is the bodily nature.

For you are to understand that the sacrament of baptism or of penance does not have such power as to hinder and utterly destroy all the stirrings of fleshly lusts and painful passions, so that a man's soul should never feel any kind of rising or stirring of them at any time. If it were so, then a soul would be fully reformed here to the honor of the first making, and that cannot be complete in this life. But it does have the power to cleanse a soul from all its former sins, and if it should be parted from the body saves it from damnation; and if it stays in the body it gives the soul grace to withstand the stirring of sin, and it keeps it in grace as well, so that no kind of lustful stirrings or passions that it feels in the flesh, however grievous, shall harm it or part it from God, as long as it does not willfully consent to it. This is what St. Paul meant when he said thus: *Nihil damnationis est hiis qui sunt in Christo qui non secundum carnem ambulant, etc.*[31] That is, Those souls who are reformed to the image of God in faith, through the sacrament of baptism or penance, shall not be damned for feelings of this image of sin, provided they do not follow the stirrings of the flesh by fulfilling them in deed.

9. That we should steadfastly believe in the reforming of this image[32] if our conscience bears witness to a full forsaking of sin and a true turning of our will to godly living.

St. Paul speaks thus about this reforming in faith: *Iustus ex fide vivit.*[33] The righteous man lives in faith. That is, Someone who is made righteous by baptism or penance lives in faith, which is sufficient for salvation and for heavenly peace, as St. Paul says: *Iustificati ex fide pacem habemus ad Deum.*[34] That is, We who are justified and reformed through faith in Christ have peace and accord made between God and ourselves, notwithstanding the vicious feelings of our body of sin. For though this reforming is secret and cannot well be felt here in this life,[35] nevertheless if anyone believes in it steadfastly, diligently shaping his works to accord with his faith and not turning again to mortal sin, it is certain that when the hour of death comes and the soul is parted from this bodily life, he shall then find the truth of what I say now.

This is how St. John speaks to comfort chosen souls that live here in faith under the feeling of this painful image: *Carissimi, et nunc sumus filii Dei; sed nondum apparuit quid erimus. Scimus quoniam cum Christus apparuerit, tunc apparebimus cum eo similes ei in gloria.*[36] That is, My dear friends, we are even now, while we live here, the sons of God, for we are reformed by faith in Christ to his likeness; but what we are does not yet show: it is all hidden. Nevertheless, we know well that when our Lord shall show himself at the last day we shall then appear—with him and like him—in eternal joy. If, then, you want to know whether your soul is reformed to the image of God or not, you can approach it by what I have said. Ransack your own conscience and examine your will, for everything stands upon that. If it is turned away from every kind of mortal sin, so that you would not for anything break the commandment of God knowingly and willingly, and if you have humbly made confession of the wrong already done against his bidding, with sorrow that you did it and with a wholehearted resolve to leave it, I say to you assuredly that your soul is reformed in faith to the likeness of God.

10. That all the souls that live humbly in the faith of holy church and have their faith quickened by love and charity are reformed by this sacrament, though they cannot feel the special gift of devotion or of good feeling.

In this reforming that is only in faith the greater part of chosen souls lead their life, who steadfastly set their will to flee every kind of mortal sin, to hold themselves in love and charity toward their fellow Christians, and to keep the commandments of God as far as they know. When it so happens that stirrings of wickedness and evil intentions rise in their hearts—of pride, envy, anger, lechery, or any other capital sin—they withstand them and strive against them with resolute displeasure, so that these wicked purposes are not followed by deeds. Nevertheless, if they carelessly fall, as it were against their will through frailty or ignorance, at once their conscience troubles them and pains them so grievously that they can have no rest until they have confessed and can receive forgiveness. Indeed I consider that all these souls living so are reformed in faith to the image of God; and if they live in this reforming and are found in it at the hour of their death, they shall be saved and come to the full reforming in the bliss of heaven, even though they could never have spiritual feeling or inward savor or special grace of devotion in all their lifetime. For otherwise, if you say that no soul shall be saved without being reformed into spiritual feeling, so that it could feel devotion and spiritual savor in God (as some souls do through special grace), then few souls should be saved in comparison with the multitude of others. No, that is not to be believed—that only for those souls that are devout and come by grace to spiritual feeling, and for no more, our Lord Jesus should have taken human nature and suffered the hard passion of death. It would have been a small gain for him, to come from so far to so near, and from so high to so low, for so few souls. No, his mercy is spread more widely than that.

Yet on the other hand, if you believe that the passion of our Lord is so precious and his mercy so great that no soul shall be damned—especially of any Christian man, whatever evil he does—as some fools suppose, you are certainly in great error. Therefore take the middle way and keep yourself there, and believe as holy church believes: that if the most sinful man that lives on earth turns his will (through grace and with true repentance) from mortal sin to the service of God, he is reformed in his soul; and if he dies in that state he shall be saved. Our Lord made such a promise through his prophet, saying thus: *In quacumque hora conversus peccator et ingemuerit, vita vivet et non morietur.*[37] That is, At whatever time the sinful man is turned to God from sin and has sorrow for it, he shall live, and he shall not die eternally. And so on the other hand, whoever lies in mortal sin, and will not leave it or correct himself from it or receive the sacrament of penance, or else if he does receive it he does not take it truly for love of God,[38] that is, for love of virtue and purity, but only for fear or shame of the world, or else only for dread of the pains of hell: he is not reformed to the likeness of God. And if he dies in that plight he shall not be saved; his faith shall not save him, for his faith is a dead faith, lacking love, and therefore it is of no avail to him. But those who have faith quickened through love and charity are reformed to the likeness of God: even though it is the least degree of charity,[39] as with simple souls who do not feel the gift of special devotion or spiritual knowledge of God as some spiritual men do, but believe in a general way as holy church believes without fully knowing what that is, for they have no need. And in that faith they keep themselves in love and charity toward their fellow Christians as far as they can, fleeing all mortal sins according to their knowledge, and doing the works of mercy toward their fellow Christians. All these belong to the bliss of heaven, for so it is written in the Apocalypse: *Qui timetis Deum, pusilli et magni, laudate eum.*[40] This is, You that fear God, both small and great, thank him. By "great" are understood souls that are proficient in grace, or else perfect in the love of God, who are reformed in spiritual feeling. By "small" are understood the imperfect souls of worldly men and women, and others that have only a child's knowledge of God and very little feeling of him but are brought up in the bosom of holy church and nourished with the sacraments as children are fed with milk.[41] All these shall praise God and thank him for the salvation of their souls by his infinite mercy and goodness. For holy church, who is mother of all these and has tender love for all her spiritual children, prays and pleads for them all tenderly to her Spouse, that is, Jesus, and gets for them healing of soul by virtue of his passion, especially for those that do not know how to speak for themselves for their own need by means of spiritual prayer.

Thus I find in the gospel that the woman of Canaan[42] asked our Lord for the healing of her daughter, who was troubled by a devil; and our Lord at first made a difficulty, because she was a foreigner. Nevertheless, she did not stop crying until he had granted her request and spoke to her like this: "Ah woman, great is your faith. May it be for you just as you wish." And in the same hour her daughter was made well. This woman signifies holy church, asking our Lord's help for the simple ignorant souls that are troubled with worldly temptations and do not know how to speak perfectly to God with fervor in devotion or burning love in contemplation; and although it may seem that our Lord at first makes a difficulty because they are as it were alienated from him, nevertheless because of the great faith and merit of holy church he grants her all she wants. And so these simple souls who believe steadfastly as holy church believes, putting themselves wholly in the mercy of God and humbling themselves beneath holy church's sacraments and laws, are made safe through the prayer and faith of their spiritual mother, who is holy church.

11. That reformed souls always need to fight and strive against stirrings of sin as long as they live here; and how a soul may know when it consents to stirrings, and when not.

This reforming in faith is easily acquired,[43] but it cannot so easily be held. And so for anyone who is reformed in faith to the likeness of God there is need for great toil and diligence if he wants to keep this image whole and clean, so that it does not relapse through weakness of will into the image of sin. He cannot be idle or heedless, for the image of sin is fastened to him so closely and so continually presses upon him with diverse stirrings of sin that unless he is very wary he will quite easily consent and fall into it again. Therefore he needs always to be striving and fighting against wicked stirrings from this image of sin, and to make no agreement or friendship with it, to be obedient to its irrational biddings, for if he does he deceives himself. But in truth if he strives with them there is not much fear of his consenting, for strife breaks peace and false accord. It is good for a man to have peace with everything except with the devil and with this image of sin, for against them he must always fight—in his thought and in his deed—until he has gained the mastery over them; and that shall never be complete in this life as long as he bears and feels this image. I do not deny that a soul may through grace have the upper hand over this image, to such an extent that he shall not follow or consent to its irrational stirrings; but to be so completely delivered from this image that he should feel no temptation, or the jabbering of any carnal affection or vain thought at any time—no man can have that in this life.

I suppose that a soul who by the ravishing[44] of love is reformed in feeling into the contemplation of God may be so far from the sensuality[45] and from vain imagination, and so far drawn out and parted for a time from the feeling of the flesh, that it shall feel nothing but God; but that does not last for ever. And therefore I say that everyone ought to strive against this image of sin, and especially the man who is reformed only in faith and can so easily be deceived. In the person of these men St. Paul speaks thus: *Caro concupiscit adversus spiritum, et spiritus adversus carnem.*[46] That is, A soul reformed to the likeness of God fights against the carnal stirrings of this image of sin, and in the same way this image of sin strives against the will of the spirit. St. Paul knew this kind of fighting with this double image when he spoke thus: *Inveni legem in membris meis repugnantem legi mentis meae, et captivum me ducentem in legem peccati.*[47] That is, I have found two laws in myself: one law in my soul within, and another outside in my bodily limbs, fighting with it, that often leads me like a wretched prisoner to the law of sin. By these two laws in a soul I understand this double image: by the law of the spirit I understand the reason of the soul when it is reformed to the image of God; by the law of the flesh I understand the sensuality, which I call the image of sin. In these two laws a reformed soul leads his life as St. Paul says: *Mente enim servio legi Dei, carne vero legi peccati.*[48] In my soul, that is, in my will and in my reason, I serve the law of God; but in my flesh, that is, in my carnal appetite, I serve the law of sin. Nevertheless, so that a reformed soul shall not despair, even though he serves the law of sin by feeling the vicious sensuality against the will of the spirit, because of the corruption of the bodily nature, St. Paul excuses it, speaking like this in his own person: *Non enim quod volo bonum hoc ago; sed malum quod odi, hoc facio. Si autem malum quod odi hoc facio, non ego operor illud, sed quod habitat in me, peccatum.*[49] I do not perform the good that I would like to do, that is, I would like to feel no carnal stirring, and that I do not; but I do the evil that I hate, that is, the sinful stirrings of my flesh. I hate them and yet I feel them. Nevertheless, since it is the case that I hate the wicked stirrings of my flesh and yet I feel them and often delight in them against my will, they shall not be brought against me for condemnation as if I had done them, and why? Because the corruption of this image of sin does them, and not I.

See, here in his own person St. Paul comforts all souls that through grace are reformed in faith, so that they should not fear the burden of this image too much with its irrational stirrings, provided they do not deliberately consent to them. Nevertheless, on this point many souls that are reformed in faith are often much tormented and troubled in vain. For example, when they have felt carnal stirrings of pride, envy, covetousness or lechery, or of any other capital sin, they sometimes do not know whether they consented to them or not. And that is no great wonder, for in time of temptation a frail man's thought is so troubled and so oppressed that he has no clear sight or freedom[50] in himself, but is often caught unwarily with pleasure and goes on a long time before he notices it. And therefore some fall into doubt and bewilderment as to whether they have sinned in time of temptation or not.

On this point, I say (as it appears to me) that a soul may have proof in this way as to whether he has consented or not. If it so happens that anyone is stirred to any kind of sin, and the pleasure is so great in his carnal feeling that it disturbs his reason and occupies the affection of the soul as if by force; and if nevertheless he keeps hold of himself, in that he does not follow it in deed, and would not want to if he could, but rather finds it painful to feel the pleasure of that sin, and would willingly put it away if he could; and if then, when the stirring has passed off, he is glad and well-content to be delivered from it: by this test he may know that he did not consent, however great the pleasure might be in the carnal feeling; and he did not sin, at any rate mortally.

Nevertheless, there is a sure remedy for such a simple soul that is troubled in itself and does not know how to help itself: not to be too bold in himself, fully reckoning that such fleshly stirrings with pleasure are not sins, for in that way he could fall into heedlessness and false confidence. Neither should he be too fearful, or too simple in wit, rating them all as mortal sins, or as great venial ones: for neither is true; but let him regard them all as sins and wretchedness of his own, and let him have sorrow for them, and not be too much concerned with judging them mortal or venial.[51] But if his conscience is greatly troubled, he should hasten to show his confessor such stirrings, in general or in particular, and especially any evil stirring that begins to take root in the heart and occupy it most, to draw it down to sin and worldly vanities. When he has thus made confession in general or in particular, let him believe steadfastly that they are forgiven, and not debate any more about those that are forgiven and past, as to whether they were mortal or venial; but let him take more care and guard himself better against those that are to come. And if he does so, then he can come to rest of conscience.

But some are then so carnal and so ignorant that they want to feel or hear or see the forgiveness of their sins as openly as they can feel or see a bodily thing, and because they do not feel like this they often fall into such hesitations and doubts about themselves, and can never come to rest. In that they are not wise, for faith goes before feeling. Our Lord said so to a man who was paralyzed, when he healed him: *Confide fili, remittuntur tui peccata tua.*[52] That is, Son, believe steadfastly, your sins are forgiven you. He did not say to him, "See or feel how your sins are forgiven you"—for forgiveness of sin is done spiritually and invisibly through the grace of the Holy Spirit—but *believe* it.

In just the same way, everyone who wants to come to rest of conscience should first do all that in him lies to believe in the forgiveness of his sins, without spiritual feeling; and if he first believes it he shall afterward through grace feel it and understand it, that it is so. Thus spoke the Apostle: *Nisi credideritis non intelligetis.*[53] That is, Unless you first believe, you cannot understand. Faith goes before, and understanding comes after;[54] and that understanding I call the sight of God (if it is by his grace), which a soul cannot have except through great purity, as our Lord says: *Beati mundo corde, quoniam ipsi Deum videbunt.*[55] Blessed be the pure of heart, for they shall see God. That is, They shall see God—not with their fleshly eye, but with the inner eye that is understanding, cleansed and illumined through grace of the Holy Spirit to see the truth. A soul cannot feel this purity unless he already has a firm faith, as the Apostle says: *Fide mundans corda eorum,*[56] That is, Our Lord cleanses the hearts of his chosen through faith. Therefore, a soul needs first to believe in the reforming of himself made through the sacrament of penance, even though he does not see it, and to prepare himself fully to live a just and virtuous life as his faith asks, so that he may afterward come to the sight, and to the reforming in feeling.

12. That this image is both fair and foul while it is in this life, even though it is reformed; and the difference in hidden feeling between reformed and unreformed souls.

Therefore a man's soul is fair, and a man's soul is foul: fair inasmuch as it is reformed in faith to the likeness of God, but foul inasmuch as it is still mixed with the fleshly feelings and irrational stirrings of this foul image of sin. Foul without as if it were a beast; fair within like an angel. Foul in the feeling of the sensuality; fair in the faith of the reason. Foul for the fleshly appetite; fair for the good will. So fair and so foul is a chosen soul, as holy scripture says: *Nigra sum sed formosa, filiae Jerusalem, sicut tabernacula cedar et sicut pellis Salomonis.*[57] That is, I am black, but I am fair and shapely, you daughters of Jerusalem, as the tabernacles of cedar and as the skin of Solomon. That is, You angels of heaven who are daughters of the Jerusalem on high, do not wonder at me or despise me for my black shadow, for though because of my carnal nature I am outwardly black like a tabernacle of cedar, nevertheless I am wholly fair within, like the skin of Solomon, for I am reformed to the likeness of God.

By cedar is understood darkness,[58] and that is the devil; by a tabernacle of cedar is understood a damned soul, which is a tabernacle of the devil. By Solomon, which means *peaceable*,[59] is understood our Lord Jesus, for he is peace, and peaceable. By the skin of Solomon is understood a blessed angel[60] in whom our Lord dwells and is hidden, as life is hidden within the skin of a living body; and therefore an angel is likened to a skin. Therefore, a chosen soul with humble trust in God and gladness of heart can speak like this: "Although because of my body of sin I am black like a damned soul—that is, one of the tabernacles of the devil—nevertheless through faith and a good will I am all fair within, like an angel of heaven." For so he says in another place: *Nolite considerare me quod fusca sum, quoniam decoloravit me sol.*[61] That is, Do not look at me because I am dark, for the sun has disfigured me. The sun makes a skin dark only on the outside, and not within, and it signifies this life in the flesh. And so a chosen soul speaks thus: "Do not condemn me because I am dark; for the darkness that I have is all without, through touching and bearing this image of sin; but it is nothing within." There-fore, although it so happens that a chosen soul reformed in faith dwells in this body of sin, feels the same carnal stirrings, and does in its body the same works as a tabernacle of cedar, to such a length that in the judgment of man there should be no difference between the one and the other: nevertheless inwardly in their souls there is a very great differ-ence, and in the sight of God there is a very great distinction; but the knowledge of this—which is one and which the other—is kept for God alone, for it surpasses the judgment and feeling of man. Therefore, we should judge nobody as evil for something that may be used both well and ill, for a soul that is not reformed is so completely taken with the love of the world and so far overwhelmed with the pleasure of his flesh in all his sensuality that he chooses it as the full rest of his heart; and in his hidden purpose he wants nothing else, but always to be sure of it. He feels no liquor of grace stirring him to loathe this fleshly life or to desire heavenly joy; and therefore I can say that he does not bear this image of sin, but he is borne by it, like a man so sick and so weak that he could not carry himself, and therefore he is laid on a bed and carried on a litter. In just this way such a sinful soul is so weak and so powerless for lack of grace that he can move neither hand nor foot to do any good deed, or to set the displeasure of his will against the least stirring of sin when it comes, but he falls upon it like a beast upon a carcass.

But even though a soul that is reformed may use his carnal senses and feel carnal stirrings, he loathes them nevertheless in his heart, since he would not fully rest in them for anything; but he flees from that rest as from the bite of an adder, and would rather have his rest and the love of his heart in God if he knew how, sometimes longing for it and often finding the pleasure of this life irksome for love of the life everlasting. This soul is not carried in the image of sin like a sick man, even though he feels it, but he carries it; for through grace he is made mighty and strong to suffer and bear his body, with all its evil stirrings, without hurting or defiling himself; and that is inasmuch as he does not love them or pursue them or consent to those which are mortal sins, as the other does.

This was given bodily fulfilment in the gospel story of a man with paralysis who was so feeble that he could not walk, and therefore was laid and carried on a litter and brought to our Lord. When our Lord saw him in trouble, of his goodness he spoke to him like this: *Surge et tolle grabatum tuum, et vade in domum tuam.*[62] That is, Rise up and take your bed and go into your house. And so he did, and was well. And indeed, just as this man when he was healed carried on his back the bed that before carried him, so it may be said spiritually that a soul reformed in faith carries this image of sin which carried him before. Therefore, do not be too afraid of the blackness that you have from bearing this image of sin, except for the shame and discomfort that you have from beholding it, and also the upbraiding that you feel in your heart from your spiritual enemies, when they speak to you thus: "Where is your Lord Jesus? What are you looking for? Where is your fairness that you talk about? What do you feel apart from blindness and sin? Where is that image of God that you say is reformed in you?" Fortify yourself strongly with faith, as I have said before, and if you do so you shall by this faith destroy all the temptations of your enemies. The apostle Paul said this: *Accipe scutum fidei in quo tela hostis nequissima poteris extinguere.*[63] That is, Take to yourself a shield of steadfast faith through which you can quench all the burning darts of your enemy.

13. Three kinds of people, of whom some are not reformed, some are reformed only in faith, and some in faith and in feeling.

By what I have said before you can see that according to the diverse parts of the soul there are diverse states of people.[64] Some are not reformed to the likeness of God, some are reformed only in faith, and some are reformed in faith and in feeling.

For you are to understand that a soul has two parts.[65] One is called the sensuality: that is the carnal feeling through the five outward senses which is common to man and beast. From this sensuality, when it is irrationally and inordinately ruled, is made the image of sin, as I have said before, for the sensuality is sin when it is not ruled according to reason.

The other part is called reason, and that is divided in two, into the higher part and the lower part. The higher part is compared to a man, for it should be master and sovereign, and that is properly the image of God, for by that alone the soul knows God and loves him. The lower part is compared to a woman, for it should be obedient to the higher part of reason as woman is obedient to man, and that lies in the knowledge and rule of earthly things, to use them discerningly according to need and to refuse them when there is no need; at the same time always to have an eye raised to the higher part of reason, with reverence and fear, in order to follow it. Now, I can say that a soul living according to the pleasures and lusts of his flesh like a beast without reason, and having neither knowledge of God nor the desire for virtues or the good life, but all blinded with pride, gnawed by envy, oppressed with covetousness, and defiled with lechery and other great sins, is not reformed to the likeness of God, for it lies and rests wholly in the image of sin, that is, the sensuality. Another soul that fears God, withstands the impulses of the sensuality to mortal sin and does not follow them, but lives rationally in the rule and control of worldly things, directing his purpose and his will to please God by his outward works: he is reformed in faith to the likeness of God; and though he feels the same stirrings of sin as the other did it shall not harm him, for he does not rest in them as the other does. But another soul that through grace flees all the stirrings of the sensuality to mortal sin—and to venial sins as well—to such a length that he does not feel them: he is reformed in feeling, for he follows the higher part of reason in beholding God and spiritual things, as I shall tell you later.

14. How people in sin deform themselves into the likeness of various beasts, and they are called lovers of this world.

Anyone is wretched, then, if he does not know the dignity of his soul[66] and does not want to know it: how it is the most honorable creature that God ever made, except an angel, whom it resembles; high above every other bodily race, whom no rest can fully satisfy save God alone.[67] And therefore he should not love or like anything but him, neither desiring nor seeking anything but how he could be reformed to his likeness. But because he does not know this he seeks and desires his rest and his pleasure outwardly, in bodily creatures worse than he is himself. He behaves unnaturally and acts unreasonably[68] when he leaves the supreme good and everlasting life that is God unsought and unloved, unknown and unworshipped, and chooses his rest and his glory in the passing delight of an earthly thing.[69] Nevertheless so do all the lovers of this world who have their joy and their glory in this wretched life. Some have it in pride and vainglory in themselves, so that when they have lost the fear of God they toil and study night and day how to come to the honor and praise of the world, and do not care how, provided they get to it and surpass all others in learning or in a craft, in name or in fame, in riches and in reverence, in sovereignty and power, in high estate and lordship. Some men have their delight and their rest in riches and in having outrageous earthly wealth, setting their hearts so fully on getting it that they seek nothing else but how they might come by it. Some have their pleasure in the fleshly lust of gluttony and lechery, and in other bodily uncleanness, and some in one thing and some in another.

This is the wretched way that people behave when they misshape themselves from the dignity of man and turn into the likeness of various beasts.[70] The proud man is turned into a lion because of his pride, for he would be feared and honored by all men, wanting no one to withstand the fulfillment of his worldly will either by word or by deed; and if anyone wants to hinder the wrongful pride of his will, he grows cruel and angry, desiring his revenge on him as a lion avenges himself on a little beast. The man who behaves thus is no man, for he acts unreasonably, against the nature of man, and so he is turned and transformed into a lion. Envious and angry men are turned into dogs through wrath and envy: they bark against their fellow Christians and bite them with wicked and malicious words, harassing those that have not trespassed with wrongful deeds, and harming them in body and soul against God's command. Some men are changed into asses; these are slow in the service of God and grudge doing any good deed to their fellow Christians. They are ready enough to run to Rome for worldly profit and for earthly honor, or to give pleasure to an earthly man, but they are soon irked if it is for spiritual reward—to help their own souls—or for the honor of God. They want nothing of it, and if they do anything they go only a step—and that with a contrary will. Some are turned into pigs, for they are so blind in their wits and so like beasts in their ways that they have no fear of God, but follow only the lusts and pleasures of their flesh, without regard to the decency of man, either to rule themselves as reason bids, or to restrain the irrational stirrings of the carnal nature; but as soon as a carnal stirring of sin comes they are ready to fall to and follow it as pigs do. Some men are turned into wolves that live by seizing their prey, like false covetous men who through force and oppression rob their fellow Christians of their worldly goods. Some men are turned into foxes, like false and deceitful men that live in trickery and fraud.

All these, and many more who do not live in fear of God but break his commandments, deform themselves from the likeness of God and make themselves like beasts, yes, and worse than beasts! For they are like the devil of hell. And therefore it is certain, if these men who live so are not reformed when the hour of death comes and their souls have left their bodies, then their eyes (which now are blocked with sin) shall be opened, and then they shall feel and find the punishment for their wickedness that they lived in here; and because here in this life the image of God was not reformed in them through the sacrament of penance, either in faith or in feeling, they shall be cast out as accursed from the blessed face of our Creator, and they shall be damned with the devil into the depths of hell, there to stay forever, without end. John says so in the Apocalypse: *Tumidis et incredulis, execratis et homicidis, fornicatoribus, veneficis et idolatris et omnibus mendacibus, pars illorum erit in stagno ardenti igne et sulphure.*[71] That is, to proud men and unbelievers, to the accursed and to murderers, to the lecherous and the covetous, to poisoners and to worshippers of idols, and to all false liars: their lot shall be with the devil in the pit of hell, burning with fire and brimstone. If the lovers of this world would often think about this—how all this world shall pass and draw to an end, and how hard all wicked love shall be punished—in a short time they would loathe all the worldly pleasure that they now like most, and they would lift up their hearts to love God, and they would busily search and labor to be reformed to his likeness before they pass away.

15.　How in various ways the lovers of this world make themselves unable to reform their own souls.

But now some of them speak like this: "I would willingly love God, be a good person and forsake the love of the world if I could, but I have no grace for it. If I had the same grace as a good man has I should do as he does, but because I do not have it, I cannot; and so I am not to blame, but I am excused."

To these people I speak thus: What they say is true—that they have no grace and therefore lie still in their sin and cannot rise out of it—but that does not avail them or excuse them before God, for it is their own fault. In various ways they so disenable themselves that the light of grace cannot shine on them or rest in their hearts; for some are so perverse that they do not want grace, and will not be good, since they well know that if they were to be good they would have to abstain from the great pleasure and delight of this world that they find in earthly things: and that they will not do, for it seems to them so sweet that they do not want to forgo it. And also they would have to undertake works of penance such as fasting, waking, praying and other good practices in order to chastise their flesh and restrain their carnal will: and that they cannot do, for it is made so sharp and so frightful to their mind that they dread and loathe thinking about it; and in this cowardly and wretched way they go on living in their sin. Some—so it seems—do wish for grace and begin to fit themselves for it, but their will is very weak, for as soon as any stirring of sin comes they at once fall in with it, although it is contrary to God's bidding. They are so bound by their previous habit of often falling into sin and consenting to it that it seems to them impossible to resist, and thus the pretended hardness of performance weakens their will and knocks it down again. Others too feel the stirring of grace, as when their conscience bites them for their evil living and urges them to leave it; but that is so painful for them and so burdensome that they will not endure it or stay with it, but escape from it and forget it if they can, to such lengths that they seek pleasure and comfort outwardly in fleshly creatures, rather than feel this biting of conscience[72] within their soul.

Moreover, some people are so blind and so bestial that they suppose there is no other life but this, and that a man has no more soul than a beast, but that the soul of man dies with the body like the soul of a beast; and therefore they say, "Let us eat, drink and make merry here, for we are sure of this life: we see no other heaven." Certainly there are some wretches who say such things in their hearts, though they do not say them with their mouths. The prophet speaks like this of such people: *Dixit insipiens in corde suo, non est Deus.*[73] That is, The unwise man said in his heart, there is no God. This unwise man is every wretched person who lives loving sin and choosing the love of this world as rest for his soul. He says there is no God: not with his mouth, for he will speak of him sometimes when he is doing well materially, as it were in reverence, when he says, "Blessed be God"; and sometimes in defiance when he is angry against God or his fellow Christian and swears by his blessed body or any of his parts. But in his thought he says there is no God; and that is either because he thinks God does not see his sin, or that he will not punish it as hard as holy scripture says, or that he will forgive him his sin even though he does not leave it, or else that no Christian man shall be damned however wickedly he behaves; or else—if he fasts on our Lady's fast,[74] daily says a certain prayer, or hears two or three Masses every day, or does a certain bodily deed as if to honor God—he shall never go to hell however great his sin, and even though he does not forsake it. This man says in his heart, There is no God; but he is unwise, as the prophet says. For in pain he shall feel and find that God is the one whom he forgot and thought nothing of in the prosperity of this world; as the prophet says, *Sola vexatio dabit intellectum auditui.*[75] That is, Only pain shall give understanding. For anyone who does not know this here, and will not know it, shall know it well when he is in pain.

16. A little advice on what lovers of this world should do if they want to be reformed in soul before they leave here.

Although these people well know that they are out of grace and in mortal sin, they have no care, sorrow or thought for it but get as much carnal enjoyment and worldly solace as they can; the further they are from grace, the more they make merry; and perhaps some feel well pleased to have no grace, so that they can (as it were) pursue the pleasure of carnal desires the more fully and freely, as though God were asleep and could not see them: and this is one of the greatest offenses. And so by their own perversity they block out the light of grace from their own soul, so that it cannot rest there. This grace shines—as much as in it lies—for all spiritual creatures, ready to enter wherever it is received, just as the sun shines upon all material creatures wherever it is not impeded. St. John says so in the gospel: *Lux in tenebris lucet, et tenebrae eam non comprehenderunt.*[76] That is, The light of grace shines in darkness, that is, into men's hearts that are darkened by sin, but the darkness does not take it. That is, These blind hearts do not receive that light of grace and do not have the benefit of it, but, just as a blind man is all enfolded[77] by the light of the sun when he stands in it, and yet he neither sees it nor has the advantage of walking by it, likewise in the spirit a soul blinded by mortal sin has this spiritual light all about him, and yet he is none the better, for he is blind and will not see or admit his blindness. And that is one of the greatest hindrances to grace, that from pride in himself a wretched man will not acknowledge his own blindness; or if he does he gives it no weight, but jokes and makes fun of it as if he were secure on all sides.

Therefore, I speak to all these people who are thus blinded and bound with the love of this world and are so vilely misshapen from the beauty of man, and I counsel them to think of their souls, and to fit themselves for grace as much as they can; and if they will, they can do it like this. When they feel themselves to be out of grace and overwhelmed with mortal sin, then let them think how bad and how perilous it is for them to be out of grace, and separated from God as they are, for there is nothing to hold them from the pit of hell and keep them from falling straight into it but the one bare single thread of this bodily life on which they hang. What can be lost more easily than a single thread [that] may be broken in two? For if the breath were stopped in their body (as can easily happen), their soul would pass forth and at once be in hell, eternally. And if only they would think in this way, they would quake and tremble for dread of the righteous judgments of God and of the hard punishment for sin; and they would sorrow and mourn for their sin and for their lack of grace. Then they would call out and pray that they might have grace; and if they did so, then grace would fall upon them and drive out the darkness and hardness of heart and weakness of will, and give them power and strength to forsake the false love of this world, inasmuch as it is[78] mortal sin. For there is no soul so far from God through wickedness of will in mortal sin—I except no one that lives in this body of sin—that he cannot through grace be set right and reformed to cleanness of living, if in humility he will bow his will to God in order to amend his life, and heartily ask him for grace and forgiveness, acquitting our Lord and taking all the blame upon himself. For holy scripture says: *Nolo mortem peccatoris, sed magis ut convertatur et vivat.*[79] That is, Our Lord says, I do not want the death of a sinner, but I would rather he were turned to me and should live. For our Lord wants the most perverse man alive—distorted through sin—to be reformed to his likeness, if he turns his will and asks for grace.

17. That reforming in feeling and in faith cannot be acquired suddenly, but over a long time, by grace and much toil of body and spirit.

This reforming is in faith, as I have said before, and it can be had easily; but after this comes reforming in faith and in feeling, which may not so easily be acquired, but through long toil and great effort. Reforming in faith is common to all chosen souls, though they are only in the lowest degree of charity; but reforming in feeling pertains especially to such souls as can come to the state of perfection—and that cannot be had suddenly: but a soul can come to it after great abundance of grace and great spiritual labor, and that is when he is first healed of his spiritual sickness, when all bitter passions, carnal pleasures and other old feelings are burnt out of the heart with the fire of desire, and new gracious feelings are brought in, with burning love and spiritual light: then a soul draws near to perfection and to reforming in feeling. For certainly, if anyone is brought near to death through bodily sickness and receives a medicine by which he is restored and made sure of his life, he cannot as a result get up at once and go to work like a fit man, since the feebleness of his body holds him down; so he must wait a good while, looking after himself well with medicines and taking a measured diet—on the instructions of a doctor—until he can fully recover his bodily health. Just so in the spirit: someone who is brought to spiritual death through mortal sin is not at once healed of all his passions and all his fleshly desires, nor is he capable of contemplation, even though he is restored to life through the medicine of the sacrament of penance, so that he shall not be damned. But he ought to wait a great while and take good care of himself and rule himself, in order to recover full health of soul, for he shall languish a great while before he is fully healed. However, if he takes medicines from a good doctor and uses them at the right time, with careful measurement, he shall be restored to his spiritual strength much the sooner, and come to reforming in feeling.

For reforming in faith is the lowest state of all chosen souls, since below that they could not well be,[80] but reforming in feeling is the highest state that the soul may come to in this life. But a soul cannot suddenly jump from the lowest to the highest,[81] any more than someone wanting to climb a high ladder[82] and setting his foot upon the lowest rung can next fly up to the highest. He needs to go gradually, one after another, until he can come to the top. It is just the same spiritually. Nobody is suddenly made perfect in grace, but through long exercise and skilled working a soul may come to it, especially when a wretched soul is taught and helped by him in whom lies all grace. For no soul can come to it without special help[83] and inward teaching from him.

18. The reason why so few souls come to this reforming in faith and in feeling, compared with the multitude of others.

But now you say, "Since our Lord is so courteous in his goodness, and so free with his gracious gifts, it is a wonder that so few souls—as it seems in comparison with the multitude of others—can come to this reforming in feeling. It seems as if he were hard to please—and that is not true—or that he had no concern for his creatures who by receiving faith have become his servants."

To this I may answer and say, as it seems to me, that one reason is this. Many people that are reformed in faith do not set their hearts on profiting[84] in grace, or on seeking any higher state of godly living through diligence in prayer and meditation, and other work of body and spirit. They are satisfied to stand still in their present state by keeping themselves out of mortal sin; for they say that to be saved is enough for them, and to have the lowest degree in heaven. They have no desire for more. So perhaps do some of the chosen souls that lead the active life in the world, and in them that is not surprising, for they are so occupied with the worldly business that has to be done that they cannot set their hearts entirely on profiting in spiritual working. Nevertheless it is perilous for them, for they fall out and in all day, and are now up and now down, and cannot come to the stability of godly living. However, they can to some extent be excused because of their state of living. But other men and women who if they wish are free from worldly business, and can have their needs supplied without great practical effort, as can religious men and women particularly, who bind themselves to the state of perfection by taking religious vows, and others too in secular state who have great reasoning power and natural judgment, and could if they wished prepare themselves to come to abundant grace: these people are more to blame, because they stand still as if they were idle, and will not profit in grace or seek any further to come to the love and knowing of God.

There is indeed danger for a soul that is reformed only in faith and does not want to seek or profit any more, or give himself diligently to labor of body or spirit, because like this he may easily lose what he has and fall again into mortal sin. While a soul is in the flesh it cannot stand still all the time in one condition,[85] for it is either profiting in grace or lapsing in sin. It happens with him as it does with a man dragged out of a pit,[86] who, when he was up, wanted to go no further than the brink: he would certainly be a great fool, for a little puff of wind or some unwary movement of his own could quickly throw him down again, worse than he was before. Nevertheless, if he escapes as far as he can from the brink, and moves forward over the ground, then he is safer—even though there came a great storm—for he does not fall into the pit. And so spiritually with someone who is pulled out of the pit of sin through reforming in faith; when he is out of mortal sin he thinks himself safe enough and therefore will not profit, but keeps still as he is, as near as possible to the pit's brink; indeed he is not wise, for at the least temptation of the Enemy or of his flesh he falls into sin again. However, if he flees from the pit—that is, if he fully sets his heart on coming to more grace and on toiling busily in order to come to it, and gives himself with a will to prayer, meditation and doing other good works—he will not easily fall into mortal sin again, even though great temptations rise against him.

And certainly it is a wonder to me, since grace is so good and so profitable, why someone having only a little of it—yes, so little that he could not have less—will say, "Ho! I don't want any more of this, for I have enough." At the same time I see that a secular person with far more worldly goods than he needs will never say, "Ho! I have enough, I want [no] more of this." But he will always crave more and more, toiling with all his faculties and all his powers, and will never stop coveting until he can have more. Much more, then, should a chosen soul crave spiritual goods, which are everlasting and make a soul blessed; and if he did well he should never stop coveting, but get what he can, for the one who covets most shall have the most; and indeed if he did this he should greatly profit and increase in grace.

19. Another reason for the same, and how self-imposed bodily practices, indiscreetly observed, sometimes hinder souls from feeling more grace.

Another reason is this. Some people who are reformed in faith at the beginning of their turning to God set themselves in a certain kind of exercise (whether of body or of spirit) and think always to keep to that way of working, and not to change it for any other that comes through grace, even though it were better, for they suppose that practice always to be best for them to keep, and therefore they rest in it, and so bind themselves to it by habit that when they have completed it they feel wonderfully at ease, thinking they have done a great thing for God; and if it happens by chance that they are hindered from their custom, they are angry and despondent—even though it may be for a reasonable cause —and their conscience is as troubled as if they had done a great mortal sin. To some degree these people hinder themselves from feeling more grace, for they set their perfection in a bodily work, and so they make an end in the middle of the way, where there is no end; for which reason the bodily practices that people use in their beginning are good, but they are only ways and means[87] of leading a soul to perfection; therefore if someone founds his perfection on a bodily work, or on a spiritual work that he feels at the beginning of his turning to God, and wants to seek no further, but always to rest there, he seriously hinders himself, for that is a feeble craft in which an apprentice has the same skill at all times, and which he knows as much of on the first day as he does twenty winters later, or else—if the craft is good and subtle—the man who makes no progress in it has a dull mind or a contrary will.

But then it is true that of all crafts that there are, the service of God is the most excellent and subtle, the highest and hardest to reach in its perfection, and also it is the most profitable, and most often gainful for one who can truly practice it. And therefore it seems that those apprentices who are always equally far on in learning it are either dull witted or else unwilling.

I do not condemn these practices that people use in the state of beginning, whether bodily or spiritual, for I say that they are very good and helpful for them to use; but I would like them to consider these only as an entrance and a way toward spiritual feeling, and to use them as a convenient means till better come. In using them they should long for something better: so if a better [gift[88]] should come—more spiritual, and stronger in drawing the thought from fleshliness and from the sensuality and vain imagination—and if that should be hindered through their usual practice, then let them then leave it, provided it can be left without scandal or distress to others, and follow what they feel. But if neither hinders the other, than let them use both if they can. I do not mean practices that are obligatory through bonds of law or rule, or of penance, but others taken by choice. So the prophet teaches us in the psalms, saying thus: *Etenim benedictionem dabit legislator, ibunt de virtute in virtutem, videbitur Deus deorum in Syon.*[89] That is, In truth the bringer of the Law shall give blessing; they shall go from strength to strength, and the God of gods shall be seen in Syon. The bringer of the law—that is, our Lord Jesus Christ—shall give his blessing; that is, he shall give his gifts of grace to his chosen souls, calling them from sin and justifying them by good works to his likeness, through which grace they shall profit and grow from strength to strength till they come to Syon; that is, until they come to contemplation, in which they shall see the God of gods; that is, they shall see clearly that there is no God but One, and they shall see that there exists nothing but God.

20. How souls cannot be reformed in feeling, or kept in it after attaining it, without great diligence in body and spirit, and without great humility and grace.

Now you say, "Since it is the case that reforming in faith is so low and so perilous to rest in, for fear of falling again, and reforming in feeling is so high and so secure for anyone who can come to it, then you long to know what kind of labor would be most useful in helping a man to be proficient and achieve it; or if there were any certain task or special work by which a man could come to that grace and reforming in feeling." To this I reply thus. You well know that any man or woman wishing to prepare for purity of heart and for a feeling of grace has need of great effort and hard fighting in will and in deed, to persevere against the wicked stirrings of all the capital sins: not only against pride or envy, but against all the others, with all the different kinds that come out of them, as I have said before in the first part of this writing, because passions and carnal desires hinder purity in the heart and peace in conscience. He should also labor in order to get all the virtues: not only chastity and abstinence, but also patience and mildness, charity and humility and all the others; and this cannot be done by one kind of work but through many different tasks, according to people's various dispositions: for instance, now praying, now meditating, now doing some good work, now trying himself in different ways—in hunger, thirst and cold,[90] in suffering shame and contempt, if need be, and in other bodily distresses—for love of virtue and righteousness. This you know well, for you read it in every book that teaches godly living. So also says everyone who wants to stir men's souls to the love of God.

And so it seems there is no special task or certain kind of work through which alone a soul might come to that grace, but it is chiefly through the grace of our Lord Jesus, and by many great works in all that he can do: and yet all is little enough. And one reason may be this. Since our Lord Jesus himself is the special master of this craft, and he is the special healer[91] of spiritual sickness (for without him all is nothing), it is therefore reasonable that as he teaches and stirs,[92] so a man follows and works. But it is a simple master who has the skill to teach his pupil only one lesson all the time he is learning, and only a foolish doctor who tries to heal all diseases with one medicine; therefore our Lord Jesus—who is so wise and so good—teaches various lessons to his disciples to show his wisdom and his goodness, according to their proficiency in learning; and to different souls he gives various medicines to suit the sickness that they feel.

And this too is another reason. If there were one certain deed by which a soul could come to the perfect love of God, a man should then suppose that he could come to it by his own work and through his own labor, as a merchant gets his profit by his own efforts alone, and by his own work. No, it is not like this spiritually, in the love of God. For anyone who wants to serve God wisely and come to the perfect love of God shall not covet any other reward, but him alone.[93] But then, no created being can deserve to have him by his own sole effort, for even if a man could labor as hard in body and spirit as all the creatures that ever existed, he could not by his works alone deserve to have God as his reward; for he is supreme bliss and infinite goodness, and beyond comparison surpasses all men's deserts; and therefore he may not be gained by any man's special work, as can a material prize. For he is free, and gives himself where he will[94] and when he will, neither for this work nor for that, neither in this time nor after that time. Although a soul works all his life with all his skill and strength, he shall never have a perfect love of Jesus until our Lord Jesus will freely give it.

Nevertheless, I say on the other hand that I do not think he gives it unless a man works and labors with all his skill and strength—yes, until he feels he can do no more—or else he fully intends to if he could. And so it seems that neither grace alone without the full working of a soul that is in it, nor work by itself without grace, brings a soul to that reforming in feeling which stands upon perfect love and charity.[95] But the one joined to the other—that is, grace joined to working—brings into a soul the blessed feeling of perfect love; and that grace cannot fully rest except on a humble soul full of the fear of God. I can therefore say that anyone without humility, or who neglects his duty, cannot come to this reforming in feeling. He has not complete humility if he does not know how to feel himself truly as he is,[96] as in this way. If anyone does all the good works that he knows, such as fasting, waking, wearing a hairshirt, and the suffering of every other bodily penance; or performs all the outward works of mercy to his fellow Christians, or else the inward ones such as praying, weeping, sighing and meditating; and if he always rests in them, leaning so much on them and regarding them so highly in his own sight that he presumes on his own merits and thinks himself always rich and good, holy and virtuous: certainly, as long as he feels like this he is not humble enough. And although he says or thinks that all he does is by the gift of God, and not from himself, he is not yet humble enough; for he cannot yet strip himself naked of all his good works, or make himself truly poor in spirit, or feel himself to be nothing —as he is. And certainly until a soul knows palpably by grace how to think himself nothing, and how to bare himself of all the good works that he does[97] through beholding the truth[98] of Jesus, he is not perfectly humble. For what is humility but truth?[99] It is indeed nothing else. And therefore the man who through grace may see Jesus—how he [Jesus] does everything, and how he himself does nothing at all, but allows Jesus to work in him whatever he pleases—he is humble. But this is very hard,[100] and as it were impossible and irrational for a man who works entirely by human reason and sees no further: to do many good works and then to ascribe them all to Jesus and value himself at nothing. Nevertheless for anyone with a spiritual sight of truth it should seem altogether true and reasonable to do so; and indeed anyone who has this sight shall never do less,[101] but he shall be stirred to labor much harder in body and spirit, and with a better will. And this may be one reason why some people perhaps toil and sweat and hurt their wretched body with outrageous penance all their life, and are always saying prayers and psalters and many other devotions, and yet they cannot come to that spiritual feeling of the love of God as it seems that some do in a short time with less pain: it is because they do not have that humility that I speak of.

Similarly, I say on the other hand that anyone who does not work diligently cannot come to the feeling of grace. He is not diligent in his duty if he thinks like this: To what purpose should I labor? To what end should I pray or meditate, wake or fast, or do any other bodily penance in order to come to such grace, since it cannot be acquired or had except by the free gift of Jesus? Therefore I will continue in the carnal state I am in, and do none at all of such works in body or spirit until he gives grace; for if he wishes to give it he asks for no labor from me: I shall have it whatever I do, and however little I do. And if he will not give it, I shall get it none the sooner however fast I labor for it.

Anyone who talks like this shall not come to this reforming, for he willfully turns to the idleness of the fleshly nature and disenables himself for the gift of grace, inasmuch as he rejects both the inward work that consists of lasting desire and longing for Jesus and the outward working done through the labor of his body in outward deeds. And in this way he cannot have it. Therefore I say that if a man is without true humility and heartfelt diligence—either inwardly alone by great fervor, lasting desire and busy prayer and meditation in God, or else both inwardly and outwardly—he cannot come to this spiritual reforming of his image.

21.   An introduction as to how a soul should behave in purpose and in practice if it wants to come to this reforming, through the example of a pilgrim going to Jerusalem; and the two kinds of humility.

Nevertheless, because you desire to have some kind of practice by which you could approach that reforming more quickly, I shall tell you by the grace of our Lord Jesus what seems to me the shortest and promptest aid that I know in this work. And how that shall be I will tell you in this manner, through the example of a good pilgrim.

There was a man wanting to go to Jerusalem,[102] and because he did not know the way he came to another man who he thought knew it and asked whether he could reach that city. The other man told him he could not get there without great hardship and labor, for the way is long and the perils are great, with thieves and robbers as well as many other difficulties to beset a man on his journey; also there are many different ways seeming to lead in that direction, yet people are being killed and robbed daily and cannot come to the place they desire. However, there is one way, and he would undertake that anyone who takes and keeps to it shall come to the city of Jerusalem, and never lose his life or be slain or die of want. He would often be robbed and badly beaten and suffer great distress on his journey, but his life would always be safe. Then the pilgrim said: "If it is true that I can keep my life and come to the place I desire, I do not care what trouble I suffer on the journey, and therefore tell me what you will, and I promise faithfully to do as you say." The other man answered and said this: "See, I am setting you on the right road. This is the way, and be sure to keep the instructions I give you."

"Whatever you hear, see or feel that would hinder you on your way, do not willingly stay with it,[103] and do not tarry for it, taking rest; do not look at it, do not take pleasure in it, and do not fear it; but always go forth on your way and think that you want to be in Jerusalem. For that is what you long for and what you desire,[104] and nothing else but that; and if men rob you, strip you, beat you, scorn you and despise you, do not fight back if you want to have your life, but bear the hurt that you have and go on as if it were nothing, lest you come to more harm. In the same way, if men want to delay you with stories and feed you with lies, trying to draw you to pleasures and make you leave your pilgrimage, turn a deaf ear and do not reply, saying only that you want to be in Jerusalem. And if men offer you gifts and seek to enrich you with worldly goods, pay no attention to them; always think of Jerusalem. And if you will keep on this way and do as I have said, I promise you your life—that you shall not be slain but come to the place that you desire."

According to our spiritual proposition, Jerusalem is as much as to say *sight of peace*[105] and stands for contemplation in perfect love of God, for contemplation is nothing other than a sight of Jesus, who is true peace. Then if you long to come to this blessed sight of true peace and to be a faithful pilgrim toward Jerusalem—even though it should be that I was never there, yet as far as I know—I shall set you in the way that leads toward it.

The beginning of the highway along which you shall go is reforming in faith, grounded humbly in the faith and in the laws of holy church, as I have said before, for trust assuredly that although you have formerly sinned, you are on the right road, if you are now reformed by the sacrament of penance according to the law of holy church. Now since you are on the sure way, if you want to speed on your travels and make a good journey each day, you should hold these two things often in your mind—humility and love. That is: *I am nothing; I have nothing; I desire only one thing.* You shall have the meaning of these words continually in your intention, and in the habit of your soul, even though you may not always have their particular form in your thought, for that is not necessary. Humility says, I am nothing; I have nothing. Love says, I desire only one thing, and that is Jesus. These two strings,[106] well-fastened with mindfulness of Jesus, make good harmony on the harp of the soul when they are skillfully touched with the finger of reason. For the lower you strike upon the one, the higher sounds the other; the less you feel that you are or that you have of yourself through humility, the more you long to have of Jesus in the desire of love. I do not mean only that humility[107] that a soul feels as it looks at its own sin or at the frailties and wretchedness of this life, or at the worthiness of his fellow Christians, for although this humility is true and medicinal, it is comparatively rough and carnal, not pure or soft or lovely. But I mean also this humility that the soul feels through grace in seeing and considering the infinite being and wonderful goodness of Jesus, and if you cannot see it yet with your spiritual eye, that you believe in it, for through the sight of his being—either in full faith or in feeling—you shall regard yourself not only as the greatest wretch[108] that there is, but also as nothing in the substance of your soul, even if you had never committed sin. And that is lovely humility, for in comparison with Jesus who is in truth All, you are but nothing. In the same way think that you have nothing, but are like a vessel that always stands empty, as if with nothing in it of your own: for however many good works you do, outwardly or inwardly, you have nothing at all until you have—and feel that you have—the love of Jesus. For your soul can be filled only with that precious liquor, and with nothing else; and because that thing alone is so precious and so valuable, regard anything you have or do as nothing to rest in, without the sight and the love of Jesus. Throw it all behind you and forget it,[109] so that you can have what is best of all.

Just as a true pilgrim going to Jerusalem leaves behind him house and land, wife and children,[110] and makes himself poor and bare of all that he has in order to travel light and without hindrance, so if you want to be a spiritual pilgrim you are to make yourself naked of all that you have— both good works and bad—and throw them all behind you; and thus become so poor in your own feeling that there can be no deed of your own that you want to lean upon for rest, but you are always desiring more grace of love, and always seeking the spiritual presence of Jesus. If you do so, you shall then set in your heart, wholly and fully, your desire to be at Jerusalem, and in no other place but there; and that is, you shall set in your heart, wholly and fully,[111] your will to have nothing but the love of Jesus and the spiritual sight of him, as far as he wishes to show himself. It is for that alone you are made and redeemed, and that is your beginning and your end, your joy and your glory. Therefore, whatso-ever you have, however rich you may be in other works of body and spirit, unless you have that, and know and feel that you have it, consider that you have nothing at all. Print this statement well on the intention of your heart, and hold firmly to it, and it will save you from all the perils of your journey, so that you will never perish. It shall save you from thieves and robbers (which is what I call unclean spirits),[112] so that though they strip you and beat you with diverse temptations, your life shall always be saved; and in brief if you guard it as I shall tell you, you shall within a short time escape all perils and distresses and come to the city of Jerusalem.

Now that you are on the road and know the name of the place you are bound for, begin to go forward on your journey. Your going forth is nothing else but the work of the spirit—and of the body as well, when there is need for it—which you are to use with discretion in the follow-ing way. Whatever work it is that you should do, in body or in spirit, according to the degree and state in which you stand,[113] if it helps this grace-given desire that you have to love Jesus, making it more whole, easier and more powerful for all virtues and all goodness, that is the work I consider the best, whether it be prayer,[114] meditation, reading or working; and as long as that task most strengthens your heart and your will for the love of Jesus and draws your affection and your thought farthest from worldly vanities, it is good to use it. And if it happens that the savor of it becomes less through use, and you feel that you savor another kind of work more, and you feel more grace in another, take another and leave that one. For though your desire and the yearning of your heart for Jesus should always be unchangeable, nevertheless the spiritual practices that you are to use in prayer or meditation to feed and nourish your desire may be diverse, and may well be changed according to the way you feel disposed to apply your own heart, through grace.

For it goes with works and desire as it does with a fire and sticks.[115] The more sticks are laid on a fire, the greater is the flame, and so the more varied the spiritual work that anyone has in mind for keeping his desire whole, the more powerful and ardent shall be his desire for God. Therefore notice carefully what work you best know how to do and what most helps you to keep whole this desire for Jesus (if you are free, and are not bound except under the common law), and do that. Do not bind yourself unchangeably to practices of your own choosing[116] that hinder the freedom of your heart to love Jesus if grace should specially visit you, for I shall tell you which customs are always good and need to be kept. See, a particular custom is always good to keep if it consists in getting virtue and hindering sin, and that practice should never be left. For if you behave well, you will always be humble and patient, sober and chaste; and so with all other virtues. But the practice of any other thing that hinders a better work should be left when it is time for one to do this: for instance, if somebody has the custom of saying so many prayers, or meditating in a certain way for a particular length of time, or waking or kneeling for a certain time, or doing other such bodily work, this practice is to be left off sometimes when a reasonable cause hinders it, or else if more grace comes from another quarter.

22.   The delays and temptations that souls shall feel from their spiritual enemies on their spiritual journey to the heavenly Jerusalem, and some remedies against them.

Now you are on the way and know how you shall go. Now beware of enemies that will be trying to hinder you if they can, for their intention is to put out of your heart that desire and that longing that you have for the love of Jesus, and to drive you home again to the love of worldly vanity, for there is nothing that grieves them so much. These enemies are principally carnal desires and vain fears that rise out of your heart through the corruption of your fleshly nature, and want to hinder your desire for the love of God, so that they can fully occupy your heart without disturbance. These are your nearest enemies. There are other enemies too, such as unclean spirits that are busily trying to deceive you with tricks and wiles. But you shall have one remedy, as I said before: whatever it may be that they say, do not believe them, but keep on your way and desire only the love of Jesus. Always give this answer: I am nothing; I have nothing; I desire nothing but the love of Jesus alone. If your enemies speak to you first like this, by stirrings in your heart, that you have not made a proper confession,[117] or that there is some old sin hidden in your heart that you do not know and never confessed, and therefore you must turn home again, leave your desire and go to make a better confession: do not believe this saying, for it is false and you are absolved. Trust firmly that you are on the road, and you need no more ransacking of your confession for what is past: keep on your way and think of Jerusalem. Similarly, if they say that you are not worthy to have the love of God, and ask what good it is to crave something you cannot have and do not deserve, do not believe them, but go forward, saying thus: "Not because I am worthy, but because I am unworthy—that is my motive for loving God, for if I had that love, it would make me worthy; and since I was made for it, even though I should never have it I will yet desire it; and therefore I will pray and meditate in order to get it." And then, if your enemies see that you begin to grow bold and resolute in your work, they start getting frightened of you; however, they will not stop hindering you when they can as long as you are going on your way. What with fear and menaces[118] on the one hand and flattery and false blandishment on the other, to make you break your purpose and turn home again, they will speak like this: "If you keep up your desire for Jesus, laboring as hard as you have begun, you will fall into sickness[119] or into fantasies and frenzies, as you see some do; or you will fall into poverty and come to bodily harm, and no one will want to help you; or you might fall into secret temptations of the devil, in which you will not know how to help yourself. It is very dangerous for any man to give himself wholly to the love of God, to leave all the world and desire nothing but his love alone; for so many perils may befall that one does not know of. And therefore turn home again and leave this desire, for you will never carry it through to the end, and behave as other people do in the world."

So say your enemies; but do not believe them. Keep up your desire, and say nothing else but that you want to have Jesus and to be in Jerusalem. And if they then perceive your will to be so strong that you will not spare yourself—for sin or for sickness, for fantasies or frenzy, for doubts or fears of spiritual temptations, for poverty or distress, for life or for death—but that your will is set ever onward, with one thing and one alone, turning a deaf ear to them as if you did not hear them, and keeping on stubbornly and unstintingly with your prayers and your

231

other spiritual works, and with discretion according to the counsel of your superior or your spiritual father: then they begin to be angry and to draw a little nearer to you. They start robbing you and beating you and doing you all the injury they know: and that is when they cause all your deeds—however well done—to be judged evil by others and turned the worst way. And whatever you may want to do for the benefit of your body and soul, it will be hampered and hindered by other men, in order to thwart you in everything that you reasonably desire. All this they do to stir you to anger, resentment or ill-will against your fellow Christians.

But against all these annoyances, and all others that may befall, use this remedy: take Jesus in your mind, and do not be angry with them; do not linger with them, but think of your lesson—that you are nothing, you have nothing, you cannot lose any earthly goods, and you desire nothing but the love of Jesus—and keep on your way to Jerusalem, with your occupation. Nevertheless, if through your own frailty you are at some time vexed with such troubles befalling your life in the body through the ill-will of man or the malice of the devil, come to yourself again as soon as you can; stop thinking of that distress and go forth to your work. Do not stay too long with them, for fear of your enemies.

23. A general remedy against wicked stirrings and painful vexations that befall the heart from the world, the flesh and the devil.

And after this your enemies will be much abashed, when they see you so well-disposed that you are not annoyed, heavyhearted, wrathful, or greatly stirred against any creature, for anything that they can do or say against you, but that you fully set your heart upon bearing all that may happen—ease and hardship, praise or blame—and that you will not trouble about anything, provided you can keep whole your thought and your desire for the love of God. But then they will try you with flattery and vain blandishment, and that is when they bring to the sight of your soul all your good deeds and virtues,[120] and impress upon you that all men praise you and speak of your holiness; and how everybody loves you and honors you for your holy living. Your enemies do this to make you think that their talk is true, and take delight in this vain joy and rest in it; but if you do well you shall hold all such vain jabbering as the falsehood and flattery of your enemy, who proffers you a drink of venom tempered with honey. Therefore refuse it: say you do not want any of it, but you want to be in Jerusalem.

You shall feel such hindrances, or others like them—what with your flesh, the world and the devil—more than I can recite now. For as long as a man allows his thoughts to run willingly all over the world to consider different things, he notices few hindrances; but as soon as he draws all his thought and his yearning to one thing alone—to have that, to see that, to know that, and to love that (and *that* is only Jesus)—then he shall well feel many painful hindrances, for everything that he feels and is not what he desires is a hindrance to him. Therefore, I have told you particularly of some as an example. Furthermore, I say in general that whatever stirring you feel from your flesh or from the devil, pleasant or painful, bitter or sweet, agreeable or dreadful, glad or sorrowful —that would draw down your thought and your desire from the love of Jesus to worldly vanity and utterly prevent the spiritual desire that you have for the love of him, so that your heart should stay occupied with that stirring: think nothing of it, do not willingly receive it, and do not linger over it too long. But if it concerns some worldly thing that ought to be done for yourself or your fellow Christian, finish with it quickly and bring it to an end so that it does not hang on your heart. If it is some other thing that is not necessary, or does not concern you, do not trouble about it, do not parley with it, and do not get angry; neither fear it nor take pleasure in it; but promptly strike it out of your heart, saying thus: "I am nothing; I have nothing; I neither seek nor desire anything but the love of Jesus." Knit your thought to this desire and make it strong; maintain it with prayer and with other spiritual work so that you do not forget it; and it shall lead you in the right way and save you from all perils, so that although you feel them you shall not perish. And I think it will bring you to perfect love of our Lord Jesus.

On the other hand I also say: Whatever work or stirring it may be that can help your desire, strengthen and nourish it, and make your heart furthest from the enjoyment and remembrance of the world, and more whole and more ardent for the love of God—whether it be prayer or meditation, stillness or speaking, reading or listening, solitude or company, walking or sitting—keep it for the time and work in it as long as the savor lasts, provided you take with it food, drink and sleep like a pilgrim, keeping discretion in your labor as your superior advises and ordains. For however great his haste on his journey, yet at the right time he is willing to eat, drink and sleep. Do so yourself, for although it may hinder you at one time it shall advance you at another.

24. An evil day and a good night: what it means, and how the love of the world is compared to an evil day, and the love of God to a good night.

If you then want to know what this desire is, it is in truth Jesus, for he makes this desire in you,[121] and he gives it you, and he it is that desires in you, and he it is that is desired: he is all, and he does all, if you could see him. You do nothing, but allow him to work in your soul and consent to him,[122] with great gladness of heart that he vouchsafes to do this in you. You are nothing but a rational instrument[123] in which he works. And therefore, when you feel your thought taken up with desire for Jesus by the touching of his grace, with a strong and devout will to please him and love him: think then that you have Jesus, for he it is that you desire. Behold him well, for he goes before you[124] not in bodily likeness but invisibly, through the secret presence of his power.[125] Therefore see him in the spirit if you can, or else trust him and follow him wheresoever he goes, for he shall lead you in the right way to Jerusalem: that is, the sight of peace in contemplation. So prayed the prophet to the Father of heaven, saying: *Emitte lucem tuam et veritatem tuam; ipsa me deduxerunt, et adduxerunt in montem sanctum tuum, et in tabernacula tua.*[126] That is: Father of heaven, send out your light and your truth—that is, your Son Jesus—and by desire within me he shall lead me into your holy hill, and into your tabernacles—that is, to the feeling of perfect love and to height in contemplation.

The prophet speaks thus about this desire: *Memoriale tuum Domine in desiderio animae. Anima mea desideravit te in nocte, sed et spiritus meus in praecordiis meis.*[127] That is: Lord Jesus, the remembrance of you is impressed on the desire of my soul, for my soul has desired you in the night, and my spirit has longed for you in all my thoughts. And why the prophet says he has desired God all in the night, and what he means by it, I shall tell you.

You know well that a night is a space of time between two days, for when one day is ended another comes: not at once, but night comes first to divide the days—sometimes long and sometimes short—and then after that there comes another day. The prophet meant not only this kind of night but he meant by it also a night of the spirit. You shall understand that there are two days or two lights. The first is a false light; the second is a true light. The false light is the love of this world that a man has in himself from the corruption of his flesh; the true light is the perfect love of Jesus felt in a man's soul through grace. The love of the world is a false light, for it passes away and does not last, and so it does not perform what it promises.

This light was promised to Adam by the devil when he stirred him to sin and spoke thus: *Aperientur oculi vestri, et eritis sicut dei.*[128] That is: Your eyes shall be opened, and you shall be like gods. And he spoke the truth there, for when Adam had sinned, at once his inner eye was shut and the light of the spirit withdrawn; and his outer eyes were opened, and he felt and saw a new light of carnal pleasure and worldly love that he had not seen before; and so he saw a new day. But this was an evil day, for this was the one that Job cursed when he spoke thus: *Pereat dies in qua natus sum.*[129] That is: May the day perish on which I was born! He did not curse the day running in the year that God made, but he cursed this day that man made: that is, the covetousness and love of this world in which he was born, although he did not feel it. Then he asked God that this day and this light should perish, and last no longer.

But the everlasting love of Jesus is a true day and a blessed light, for God is both love and light; and he is everlasting; and therefore the man who loves him is in everlasting light, as St. John says: *Qui diligit Deum manet in lumine.*[130] He who loves God stays wholly in light. Then whoever perceives and sees the love of this world to be false and failing, and is therefore ready to forsake it and seek the love of God, cannot at once feel the love of him but has to abide awhile in the night. For he cannot suddenly come from the one light to the other, that is, from the love of the world to perfect love of God.

This night is nothing but a separation and withdrawal of the thought of the soul from earthly things, by great desire and yearning to love, see and feel Jesus and the things of the spirit. This is the night. For just as the night is dark, a hiding place for all bodily creatures, and a rest from all bodily works, so someone who fully intends to think of Jesus and to desire only the love of him takes care to hide his thought from vain regarding, and his affection from carnal pleasure in all bodily creatures, so that his thought may be set free—not fixed—and his affection neither bound, pained nor troubled with anything lower or worse than he is himself. And if he can do so, then it is night for him; for then he is in darkness.

But this is a good night[131] and a luminous darkness,[132] for it is a shutting out of the false love of this world, and it is a drawing near to the true day. And certainly the darker this night is, the nearer is the true day of the love of Jesus, since the more the soul can be hidden from the noise and din of carnal affections and unclean thoughts, through longing for

God, the nearer it is to feeling the light of the love of him, for it is almost there. This, it seems, is what the prophet meant when he said: *Cum in tenebris sedeo, Dominus lux mea est.*[133] That is: When I sit in the darkness, our Lord is my light, that is, When my soul is hidden from all stirrings of sin—as it were in sleep—then our Lord is my light. For then he draws near by his grace to show me something of his light.

Nevertheless, this night is sometimes painful, and sometimes it is easy and comforting.[134] It is painful at first when someone is very unclean and not accustomed by grace to be often in this darkness, yet would like to have it. Therefore he sets his thought and his desire toward God as much as he can, not wanting to feel or think of anything but him. And because he cannot easily have it, he finds it painful; for the habit and the familiarity that he has had before with sins of the world, carnal affections and earthly things, and his fleshly deeds, so press upon him and continually strike inward by force and drag down all his soul to themselves, that he cannot well hide from them as quickly as he would wish. Therefore this darkness is painful to him, especially when grace does not touch him in abundance. Nevertheless, if it should be like this with you, do not be too heavyhearted and do not strive too hard,[135] as if you would put them out of your soul by force, for you cannot do it; but wait for grace, bear this quietly, and do not break yourself too much. And skillfully—if you can—draw your desire and the regard of your spirit toward Jesus, as if you would not trouble with them. For you must know, when you want to desire Jesus and think of him alone, and you cannot do this freely for the pressure of such worldly thoughts: you are truly out of the false day and entering this darkness; but your darkness is not restful because of disuse and ignorance and impurity of your own; and therefore make use of it often, and in due course it will become easier and more restful for you through the feeling of grace. That is when your soul is made so free, so powerful and so gathered into itself through grace that it has no desire to think of anything at all, and it can think of nothing, without hindrance from any bodily thing: then it is in a good darkness.

This is what I mean by such darkness: that a soul can through grace be gathered into itself and stay still in itself, freely and wholly, and not be driven against the will or dragged down by force to ponder or enjoy any sin or any earthly thing vainly, or to let the affection cleave to it in love. Then the soul indeed thinks of nothing, for then it thinks of no earthly thing in a way that can attach it. This is a rich nothing; and this nothing and this night is a great ease for the soul that desires the love of Jesus. It is at ease from the thought of any earthly thing, but not toward Jesus, for though the soul does not think of any earthly thing, it is thinking of him very busily.

Then what is the thing that makes this darkness? Certainly, only a grace-given desire to have the love of Jesus, for the desire and the longing that it has at that time for the love of God—to see him and have him—drives out of the heart all worldly vanities and carnal affections, gathers the soul into itself, and occupies it only with thinking how it could come to the love of him; and so brings it into this rich nothing. And indeed it is not all dark or negative[136] when it thinks like this, for although it is dark from false light it is not all dark from the true light,[137] since Jesus, who is both love and light, is in this darkness. Whether it is painful or restful he is in the soul, as if toiling in desire and longing for light, but he is not yet resting as in love and showing his light; and therefore it is called night and darkness, inasmuch as the soul is hidden from the false light of the world and does not yet have the full feeling of true light, but is awaiting that blessed love of God which it desires.

Then if you want to know when you are in this secure darkness and when not, you can test it like this, and seek no further. When you feel your intention and your will fully set to desire God and think only of him, you can, as it were, first ask yourself in your own thought whether you desire to have anything from this life for love of itself, or to have the use of any of your bodily senses in any created thing, and then perhaps your eye begins and answers thus:[138] "I want to see nothing at all"; and after that, your ear: "I want to hear nothing at all"; and your mouth: "I want to taste nothing at all, and I want to say nothing at all of earthly things"; and your nose: "I want to smell nothing at all"; and your body: "I want to feel nothing at all"; and afterward perhaps your heart says: "I do not want to think of any earthly thing or bodily deed, neither do I want to have affection carnally attached to any created being, but only in God and toward God, if I knew how." And when they all answer you so (and that is done very promptly if grace touches you), then you have entered a little into this darkness. For although you feel and perceive glimpses and gestures of vain thoughts and the pressing in of carnal affections, nevertheless you are in this profitable darkness, provided your thought is not fixed in them. For such vain imaginations that fall unforeseen to the heart trouble this darkness and somewhat hurt the soul, because it would like to be hidden from them and cannot be; but they do not take away the profit of this darkness, for the soul shall by that way come to restful darkness. And this darkness is restful when for a time the soul is hidden from the painful feeling of all such vain thoughts, and is rested only in desire and longing for Jesus, with a spiritual consideration of him, as shall be told later. That lasts for only a while in its wholeness; nevertheless it is most profitable, even though it lasts but a short time.

25.   How the desire of Jesus felt in this luminous darkness slays all stirrings of sin and enables the soul to perceive spiritual illuminations from the heavenly Jerusalem, which is Jesus.

Then since this darkness and night is so good and restful even though it is only short, standing only in desire and longing for the love of Jesus, with a blind thinking[139] of him: then how good and how blessed it is to feel his love, and to be illuminated with his blessed invisible light[140] in order to see truth. And this is the light that a soul receives when the night passes and the day springs.[141] This, I consider, was the night that the prophet meant when he said, "My soul has desired you in the night."[142] As I have said before, it is much better (even though it might be painful) to be hidden in this dark night from looking at the world than to be out in the false pleasure of it, which seems to shine with such cheer for those who are blind in the knowing of spiritual light. For when you are in this darkness you are much nearer Jerusalem than when you are in the midst of that false light. Therefore apply your heart fully to the stirring of grace, grow used to staying in this darkness,[143] and try often to feel at home[144] in it. It will soon be made restful to you, and the true light of spiritual knowledge shall arise for you: not all at once, but secretly and little by little, as the prophet says: *Habitantibus in regione umbrae mortis lux orta est eis.*[145] That is: For the dwellers in the land of the shadow of death, light has arisen. That is, The light of grace rose and shall rise for those that know how to stay in the shadow of death, that is, in this darkness that is like death. For as death kills a living body and all the feelings of its flesh, just so the desire to love Jesus, felt in this darkness, kills all sins, all carnal affections and all unclean thoughts for the time, and then you are fast drawing near to Jerusalem. You are not there yet, but before you come to it you will be able to see it from afar, by the small sudden gleams that shine through little crannies[146] from that city.

For you must know, although your soul may be in this restful darkness without being troubled by worldly vanities, it is not yet where it should be; it is not yet all clothed in light, or wholly turned into the fire of love. It well feels that there is something above itself that it does not know and does not yet have, but it wants to have it and ardently yearns for it: and that is nothing else but the sight of Jerusalem from without, which is like a city that the prophet Ezekiel[147] saw in his visions.

He says that he saw a city set on a hill facing south, which in his sight measured no more in length and breadth than a rood: that was six cubits and a palm long; but as soon as he was brought into the city and looked about him it seemed to him very large, for he saw many halls and chambers, both public and private. He saw gates and porches outward and inward, and building much greater than I say now, many hundred cubits in length and in breadth. Then this was a wonder to him: how this city, which seemed to him so small when he was outside, was so long and so broad within.

This city signifies the perfect love of God set on the hill of contemplation, which appears as something to the sight of a soul that is outside the feeling of it and is toiling toward it in desire: yet it seems only a little thing, no more than a rood—that is, six cubits and a palm in length. By six cubits is understood the perfection of man's work; by the palm a little touching of contemplation. He sees well that there is such a thing, surpassing all that man's labor can deserve by a little, as the palm exceeds the six cubits; but he does not see what it is inside. Nevertheless, if he can come inside the city of contemplation, then he sees much more than he saw at first.

26. How one is to know false illuminations feigned by the devil from the true light of knowledge that comes from Jesus, and by what signs.

But now beware of the midday devil[148] that feigns light as if it came out of Jerusalem, and does not, for the devil sees that our Lord Jesus shows to his lovers the light of truth. Therefore to deceive those who are unwise he shows a light that is not true in the guise of a true light, and deceives them. However, through an example from the firmament I shall say how, as it seems to me, a soul can recognize the light of truth when it shines from God, and know when it is pretended by the Enemy.

Sometimes the firmament shows a light from the sun which seems to be the sun and is not, and sometimes it shows the true sun truly. This is how to know one from the other. The false sun shows itself only between two black rainy clouds; then, because the sun is near, there shines out from the clouds a light as if it were a sun, and it is not. But the true sun shows itself when the firmament is clear, or mostly cleared, from the black clouds. Now to our proposition. Some men do, as it seems, forsake the love of the world and want to come to the love of God and to the light of understanding of him, but they are not willing to come through this darkness that I have spoken of before. They do not want to know themselves truly or humbly: what they have been before—or what they still are—through sin, or how in their own nature they are nothing beside God. They are not trying to enter into themselves, leaving all other things outside, and to slay all wicked stirrings of sins that arise in their hearts—of pride, envy, wrath and other sins—through lasting desire for Jesus in prayer, meditation, silence, weeping and other exercise of body and spirit as devout men and holy men have done. But as soon as they have forsaken the world[149] as it were in outward appearance, or else soon after, they consider themselves to be holy, and able to have the spiritual understanding of the gospel and of holy scripture. And especially if they can fulfil the commandments of God literally and keep themselves from bodily sins, then they suppose that they love God perfectly; and therefore they want to teach everyone else and preach to them, as if they had received the grace of understanding and the perfection of charity by special gift of the Holy Spirit. And also they are much more stirred to do this inasmuch as they sometimes feel great knowledge, as if it were suddenly given to them without great study beforehand, and also great fervor of love (as it seems) to preach faith and justice to their fellow Christians. Therefore they hold it as a grace of God that visits them with his blessed light before other souls. Nevertheless, if they will look about them well, they shall see clearly that this light of knowing and that heat[150] which they feel does not come from the true sun, that is, our Lord Jesus, but from the midday devil that feigns light and makes himself like the sun; and therefore he shall be known by the example given before.

The light of knowledge that is pretended by the devil before a dark soul is always shown between two black rainy clouds.[151] The upper cloud is presumption and exaltation of the self; the lower cloud is the abasement and humiliation of his fellow-Christian. Then whatever light of knowing or feeling of fervor it may be that shines upon a soul in presumption and self-praise, together with disdain for his fellow-Christian, felt at the same time: that is not the light of grace given by the Holy Spirit, even though the knowledge were true in itself; but it is either from the devil, if it comes suddenly, or from man's own mind, if it comes by study.[152] And so it may well be known that this feigned light of knowing is not the light of the true sun, for those who have such knowledge in this way are full of spiritual pride, and do not see it.

They are so blinded with this false light that they regard the haughtiness of their own hearts and their disobedience to the laws of holy church[153] as perfect humility before the gospel and the laws of God. They suppose the following of their own will to be freedom of spirit, and therefore like black clouds they begin to rain the water of errors and heresies, for the words that they sow[154] by preaching all tend to backbiting, strife and the making of discord, and to the condemnation of certain classes and people, and yet they say that all this is charity and zeal for righteousness. But that is not true, for St. James the Apostle says: *Ubi enim zelus et contentio, ibi inconstantia et omne opus pravum. Non est sapientia haec desursum descendens a Patre luminum, sed terrena, animalis et diabolica.*[155] That is: Wherever there is envy and quarrelling there is inconstancy and all evil doing; and therefore that learning which brings forth such sins does not come from the Father of light, that is, God, but it is earthly, bestial and devilish. And so by these tokens[156]—which are pride, presumption, disobedience, disdain, backbiting and other such sins (for these follow later)—may the feigned light be known from the true. For the true sun does not show himself by special visitation to give light of understanding or perfect charity to a soul, unless the firmament is first made bright and clear of clouds; that is, unless the conscience is made clean by the fire of burning desire for Jesus in this darkness, which lays waste and burns all wicked stirrings of pride, vainglory, wrath, envy, and all other sins in the soul, as the prophet says: *Ignis ante ipsum praecedet, et inflammabit in circuitu inimicos eius.*[157] Fire shall go before him—that is, desire of love shall go before Jesus in a man's soul—and it shall burn all his enemies. That is, it shall lay waste all sins.

For unless a soul is first struck down from pride in itself by fear, and is well assayed and burnt[158] in this fire of desire, and (as it were) purified from all spiritual filth by long time in devout prayers and other spiritual exercises, it is not able to suffer the shinings of spiritual light, or to receive the precious liquor of perfect love of Jesus.[159] But when it is thus purified and refined through this fire, then it can receive the grace-given light of spiritual knowledge and the perfection of love that is the true sun. Holy Scripture speaks thus: *Vobis qui timetis Deum orietur sol iustitiae.*[160] The true Sun of Righteousness, that is, our Lord, shall arise for you that fear him, that is, to humble souls that lower themselves beneath their fellow Christians by acknowledging their own wretchedness, and that cast themselves down below God by regarding themselves

241

as nothing in their own substance, through reverent fear and through continually beholding him in the spirit. For that is perfect humility.

To these souls the true sun shall rise and illumine their reason in the knowledge of his truth, and kindle their affection in the burning of love; and then they shall both burn and shine. Through the strength of this heavenly sun they shall burn in perfect love, and shine in the knowledge of God and spiritual things. For then they are reformed in feeling.

Therefore I think it is good for anyone who does not want to be deceived to draw himself down and hide in this darkness—first from concerning himself with others, as I have said—and forget all the world if he can, and follow Jesus with lasting desire, offered in prayer and in meditation on him. Then I believe that the light that comes after this darkness is sure and true, and that it shines out of the city of Jerusalem from the true sun upon a soul that toils in darkness and cries for light, to teach it the way and comfort it in travail. For I think that true darkness is never followed by false light; that is, if a man truly and entirely sets himself to forsake the love of the world and can through grace come to the feeling and knowledge of himself, keeping himself humbly in that feeling, he shall not be deceived with any errors, heresies or fantasies. For all these come in by the gate of pride. Then if pride is blocked out, nothing of this kind shall rest in a soul, and although they may come and present themselves, they shall not enter, for the grace that the soul feels in this humble darkness shall teach the soul truth, and show it that all such suggestions are from the Enemy.

27. What great profit there is for a soul in being brought through grace into luminous darkness, and how someone is to prepare himself if he wants to come to it.

There are many devout souls who come into this darkness through grace and feel the knowledge of themselves, and yet do not fully know what the darkness is; and that ignorance hinders them somewhat. Very often they feel their thought and their affection drawn out and separated from the awareness of earthly things and brought into great rest of a delightful softness, without the painful troubling of vain thoughts, or of their bodily senses, and at that time they feel such great freedom of spirit that they can think of Jesus peacefully, offering him their prayers and their psalms with much savor and sweetness for as long as the frailty of the bodily nature can bear it. They know well that this feeling is good, but they do not know what it is. Therefore, to all such souls I say, as it seems to me, that this kind of feeling is indeed this darkness that I speak of, although it may be only short and seldom. For it is a feeling of themselves first, and a rising above themselves through burning desire to the sight of Jesus; or else, if I am to speak more truthfully, this grace-given feeling is a spiritual sight of Jesus. And if they can keep themselves in that rest, or bring it through grace into custom,[161] so that they could have it easily and freely when they liked, and hold themselves in it, they shall never be overcome by temptation of the devil or of the flesh, or by errors or heresies, for they are set in the gate of contemplation,[162] able and ready to receive the perfect love of Jesus. Therefore if anyone has it, it is good for him to acknowledge it humbly, keep it tenderly and pursue it fervently, so that no created thing may altogether hinder him from following it when he can; and to forget and not care at all for anything that should distract him from this, if he is free of himself and can do as he wills without scandal or harm to his fellow Christian. For it seems to me that he cannot easily come to this rest unless he has a great abundance of grace and sets himself to follow the stirring of it: and that he ought to do, for grace always wants to be free, especially from sin and worldly business and from all other things that hinder its working, even though they are no sin.

Nevertheless, if another soul that has not yet received this fullness of grace desires to come to this spiritual knowledge of Jesus, he must enable himself for it as much as in him lies, and put away all hindrances that block grace, as far as he can. He must learn to die to the world[163] and truly forsake the love of it. First, pride of body and spirit, so that he desires no honor or praise from the world,[164] no name or fame, state or rank, authority or lordship, worldly learning or worldly art, benefices or riches, precious clothing or worldly array, or anything else through which he should be honored above other men. He shall desire none of all these, but if they are imposed upon him take them with fear, so that he may be poor either outwardly and inwardly together, or else fully within. And let him desire to be forgotten by the world, so that people have no more regard for him than for the poorest man that lives, however rich or learned he may be. Similarly, he may not allow his heart to rest in the consideration of his own deeds, or in his virtues, supposing himself to do better than someone else because he forsakes the world and others do not, and therefore thinking highly of himself.

He must also give up all resentful feelings and evil wishes of wrath and envy against his fellow Christians, and not annoy anyone or anger him unreasonably in word or deed, or give anyone reasonable grounds to be angry or vexed: so that he can be free of all men, and so that nobody has any dealings with him, or he with anyone else. Let him also forsake covetousness, so that he desires no earthly goods at all, but asks only for his bodily sustenance according to his need, and thinks himself content whatever God stirs others to give him; and let him put no kind of trust in the possession of any worldly goods, or in the help or favor of any worldly friend, but principally and entirely in God. For if he does otherwise, he binds himself to the world, and therefore he cannot be free to think about God.

In the same way he must utterly forsake gluttony and lechery and every other impurity of the flesh, so that the affection may not be bound to any woman by carnal love or familiarity, for there is no doubt that such blind love as sometimes exists between a man and a woman[165] and seems good and honest—inasmuch as they do not intend to sin in deed —is most unclean in the sight of God, and a very great sin. For it is a great sin for a man to allow his affection (that should be fastened to Jesus and to all virtues and to all purity of spirit) willfully to be bound with the carnal love of any created being, especially if it is so much that it bears down the thought and makes it too restless to have any savor in God. Thus I regard it as willful if a man does it and says it is no sin, or else is so blinded with it that he is unwilling to see it. Similarly, a man must not desire delicacies in food and drink[166] only for the pleasure of his flesh, but be content with such food as he can have easily without great ado, especially if he is well—whatever meat it may be that will get rid of hunger and keep the body in ordinary strength for the service of God. Let him not grumble or contend or be angry over his food, even though he is not always served as the flesh would have it.

He must utterly forsake all these sins—and all others—in will and in deed, when he can, as well as other things that hinder him, so that he may prepare himself to think freely of Jesus. For as long as these hindrances and others like them hang upon him he cannot die to the world or come into this darkness of self-knowing, and therefore in order to come to it he must do all this as St. Paul did, speaking thus: *Mihi mundus crucifixus est et ego mundo*.[167] The world is slain and crucified to me, and I to the world. That is, if someone for love of God forsakes the love of the world in honors, riches and all other worldly things mentioned before, and neither loves it nor pursues it, but is content to have nothing of it, and would not have it if he could, for him the world is truly dead, for he has no savor or delight in it. Similarly, if the world has no opinion of him and no regard for him, does him no favor or honor and sets no value on him, but forgets him like a dead man, then he is dead to the world.

This dying to the world is this darkness, and it is the gate to contemplation[168] and to reforming in feeling, and no other than this. There can be many different ways and diverse practices leading different souls to contemplation, for there are diverse exercises in working according to people's various dispositions and the different states they are in,[169] such as seculars and those in religious orders. Nevertheless, there is only one gate. For whatever exercise a soul may have, unless he can come by it to this knowledge and to a humble feeling of himself—mortified and dead to the world as regards his love, and able sometimes to feel himself set in this restful darkness whereby he can be hidden from the world's vanity, and to see himself, what he is—indeed, he has not yet come to reforming in feeling, and does not have contemplation in its fullness. He is very far from it; and if he wants to come by any other gate, he is no more than a thief and a breaker of the wall; and therefore he shall be cast out as unworthy. But the man who can bring himself first to nothing through grace of humility, and in this way die, he is in the gate, for he is dead to the world and lives to God. St. Paul speaks of it like this: *Mortui enim estis, et vita vestra abscondita est cum Christo in Deo.*[170] You are dead: that is, you that for the love of God forsake all the love of the world are dead to the world; but your life is hidden from worldly men, as Christ lives and is hidden in his divinity from the love and the sight of carnal lovers.

This is the gate shown by our Lord himself in the gospel, when he spoke thus: *Omnis qui reliquerit patrem aut matrem, fratrem aut sororem propter me, centuplum accipiet et vitam eternam possidebit.*[171] Everyone who for my sake forsakes father or mother, sister or brother, or any earthly possession, shall have a hundredfold in this life, and afterward the glory of heaven. This hundredfold that a soul shall have if he forsakes the world is nothing else but the profit of this luminous darkness which I call the gate of contemplation, for someone that is in this darkness, hidden through grace from worldly vanity, does not desire any worldly wealth. He does not seek it, is not troubled by it, does not look forward to it and does not love it; and therefore he has a hundredfold more than the king or than anyone who most desires earthly goods. The man who covets nothing but Jesus has a hundredfold, because he has more rest and more peace of heart, more true love and delight in his soul in one day than is felt in a lifetime by a man who craves most of the world and has all the wealth of it at his will.

This is, then, a good darkness and a rich nothing,[172] bringing a soul to so much spiritual ease and such still softness. I believe David meant this night or this nothing when he said: *Ad nihilum redactus sum, et nescivi.*[173] That is: I was brought to nothing, and I did not know it. That is, the grace of our Lord Jesus sent into my heart has slain in me and brought to nothing all the love of the world, and I did not know how, for it is not mine through my own doing or by my own feeling, but by the grace of our Lord Jesus. And therefore it seems to me that anyone wanting to have the light of grace and to feel abundantly the love of Jesus[174] in his soul must forsake all the false light of worldly love and abide in this darkness. And nevertheless, if he is at first afraid to stay in it let him not turn again to the love of the world, but suffer awhile and put all his hope and trust in Jesus, and he shall not for long be without some spiritual light.

This was the prophet's teaching: *Qui ambulavit in tenebris, et non est lumen ei, speret in Domino, et innitatur super Deum suum.*[175] Whoever walks in darkness and has no light—that is, Whoever will hide himself from the love of the world and cannot quickly feel the light of spiritual love—let him not despair or turn again to the world; but hope in our Lord and lean upon him, that is, trust in God and hold fast to him by desire, and abide awhile; and he shall have light. For it happens to him as it does if someone has been a great while in the sun and afterward comes suddenly into a dark house where no sun shines. At first he shall be as if blind,[176] seeing nothing at all, but if he will wait awhile he shall soon be able to see around him: first large things and then small ones, and later all that is in the house. It is just the same spiritually. For someone who forsakes the love of the world and comes to himself into his own con-science, it is at first rather dark and blinding to his sight; but if he still stands and keeps up the same will to the love of Jesus, with diligent prayer and frequent meditation, he shall afterward be able to see both large and small things that he at first did not recognize. This seems to be what the prophet promised, saying: *Orietur in tenebris lux tua, et tene-brae tuae erunt sicut meridies. Et requiem dabit tibi Dominus Deus tuus, et implebit animam tuam splendoribus.*[177] Light shall arise for you in dark-ness, that is, you that truly forsake the light of all worldly love and hide your thought in this darkness, the light of blessed love and spiritual knowing of God shall rise upon you. *And your darkness shall be like noon,* that is, your darkness of wearisome desire and the blind trust in God that you have at first shall turn into clear knowing, and into the assurance of love. *And your Lord God shall give you rest,* that is, your carnal desires, your painful dreads and doubts, and the wicked spirits which have continually tormented you hitherto: all these shall grow weak and lose much of their might, and you shall be made so strong that they shall not harm you, for you shall be hidden from them in rest. *And then our Lord Jesus shall fill your soul with splendors,* that is, when you are brought into this spiritual rest, then you shall attend more easily to God and do nothing else but love him; and then he shall fill all the powers of your soul with beams of spiritual light. Do not wonder at my calling the forsaking of worldly love "darkness," for the prophet called it so, speaking like this to a soul: *Intra in tenebras tuas, filia Caldeorum.*[178] Go into your darkness, O daughter of Chaldea. That is, O soul—like a daughter of Chaldea because of your love of the world—leave it and go into your darkness.

28.   That in reforming a soul the work of our Lord Jesus is divided into four times: calling, correcting, magnifying and glorifying.

See, I have told you a little about preparing yourself to go forward, if you desire to be reformed in feeling. Nevertheless, I do not say that you can do it by yourself, since I well know that it is our Lord Jesus who brings all this to completion wherever he will. For he alone stirs a soul through his grace, bringing it first into darkness and afterward into light, as the prophet says: *Sicut tenebrae eius, ita et lumen eius.*[179] That is, Just as the light of knowledge and the feeling of spiritual love are from God, so the darkness—that is, the forsaking of worldly love—is from him; for he does all. He forms and reforms: he forms by himself alone, but he reforms us with us;[180] for all this is done by the giving of grace, and by applying our will to grace. And the way in which he does that is stated by St. Paul: *Quos Deus praescivit fieri conformes imaginis Filii eius, hos vocavit; et quos vocavit, hos iustificavit; et quos iustificavit, hos magnificavit; et quos magnificavit, hos et glorificavit.*[181] These that God knew before, that were to be made to conform to the image of his Son: these he called; these he corrected; these he magnified; and these he glorified.

Although these words can be said of chosen souls in the lowest degree of charity, reformed only in faith, they can yet be understood more specially of these souls that are reformed in feeling, to whom our

Lord God shows a great abundance of grace and over whom he goes to much more trouble. For they are especially his own sons, who bear the full shape and likeness of his Son Jesus. In these words St. Paul divides our Lord's work into four times. The first is the time of a soul's calling from worldly vanity, and that time is often easy and full of comfort. For at the beginning of conversion a person who is disposed to abundant grace is so vitally and perceptibly inspired, and often feels such great sweetness of devotion, with so many tears in compunction, that he sometimes feels as if he were half in heaven.

But afterwards this softness passes away for awhile; and then comes the second time, that is, the time of correcting. That is wearisome, for when he begins to press forward strongly[182] in the way of righteousness and to set his will fully against all sin, within and without, and he stretches out his desire to virtues and the love of Jesus, then he feels great hindrance both inside himself, from the perversity and hardness of his own will, and from without, through the temptation of his enemy, so that he is often in very great torment. And that is no wonder, for he has so long been crooked toward the false love of the world[183] that he cannot be made straight and even without great baking and bending, just as a crooked staff cannot be straightened without being cast in the fire and baked. Therefore our Lord Jesus, seeing what is good for an obstinate soul, allows it to be troubled and vexed by various temptations, and well tried through tribulations of the spirit, until all the rust of impurity[184] can be burnt out of it. And that shall be inward, through fear, doubts and perplexities, so that the soul nearly falls into despair, and it will seem as if forsaken by God[185] and left altogether in the hands of the devil, except for a little secret trust that it shall have in the goodness of God and in his mercy; for however far our Lord Jesus may go from such a soul he leaves in it that secret trust, by which it is borne up from despair and saved from spiritual harms. Outside itself, too, it shall be mortified and punished in the sensuality, either by sickness of various kinds or through feeling itself tormented by the devil, or else through a secret power of God. The poor soul shall be so punished by feeling and bearing the wretched body—and it shall not know where or how—that it could not endure being in the body were it not that Lord Jesus keeps it there. Nevertheless, the soul would rather be in all this pain than be blinded with the false love of the world: for that would be hell to such a soul. But the suffering of this kind of pain is nothing but purgatory, and therefore he suffers it gladly and would not put it away even if he could, because it is so profitable. Our Lord does all this for the great benefit of the soul, in order to drive it out from rest in carnal living and to separate it from the love of the sensuality, so that it might receive spiritual light.

For after this, when the soul is thus mortified and brought from worldly love into this darkness—so that it has no more savor or delight in worldly pleasure than in a straw, but finds it bitter as wormwood—then comes the third time, of <u>magnifying</u>, and that is when the soul is partly reformed in feeling, and receives the gift of perfection and the grace of contemplation; and that is a time of great rest.

And after this comes the fourth time, of glorifying. That is when the soul shall be fully reformed in the bliss of heaven. For these souls that are thus called from sin and corrected—or else in another way, by various kinds of assaying through both fire and water[86]—and afterward are thus magnified: they shall be glorified, for our Lord shall then give them in full what they here desired, and more than they knew how to desire. For he shall raise them above all other chosen souls to equality with the Cherubim and Seraphim, since they surpassed all others in the knowledge and love of God here in this life.

Therefore, anyone who wants to come to this magnifying should not fear this correcting, for that is the way. Our Lord spoke a word of great comfort by his prophet to all such souls that are tried with the fire of tribulation: *Puer meus noli timere, si transieris per ignem, flamma non nocebit te.*[87] That is: My child, if you pass through fire, do not be afraid, for the flame shall not harm you. It shall cleanse you from all fleshly filth and make you able to receive the spiritual fire of the love of God. And that needs to be done first, for as I have said, the soul cannot otherwise be reformed in feeling.

29. How it sometimes happens that souls beginning and proficient in grace seem by outward signs to have more love than some that are perfect, and yet it is not truly so within.

But now you say, "How can this be true?" For there are many souls newly turned to God[188] that have many spiritual feelings. Some have great feelings of compunction for their sins, while others have great devotions and fervors in their prayers, and often various touchings of spiritual light in their understanding; some have feelings of other kinds: of comforting heat and great sweetness. However, these souls never come fully into this restful darkness that I speak of, with fervent desire and lasting thought in God. Then you ask whether these souls are re-formed in feeling or not: it seems, Yes, inasmuch as they have these great spiritual feelings that are not sensed by other people standing only in faith. To this I can say, as it seems to me, that these spiritual feelings, whether they stand in compunction, in devotion, or in spiritual imagina-tion, are not the feelings which a soul shall have and feel in the grace of contemplation. I do not deny that they are true and graciously given by God, but the souls that feel such things are not yet reformed in feeling, neither do they yet have the gift of perfection, or the spiritually burning love in Jesus, that they may come to.

Nevertheless, it often seems otherwise: that such souls feel more of the love of God than others who have the gift of perfection, inasmuch as the feeling shows more outwardly by great fervor of bodily signs—in weeping, praying, kneeling and speaking, and other bodily movement—to such an extent that it appears to someone else that they are always ravished in love. And although in my opinion it is not so, I well know that such feelings and fervors of devotion and compunction felt by these people are gracious gifts of God sent into chosen souls to draw them out of the worldly love and fleshly lust that have long been rooted in their hearts, and from that love they are not to be drawn except by feeling such stirrings of great fervor.

However, the great outward showing of the fervor is due not only to the abundance of love that they have but to the smallness and weak-ness of their souls, which cannot bear a little touching of God. For it is still, as it were, carnally fastened to the flesh, and has never yet been separated from it through spiritual mortifying; and therefore the least touching of love and the least sparkle of spiritual light sent from heaven into such a soul is so much and so comforting, so sweet and so delightful, beyond all the pleasure that it ever felt before in the carnal love of earthly things, that it is overcome by it; and also it is so new, so sudden and so unknown that it cannot bear to suffer it, but bursts out and reveals it in weeping, sobbing and other bodily movement.

When an old cask[189] receives new wine that is fresh and potent, it swells out and is on the point of splitting and bursting, until the wine has fermented and purged away all impurity; but as soon as the wine is fined and cleared, then it stands still, and the cask is whole. It is just the same when a soul that is old through sin receives a little of the love of God, which is so fresh and potent that the body is on the point of splitting and breaking, were it not that God keeps it whole; but still it bursts out at the eyes by weeping, and at the mouth in speaking, and that is more from the weakness and feebleness of the soul than from the abundance of love. For afterward, when love has boiled out all the impurity of the soul by such great fervors, then the love is clear and stands still, and then both body and soul are much more at peace; and yet the same soul has far greater love than it had before, even though less appears outwardly, for it is now wholly at rest within, having only a little outward showing of fervor. And therefore I say that these souls who feel such great bodily fervors are not yet reformed in feeling, even though they are in much grace, but they are greatly disposed to it. For I believe that such a man, particularly who has been greatly defiled in sin, shall not be reformed in feeling without first being burnt and purified beforehand with such great compunctions. Another soul that was never much defiled with love of the world, but has always been kept in innocence from great sins, may more easily and secretly come to this reforming, without showing great outward fervor.

Then this is true, as I suppose: that such comforts and fervors as a soul feels in the state of beginning or of proficient are as it were his spiritual food, sent from heaven to strengthen him in his labor. Just as a pilgrim travelling all day without food or drink and nearly overcome with weariness comes upon a good inn at last, there has food and drink, and is well refreshed for the time: so in the spiritual sense a devout soul eager to forsake the love of the world and to love God, and doing its utmost toward it, prays and travails all day in body and spirit and sometimes feels no comfort or savor in devotion. Then our Lord, having pity for all his creatures,[190] sends it amid his spiritual food, and comforts it in devotion as he vouchsafes, lest it should perish for need or turn to sadness or grumbling. And when the soul feels any spiritual comfort, then he thinks himself well content with all his travail and all the distress he had during the day, in that he does well in the evening by the feeling of some grace.

It happens in the same way to other souls who are proficient, and further on in grace: they often feel gracious touchings of the Holy Spirit in their souls, both in understanding and in sight of spiritual things, and in the affection of love; but they are not yet reformed in feeling, neither are they yet perfect, for the reason that all such feelings come to them in that state as if without warning, for they come before they notice it and leave them before they notice, and they do not know how to come to them again, where they should look for them or where they should find them; they are not yet at home[191] with these feelings, but they suddenly go and suddenly come. They are not yet made lords of themselves by stability of thought and the lasting desire of Jesus, neither is the eye of their soul yet opened to the beholding of spiritual things, though they are fast drawing near it. Therefore, they are not yet reformed in feeling, and they do not yet have the full gift of contemplation.

30.   How a man is to have knowledge of his own soul, and how he should set his love in Jesus, God and Man: one Person.

A soul that wants to have knowledge of spiritual things needs first to have knowledge of itself.[192] For it cannot have knowledge of a nature above itself unless it has knowledge of itself; and that is when the soul is so gathered into itself,[193] separated from the consideration of all earthly things and from the use of the bodily senses, that it feels itself as it is in its own nature, without a body. Then if you desire to know and see what your soul is, you shall not turn your thought into your body in order to search for it and feel it, as if it were hidden inside your heart as your heart is hidden and held inside your body. If you search like this, you shall never find it in itself. The more you seek to find and feel it in the way you would feel a bodily thing, the further you are from it. For your soul is not a body, but a life invisible;[194] it is not hidden and held inside your body as a smaller thing is hidden and held within a greater, but holding your body and giving it life, much greater in power and virtue than your body is.

Then if you want to find it, withdraw your thought from every outward bodily thing, and so from the awareness of your own body and from all your five senses, as much as you can; and think spiritually of the nature of a rational soul, as you would think in order to know any virtue, such as truth, humility or any other. Just so think that a soul is a life—deathless and invisible—having power in itself to see and know the supreme truth and to love the supreme goodness that is God. When you see this, then you feel something of yourself. Do not seek yourself in any other place, but the more fully and clearly that you can think about the nature and dignity of a rational soul—what it is, and what is the natural working of it—the better you see yourself. It is very hard for a soul that is rough and much in the flesh to have sight and knowledge of itself, or of an angel or of God: it falls at once into the imagination of a bodily shape, and it supposes by that to have the sight of itself, and so of God, and so of spiritual things; and that cannot be. For all spiritual things are seen and known by the understanding of the soul, not by imagination. Just as a soul sees by understanding that the virtue of justice is to yield to each thing what it ought to have, so likewise the soul can see itself by understanding.

Nevertheless, I do not say that your soul is to rest still in this knowledge, but by this it shall seek higher knowledge above itself, and that is the nature of God. For your soul is only a mirror[195] in which you shall see God spiritually. Therefore, you shall first find your mirror and keep it bright and clean from fleshly filth and worldly vanity, and hold it well up from the earth so that you can see it, and in it likewise our Lord. For this is the end for which all chosen souls labor in this life, in their purpose and their intention, even though they have no special feeling of this. Therefore, it is as I have said before: that many souls—beginning and proficient—have many great fervors and much sweetness in devotion, and are all burning in love, as it seems; and yet they do not have perfect love or spiritual knowledge of God. For you must know that however great the fervor that a soul feels—so much that it seems to him that the body cannot bear it—or even though he melts altogether into weeping: as long as his thinking and his consideration of God is mainly or entirely in imagination and not in understanding,[196] he has not yet come to perfect love or to contemplation.

For you are to understand that the love of God is of three kinds. All are good, but each one is better than another. The first comes through faith alone, without the grace of imagination or spiritual knowledge of God: this love is in the least soul that is reformed in faith, in the lowest degree of charity, and it is good, since it is enough for salvation. The second love is what a soul feels through faith and the imagination of Jesus in his humanity. This love is better than the first, when the imagination is stirred by grace, for the eye of the spirit is opened to behold our Lord's manhood. The third love is what the soul feels through spiritual sight of the divine nature in the manhood, as it may be seen here: that is the best and most valuable, and that is perfect love. A soul does not feel this love until he is reformed in feeling. Beginners and proficient souls do not have this love, for they do not know how to meditate upon Jesus or love him spiritually, but (as it were) all humanly and carnally, according to the conditions and likeness of man; and with that point of view they shape all their work, by their thoughts and their affections. They fear him as a man, and worship him principally in human imagery, and go no further. For instance, if they have done wrong and trespassed against God, they then think that God is angry with them, as a man would be if they had trespassed against him. Therefore they fall down as if at our Lord's feet with sorrow of heart, and cry for mercy, and when they do so they have a good trust that our Lord will of his mercy forgive them their trespass. This kind of practice is very good, but it is not as spiritual as it might be. In the same way, when they want to worship God they present themselves in their thought as it were before our Lord's face in a bodily likeness, and imagine a wonderful light[197] where our Lord Jesus is; and then they bow before him, honor him and fear him, and put themselves fully at his mercy, for him to do with them whatever he will. Similarly, when they want to love God they behold him, honor him and fear him as a man, not yet as God in man—either in his passion or in some other thing to do with his manhood—and in that beholding they feel their hearts greatly stirred to the love of God.

M.K.?

This kind of practice is good and comes of grace, but it is much less and lower than the practice of understanding: that is when the soul by grace beholds God in man. For in our Lord Jesus there are two natures: the manhood and the divinity. Then just as the divine nature is more excellent and honorable than the manhood, so the spiritual consideration of the divinity in Jesus the man is more honorable, more spiritual and more deserving of reward than the consideration of the manhood alone, whether one beholds the manhood as mortal or as glorified. And just so, for the same reason, the love that a soul feels in considering and thinking of the divinity in man, when it is shown by grace, is more honorable, spiritual and deserving of reward than the fervor of devotion that the soul feels by imagining only the manhood, however much it shows outwardly. For in comparison with that, this is only human, since in the imagination our Lord does not show himself *as* he is, or *that* he is; for the soul could not at that time bear such a thing, because of the frailty of the fleshly nature.

Nevertheless, to such souls that do not know how to think spiritually of the divine nature our Lord Jesus tempers the invisible light of his divinity,[198] so that they should not err in their devotion but be comforted and strengthened through some kind of inward beholding of Jesus, to forsake sin and the love of the world. He clothes that invisible light in the bodily likeness of his manhood and shows it to the inner eye of a soul, which he feeds spiritually with the love of his precious body: a love of such great power that it slays all wicked love in the soul and strengthens it to suffer bodily penance for love of Jesus, as well as other bodily distress in time of need. And this is the shadowing of our Lord Jesus over a chosen soul, in which shadowing a soul is kept from the burning of worldly love; for just as a shadow is made by a light and a body, so this spiritual shadow is made by the blessed invisible light of the divinity and the manhood united to it, shown to a devout soul. Of this shadow the prophet speaks thus. *Spiritus ante faciem nostram Christus Dominus: sub umbra eius vivemus inter gentes.*[199] Our Lord Jesus Christ is a spirit before our face: under his shadow we shall live among the nations. That is, our Lord Jesus in his divinity is a spirit that cannot be seen as he is in his blessed light by us living in the flesh: therefore as long as we are here we shall live under the shadow of his humanity. But although it is true that this love in imagination is good, nevertheless a soul should desire to have spiritual love in the understanding of the divine nature, for that is the end and the full blessedness of the soul, and all other considerations in the body are but means leading the soul to it. I do not say that we should separate God from man, but we are to love Jesus, both God and man: God in man, and man in God; spiritual, not carnal.

This was our Lord's teaching to Mary Magdalene[200] (who was to be contemplative), when he spoke thus, *Noli me tangere; nondum enim ascendi ad Patrem meum.*[201] Do not touch me; I have not yet ascended to my Father. That is to say, Mary Magdalene ardently loved our Lord Jesus before the time of his passion, but her love was much in the body, little in the spirit; she well believed that he was God, but she loved him little as God, for at that time she did not know how; and therefore she allowed all her affection and all her thought to go to him as he was, in the form of man; and our Lord did not blame her then, but greatly praised it. But afterward, when he had risen from death and appeared to her, she would have honored him with the same kind of love as she did before, and then our Lord forbade her, saying thus: "Do not touch me"—that is, Do not set the rest or the love of your heart upon that human form you see with your bodily eye alone, to rest in it, because in that form I have not ascended to my Father, that is, I am not equal to the Father. For in human form I am less than he. Do not touch me thus: but set your thought and your love upon that form in which I am equal to the Father

—that is, the form of the divinity—and love me, know me, and honor me as God and man divinely, not as a man humanly. That is how you shall touch me, because I am both God and man, and the whole reason why I shall be loved and honored is that I am God and took the nature of man; therefore make me a God in your heart and in your love, and worship me in your understanding as Jesus, God in man—supreme truth, supreme goodness and blessed life—for that is what I am. This is how our Lord taught her, as I understand, and also all other souls who are disposed to contemplation and fit for it, that they should do the same.

Nevertheless, for other souls that are neither subtle by nature nor made spiritual through grace, it is good to keep on with their own practice—in imagination with human affection—until more grace comes to them freely. It is not safe for anyone to abandon one good thing before he sees and feels a better. The same may be said of other kinds of feeling that are like bodily ones, such as hearing delightful song, feeling a comfortable heat in the body, or perceiving light or the sweetness of bodily savor. These are not spiritual feelings, for spiritual feelings are felt in the powers of the soul; principally in understanding and love, and little in imagination; but these feelings are in the imagination, and therefore they are not spiritual feelings. Even when they are best and most true, they are still only outward signs of the inward grace that is felt in the powers of the soul.

This can be clearly proved by holy scripture, which says this: *Apparuerunt apostolis dispertitae linguae tanquam ignis, seditque supra singulos eorum Spiritus Sanctus.*[202] The Holy Spirit appeared to the apostles on the day of Pentecost in the likeness of burning tongues, and inflamed their hearts and sat upon each of them. Now, it is true that the Holy Spirit, who is God invisible in himself, was neither that fire nor those tongues that were seen, nor that burning which was felt in the body, but he was felt invisibly in the powers of their souls, for he enlightened their reason and kindled their affection through his blessed presence so clearly and so ardently that they suddenly had the spiritual knowledge of truth and the perfection of love, as our Lord promised them, saying thus: *Spiritus Sanctus docebit vos omnem veritatem.*[203] That is: The Holy Spirit shall teach you all truth. Then that fire and that burning was nothing else but a bodily sign, shown outwardly as witness to that grace which was felt within; and as it was in them, so it is in other souls that are visited and illuminated inwardly by the Holy Spirit and have with it such outward feeling, in comfort and as witness to the inward grace. But that grace is not, as I suppose, in all souls that are perfect, but where our Lord wills. For other souls that are imperfect and have such feelings outwardly, not having yet received the inward grace, it is not good to rest too much in such feelings, except inasmuch as they help the soul to more stability of thought in God, and to more love. For some may be true and some may be pretended, as I have said before.

31. How this manner of speaking about a soul's reforming in feeling shall be taken, in what way it is reformed, and how this is based on the words of St. Paul.

Now I have said a little to you about reforming in faith, and in the same way I have shortly touched on the progress from that reforming to the higher reforming which is in feeling; not with the intention or wish to set God's works under a law of my own speaking, as if to say that God works thus in a soul, and in no other way; no, I do not mean that. But I speak in accordance with my simple feeling, that our Lord Jesus works thus in some creatures, as I suppose. I fully expect that he also works in other ways, beyond my understanding and feeling. Nevertheless, whether he works thus or otherwise—by various means, in longer or shorter time, with great or little labor—if everything leads to one end (that is, to the perfect love of him) then it is good enough. For if he will give one soul the full grace of contemplation on one day and without any labor,[204] as he is well able to do: it is as good for that soul as if he had been tried, punished, mortified and purified for the length of twenty winters. Therefore take what I say as I have said, and especially as I intend to say; for now by the grace of our Lord Jesus I shall speak a little—more openly, as it seems to me—about reforming in feeling: what it is and how it is made, and what are the spiritual feelings that a soul receives.

First, however, so that you do not take as pretense or fantasy this way in which I speak of the soul's reforming in feeling, I shall base it upon St. Paul's words, where he speaks like this. *Nolite conformari huic saeculo, sed reformamini in novitate sensus vestri.*[205] That is, You who are through grace reformed in faith, do not henceforth conform yourselves to the manners of the world in pride, covetousness or other sins, but be reformed in newness of feeling. Look, here you can see that St. Paul speaks of reforming in feeling; and what that new feeling is he explains in another place like this: *Ut impleamini in agnitione voluntatis eius, in omni intellectu et sapientia spirituali.*[206] That is, We pray God that you may be filled with knowledge of God's will in all understanding and in every kind of spiritual wisdom. This is reforming in feeling.

For you are to understand that the soul has two kinds of feelings: one outwardly, of the five bodily senses, and the other within, of the spiritual senses, which are properly the powers of the soul, mind, reason and will. When through grace these powers are filled with all understanding of the will of God and spiritual wisdom, then the soul has new and gracious feelings. That this is true he shows like this in another place: *Renovamini spiritu mentis vestrae, et induite novum hominem qui secundum Deum creatus est in iustitia, sanctitate, et veritate.*[207] Be renewed in the spirit of your soul. That is, you are to be reformed, not in bodily feeling or in imagination, but in the higher part of your reason, and clothe yourselves in a new man, who is created according to God, in righteousness. That is, your reason, which is properly the image of God through grace of the Holy Spirit, shall be clothed in a new light of truth, holiness and righteousness, and then it is reformed in feeling. For when the soul has perfect knowledge of God, then it is reformed. St. Paul speaks like this: *Exspoliantes veterem hominem cum actibus suis, induite novum qui renovatur in agnitione Dei, secundum imaginem eius qui creavit illum.*[208] Strip yourselves of the old man with all his deeds—that is, cast off from yourselves the love of the world, with all worldly behavior—and clothe yourselves in a new man; that is, you shall be renewed in the knowledge of God after the likeness of him who made you. By these words you can understand that St. Paul wanted to have men's souls reformed in perfect knowledge of God, for that is the new feeling that he speaks of in general. Therefore, according to his word I shall speak more openly of this reforming, as God gives me grace. For there are two ways of knowing God. One is held principally in the imagination and little in understanding: this knowledge is in chosen souls beginning and proficient in grace who know God and love him in a wholly human manner—not spiritually—with human affections and in bodily likeness, as I have said before. This knowledge is good and it is compared to milk,[209] by which they are tenderly nourished like children until they are able to come to the Father's table and take whole bread from his hand. Another kind of knowledge is felt principally in understanding, when it is comforted and illumined by the Holy Spirit, and little in imagination; for the understanding is [the] lady,[210] and the imagination is like a serving maid to the understanding, when there is need. This knowledge is whole bread, food for perfect souls, and it is reforming in feeling.

32. **How God opens the inner eye of the soul for it to see him: not all at once, but at different times; and an illustration of three ways of reforming a soul.**

After a soul is called away from love of the world and is later corrected and assayed, mortified and purified—as I have said before—our Lord Jesus of his merciful goodness reforms it in feeling, when he deigns. As he illuminates the reason through the touch and shining of his blessed light he opens the inner eyes of the soul, to see him and know him; not all at once, but little by little at different times, as the soul may allow him. He [the soul] does not see *what* he [God] is, for no created being can do that in heaven or earth; and he [the soul] does not see him *as* he is, for that sight is only in the glory of heaven. But he sees *that* he is:[211] an unchangeable being;[212] a supreme power, supreme truth, supreme goodness; a blessed life, an endless beatitude.[213] This the soul sees, and much more that comes with it; not blindly, nakedly and without savor, as with a scholar who sees him by his learning, only through the power of his naked reason; but he sees him through an understanding which is strengthened and illuminated by the gift of the Holy Spirit, with a wonderful reverence and a secret burning love, and with spiritual savor and heavenly delight—more clearly and more fully than it may be written or told.

Although this sight may be only little and for a short time, it is so excellent and so strong that it draws to itself and ravishes the entire affection of the soul from the consideration and awareness of all earthly things, to rest in it forever if it could. And from this kind of seeing and knowing the soul grounds all its inward practice in all the affections,[214] for then it fears God in man as truth, wonders at him as power, and loves him as goodness.

This sight and knowledge of Jesus, with the blessed love that comes out of it, may be called the reforming of a soul that I speak of, in faith and in feeling. It is in faith because it is still dark[215] in comparison with the full knowledge that shall be in heaven, for there not only shall we see *that* he is but we shall see him *as* he is. As St. John says: *Tunc videbimus eum sicuti est.*[216] That is, Then we shall see him as he is. Nevertheless, it is also in feeling, compared with that blind knowledge which a soul has, based only on faith. For this soul knows something of the nature of Jesus God through this grace-given sight, while the other does not know, but only believes that it is true.

However, so that you may have a better conception of what I mean I shall show these three ways of reforming a soul by the example of three men standing in the light of the sun.[217] One of the three is blind, another can see but has his eyes shut, and the third looks out with full sight.

The blind man has no way of knowing that he is in the sun, but he believes it if a trustworthy man tells him; and he signifies a soul who is reformed only in faith, believing in God as holy church teaches, but not knowing what. This is sufficient for salvation.

The second man sees a light from the sun but does not see clearly what it is, and neither does he see it as it is, for his eyelid hinders him from seeing, yet through his eyelid he sees a gleam of great light. He signifies a soul who is reformed in faith and in feeling, and so is contemplative, for he sees something of the divinity of Jesus through grace: not clearly or fully, since the lid (that is, his bodily nature) is still a wall between his nature and the nature of Jesus God, and hinders him from the clear sight of him. But as grace touches him more or less, he sees through this wall that Jesus is God, and that Jesus is supreme goodness, supreme being and a blessed life,[218] and that all other goodness comes from him. This the soul sees through grace, notwithstanding the bodily nature; and the purer and more subtle that the soul is made and the further it is parted from carnality, the sharper the sight it has and the stronger its love for the divinity of Jesus. This sight is so powerful that although no other man living would believe in Jesus or love him, he himself would never believe the less or love Him the less; for he sees it so certainly that he cannot disbelieve it.

The third man, who has full sight of the sun, does not need to believe it, because he sees it fully; and he signifies a fully blessed soul who without any wall of body or of sin openly sees the face of Jesus in the glory of heaven, where there is no faith; and therefore he is fully reformed in feeling.

There is no state above the second reforming that a soul can come to here in this life; for this is the state of perfection, and the way toward heaven. Nevertheless, not all the souls that are in this state are equally far advanced. For some have it little, briefly and seldom; and some longer, clearer and more often; and some have it clearest and longest of all, according to the abundance of grace—and yet all these have the gift of contemplation. For the soul does not have the perfect sight of Jesus all at once, but first a little, and after that it becomes proficient and comes to more feeling; and as long as it is in this life it can grow more in knowledge and in this love of Jesus. And indeed I do not know what should be more desirable for such a soul that has felt a little of it than to leave and utterly disregard everything else and aim at this alone: to have a clearer sight and purer love of Jesus, in whom is all the blessed Trinity.

This way of knowing Jesus, as I understand, is the opening of heaven to the eye of a pure soul, of which holy men speak[219] in their writings. Not as some suppose, that the opening of heaven is as if a soul could see by imagination through the skies above the firmament, how our Lord Jesus sits in his majesty in a bodily light as great as a hundred suns. No, it is not so: and however high he sees in that manner, he does not truly see the spiritual heaven. The higher he climbs above the sun, to see Jesus God thus, by such imagination, the lower he falls beneath the sun. Nevertheless, this kind of sight is tolerable for simple souls, that know no better way to seek him who is invisible.

33. How Jesus is heaven to the soul, and why he is called fire.

What is heaven to a rational soul? Truly, nothing but Jesus, God. For if that only is heaven which is above everything, then God alone is heaven to the soul of man, for he alone is above the nature of a soul. Then if through grace a soul can have knowledge of that blessed nature of Jesus, he truly sees heaven, for he sees God.

Therefore there are many who err[220] in their understanding of some words that are spoken about God, for they do not understand them in a spiritual sense. It is said in holy writings[221] that a soul who wants to find God is to lift the inner eye upward and seek God above itself. Then some who want to follow this saying take these words above themselves to mean setting the self in a higher position and place of honor, in the same way as one element and one planet are above another in the setting and dignity of their physical position; but spiritually it is not so. For a soul is above every bodily thing not because of its position but for the subtlety and dignity of its nature. In the very same way God is above all material and spiritual creatures: not by the placing of his position but through the subtlety and dignity of his unchangeable and blessed nature. Therefore whoever wants to seek God wisely, and to find him, is not to run out with his thought as if he would climb above the sun, pierce the firmament and form an image of the majesty something like the light of a hundred suns: he should rather draw down the sun and all the firmament, forget it,[222] and cast it beneath him where he stands, setting at nought all this and every material thing as well. Let him then think spiritually—if he knows how—both of himself and of God. If he does so, then the soul sees above itself; and then it sees heaven.

This word *within* is to be understood in the same way. It is commonly said that a soul shall see our Lord within all things, and within itself. It is true that our Lord is within all creatures,[223] but not in the way that a kernel is hidden inside the shell of a nut, or as a little bodily thing is held inside another big one. But he is within all creatures as holding and keeping them in their being, through the subtlety and power of his own blessed nature and invisible purity. For just as a thing that is most precious and most pure is laid furthest inside, so by that example it is said that the nature of God (which is most precious, most pure and most spiritual, and furthest from the material nature) is hidden within all things. Therefore anyone who will search for God within is first to forget all material things—for all that is outside—and his own body; and he shall forget to think of his own soul, and he shall think of that uncreated nature which is Jesus, who made him, gives him life and holds him, granting him reason, memory and love; and he is within him through his power and supreme subtlety. This is what the soul is to do when grace touches it, or else it will be of little use to seek Jesus and find him within itself or within all creatures,[224] in my opinion.

It is also said in holy scripture that God is light. So says St. John, *Deus lux est.*[225] That is, God is light. This light shall not be understood as material light, but it is understood thus. God is light. That is, God is faith and truth, for truth is spiritual light; then anyone who with most grace knows truth, best sees God; and nevertheless it is compared to material light, for this reason. Just as the sun shows itself to the eye of the body, and shows all material things by itself, so the truth—which is God—shows itself first to the reason of the soul, and then through itself reveals all the other spiritual things that need to be known by a soul. So says the prophet: *Domine, in lumine tuo videbimus lumen.*[226] Lord, by your light we shall see your light. That is, we shall see you (who are truth) through yourself.

incendium

In the same way it is said that God is fire: *Deus noster ignis consumens est.*[227] That is: Our Lord is fire, laying waste. That is to say, God is not the elemental fire that heats a body and burns it, but God is love and charity. For as fire consumes all material things that can be destroyed, so the love of God burns and consumes all sin[228] out of the soul, making it clean, as fire purifies every kind of metal. These words—and all others in holy scripture that speak of our Lord by <u>material similes</u>—must needs be understood in a spiritual way, or else there is no savor in them. Nevertheless, the reason why such words are spoken of our Lord in holy scripture is this: because we are so carnal that we do not know how to speak of God, or to understand about him, unless we are first introduced through words of this kind. However, when the inner eye is opened through grace to have a little sight of Jesus, then the soul will easily enough turn all such words for material things into spiritual meaning.

This spiritual opening of the inner eye into knowledge of the Deity is what I call reforming in faith and in feeling. For then the soul feels in understanding a little of the thing that it had before only in bare believing; and that is the beginning of contemplation, of which St. Paul speaks thus: *Non contemplantibus nobis quae videntur sed quae non videntur; quia quae videntur temporalia sunt, quae autem non videntur aeterna sunt.*[229] That is, Our contemplation is not of things that are seen, but of things invisible; for things that are seen are passing away, but invisible things are everlasting. To this sight every soul should desire to come: both here in part, and fully in the bliss of heaven. For the full glory of a rational soul, and its eternal life, lies in that sight and in that knowledge of Jesus. *Haec est autem vita aeterna, ut cognoscant te unum Deum, et quem misisti, Jhesum Christum.*[230] That is, Father, this is eternal life: that your chosen souls may know you and your Son whom you have sent, one true God.

34. Two kinds of love, created and uncreated: what it means and how we are obliged to love Jesus—much for our creation, and more for our redemption, but most of all for our salvation through the gift of his love.

But now you are wondering: since this knowledge is the glory and the end of a soul,[231] why then have I said before that a soul should desire nothing but the love of God, without saying anything about this sight— that this is what a soul ought to desire?

To this I can reply thus: that the sight of Jesus is the full glory of a soul, and that is not only for the sight, but also for the blessed love[232] that comes from that sight. Nevertheless, because love comes out of knowledge and not knowledge out of love, it is said that the glory of a soul consists in the first place in the knowledge and sight of God, with love; and the more he is known, the better he is loved. But as the soul cannot come to this knowledge—or to this love that comes from it—without love,²³³ I therefore said that you should desire only love, for love is the cause of a soul's coming to this sight and to this knowledge. And that love is not the love that a soul has in itself for God; but the love that our Lord has for a sinful soul²³⁴ that knows nothing at all about loving him is the cause why this soul comes to this knowledge, and to this love that comes out of it. How that is, I shall tell you more plainly.

Holy writers say, and it is true, that there are two kinds of spiritual love.²³⁵ One is called uncreated, and the other is called created. Love uncreated is God himself, the third person in the Trinity, who is the Holy Spirit. He is love uncreated and unmade, as St. John says in this way: *Deus dilectio est*.²³⁶ God is love, that is, the Holy Spirit. Love created is the affection of the soul, made by the Holy Spirit from the sight and the knowledge of truth—that is, God alone—stirred and established in him. This love is called created, for it is made by the Holy Spirit. It is not God in himself, because it is created, but it is the love of the soul felt through the sight of Jesus and stirred toward him alone. Now you can see that created love is not the cause²³⁷ of a soul's coming to the spiritual sight of Jesus, as some men would think—that they would want to love God so ardently (as if in their own strength) that they were worthy to have the spiritual knowledge of him. No, it is not like that: but love uncreated, which is God himself, is the cause of all this knowledge; for a blind wretched soul is so far from the clear knowledge and blessed feeling of his love, through the sin and frailty of the bodily nature, that it could never come to it were it not for the infinite greatness of the love of God. But then because he loves us so much he gives us his love, which is the Holy Spirit. He is both the giver and the gift,²³⁸ and by that gift he then makes us know and love him.

See, this is the love that I spoke of: that you should covet and desire only this uncreated love that is the Holy Spirit, for indeed a lesser thing or a lesser gift than he is cannot avail to bring us to the blessed sight of Jesus. And therefore we shall fully desire and ask of Jesus only this gift of love:²³⁹ that he would for the greatness of his blessed love touch our hearts with his invisible light to the knowledge of himself, and share with us his blessed love, so that as he loves us we might love him in return. So says St. John: *Nos diligamus Deum, quoniam ipse prior dilexit nos*.²⁴⁰ That is, Let us love God now, for he first loved us. He loved us much when he made us in his likeness, but he loved us more when through willing acceptance of death in his manhood he bought us with his precious blood from the power of the devil and from the pain of hell. But he loves us most²⁴¹ when he gives us the gift of the Holy Spirit—that is love—by which we know him and love him and are made sure that we are his sons, chosen for salvation. For this love we are more bound to him than for any other love that he ever showed for us, either in our making or in our redemption. For even though he had made us and bought us, what use would our making or redemption be to us unless he also saved us? Indeed, none at all.

Therefore the greatest token of love shown to us is this, as it seems to me: that he gives himself to our souls in his divinity. He gave himself first to us in his humanity, for our ransom, when he offered himself to the Father of heaven upon the altar of the cross. This was a beautiful gift, and a great token of love. But when in his divinity he gives himself spiritually to our souls, for our salvation, and makes us know him and love him, then he loves us fully; for then he gives us himself, and he could not give us more; and less could not suffice for us.[242] For this reason it is said that the justification of a sinful soul through forgiveness of sins is ascribed and appropriated principally to the working of the Holy Spirit, for the Holy Spirit is love, and in the justification of a soul our Lord Jesus shows his greatest love to a soul, for he does away with all sin and unites the soul with himself. And that is the best thing that he can do for a soul, and therefore it is appropriated to the Holy Spirit.

The making of a soul is appropriated[243] to the Father, for the supreme might and power that he shows in the making of it. The redemption is ascribed and appropriated to the Son, for the supreme understanding and wisdom that he showed in his humanity, for he overcame the devil principally through wisdom, and not through strength. But the justifying and full salvation of a soul by the forgiveness of sins is appropriated to the third Person, that is, the Holy Spirit, for Jesus in that shows most love to man's soul, and for that thing we shall most love him in return. His creation is common to us and to all creatures lacking reason, for as he made us from nothing, so did he make them; and therefore this work is greatest in power, but not most in love. Likewise the redemption is common to us and to all rational souls, such as Jews, Saracens and false Christian people, since he died for all souls alike and redeemed them, if they wish to have the profit of it; and in the same way it was sufficient for the redemption of all, even though it may be that not everyone has it. This work came most from wisdom, not from love. But our souls are justified and made holy through the gift of the Holy Spirit, and it is the working of love alone; it is not in common, but a special gift only for chosen souls; and that is in truth the greatest work of love toward us who are his chosen children.

This is the love of God that I spoke of, which you should long for and desire, for this love is God himself, and the Holy Spirit. When this uncreated love is given to us it works all that is good in our souls, and all that belongs to goodness. This love loves us before we love him, for it cleanses us first from our sins and makes us love him, and makes our will strong to withstand all sins; and it stirs us to test ourselves through various exercises—both bodily and spiritual—in all virtues. It also stirs us to forsake the love and pleasure of the world; it slays in us all wicked stirrings of sin, and carnal affections and worldly fears; it keeps us from the malicious temptations of the devil, and it drives us out from the business and vanity of the world, and from the company of those who love it. All this is done by the uncreated love of God when he gives himself to us. We do nothing at all but submit to him[244] and assent to him, for that is the most that we do: that we willingly assent to his gracious working in us. And yet that will is not from ourselves[245] but of his making, so that in my opinion he does in us all that is well done; and still we do not see it. And he not only does thus, but afterward love does more, for he opens the eye of the soul and wonderfully shows to the soul the sight of Jesus, and the knowledge of him, as the soul can bear it, little by little. And by that sight he ravishes all the affection of the soul to himself, and then the soul begins to know him spiritually and to love him ardently. Then the soul sees[246] something of the nature of the blessed divinity of Jesus: how he is all, and that he works all, and that all good deeds that are done—and good thoughts—are from him alone. For he is all supreme power, all supreme truth and all supreme goodness;[247] and therefore every good deed that is done is from him and by him, and he alone shall have the honor and thanks for all good deeds, and no thing but he. Wretched men steal his honor[248] here for a while, but at the last end truth shall reveal that Jesus did all, and that man by himself did nothing whatever. Then the thieves of God's property that are not reconciled with him here in this life shall be condemned to death, and Jesus shall be fully honored and thanked by all blessed creatures for his gracious working.

This love is nothing else but Jesus himself, who for love works all this in a man's soul and reforms it in feeling to his likeness, as I have said before, and as in part I am about to say. This love brings into the soul the fullness of all virtues,[249] making them all pure and true, soft and easy, and turns them all into love and pleasure; I shall tell you a little later of the manner in which he does that. This love draws the soul from the carnal to the spiritual, from earthly feeling into heavenly savor, and from the vain beholding of worldly things into the contemplation of spiritual creatures and of the mysteries of God.

35. How some souls love Jesus through fervors of the body and their own human affections, which are stirred by grace and reason: and how some love Jesus more restfully by spiritual affections alone, stirred inwardly through the special grace of the Holy Spirit.

I can therefore say that anybody who has most of this love here in this life pleases God most and shall have the clearest sight of him in the glory of heaven,[250] for he has the greatest gift of love here on earth. This love cannot be had by one's own effort, as some suppose; it is freely received[251] by the gracious gift of Jesus after the great labor of body and soul that goes before, for there are some lovers of God that make themselves love God as if by their own strength:[252] they strain themselves through great violence and pant so strongly that they burst into bodily fervors, seeming ready to draw God down from heaven to themselves, and saying in their hearts and with their mouths, "Ah, Lord, I love you and I want to love you; for your love I would suffer death." In this kind of operation they feel great fervor and much grace, and in my opinion it is true that this practice is good and worthy of reward if it is well-tempered with humility and discretion. But nevertheless these men neither love nor have the gift of love in the manner I speak of, and like that they do not ask for it.

For a soul who has the gift of love as I mean, through the grace-given beholding of Jesus[253]—or else would like it, if he does not have it yet—is not eager to overstrain himself as if by bodily strength, in order to have it by fervors of the body, and in this way to feel some part of the love of God; but it seems to him that he is nothing at all, and that by himself he does not know how to do anything whatever, but hangs upon the mercy of God and is borne up by it like no more than a dead thing. He sees well that Jesus is all and does all, and therefore he asks for nothing else but the gift of his love. For since the soul sees that its own love is nothing, it therefore wants his love, for that is enough; for that he prays and that he desires: that the love of God would touch him with its blessed light, so that he could see a little of him by his gracious presence; for then he should love him; and so by this way the gift of love that is God comes into a soul.

The more that through grace the soul makes itself nothing by the sight of this truth (sometimes without any fervor shown outwardly), and the less it thinks that it loves or sees God, the nearer it approaches to perceiving the gift of blessed love. For then love is master and works in the soul, making it forget itself and see and consider only how love acts, and then the soul is more passive than active: and that is pure love. This was St. Paul's meaning when he said: *Quicumque Spiritu Dei aguntur, hii filii Dei sunt.*[254] All who are acted upon by the Spirit of God are the sons of God. That is, These souls who are made so humble and obedient to God[255] that they do not work of themselves, but allow the Holy Spirit to stir them and work in them the feelings of love, with a very sweet accord to his stirrings: these are especially God's sons, most like him.

Other souls do not know how to love thus, but harass themselves by their own affections; through thinking of God and through bodily practice they stir themselves to draw out the feeling of love forcibly, by fervors and other bodily signs: these do not love spiritually. They do well and are worthy of reward, provided they will humbly acknowledge that what they do is not naturally the feeling of love, through grace; but it is the human action of a soul, done at the bidding of reason.[256] And nevertheless, through the goodness of God, because the soul does what in it lies, these human affections of the soul stirred toward God by the operation of man are turned into spiritual affections, and are made worthy of reward as if they had been done spiritually in the first place. And this is a great courtesy of our Lord, shown to humble souls, who turns all these human affections[257] of natural love into the affection and into the reward of his own love, as if he had wrought them all entirely by himself. And so these affections thus turned may be called the affections of spiritual love through purchase,[258] not through natural bringing forth by the Holy Spirit. I do not say that a soul can bring about such human affections from itself alone, without grace, for I well know St. Paul's saying that by ourselves and without grace we cannot either do or think anything that is good. *Non enim quod sumus sufficientes cogitare aliquid ex nobis, quasi ex nobis; sed sufficientia nostra ex Deo est.*[259] That is, We who love God do not suppose that we are sufficient in ourselves alone to love, or to think what is good, but our sufficiency comes from God. For God works everything in us, both good will and good work, as St. Paul says: *Deus est qui operatur in nobis, et velle et perficere pro bona voluntate.*[260] That is, It is God who works in us good will and the fulfilling of good will. But I say that such affections are good, made by means of a soul according to the general grace that he gives to all his chosen souls: not from special grace made spiritual by the touching of his gracious presence, as he works in his perfect lovers in the way I have said before. For in imperfect lovers[261] of God, love works distantly, through the affections of man; but in perfect lovers, love works closely by his own spiritual affections, slaying for the time all other affections in a soul— those carnal, natural and human: and that is properly the working of love himself. In a pure soul, a small part of this love can be had here, through the spiritual sight of Jesus; but in the joy of heaven it is fulfilled by clear sight in his Deity, for there no affection shall be felt in a soul but what is divine and spiritual.

36. That among all the gifts of Jesus,[262] love is the most valuable and profitable; and how in his lovers Jesus does all that is well done, for love alone, and how love makes it light and easy to practice all virtues and all good deeds.

Then ask from God nothing but this gift of love, which is the Holy Spirit. For of all the gifts that our Lord gives, none is so good or so profitable, so valuable or so excellent as this; for there is no gift of God that is both the giver and the gift, except this gift of love; and therefore it is the best and the most worthy of honor. The gift of prophecy, the gift of working miracles, the gift of great knowledge and counselling, and the gift of great fasting or of doing great penance, or any others like them, are great gifts of the Holy Spirit; but they are not the Holy Spirit, for a reprobate fit for damnation could have those gifts as fully as a chosen soul.

And therefore all these kinds of gift are not greatly to be desired or much to be valued, but the gift of love is the Holy Spirit, God himself, and no soul can have him and also be damned, because that gift alone saves it from damnation and makes it God's son, a partner in the heavenly heritage.[263] That love, as I have said before, is not the affection of love that is created in a soul, but it is the Holy Spirit himself—Love uncreated—who saves a soul, for he gives himself to a soul first before the soul loves him, and he forms the affection in the soul and makes the soul love him only for himself. And not only that, but also by this gift the soul loves itself and all its fellow Christians as itself,[264] for God alone; and this is the gift of love that makes a distinction[265] between chosen souls and the damned; and this gift makes complete peace between God and a soul, and unites all blessed creatures wholly in God. For it causes Jesus to love us, and us to love him in return; and all of us to love one another in him.

Desire this gift of love first of all, as I have said; for if he will give it of his grace in that way, it shall open and illuminate the reason of your soul to see truth, which is God, and spiritual things; and it shall stir your affection to love him wholly and fully. It shall work in your soul only as he wills, and you shall behold Jesus reverently with the softness of love and see how he acts. This is what he tells us to do, speaking thus by his prophet: *Vacate et videte quoniam ego sum Deus.*[266] Be still and see that I am God. That is, You who are reformed in feeling and have your inner eye opened to the sight of spiritual things, cease sometimes from outward activity and see that I am God. That is, See only how I, Jesus—God and man—act. Behold me, for I do all. I am love, and for love I do all that I do: and you do nothing. And that this is true I shall show you; for there is no good deed done in you, or any good thought felt in you, unless it is done through me—that is, through power, wisdom and love, powerfully, wisely and lovingly—otherwise it is not a good deed. But now it is true that I Jesus am power, wisdom and blessed love, and you are nothing; for I am God. Then you can well see that in you I do all your good deeds, all your good thoughts and all your good loves, and you do nothing at all; and yet these good deeds are nonetheless called yours: not because you do them in the first place, but because I give them to you for the love that I have for you. Therefore, since I am Jesus and do all this for love, stop considering yourself, think nothing of yourself, and look upon me. See then that I am God, for I do all this. This is something of the meaning of that verse of David's given above.

See then and consider what Love works in a chosen soul which he reforms in feeling to his likeness, when the reason is given a little light for the spiritual knowledge of Jesus and the feeling of his love. Then Love brings into the soul the fullness of virtues,[267] and turns them all into softness and delight as if without effort from the soul, for the soul does not struggle hard to get them as it did before, but it has them easily and feels them restfully only through the gift of Love, which is the Holy Spirit. And that is a very great comfort and unspeakable gladness, when it suddenly feels—and never knows how—that the virtues of humility and patience, sobriety and constancy, chastity and purity, kindness toward his fellow Christian, and all the other virtues, which were burdensome to him and painful and hard to keep, are now turned into softness and pleasure and wonderful lightness of heart: to such an extent that he does not find it difficult or hard to keep any virtue, but very pleasing; and all this is the work of Love.

There are others who stand in the common way of charity[268] and are not so far advanced in grace, but work under the orders of reason: in order to acquire[269] virtues, these continually strive and fight against sins, and like wrestlers they are sometimes on top and sometimes underneath. These people do very well. They have virtues in reason and in will,[270] not in savor or in love, for they themselves fight for them, as if by their own strength. And therefore they cannot have complete rest or fully gain the upper hand. They shall nevertheless have great reward, but they are not yet humble enough. They have not put themselves completely in God's hand, for they do not yet see him. But a soul which has the spiritual sight of Jesus pays little attention to the struggle for virtues[271] and is not specially concerned with them; but he directs all his efforts toward keeping that sight and that consideration of Jesus that he has: to hold his mind firmly upon it and bind his love to it alone, so that it does not fall away, and forgets all other things as much as possible. And when it does this, then Jesus is truly master in the soul against all sins, sheltering it with his blessed presence and getting for it all virtues. And the soul is so comforted and borne up with the soft feeling of love that it has from the sight of Jesus that it feels no great outward distress. In this way love slays all sins generally in a soul, and reforms it in a new feeling of virtues.[272]

37. How through the grace-given beholding of Jesus love slays all stirrings of pride and makes the soul perfectly humble, for it causes it to lose the savor of all earthly honor.

Nevertheless, I will say more particularly how love slays sins[273] and reforms virtues in a soul: first, about pride and the humility that is contrary to it. You are to understand that there are two kinds of humility: one is possessed through the operation of reason, and the other is felt by the special gift of Love. Both are from Love, but Love works the former by the reason of the soul, and the other he effects by himself. The first is imperfect; the other is perfect.[274]

A person feels the first humility through considering his own sins and his own wretchedness, through which consideration he thinks himself unworthy to have any gift of grace or any reward from God; but it seems to him enough that of his great mercy he would grant him forgiveness of his sins. And it seems to him likewise that because of his own sins he is worse than the greatest sinner that lives, and that everyone does better than himself; and so by such consideration he casts himself down in his thought beneath all men. He tries busily to withstand the stirrings of pride as much as he can, in both body and soul, and despises himself, so that he does not assent to the feelings of pride. And if at any time his heart should be taken by it, and thus defiled with the vain joy of honor, knowledge, praise, or any other thing: as soon as he can perceive it, he is displeased with himself and sorrows over it in his heart; he asks God's forgiveness for it, shows himself to his confessor, humbly accuses himself, and receives his penance. This is good humility, but it is not yet perfect, for it belongs to souls that are beginning and profiting in grace, caused by consideration of their sins. Love brings about this humility through the reason of the soul.

A soul feels perfect humility from the sight and spiritual knowledge of Jesus, for when the Holy Spirit illuminates the reason to the sight of truth—how Jesus is all and that he does all—the soul has such great love and such great joy in that spiritual sight, because it is so true, that it forgets itself and wholly leans upon Jesus with all the love that it has, to gaze on him. It takes no heed of its own unworthiness,[275] or of sins already committed, but values itself at nothing, with all the good deeds that it ever did, as if nothing existed but Jesus. David was humble like this when he spoke thus: *Et substantia mea tanquam nihilum ante te.*[276] That is, Lord Jesus, the sight of your blessed uncreated substance and your infinite being shows me clearly that my substance—and the being of my soul—is as nothing beside you. As for his fellow Christians, he pays no attention to them and does not judge them to be either better or worse than himself, for he regards himself and all other people equally, as nothing in themselves compared with God. And that is true: for all the goodness that is done in himself or in them is from God alone, whom he beholds as all. Therefore he considers all other creatures to be nothing, as he does himself. The prophet was humble in this way when he said: *Omnes gentes quasi non sint, sic sunt coram eo, et quasi nichilum et inane reputatae sunt ei.*[277] All men are as nothing before our Lord, and as vain and without being are they accounted to him. That is, compared with the eternal being and unchangeable nature of God, mankind is as nothing, for it is made from nothing and to nothing it shall return, unless he who made it from nothing holds it in existence.

This is truth, and this ought to make a soul humble, if it might see this truth through grace. Therefore, when love opens the inner eye of the soul to see this truth, with other circumstances that come with it, then the soul begins to be truly humble, for then by the sight of God it feels and sees itself as it is. And then the soul stops looking and leaning toward itself and turns entirely to the beholding of him; and when it does so, then the soul thinks nothing of all the joy and honor of the world, for the joy of worldly honor is so little and so worthless in comparison with the joy and love that it feels in the spiritual sight of Jesus and the knowledge of truth, that he would want none of it, even if he could have it without any sin. And although people should want to honor him, praise him, favor him and set him in great eminence, it is no pleasure to him. Even to have the knowledge of all the seven liberal arts and of all arts under the sun, with the power to work miracles of all kinds: all this gives him no more delight or savor than gnawing on a dry stick. He would much rather forget all these and be alone, out of sight of the world, than think about them and be honored by everyone.

For the heart of a true lover of Jesus is made so great and so large[278] through a little sight of him and a little feeling of his spiritual love, that all the pleasure and all the joy of the whole earth cannot suffice to fill a corner of it. Then it well seems that for these wretched lovers of the world, who are (as it were) ravished with love of their own honor[279] and pursue the gaining of it with all the strength and wit that they have, there is no savor in this humility, and they are very far from it. But the lover of Jesus has this humility enduringly, and it is not with sullenness or striving for it, but with pleasure and gladness; and it has this gladness not because it forsakes the honor of the world—for that would be a proud humility that belongs to a hypocrite—but because it has a sight and a spiritual knowledge of the truth and dignity of Jesus, through the gift of the Holy Spirit.

That reverent sight and loving consideration of Jesus comforts the soul so wonderfully and bears it up so powerfully and softly that it cannot take pleasure or fully rest in any earthly joy, neither does it wish to. For himself he does not care whether people abuse or praise him, honor or despise him; he does not take it to heart, either to be pleased if men despise him—so seeming to have more humility—or to be displeased that he should be honored or praised: he would rather forget both the one and the other, to think of Jesus alone and get humility in that way. And that is much the safer if anyone could reach it, as David did when he said: *Oculi mei semper ad Dominum, quoniam ipse evellet de laqueo pedes meos.*[280] That is, My eyes are always open to Jesus our Lord, because he shall keep my feet from the snares of sins; for when he does so, he then utterly forsakes himself and submits himself wholly to Jesus. Then he is under secure guard, for the shield of truth he holds keeps him so safe that he shall not be hurt through any stirring of pride as long as he stays within that shield, as the prophet says: *Scuto circumdabit te veritas eius,*[281] *non timebis a timore nocturno.*[282] That is, Truth shall encircle you with a shield—and that is, if you look only upon him, leaving all other things—for then you shall not fear for the terror by night, that is, you shall not fear the spirit of pride, whether he comes by night or by day, as the next verse says afterward, *A sagitta volante in die.*[283] Pride comes by night[284] to attack a soul when it is despised and condemned by other men, to make it fall into discouragement and sorrow. It comes also like an arrow flying by day when a man is honored and praised by all—whether for worldly or for spiritual deeds—to give him vain joy to rest upon, in himself and in a passing thing. This is a sharp arrow, and a dangerous one: it flies swiftly, it strikes softly, yet it wounds mortally; but the lover of Jesus, who steadily beholds him through devout prayers and diligent thought of him, is so wrapped round with the safe shield of truth that he is not afraid, for this arrow cannot enter the soul, and even though it comes it does not hurt, but glances away and passes on.

And thus the soul is made humble, as I understand, by the working of the Holy Spirit: that is, the gift of love; for he opens the eye of the soul to see and love Jesus, and he keeps the soul restfully and safely in that sight, slaying all the stirrings of pride very secretly and softly: and the soul never knows how. He likewise brings in by that way—in truth and in love—the virtue of humility. All this is done by Love, but not with the same fullness in all his lovers; for some have this grace only briefly and slightly, as if they were at the beginning, making a little attempt toward it, because their conscience is not yet fully cleansed through grace. Others have it more fully, because they have clearer sight of Jesus, and they feel more of his love; and some have it most fully, for they have the full gift of contemplation. Nevertheless, he who has it least in the way that I have said, truly has the gift of perfect humility, for he has the gift of perfect love.

38. How Love quietly slays all stirrings of wrath and envy, and reforms in the soul the virtues of peace, patience and perfect charity toward its fellow Christian, as he did particularly in the apostles.

Love works wisely and gently[285] in a soul where he wills, for he powerfully slays wrath, envy, and all sufferings of distress and resentment in it, and brings into the soul the virtues of patience and mildness, peacemaking and kindness toward its fellow Christian. It is very hard and very difficult for a man who relies only on the operation of his own reason to keep patience, holy rest and gentleness in his heart, and charity toward his fellow Christians, if they harass him and do him wrong without reason, and not to do something to them in return through the stirring of wrath or resentment—in speech, in action or in both. Nevertheless, if anyone is stirred or troubled in himself and made unquiet, provided that it is not too much—beyond the bounds of reason—and that he guards his hand and tongue and is ready to forgive the trespass when mercy is asked: this man still has the virtue of patience, even though it may be only weakly and nakedly, for he wants to have it, and in order to do so works hard to bridle his irrational sufferings; also, he is sorry that he does not have it as he should.

For a true lover of Jesus, however, there is no great difficulty[286] in suffering all this, because Love fights for him and very softly slays such stirrings of wrath and resentment, making his soul so easy, peaceable, long suffering and godly through the spiritual sight of Jesus, with the feeling of his blessed love, that he cares nothing for them, even though he is despised and condemned by others or is wronged, harmed, shamed or disgraced. He is not much stirred against them,[287] and he does not want to be angered or stirred against them, for if he were greatly stirred he would lose the comfort that he feels in his soul—and that he will not do. He can more easily forget all the wrong done to him than another man can forgive it, even though mercy were asked; and so he would much rather forget it than forgive it, for to him this seems the easier way. And all this is done by Love, for Love opens the eye of the soul to the sight of Jesus and confirms it with the pleasure of love that it feels from that sight, comforting it so powerfully that it does not heed what-

275

ever people chatter or do against him—it does not weigh upon him at all. The greatest harm that could come to him would be a loss of that spiritual sight of Jesus, and therefore he would rather suffer every other injury than that one alone.

The soul can do all this well and easily, without great troubling of the spiritual sight, when harm comes entirely from without and does not touch the body, like backbiting, scorning or the robbery of such things as he has. All this does not grieve him. But it goes somewhat nearer when the flesh is touched and he feels pain: then it is harder. Nevertheless, though it is hard and impossible for frail human nature to suffer bodily penance gladly and patiently, without bitter stirrings of wrath, vexation and resentment, it is not impossible for Love—that is, the Holy Spirit— to effect this in a soul which he touches with the blessed gift of love. He gives to a soul that is in that state powerful feelings of love, and wonderfully fastens it to Jesus, separating it very far from the sensuality through his hidden might and comforting it so sweetly by his blessed presence that the soul feels little or no pain from the sensuality; and this is a special grace given to the holy martyrs.[288]

The apostles had this grace, as holy scripture says of them: *Ibant apostoli gaudentes a conspectu concilii quoniam digni habiti sunt pro nomine Christi contumeliam pati.*[289] That is, The apostles went rejoicing from the council of the Jews when they were beaten with scourges, and they were glad that they were worthy to suffer any bodily distress for the love of Jesus. They were not stirred to wrath or fierceness, to be avenged on the Jews that beat them, as a worldly man would be when he suffered a little harm, however slight, from a fellow Christian; neither were they stirred to pride or self-righteousness, or to contempt and judgment of the Jews, as are hypocrites and heretics who are willing to suffer[290] great bodily pain and are sometimes ready to suffer death— with great gladness and strong will—as if in the name of Jesus, for love of him. Truly that love and gladness that they have in suffering bodily misfortune is not from the Holy Spirit: it does not come from the fire that burns on the high altar of heaven,[291] but it is pretended by the devil and set alight by hell, for it is all mingled with the haughtiness of pride and of presumption in themselves, and contempt and judgment and disdain for those who punish them in this way. Yet they suppose that all is charity, and that they suffer all that for the love of God; but they are deceived by the midday devil.[292]

When a true lover of Jesus suffers harm from his fellow Christian, he is so strengthened through the grace of the Holy Spirit and is made so humble, patient and peaceable (and that truly), that whatever wrong or harm it may be that he suffers from his fellow Christian he always keeps humility; he does not despise him or judge him, but prays for him in his heart, and has pity and compassion much more tenderly for him than for someone else who never did him harm. In truth, he loves him better, and more fervently desires the salvation of his soul, because he sees that he himself shall have so much spiritual profit from the evil deed of that other man, even though it is against his will. But this love and humility is the work of the Holy Spirit alone, above human nature, in those whom he makes true lovers of Jesus.

39. How love slays covetousness, lechery and gluttony, and slays carnal savor and delight in all the five senses of the body quietly and easily, through a grace-given beholding of Jesus.

Covetousness is also slain in a soul by the working of love, for it makes the soul so desirous of spiritual goods and so ardent toward heavenly riches that it sets no value on any earthly wealth. It has no more delight in a precious stone than in a piece of chalk, and no more love for a hundred pounds of gold than for a pound of lead. It puts one price on all things that shall perish, and no one thing is worth more than another in its love. For it seems clear that all these earthly things, which worldly men prize so greatly and love so dearly, shall pass away and turn to nothing: both the thing in itself and the love of it. Sometimes, therefore, he brings it to mind in that state it shall come to later, and so he counts it as nothing. When lovers of the world strive and fight and sue for earthly goods, over who can have them first, the lover of Jesus contends with no one, but keeps himself at peace and feels content with what he has. He has no wish to strive for more, for it seems to him he does not need any more of all the riches on earth than a scant bodily sustenance to preserve the life of the body as long as God wills; he can have that easily, and therefore he wants no more. He is content when he has no more than he barely needs for the time, so that he can freely be discharged from the business of keeping and spending it, and fully give his heart and his efforts to the seeking of Jesus, to find him in purity of spirit: that is the sum of his desire, because only the pure of heart shall see him.

In the same way the carnal love of father and mother,²⁹³ and of other friends in the world, does not weigh upon him: it is cut right out of his heart with the sword of spiritual love, so that he has no more affection toward father, mother or any secular friend than he has for another person, unless he sees or feels in them more grace or more virtue than in other people, except for this: he would rather[294] that his father and mother had the same grace that some other people have, but nevertheless if they are not like that, then he loves others better than them; and that is charity. And so God's love slays covetousness of the world, and brings into the soul poverty of spirit.

Love does that not only in those who have no worldly goods at all[295] but also in some creatures who are in great positions in the world and have the dispensing of earthly riches. In some of them Love slays covetousness to such a length that they have no more pleasure or savor in possessing them than in a straw; and even though they are lost through the fault of those that should look after them, they do not care, since through the gift of the Holy Spirit the heart of God's lover is taken up so fully with the sight and the love of something else; and that is so precious and so honorable that it will not lastingly receive any other love that is contrary to it.

And Love not only does this but it also slays the pleasure of lechery and all other uncleanness of the body, bringing true chastity into the soul and turning it into pleasure. The soul feels such great delight in the sight of Jesus that it is glad to be chaste, and it finds no great hardship in keeping chastity, for like that it is most at ease and most at rest.

In the same way, the gift of love slays the carnal lusts of gluttony, making the soul sober and temperate and bearing it up so strongly that it cannot rest in the pleasure of food and drink, but it takes whatever is least harmful to the constitution of the body, if he can come by it easily: not for the love of itself but for love of God.[296] In this way the lover of God clearly sees his own need to look after his bodily life with food and drink as long as God wishes to allow body and soul to stay together. Such, then, as I understand, shall be the discretion[297] of the lover of Jesus who has the feeling and practice of love: that in whatever way he can best keep his grace whole, and be least hindered from working in it through taking sustenance for the body, that is how he shall do it. The kind of food that least hinders and troubles the heart and can keep the body in strength—be it meat, fish or only bread and ale—that is what I believe the soul chooses to have if it can come by it, for the whole business of the soul is to think always about Jesus with reverend love, if it can, without being hindered by anything. Therefore, since it must needs be delayed and hindered a little, the less it is delayed and hindered by food, drink, or anything else, the better it is pleased. It would rather use the best and most costly food under the sun,[298] if that less hindered the keeping of his heart, than take only bread and water, if that should hinder him more. He has no interest in getting great reward for the pain of fasting, and in being driven by it from quietness of heart, but his whole concern is to keep his heart as steady as he can in looking at Jesus and in feeling his love. And truly, as I believe, he could make use of the best food—good in its own nature—with less pleasure than another man could use the worst, working entirely by reason without the special gift of love. (I except that food which through the craft of cookery is made for pleasure alone: he cannot well assent to food of that kind.) And so on the other hand, if light food such as bread and ale helps him most, easing his heart and keeping it most at peace, it then pleases him best to use it in this way, especially if he feels bodily strength with it, only by the gift of love.

And Love does even more, for it slays *accidie* and the idleness of the flesh, making the soul lively and swift for the service of Jesus, so far that it always desires to be occupied with goodness, especially in beholding him within. By virtue of this the soul has savor and spiritual delight in prayer, in meditation, and in all other kinds of work that need to be done, according to the demands of the state or rank[299] in which he stands (whether he is religious or secular), without reluctance or painful bitterness.

In the same way it slays the vain pleasure of the five bodily senses: first the sight of the eye, so that the soul has no pleasure in the sight of any worldly thing, but rather feels pain and distress in beholding it, however beautiful it may be, however precious or however wonderful. And therefore as lovers of the world sometimes run out to see new things and wonder at them, and so to feed their hearts with the vain sight of them, in just the same way a lover of Jesus is eager to run away and withdraw himself from the sight of such things, so that the inner sight may not be hindered; for in the spirit he sees another kind of thing which is fairer and more wonderful, and he does not want to let it go.

It is the same with speaking and hearing. It is a pain for the soul of a lover to speak or hear anything that might hinder the freedom of his heart to think of Jesus. Whatever outward song or melody or minstrelsy[300] it may be, if it hinders the thought so that it cannot freely and quietly pray or think of him, it does not please him at all; and the more delightful it is to others the less savor it has for him. Similarly, to hear anything said by others does not please him at all, unless it has some concern with the work of his soul in loving Jesus: otherwise he is very soon irked by it. He would much rather be in peace, hear nothing and say nothing, than hear the speaking and teaching of the greatest scholar on earth, telling him all the propositions that he could say through the wit of man, unless he could speak feelingly and stirringly of the love of Jesus. For that is his principal art, and therefore he does not want to speak, hear or see anything but what could help him and advance him into more knowledge and better feeling of him. Regarding worldly speech, there is no doubt that he has no savor in speaking or in hearing it, either in worldly tales or in rumors or in any such vain chattering that does not concern him.

And so it is with smelling, tasting and touching: the more the thought should be distracted and broken from spiritual quietness by the use of smell, taste, or any of the bodily senses, the more he runs from it. The less he feels of them, the better he is pleased, and if he could live in the body without the feeling of any of them, he would like never to feel them, for they often trouble the heart and put it from rest, and they cannot be avoided altogether. Nevertheless, the love of Jesus is sometimes so powerful in a soul that it overcomes and slays all that is contrary to it.

40. What virtues and graces a soul receives through the opening of the inner eye into the grace-given beholding of Jesus, and how this cannot be acquired through human labor alone, but through special grace, and labor as well.

In this way Love works in a soul, opening the spiritual eye to gaze upon Jesus by the inspiration of special grace, and making it pure, subtle and fit for the work of contemplation.[301] The greatest scholar on earth cannot with all his wit imagine what this opening of the spiritual eye is, or fully declare it with his tongue, for it cannot be acquired by study or through human toil alone, but principally by the grace of the Holy Spirit, together with the work of man. I am afraid to speak of it at all, for I feel myself to be ignorant; it goes beyond my experience, and my lips are unclean. Nevertheless, because I think Love asks and Love commands, I shall for that reason say a little more of it, as I suppose Love to teach. This opening of the spiritual eye is that luminous darkness and rich nothing that I spoke of before, and it may be called *purity of spirit and spiritual rest, inward stillness and peace of conscience, highness of thought and solitude of soul, a lively feeling of grace and secrecy of heart, the waking sleep of the spouse and tasting of heavenly savor, burning in love and shining in light, entrance to contemplation and reforming in feeling.*[302] All these terms are given by various men in holy writing, for each of them spoke of it as he felt in grace, and although they all show it in diverse words, nevertheless all are one in the truth they affirm.

For a soul that through the visitation of grace has one, has all,[303] because when a soul sighing to see the face of Jesus is touched through special grace of the Holy Spirit, it is suddenly changed and turned from the plight that it was in to another way of feeling. It is wonderfully separated from the love and pleasure of all earthly things and drawn first into itself, so much that it has lost the savor of the bodily life and of everything that is, save only Jesus. And *then it is clean from all the filth of sin,* so far that the memory of it and all inordinate affection for any creature is suddenly washed and wiped away, so that there is no obstacle in the middle[304] between Jesus and the soul, but only the life of the body. And *then it is in spiritual rest,* because all painful doubts and fears and all other temptations of spiritual enemies are driven out of the heart, so that they do not trouble it or sink into it for the time. It is at rest from the annoyance of worldly business[305] and the painful vexation of wicked stirrings, but it is very busy in the free spiritual work of love, and the more it labors, the more rest it feels.

This restful labor is very far from idleness of the flesh[306] and from false confidence. It is full of spiritual work, yet it is called rest, because grace loosens the heavy yoke of carnal love[307] from the soul, making it strong and free through the gift of the spiritual love, in order to work gladly, gently and with delight in everything where it is stirred to work by grace. Therefore it is called a holy idleness and a most busy rest,[308] and so it is *in stillness* from the great shouting and bestial din of fleshly desires and unclean thoughts.

This stillness is made by the inspiration of the Holy Spirit through the beholding of Jesus, because his voice is so sweet and so strong that it puts silence in a soul instead of the chattering of all other speakers, for it is a voice of virtue, softly sounded in a pure soul, of which the prophet speaks like this: *Vox Domini in virtute.*[309] That is, The voice of our Lord Jesus is in virtue. This voice is a strong and living word, as the apostle says: *Vivus est sermo Dei et efficax, et penetrabilior omni gladio.*[310] That is, The word of Jesus is alive and strong, more piercing than any sword. Carnal love is slain through the speaking of his word, and the soul kept in silence from all wicked stirrings. Of this silence it is said in the Apocalypse: *Factum est silentium in caelo quasi dimidia hora.*[311] Silence was kept in heaven, as if for half an hour. Heaven is a pure soul,[312] lifted

[handwritten margin note: metaphors of silence]

up through grace from earthly love to heavenly conversation, and so it is in silence, but inasmuch as that full silence cannot last unbroken forever because of the corruption of the bodily nature, it is compared only to the time of half an hour: the soul thinks it a very short time, however long it is, and therefore like only a half hour. And then it has *peace in conscience,* because grace drives out the gnawing, pricking, striving and scolding of sins, and brings in peace and accord, making Jesus and a soul both at one, in full harmony of will. At that time there is no reproaching of sins, or sharp reproving of faults made in a soul, for they have kissed and made friends; all that was done amiss is forgiven.

This is how the soul feels then, with humble assurance and great gladness of spirit, and through the making of this accord it conceives a great confidence in salvation,[313] for it hears in its conscience the hidden testimony of the Holy Spirit, that he is a son chosen for the heritage of heaven. So says St. Paul: *Ipse Spiritus testimonium perhibet spiritui nostro quod filii Dei sumus.*[314] That is, The Holy Spirit bears witness to our spirit, that we are God's sons. This testimony of the conscience truly felt through grace is the real joy of the soul, as the apostle says: *Gloria mea est testimonium conscientiae meae.*[315] That is, My joy is the testimony of my conscience, and that is when it bears witness to peace and accord, true love and friendship between Jesus and a soul, and when it is in this peace it is *in highness of thought.*

When the soul is bound with love of the world, it is beneath all created things, for everything treads on it and bears it down by force, so that it can neither see Jesus nor love him. For just as the love of the world is vain and carnal, so to behold, consider and use created things is carnal, and that is a thraldom of the soul. But then through the opening of the spiritual eye into Jesus, the love is turned and the soul is raised up according to its own nature above all bodily creatures,[316] and then the beholding, consideration and use of them[317] is spiritual: for the love is spiritual. The soul then has great contempt for obedience to the love of bodily things, for it is set high above them through grace. It cares nothing for all the world, because all shall pass and perish. As long as the soul is kept to this highness of heart, no error or deceit[318] of the devil enters it, for Jesus is truly in the sight of the soul at that time, and all things are beneath him. Of this the prophet speaks: *Accedat homo ad cor altum, et exaltabitur Deus.*[319] Let man attain a high heart, and God shall be exalted. That is, A man who through grace comes to highness of thought shall see that Jesus alone is exalted above all creatures, and he in him.

And then the soul is alone, greatly estranged from the fellowship of

lovers of the world—even though her body may be right among them—
and set very far apart from the carnal affections of creatures. It does not
care if it should never see anyone, or speak with him or have comfort
from him, provided it could always be like this, in that spiritual feeling.
It feels so much at home in the blessed presence of our Lord Jesus, with
such great savor of him, that for his love it can easily forget the carnal
affection and the carnal awareness of all creatures. I do not say that it
shall not love or think of other created beings, but I say that it shall think
of them at the right time, and see them and love them spiritually and
freely, not carnally and painfully as it did before. Of this solitude the
prophet speaks thus: *Ducam eam in solitudinem, et loquar ad cor eius.*[320] I
shall lead her into solitude, and I shall speak to her heart. That is, the
grace of Jesus leads a soul from the noisy company of fleshly desires into
solitude of thought, and also makes it forget the pleasure of the world,
and by the sweetness of his inspiration sounds words of love in the ears
of the heart. A soul is alone when it loves Jesus and gives its full attention
to him, and has lost the savor and comfort of the world; the better to
keep this solitude it flees the company of everyone if it can, and seeks
solitude in the body, for that greatly helps toward solitude of soul and
the free working of love. The less hindrance it has from vain jabbering
without or vain thinking within, the freer it is for spiritual beholding,
and so it is *in secrecy of heart.*

A soul is all outside while it is oppressed and blinded by love of the
world. It is as common as the highway, for every stirring that comes
from the flesh or from the devil sinks in and goes through it. But then
through grace it is drawn into the private chamber, into the sight of our
Lord Jesus, and hears his secret counsels, and is wonderfully comforted
in the hearing. The prophet speaks of this: *Secretum meum mihi; secretum meum mihi.*[321] My secret for myself; my secret for myself. That is,
the lover of Jesus, taken up from the outward feeling of worldly love
through the inspiration of His grace, and ravished into the mystery of
holy love, yields thanks to him, saying thus, *My secret for myself.* That is,
My Lord Jesus, your mystery is shown to me and secretly hidden from
all lovers of the world, for it is called hidden manna. It is easier to ask
what that is than to tell it, and our Lord Jesus promises it to his lover
thus: *Dabo sibi manna absconditum quod nemo novit nisi qui accipit.*[322]
That is, I shall give hidden manna that no one knows but him who takes
it. This manna is heavenly fare and angels' food, as holy scripture says,
because angels are fully fed and filled with clear sight and burning love
of our Lord Jesus, and that is manna. For we can ask what it is, but not

know what it is. But here the lover of Jesus is not yet filled: only fed with a little tasting of it whilst he is bound in this bodily life.

This tasting of manna is a lively feeling of grace[323] received through the opening of the spiritual eye; this grace is no other than that felt by a chosen soul at the beginning of his conversion, but it is the selfsame grace, though felt and shown to a soul in another way. For grace grows with the soul, and the soul grows with grace, and the purer the soul is and the further separated from the love of the world, the more powerful is the grace, showing the presence of our Lord Jesus more inwardly and more spiritually. So the same grace that first turns them from sin and makes them begin and profit by gifts of virtue and the exercise of good works also makes them perfect; and that grace is called *a lively feeling of grace,* for anyone who has it feels it well and knows well by experience that he is in grace.[324] It is very lively to him, because it wonderfully quickens the soul, making it so sound that it feels no painful disease of the body even if it is weak and sickly, because the body is then at its strongest, most whole and most restful, and the soul as well.

The soul does not know how to live without this grace, except in pain, for it seems that it could keep it forever, and that nothing should drive it away. However, it is not so, for it passes away very easily;[325] but nevertheless, although the best feeling of all may pass away and withdraw, the rest still remains, keeping the soul constant and making it desire its return. This is also the wakeful sleep of the spouse, of which holy scripture speaks thus: *Ego dormio, et cor meum vigilat.*[326] I sleep, and my heart is awake. That is, I sleep spiritually when through grace the love of the world is slain in me and the wicked stirrings of carnal desires are so near death that I hardly feel them; I am not vexed by them, and my heart is set free, and then it is awake, for it is keen and prompt to love Jesus and see him. The more I sleep from outward things, the more wakeful I am in the knowledge of Jesus and of inward things. I cannot wake to Jesus unless I sleep to the world, and therefore the grace of the Holy Spirit shutting the carnal eye makes the soul sleep from worldly vanity; opening the spiritual eye to wake to the sight of God's majesty, covered under the cloud of his precious humanity, as the gospel says of the apostles when they were with our Lord Jesus in his transfiguration. First they slept, and then *evigilantes viderunt maiestatem,*[327] awakening they saw his majesty. By the sleep of the apostles is understood the dying of worldly love through the inspiration of the Holy Spirit; by their awakening, contemplation of Jesus. Through this sleep the soul is brought into rest from the din of fleshly lust, and through wakening it is raised up into the sight of Jesus and spiritual things. The more that the eyes are shut in this kind of sleep from the appetite of earthly things, the keener is the inner sight in the lovely beholding of heavenly beauty. This sleeping and this waking are worked by Love in the soul of the lover of Jesus, through the light of grace.

41. How special grace in the beholding of Jesus sometimes withdraws from a soul, and how a soul shall behave in the absence and presence of Jesus; and how a soul is to desire that the gracious presence of Jesus is always in it.

Then show me a soul that through inspiration of grace has its spiritual eye opened to behold Jesus, and is so far separated and withdrawn from the love of the world that it has *purity and poverty of spirit*,[328] *spiritual rest, inward silence and peace of conscience, highness of thought, solitude and secrecy of heart, the waking sleep of the spouse; that has lost the pleasure and joys of this world, captured by delight in heavenly savor, ever thirsting and softly sighing [for] the blessed presence of Jesus;* and I dare boldly pronounce that this soul altogether burns in love and shines in spiritual light, worthy to come to the name and honor of the spouse. For it is reformed in feeling: made able and ready for contemplation. These are the tokens of inspiration in the opening of the spiritual eye; because when the eye is opened the soul is for that time in full feeling of all these virtues mentioned before.

Nevertheless, it often happens that because of the corruption of human frailty[329] this grace partly withdraws, allowing the soul to sink into its own carnal nature as it was before; and then the soul is in sorrow and pain, for it is blind and insipid and knows nothing good. It is weak and powerless, encumbered with the body and all the bodily senses; it seeks and longs for the grace of Jesus again; and it cannot find it. For holy scripture speaks of our Lord like this: *Postquam vultum suum absconderit non est qui contempletur eum.*[330] That is, After our Lord Jesus has hid his face, there is no one who can behold Him. When he shows himself the soul cannot fail to see him, for he is light; and when he hides himself it cannot see him, for the soul is dark. His hiding is only a subtle testing of the soul; his showing is most merciful goodness for the comfort of the soul.

Do not wonder that the feeling of grace sometimes withdraws from a lover of Jesus, for holy scripture says the same of the spouse, that she fares like this: *Quaesivi et non inveni illum; vocavi et non respondit mihi.*[331]

I sought and I did not find Him; I called, and he answered not. That is, when I fall down to my frailty, then grace withdraws; for my falling is the cause of it, and not his fleeing. But then I feel the pain of my wretchedness in his absence, and therefore I sought him with the great longing of my heart, and he gave me no perceptible answer. Then I cried with all my soul, *Revertere dilecte mi*,[332] Turn again, my beloved; and yet it seemed as if he did not hear me. The painful feeling of myself and the assailing of carnal loves and fears at this time, with the lack of my spiritual strength, is a continual complaint of my soul to Jesus, and nevertheless our Lord stays aloof and does not come, however hard I cry, for he is sure enough of his lover, that he will not turn again altogether to love of the world; he can have no savor in it. And therefore he waits the longer, but in the end, when he wills, he comes again, full of grace and truth,[333] and visits the soul that languishes in desire through sighings of love for his presence; he touches it and anoints it very gently with the oil of gladness, making it suddenly whole from all pain.

Then with a glad heart the soul cries thus to Jesus in the voice of the spirit: *Oleum effusum nomen tuum*.[334] Your name Jesus is oil poured out. Your name is Jesus: that is, Health. Then as long as I feel my soul sore and sick for sin, hurting from the heavy burden of my body, sorry and fearful for the perils and wretchedness of this life, so long, Lord Jesus, your name is oil shut up, not oil poured out for me. But when I feel my soul suddenly touched with the light of grace, healed and soothed from all the filth of sin, comforted in love and light with spiritual strength and unspeakable gladness, then I can say to you with joyful praise and spiritual might, "Your name Jesus is oil poured out for me; since by the effect of your gracious visiting I well feel the true interpretation of your name, you who are Jesus, Healing; for it is only your gracious presence that heals me from sorrow and from sin."

Blessed is that soul who is always fed on the feeling of love in his presence, or is borne up by desire for him in his absence.[335] He is a wise and well-taught lover who behaves soberly and reverently in his presence, and lovingly beholds him without careless levity; in his absence he behaves patiently and calmly, without venomous despair or over-painful bitterness.

This changeability[336] of absence and presence that a soul feels is not perfection of the soul; neither is it against the grace of perfection or contemplation; but perfection is so much the less. For the more hindrance that a soul has in itself from the continual feeling of grace, the less is the grace; and yet the grace in itself is nevertheless the grace of

contemplation. This changeability of absence and presence happens in
the state of perfection as well as in the state of beginning, but in another
manner, for just as there is a difference in feeling between these two
states in the presence of grace, so there is when grace is away. Therefore, anyone who does not recognise the absence of grace[337] is apt to be
deceived, and one who does not watch over the presence of grace is
ungrateful for the visiting, whether he is in the state of beginners or of
the perfect. Nevertheless, the more stability[338] that there is in grace,
unhurt and unbroken, the more lovely is the soul, and the more like him
in whom there is no kind of changeability,[339] as the apostle says; and it is
wholly fitting that the soul-spouse should be like Jesus the Spouse in
manners and in virtues, fully agreeing with him in the constancy of
perfect love. But that seldom happens: nowhere but in the special
spouse; for he who perceives no changeability in feeling his grace, but
thinks it evenly whole and stable, unbroken and unhurt, is either quite
perfect or quite blind.[340] Someone is perfect if he is sequestered from all
fleshly affections and communion with all creatures, and if all means of
corruption and sin are broken away between Jesus and his soul, fully
united to him with softness of love. But this is grace alone, above human
nature. Anyone is quite blind who pretends to be in grace without spiritual feeling of God's inspiration, and who sets himself up in a kind of
stability, as if he were always in the feeling and working of special grace;
judging that all that he does and feels is grace, both outwardly and
within; thinking that whatever he does or speaks is grace; holding himself unchangeable in the special gift of grace. If there is any such person
—as I think there is not—he is altogether blind to the feeling of grace.

But then you might speak like this: that we should live only in faith,
and not desire spiritual feelings, or regard them if they come, for the
apostle says, *Iustus ex fide vivit*.[341] That is, the righteous man lives in
faith. To this I say that we shall not desire bodily feelings, however
comforting they may be, or regard them much if they come; but we are
always to desire spiritual feelings of the kind I now speak of, if they
come in the manner I have said before. These are the slaying of all
worldly love, the opening of the spiritual eye, purity of spirit, peace in
conscience, and all the others already told. We should desire always to
feel the lively inspiration of grace caused by the spiritual presence of
Jesus in our soul, if we could, and to have him always with reverence in
our sight; and always to feel the sweetness of his love by a wonderful
homeliness of his presence. This should be our life and our feeling in
grace, according to the measure of his gift in whom all grace exists; to

some people more and to some less, for his presence is felt in various ways as he vouchsafes, and in this we should live and work, doing what it concerns us to do; for without this we should not know how to live. For just as the soul is the life of the body,[342] so Jesus is the life of the soul by his gracious presence; and nevertheless this kind of feeling, however great, is still only faith compared with what shall come from that same Jesus in the glory of heaven. See, this feeling is for us to desire, since every rational soul should long with all its powers to draw near to Jesus and to become one with him[343] through the feeling of his gracious invisible presence.

How that presence is felt can be known better by experience than through any writing, for it is the life and the love, the power and the light, the joy and the rest of a chosen soul, and therefore he who has once truly felt it cannot give it up without pain. He cannot do other than desire it, because it is so good in itself and so comforting. What is more comforting to a soul here than to be drawn out through grace from the vile annoyance of worldly business and the filth of desires, and from vain affection for all creatures, into the restfulness and ease of spiritual love; secretly perceiving the gracious presence of Jesus, feeling itself fed with the savor of his invisible blessed face? In truth, nothing, in my opinion. Nothing can fill the soul of a lover with joy but the gracious presence of Jesus, as he knows how to show himself to a pure soul. He is never sad or sorry but when he is by himself in his carnal state; he is never fully glad or merry but when he is as far out of himself as he was with Jesus in his spiritual nature. And yet that joy is not complete, for always there hangs on his soul a heavy lump[344] of bodily corruption, bearing it down and greatly hindering the spiritual gladness, and that must always be while it is here in this life.

Nevertheless, because I speak of the changeability of grace—how it comes and goes—do not misunderstand it. I do not mean the common grace that is had and felt in faith and in goodwill toward God; without having this and persevering in it no one can be saved, for it is in the lowest chosen soul that lives. But I mean the special grace felt by inspiration of the Holy Spirit in the way told before. The common grace, which is charity,[345] stays whole whatever a man does, as long as his will and his intention is true to God, so that he does not wish to sin mortally —or else the deed that he does willfully is not forbidden as a mortal sin; for this grace is not lost except through sin. And it is mortal sin when his conscience deliberately testifies that it is mortal, and nevertheless he still does it; or else his conscience is so blinded that he considers it no mortal

sin, although he willfully does a deed which as mortal sin is forbidden by
God and by holy church.

Special grace felt through the invisible presence of Jesus, making a
soul a perfect lover, does not stay equally whole, at the height of feeling,
but comes and goes changeably, as I have said before. So our Lord says:
*Spiritus ubi vult spirat, et vocem eius audis, et nescis unde veniat aut quo
vadat.*[346] The Holy Spirit breathes where he will, and you hear his voice,
but you do not know when he comes or where he goes. Sometimes he
comes secretly when you are least aware of him, but you shall know him
well before he goes, for he wonderfully stirs and mightily turns your
heart to the consideration of his goodness, and makes your heart melt
delightfully into the softness of his love, like wax before the fire; and
this is the voice that he sounds. But then he goes, before you know it, for
he withdraws a little—not altogether, but from excess into sobriety.[347]
The highness passes, but the substance and the effect of grace remains,
and that is as long as the soul of a lover keeps himself pure and does not
fall voluntarily into negligence or carelessness in the flesh, or into outward vanity, as it sometimes does through its own frailty, even though it
has no pleasure in it. It is of this changeability in grace that I speak now.

42. A commendation of the prayer offered to Jesus by a
     contemplative soul, and how stability in prayer is a safe
     work to stand in, and how every feeling of grace in a
     chosen soul may be said to be Jesus, but the purer a soul
     is, the more valuable is the grace.

As long as a person's soul is not touched with special grace it is
blunt and rough for spiritual work, knowing nothing of it and unable to
do anything in it because of its own weakness. It is both cold and dry,[348]
undevout and insipid in itself. But then comes the light of grace, and
through touching makes it sharp and subtle, ready and able for spiritual
work, giving it a great freedom, and complete readiness in will[349] to be
obedient to all the stirring of grace, prompt to work as grace stirs; and
then it so happens sometimes that grace stirs the soul to prayer: and how
the soul prays then, I shall tell you.

The most special prayer that the soul uses and has most comfort in
is, I expect, the Our Father, or else psalms of the Psalter: the Our Father
for the unlettered, and psalms, hymns and other worship of holy church
for the learned. The soul does not pray then in the way it did before, or
in the common manner of men—in a loud voice or by speaking out

fluently—but in a very great stillness of voice and gentleness of heart. The reason is that its mind is not troubled or teased with outward things but wholly gathered together in itself,[350] and the soul is set as if in a spiritual presence of Jesus; and therefore every word and every syllable is pronounced with savor, sweetness and delight, and with heart and mouth in full accord.[351] For the soul is then all turned into fire of love, and therefore each word that it secretly prays is like a spark springing out of a firebrand, warming all the powers of the soul, turning them into love, and filling them with light: so great is the comfort that the soul is pleased to pray all the time and do nothing else. The more it prays, the better it can, and the mightier it is, for grace helps the soul well and makes everything light and easy, so that it is very glad to psalm and sing the praises of God with spiritual joy and heavenly delight.

This spiritual work is food for the soul, and this prayer is of great virtue, for it destroys and brings to nought all temptations of the devil, both secret and open; it slays all thought of the world and all pleasure in it and in fleshly sins; it bears up the body and the soul from its painful feeling of the wretchedness of this life; it keeps the soul in the feeling of grace and in the work of love, nourishing it always to stay hot and fresh, as sticks nourish the fire.[352] It does away with all boredom and heaviness of heart, and holds it in joy and spiritual gladness.

David speaks thus of this prayer: *Dirigatur oratio mea sicut incensum in conspectu tuo.*[353] That is, Lord, may my prayer be directed as incense in your sight. For just as incense thrown on the fire makes a sweet smell from the smoke rising into the air, so in a burning heart a psalm said or sung with savor and softness yields a sweet smell to the face of our Lord Jesus and all the court of heaven. No fly[354] dares rest on the lip of the pot boiling over the fire;[355] just so, no carnal delight can rest on a pure soul that is all covered and warmed in the fire of love, boiling and giving off psalms and praises to Jesus. This is true prayer. This prayer is always heard by Jesus; it yields grace to him and receives grace in return; it makes a soul at home and in fellowship with Jesus and with all the angels of heaven. Let anyone make use of it who can, for the work in itself is good and full of grace.

Although in itself this kind of prayer may not be full contemplation, or by itself be the work of love, nevertheless it is a part of contemplation. For it cannot be done like this except in abundant grace, through the opening of the spiritual eye; and therefore a soul that has this freedom and this grace-given feeling in prayer, with spiritual savor and heavenly delight, has the grace of contemplation in that way. This prayer is a rich offering, all filled with the fatness of devotion,[356] received by angels[357] and presented to the face of Jesus.

The prayer of other people who are busied with active works is made of two words, for they often form one word in their hearts, through thinking of worldly affairs, and pronounce another with their mouths, of the psalm sung or said. However, if their intention is true, their prayer is still good and worthy of reward, even if it should lack savor and sweetness. But this kind offered by a contemplative is made of only one word, for as it is formed in the heart, so it sounds whole in the mouth: as if it were only one thing that both forms and pronounces. And certainly it is no more, for the soul is made whole in itself through grace, parted so far from the carnal nature that it is master of the body, and then the body is like nothing but an instrument and a trumpet of the soul, on which the soul blows sweet notes of spiritual praises to Jesus.

This is the trumpet that David speaks of: *Buccinate in neomenia tuba, in insigni die solemnitatis vestrae.*[358] Blow on a trumpet in the new moon. That is, You souls that are reformed in spiritual life through the opening of the inner eye, blow devoutly, sounding psalms with the trumpet of your bodily tongue. Therefore, because this prayer is so pleasing to Jesus and so profitable to the soul, it is good for anyone newly turned to God to desire this feeling, whatever he may be, if he wants to please him and desires to have some rare feeling of grace; that he might through grace come to this liberty of spirit and offer his prayers and psalms to Jesus continually, constantly and devoutly, with whole attention and burning affection for him, and keep it as a custom when grace will stir him to it.

This is a sure feeling, and a true one. If you can come to it and hold it, you need not run about here and there asking questions of every spiritual man as to what you are to do, how you shall love God, and how you shall serve him, and speak of spiritual matters beyond your knowledge, as perhaps some do. That kind of thing is not very useful unless greater need makes it so. First work hard to hold firmly to your prayers, so that afterward you may come to the restful feeling of this spiritual prayer, and that shall teach you wisdom enough, truthfully and without pretense or fantasy;[359] keep to it if you have it, and do not leave it unless grace should come in another way, wanting to take it from you for a time and make you work differently. Then for a while you can leave it, and afterward turn again to it. Anyone who has this grace in prayer does not ask where he shall set the point of his thought as he prays; whether upon the words that he says or else on God or on the name of Jesus, as some ask. The feeling of grace teaches him well enough, because the soul is turned into the eye, sharply beholding the face of Jesus, and is assured that it is Jesus whom it feels and sees. I do not mean Jesus as he is in himself in the fullness of his blessed divinity, but Jesus as he wishes to show himself to a pure soul held in the body, according to the purity that it has. For you are to know well that every feeling of grace is Jesus and may be called Jesus, and as the grace is more or less, so the soul feels Jesus more or less. Yes, the first feeling of special grace in a beginner, which is called the grace of compunction[360] and contrition for his sins, is truly Jesus, because he makes that contrition in a soul by his presence. But Jesus is then quite roughly and crudely felt, very far from his divine subtlety, for the soul knows no better and can do no better because of its own impurity at that time. However, if it profits and increases in virtues and in purity, the same Jesus and no other is afterward seen and felt by the same soul when it is touched with grace. But that is more spiritual, nearer to the divine nature of Jesus. And certainly this is the greatest thing that Jesus loves in a soul: that it might be made divine and spiritual through seeing and loving, to be through grace like what he is by nature,[361] for that shall be the aim of all lovers. Then you can be sure that whenever you feel your soul specially stirred by grace in the way already described—by the opening of your spiritual eye—you see and feel Jesus. Hold him fast while you can, keep yourself in grace, and do not lightly let him go. Do not look for any other Jesus than this, by feeling that same grace more divinely, so that it might grow in you more and more; and even though the Jesus that you feel may not be Jesus as he is in his full divinity, do not fear that you may therefore be deceived in bowing to your feeling. But if you are a lover of Jesus, trust firmly that your feeling is true,[362] and that by his grace Jesus is in truth felt and seen by you, as you are able to see him here; and therefore bow entirely to your feeling when it is spiritual and full of grace; keep it tenderly and set a great value upon it—not on yourself—so that you may see and feel Jesus ever better and better. For grace shall even teach you by itself, if you will yield to it, until you come to the end.

But perhaps you begin to wonder why at one time I say that grace works all this, and another time I say that love [363] works, or Jesus works, or God. To this I reply that when I say that grace works, I mean love, Jesus and God; for all is one, and one alone.[364] Jesus is love; Jesus is grace; Jesus is God; and because he works everything in us by his grace, for love, as God, I can therefore use in this writing whichever of these four words pleases me, as I am stirred.

43. How through the opening of the spiritual eye a soul receives a gracious love able to understand holy scripture, and how Jesus, who is hidden in holy scripture, shows himself to his lovers.

When the soul of a lover feels Jesus in prayer in the way described before, and thinks that it never wants to feel otherwise, it nevertheless happens sometimes that grace puts vocal prayer to silence and stirs the soul to see and feel Jesus in another way; and that is first to see Jesus in holy scripture. For Jesus, who is all truth, is hidden and concealed there, wound in a soft fine linen under fair words, so that he cannot be known or felt except by a pure heart; because truth will not show itself to enemies, but to friends that love it and desire it with a humble heart. Truth and humility[365] are faithful sisters, joined together in love and charity, and for this reason there is no break in counsel between those two. Humility relies upon truth, and not at all on itself, and truth firmly trusts humility, and so they agree wonderfully well. Then inasmuch as a lover's soul is made humble through the inspiration of grace, by the opening of the spiritual eye, and sees that it is nothing in itself but depends only on the mercy and goodness of Jesus, and continues to be borne up by his favor and help alone, truly desiring his presence: it therefore sees Jesus. For it sees the truth of holy scripture wonderfully shown and opened, above study and toil and the reasoning of man's natural wit. And that may well be called the feeling and the perception of Jesus. For Jesus is the well of wisdom,[366] and by a little pouring of his wisdom into a pure soul he makes the soul wise enough to understand all holy scripture: not all at once in a special beholding, yet through that grace the soul receives a new ability and a grace-given disposition to understand it in a special way when it comes to mind.

This openness and clarity of perception is made by the spiritual presence of Jesus: for example, the gospel speaks of two disciples going to the village of Emmaus, burning with desire and talking of Jesus. Our Lord Jesus appeared to them in person, like a pilgrim, and taught them the prophecies about himself; and as the gospel says, *Aperuit illis sensum ut intelligerent scripturas.*[367] He opened the clearness of their wit, so that they could understand holy scripture. In just the same way the spiritual presence of Jesus opens the understanding of his lover who burns in desire for him, and by the ministry of angels brings to his mind the words and the insights of holy scripture, unsought and unconsidered, one after another, and readily expounds them, however hard or secret they may be. The harder they are[368] and the further from the rational understanding of man, the more delightful is the true showing of it when Jesus is master. It is expounded and declared literally, morally, mystically and heavenly,[369] if the matter allows it. By the letter, which is easiest and plainest, the bodily nature is comforted; by the morality of holy scripture the soul is informed about vices and virtues, how to separate them wisely one from the other; by mysticism it is illuminated to see the works of God in holy church, and to apply easily the words of holy scripture to Christ our head and to holy church, which is his mystical body; and the fourth, which is heavenly, concerns only the working of love,[370] and that is when all truth in Holy Scripture is applied to love, and because that most resembles heavenly feeling, I therefore call it heavenly.

The lover of Jesus is his friend: not because he has deserved it, but because Jesus of his merciful goodness makes him his friend by true accord, and therefore he shows his mysteries as to a true friend who pleases him with love, not serving him in fear like a slave. So he says himself to his apostles: *Iam vos dixi amicos; quia quaecumque audivi a Patri meo nota feci vobis.*[371] Now I say that you are my friends, for I make known to you all that I have heard from my Father.

To a pure soul that has its palate purified from the filth of fleshly love, holy scripture is vital food, and nourishment full of delight. It tastes very sweet when it is well chewed by spiritual understanding, because in it is hidden the spirit of life,[372] which quickens all the powers of the soul and fills them full of the sweetness of heavenly savor and spiritual delight. But in truth someone needs to have sharp white teeth,[373] well-picked, if he is to bite this spiritual bread, for heretics and lovers of the flesh cannot touch the inner flour of it: their teeth are bloody and full of filth, and therefore they are fasting from the taste of this bread. By teeth are understood the inner senses of the soul, which in heretics and lovers of the flesh are bloody, and full of sin and worldly vanities. They would like to come to the true knowledge of holy scripture through the curiosity of their natural wit, but they cannot, for their understanding is corrupted by the original sin, and by actual sin as well, and it is not yet healed through grace; therefore they gnaw only the outer bark,[374] feeling nothing of the savor enclosed within, however much they talk about it. They have neither the humility nor the purity to see it, for they are not friends of Jesus and therefore he does not show them his counsel.[375]

The mystery of holy scripture is closed under key, sealed with a signet of Jesus' finger, which is the Holy Spirit.³⁷⁶ Therefore without his love and his leave nobody can come in. He alone has the key of knowledge³⁷⁷ in his keeping, as Holy Scripture says, and he himself is the key, and he lets in whom he will through the inspiration of his grace, without breaking the seal. Jesus does this for his lovers: not for all alike, but for those who are specially inspired to seek truth in holy scripture, with great devotion in prayer preceded by great diligence in study. These can come to the finding when our Lord Jesus is willing to reveal it.

See now how grace opens the eye of the spirit and clears the understanding of the soul, wonderfully above the frailty of corrupt nature. It gives the soul a new ability, whether it wants to read holy scripture, or to hear or reflect on it in order to understand and savor its truth aright in the way described before, and easily to turn all principles and words that are stated materially into spiritual understanding. That is no great marvel, for the same spirit who first made holy scripture expounds and declares it in a pure soul for its comfort, and that is the Holy Spirit. This grace may be—and is—in the unlettered as well as in the learned as regards the substance and the veritable feeling of truth, and the spiritual savor in general, though they do not see so many principles in particular, for that is not necessary. And when the soul is thus enabled and illuminated through grace, then it is pleased to be alone sometimes, away from the hindrance or conversation of all created beings, freely to try out its instrument (which is what I call its reason) on the consideration of the truth contained in holy scripture; and there come to mind words and arguments and interpretations enough to occupy it, very seriously and in good order.

The soul may know by experience—otherwise not—what comfort and spiritual delight, savor and sweetness, it can then feel in this spiritual work through various illuminations, inward perceptions, hidden intuitions and sudden touchings of the Holy Spirit. I think he will not go wrong, provided his teeth, which are his inward senses, are kept white and clean from spiritual pride and from the curiosity of his natural understanding. I suppose David felt very great delight in this kind of work when he said: *Quam dulcia faucibus meis eloquia tua! Super mel ori meo.*³⁷⁸ How sweet are your utterances to my jaws, Lord Jesus; better than honey in my mouth. That is: Lord Jesus, your holy words, written in holy scripture and brought to my mind through grace, are sweeter to my jaws (which are the affections of my soul) than honey is to my mouth. Certainly, to see Jesus in this way is a fair and honorable work, without painful toil. It is one kind of sight of Jesus, as I said before, not as he is but clothed in the likeness of works and of words, *per speculum etiam in aenigmate*,[379] by a mirror and by a likeness, as the apostle says.

Jesus is infinite power, wisdom and goodness,[380] righteousness, truth, holiness and mercy; and what this Jesus is in himself no soul can see or hear; but in the effect of his working[381] he may be seen by the light of grace, like this. His power is seen from the making of all creatures out of nothing; his wisdom in their ordered disposition; his goodness in their salvation; his mercy in the forgiveness of sins; his holiness in the gifts of grace; his righteousness in the hard punishment of sin; his truth in the faithful rewarding of good works. All this is expressed in holy scripture, and there it is seen by a soul, with all other attributes that go with it. You must know that such gracious intuitions in holy scripture— or in any other book made through grace[382]—are nothing else but sweet letters,[383] sent between a loving soul and Jesus the beloved: or else, if I am to speak more truthfully, between Jesus the true lover and the souls loved by him. He has love of very great tenderness for all his chosen children who are here enclosed in the clay of this bodily life, and therefore, although he is absent from them—hidden high above in the bosom of the Father and filled with the delights of the blessed Deity—he thinks of them none the less and visits them very often through his gracious spiritual presence; he comforts them by his letters of holy scripture, drives out of their hearts heaviness and impatience, doubts and fears, and makes them glad and joyful in him, truly believing in all his promises and humbly awaiting the fulfilment of his will.

St. Paul spoke like this: *Quaecumque scripta sunt ad nostram doctrinam scripta sunt, ut per consolationem scripturarum spem habeamus.*[384] All that is written for our teaching is written so that by the comfort of scripture we might have hope of salvation. And this is another work of contemplation: to see Jesus in the scriptures after the opening of the spiritual eye. The purer the sight as it gazes, the more comfort is given to the affection as it tastes. A very little savor—felt in a pure soul from holy scripture in the way described before—should make the soul set little value on the knowledge of all the seven arts or all worldly sciences: for the end of this knowledge is the salvation of a soul in everlasting life, and the end of the others in themselves is only vanity and a passing delight, unless through grace they are turned to this end.

44. The hidden voice of Jesus sounding in a soul: by what means it shall be known, and how all the illuminations caused by grace in a soul are called the sayings of Jesus.

See, these are fair new feelings in a pure soul, and if a soul were filled with them it might truly be said that it was partly reformed in feeling: but not yet fully. The reason is that Jesus shows more, leads the soul further inward, and begins to speak more familiarly and more lovingly to a soul; and then the soul is ready to follow the stirrings of grace, for the prophet says: *Quocumque ibat spiritus, illuc gradiebantur et rotae sequentes eum.*[385] Wherever the spirit went, the wheels went following them. By wheels are understood true lovers of Jesus, for they are round in virtue, without awkward angles, whirling easily through aptness of will to the stirring of grace. For as grace stirs and teaches,[386] so they follow and work, as the prophet says. But first, before they can do so, they have a very sure experience and true knowledge of the voice of grace, so that they may not be deceived by their own pretense, or by the midday devil. Our Lord Jesus speaks of his lovers like this: *Oves meae vocem meam audiunt, et cognosco eas, et cognoscunt me meae.*[387] My sheep hear my voice, and I know them and they know me. The hidden voice of Jesus is altogether true, and it makes a soul true; there is no deceit in it, or fantasy,[388] no pride or hypocrisy, but mildness, humility, peace, love and charity, and it is full of life and grace. Therefore, when it sounds in a soul it is so strong sometimes that the soul at once lays aside all that there is—praying, speaking, reading or meditation in the manner described before, and every kind of bodily work—and listens to it fully, hearing and perceiving the sweet sound of this spiritual voice in rest and in love, as if ravished from the awareness of all earthly things. And then in this peace Jesus sometimes shows himself as a master to be looked on with awe, and sometimes as a father to be revered, and sometimes as a beloved spouse;[389] and it keeps the soul in a wonderful reverence and in a loving gaze upon him, so that the soul is then well content, and never so well as then. For it feels such great security[390] and rest in Jesus, and so much favor from his goodness, that it wants to be like this always and never do other work. It feels it is touching Jesus, and by virtue of that ineffable touch it is made whole and constant in itself, reverently beholding only Jesus, as if nothing existed but Jesus one thing and himself another, borne up only by the favor and wonderful goodness of Him: that is, of this thing that he sees and feels.

And this feeling is often present without any special consideration of holy scripture, and with only few words formed in the heart, though among them occur sweet words in accordance with the feeling: either praising or worshipping or making such other sounds as the heart likes. In the meantime the soul is far away from the love and pleasure of the world by virtue of this gracious feeling, and from much thought of the world too. It gives no heed to it, for it has no time for it.[391] But then sometimes, together with this, various illuminations afterward fall into a soul through grace. I call these illuminations the sayings of Jesus and the sight of spiritual things; for you must know that all the trouble Jesus takes about a soul is in order to make it a true perfect spouse for himself in the height and fullness of love. Because that cannot be done at once, Jesus—who is love, and of all lovers the wisest—tries many ways and many wonderful means before it can come about; and so that it can reach the fulfillment of true marriage he therefore uses such gracious speeches to a chosen soul in the guise of a suitor. He shows his jewels, giving many things and promising more, and offering courteous talk. Often he visits with much grace and spiritual comfort, as I have said before, but I do not know how to tell you in full detail how he does this, for there is no need. I shall nevertheless tell you a little, as grace suggests.

A pure soul is fully drawn to perfect love when the spiritual eye is opened and it is first shown spiritual things: not that a soul should rest in it and find its goal there,[392] but that by this it should seek and love him alone who is highest of all, without regarding anything other than him. But you say, "What are these spiritual things?" For I often speak of spiritual things. To this I say in reply that all the truth of holy scripture may be called a spiritual thing, and therefore a soul that can see the truth of it by the light of grace sees spiritual things, as I have said before.

45. How through the opening by grace of the spiritual eye a soul is made wise, to see humbly and truly the different degrees in holy church as it labors, and to see the nature of angels: and first, of the reprobate.

However, there are also other spiritual things shown to the soul by the light of grace, which are these: the nature of all rational souls, and the gracious working in them of our Lord Jesus; the nature of angels—blessed and reprobate—and their working; and the knowledge of the blessed Trinity, as grace teaches.

In the book of the Songs of the Spouse holy scripture speaks like this: *Surgam, et circuibo civitatem, et quaeram quem diligit anima mea.*[393] I shall rise and go about the city, and I shall seek him whom my soul loves. That is, I shall rise into highness, and go about the city. By this city is understood the universe of all creatures, bodily and spiritual, ordained and ruled under God by the laws of nature, of reason and of grace. I go round this city when I consider the natures and the causes of bodily creatures, and the gifts of grace and blessed joys of spiritual creatures; and in all these I seek him whom my soul loves. It is beautiful to look with the inner eye on Jesus in bodily creatures, to see his power, his wisdom and his goodness in ordaining their nature; but it is much more beautiful to look at Jesus in spiritual creatures. First in rational souls, of both the chosen and the reprobate, to see his merciful calling to his chosen: how he turns them from sin by the light of his grace, how he helps them, teaches and chastises them, comforts and corrects them, cleanses and feeds; how he makes them ardent in love and in light through the abundance of his grace. And he does this not to one soul only but to all his chosen, according to the measure of his grace. In the same way with all the reprobate, how justly he forsakes them and leaves them in their sin, and does them no wrong; how he rewards them in this world, allowing them to have the fulfillment of their will, and afterward punishes them eternally.

See, this is a little view of holy church while it is laboring in this life: to see how black and ugly it seems in souls that are reprobate, how fair and lovely it is in chosen souls; and all this spiritual sight is nothing else but the sight of Jesus—not in himself, but in the hidden works of his mercy and in his hard righteous judgments, daily revealed and renewed for rational souls. And more than this, it is encouraging to see with the eye of the spirit the pains of the reprobate[394] and the joy and beatitude of chosen souls; for truth cannot be seen in a pure soul without great delight and the wonderful gentleness of burning love.

It is much the same with the consideration of angels' nature: first of the damned and afterward of the blessed. The contemplation of the devil is a very fine sight for a pure soul when grace makes him appear to it as a surly captive, bound by the power of Jesus so that he can do no harm. Then the soul does not behold him in the body, but in the spirit, seeing his nature and his malice, and turns him upside down; it strips him and tears him all apart; it scorns and despises him and cares nothing for his malice. This is the command of holy scripture when it says: *Verte impium, et non erit.*[395] Turn the wicked—that is, the devil—upside down, and he shall be as nothing. The soul finds it wonderful that the devil has so much malice and so little might. No creature is as powerless as he, and therefore people are great cowards to fear him so much, for he can do nothing without leave of our Lord Jesus, not so much as go into a pig, as the gospel says;[396] far less, then, can he trouble any man. And if our Lord Jesus gives him leave to harass us, what our Lord Jesus does is done worthily and mercifully; therefore may our Lord Jesus be welcome, by himself and through all his messengers. Then the soul fears the blustering of the devil no more than the stirring of a mouse. The devil is very angry if he should dare to say no, but his mouth is stopped with his own malice, and his hands are bound[397] like a thief who deserves to be judged and hanged in hell; and then the soul accuses him and rightfully judges him as he has deserved.

Do not wonder at this saying, for St. Paul meant the same when he said: *Fratres, nescitis quoniam angelos iudicabimus?*[398] My brothers, do you not know that we shall judge angels? By these are meant spirits made good angels by nature who have become wicked through malice. This judging is figured in contemplative souls before the Judgment, for they feel a little taste of all that shall be done afterward by our Lord Jesus, openly and in truth. The devil is greatly shamed[399] and confounded in himself when he is treated like this by a pure soul; he would gladly escape, but he cannot, for the power of the Most High[400] holds him still, and that hurts him more than all the fire of hell. Then the soul falls very humbly before Jesus, with heartfelt praises and thanks that he so mightily and through his great mercy saves a simple soul from all the malice of so cruel an enemy.

46. How by the same light of grace the nature of the blessed angels may be seen; and how Jesus as God and man is above all created beings, insofar as the soul can see him here.

Then after this and by the same light the soul can see spiritually the beauty of angels and their dignity by nature: the subtlety of their substance, their confirmation in grace, the fullness of their eternal glory, the diversity of their orders[401] and the distinction of their persons; how they live all in the light of eternal truth, and how they burn all in love of the Holy Spirit according to the dignity of their orders; how they see, love and praise Jesus in blessed rest, without ceasing. In this kind of work there is no vision of the body or of a figure of the imagination, but all is spiritual, and concerning spiritual creatures.[402]

Then the soul begins to have great acquaintance with these blessed spirits, and a great fellowship; they are very tender toward such a soul, and busy themselves in helping it; they are masters to teach it, and through their spiritual presence and the touching of their light they often drive out phantoms from the soul, which they illuminate through grace. They comfort the soul with sweet words quickly uttered in a pure heart, and if it meets with any spiritual distress they serve the soul and administer all that it needs. St. Paul spoke of them like this: *Nonne omnes sunt administratorii spiritus missi propter eos qui hereditatem capient salutis?*[403] Do you not know that all holy spirits are ministers sent by Jesus for those who take the heritage of salvation? These are chosen souls. As if to say, You are to understand that all this spiritual operation of words and statements brought to mind, and such fair likenesses, are done by the ministry of angels, when the light of grace shines abundantly in a pure soul. No tongue can tell the particular feelings, illuminations, graces and comforts that pure souls perceive through the fellowship and favor of blessed angels. The soul is so fully at ease with them, looking at what they do, that it has no wish to attend to anything else; but then with the help of angels it sees still more.

For in a pure soul knowledge rises above all this, to gaze upon the blessed nature of Jesus himself: first on his glorious humanity—how it is worthily exalted above the nature of all angels—and then afterward on his blessed divinity;[404] for by knowing creatures the Creator is known. Then the soul begins to perceive a little of the mysteries of the blessed Trinity. It can, well enough, for the light of grace goes before, and therefore she shall not err as long as she keeps herself with the light.

Then is truly revealed to the eyes of the soul the unity in substance and distinction of persons in the blessed Trinity, as it can be seen here, with much other truth about the blessed Trinity concerning this matter, which is openly declared and set out in the writing of holy teachers of holy church. And you must know that a pure soul can see by the same light of grace the selfsame truth of the blessed Trinity that these holy teachers, inspired through grace, write in their books for the strengthening of our faith. I will not express too much of this matter in detail here, for there is no need.

The soul feels wonderfully great love, with heavenly delight, in beholding this truth, when it is made through special grace, for love and light both go together in a pure soul. There is no love arising from knowledge and from special beholding that can touch our Lord Jesus so nearly as this love, because only this knowledge of Jesus, God and man, is highest and most valuable in itself, if it is specially shown by the light of grace; and therefore the fire of love set aflame by this is more ardent than from the knowledge of any creature, bodily or spiritual. And all these intuitions felt in a soul through grace in the way described before —of the universe of all creatures and of our Lord Jesus, maker and keeper of all this fair universe—I call them the fair words and sweet sayings of our Lord Jesus to a soul whom he will make his true spouse. He shows mysteries and offers rich gifts from his treasure, arraying the soul with them most honorably. She need not be ashamed to appear afterward with her companions before Jesus, her spouse. All this loving courtship and private talk between Jesus and a soul may be called a hidden word, of which holy scripture says: *Porro ad me dictum est verbum absconditum et venas susurri eius percepit auris mea.*[405] Truly, a hidden word has been said to me, and my ear has perceived the veins of his whispering. The inspiration of Jesus is a hidden word, for it is secretly hidden from all lovers of the world and shown to his lovers, through which a pure soul easily perceives the veins of his whispering that are special showings of his truth. For each recognition of truth through grace, felt with inward savor and spiritual delight, is a secret whisper from Jesus in the ear of a pure soul.

If anyone is to perceive these sweet spiritual whispers wisely, he needs to have great purity of soul, in humility and all other virtues, and to be half deaf to the noise of worldly jabbering. This is the voice of Jesus, of which David says thus: *Vox Domini praeparantis cervos, et revelabit condensa.*[406] The voice of our Lord Jesus making ready the harts, and he shall show the thickets. That is, the inspiration of Jesus makes souls as light as the harts that leap from the earth over the bushes and briars of all worldly vanity, and he shows them the thickets, which are his secrets: they cannot be perceived except by a sharp eye. Truly grounded in grace and humility, these contemplations make a soul wise, burning in desire for the face of Jesus. These are the spiritual things I spoke of before; they can be called new gracious feelings, and I touch on them only a little for the instruction of your soul: for a soul that is pure, stirred by grace to the practice of this work, can see more of such spiritual matter in an hour than could be written in a great book.

Explicit hic Finis

Notes

B. L. MS. Harley 6579 (H), from which we have taken our text of Book 2, contains a number of additions and corrections made by a different hand (Hc), and these are included without further comment. Unlike the "Christocentric" expansions in Book 1, most of the interpolations in Book 2 seem to restore text accidentally lost in transmission, where a previous scribe's eye has been misled by the repetition of a word or phrase, causing him to omit the words between. See S. S. Hussey, "The Text of The Scale of Perfection, Book 2," p. 88; but cf. further "Editing the Middle English Mystics," in *Spiritualität Heute und Gestern,* ed. James Hogg (Salzburg, 1982), Vol. 2 pp. 167–73.

1. *imago Dei:* Cf. 1 Corinthians 11.7—not an exact quotation.
2. *similitudinem suam:* This is not the actual text of Genesis 1.27, but a conflation of that verse with Genesis 1.26, *Faciamus hominem ad imaginem et similitudinem nostram.*
3. *The justice of God:* The argument in this chapter follows St. Anselm, *Cur Deus Homo;* see especially 1.20; 2.8;11.
4. *most honorable [deed]: opus hominis perfectissimi opusque dignissimum* Y; H's reading is slightly ambiguous.
5. *virtutem, etc.* 1 Corinthians 1.23–24.
6. *faith—either general or special:* St. Thomas draws out the distinction between explicit and implicit faith—for the "lesser ones" (*minores*) and simple (*simplices*) implicit faith, with the intention to believe what the church believes, suffices (ST 2–2, q. 2, a. 6).
7. *these men are greatly and grievously in error:* Many people today would hold this view as very probable. Christians would agree with David Knowles: "If God, who is the common Father of all men, allows himself to be known by those outside the body of the faithful of his Church—and Christ himself praised the centurion for a faith which he had not found in Israel—the God so attained is the very God who sent his Son to redeem mankind" (*What is Mysticism?* [London, 1967], p. 126). The view which Hilton rejects is expressed by William Langland in *Piers Plowman,* B Text, Passus 12, lines 284ff., as noted by Gerard Sitwell in his edition of the *Scale.* It may also be found in some academic theologians of the fourteenth century. For the views of Robert Holcot, O.P. (d. 1349) on the virtuous pagan, see his *In Quatuor Libros Sententiarum Quaestiones* (ed. Lyon, 1518) 3, q. 1 TT, discussed in W. J. Courtney, *Schools and Scholars in Fourteenth-Century England* (Princeton, 1987), p. 343.
8. *as Jews and Saracens do:* Hilton holds to the ultra-Augustinian view of his day concerning the fate of the unbaptized. This depends on the view that Adam's original sin involves all his descendants in guilt, even

if they never committed actual sin. Such a view is expressed in Pseudo-Augustine (Fulgentius of Ruspe), *De Fide ad Petrum,* cited in Gratian, *Decretum,* p. 3, d. 4, c. 3 (Friedberg, *Corpus Iuris Canonici* [Leipzig, 1879 and reprints], vol. 1, col. 1362). This is not a view generally held by Christians today!

9. *they had the faith and did not keep it:* For the thought, cf. Luke 12.48.

10. *the full feeling of God:* Amended from Y, which reads *plenam sensacionem dei.* H has *the hole and the fulfillyng of God.*

11. *without admixture of any other affection:* This suggests the distinction made by Augustine, *De Correptione et Gratia* 12.33; the first freedom of the will (*libertas voluntatis*) was that of being able not to sin (*posse non peccare*); the last will be much greater, that of not being able to sin (*non posse peccare*).

12. *in illa die:* Isaiah 2.11.

13. *It is true.* What follows is based on Anselm, *De Concordia Praescientiae* q. 3, c. 9.

14. *consummarentur:* Hebrews 11.40.

15. *in faith and in feeling:* "Feeling" is mentioned in a like sense already in *Scale* 1.19, p. 92. It is synonymous with "understanding" as the realization for oneself of what is believed by faith. See Introduction, p. 43. In the *Cloud,* ch. 9 (Hodgson, p. 34), "feeling" is likewise taken as the fullest realization of God's presence in this life, short of the open vision (*species*) which belongs to heaven.

16. *if he does not deliberately assent to it:* This is commonplace. William Flete, *De Remediis,* MS. Bodley 43, p. 140, cites from Augustine, *De Vera Religione* 14.27, on this point.

17. *beginning, proficient, perfect:* The classification of *incipientes, proficientes, perfecti* for the three stages of the spiritual life is commonplace. Gregory, *Moralia* 24.11.28, refers to *inchoatio, medietas, perfectio.*

18. *people in active life:* Cf. *Scale* 1.9 p. 83, where Hilton says that though people whose state in life is active may attain to the third degree of contemplation by occasional and special grace, the habitual use of this is generally within the reach only of those vowed to the contemplative life. Later in *Scale* 2 Hilton will be more ready to suppose that contemplation in its full sense may be within the reach of all generous souls, e.g. *Scale* 2.21, 27 (pp. 229, 245).

19. *an image of the Devil and a brand of hell:* Cf. *Scale* 2.3, p. 197.

20. *reformed to the image of God:* Occasionally Hilton blurs the distinction between "image" and "likeness," which in general he is careful to make. Cf. *Scale* 2.1, pp. 193–194 and Introduction, pp. 35–36.

21. *is suddenly turned:* St. Thomas says that justification is effected *in instanti* (ST 1–2, q. 113, a.7).

22. *contrition:* Defined as "sorrow for sins, with the purpose of confessing them and making satisfaction," according to St. Thomas (ST Suppl. q. 1, a.1), in line with Raymond of Pennafort and the *Summa Theologica* attributed to Alexander of Hales.

23. *He does not wait for great penance to be done:* What follows is based on

Epistola ad Quemdam Saeculo Renuntiare Volentem, in Clark and Taylor, pp. 265–69. The "declaratory" theory of sacramental absolution that follows, according to which absolution is a declaration in the sight of the church of the forgiveness already bestowed by God, represents a tradition that antedates St. Thomas Aquinas, for whom sacramental absolution, as an efficacious sign, really effects what it signifies. (Cf. ST 3, q. 84, a.3; a.7). Hilton's view is found in Peter Lombard, *Sent,* 4, d.17; d.18. This older tradition is perpetuated by Franciscan theologians, e.g., St. Bonaventure, *In Sent,* 4, d.17. For the motive of humility in going to confession with a priest, cf. Peter Lombard, *Sentences* 4, d.16, c.1.

24. *full forsaking: forsasyng* H; *relinquat* Y; H's reading is probably an error for either *forsakyng* ("forsaking" in Underhill), or *forsaying,* which would here be rendered *renouncing.*

25. *grace of compunction:* The expression is a common one; cf. Gregory, *Moralia* 29.26.53: *gratia compunctionis.*

26. *holy church ordained:* Cf. *Decretalium Gregorii* IX Lib. 5, tit. 38, c.12 (*Corpus Iuris Canonici,* vol. 2, col. 887), *Omnis utriusque sexus.*

27. *anyone is greatly mistaken:* One of the conclusions distilled from Wyclif's teaching, and condemned at the Blackfriars Synod of 1382, was that confession in the presence of a priest was superfluous, cf. Workman, appendix T, pp. 416ff.

28. *this image: grace* H; *imago* Y.

29. *to believe what you do not see:* Hebrews 11.1.

30. *though he may neither feel it nor see it:* Cf. *Scale* 1.21, p. 94.

31. *ambulant, etc.:* Romans 8.1.

32. *image: ymaginis* Y; *grace* H.

33. *Iustus ex fide vivit:* Romans 1.17/Hebrews 10.38. The antithesis between faith and sight is a commonplace in Augustine; see for instance *De Trinitate* 14.2.4, citing 2 Corinthians 5.6–7, 1 Corinthians 13.12; and Romans 1.17.

34. *habemus ad Deum:* Romans 5.1.

35. *life: vita* Y; *luf* H.

36. *in gloria:* 1 John 3.2.

37. *non morietur:* Ezekiel 18.21.

38. *if he ... does not take it truly for love of God:* In line with the "declaratory" view of absolution which he has given in *Scale* 2.7, Hilton demands "perfect contrition," which he takes itself to be a gift of God, as prerequisite for forgiveness. For the demand for "perfect contrition," cf. Peter Lombard, *Sentences* 4, d.16, c.1. St. Bonaventure accepts that not everyone comes to confession with "perfect contrition," but assumes that the process of confession and absolution may effect a real purification of intention. Cf. *In Sent.* 4, d.17, p. 2, a.2, q.3. St. Thomas accepts that "imperfect contrition" suffices for justification through the sacrament of absolution, provided that one does not put obstacles in the way of grace. Cf. ST Suppl, q. 18, a.1.

39. *the least degree of charity:* The stages of spiritual progress—*incipientes,*

proficientes, perfecti—are reckoned as so many stages of charity. ST 2–2, q.24, a.9.

40. *laudate eum:* Revelation 19.5. Cf. the use of Canticle 5.1 in *Scale* 1.44, p. 117.

41. *A child's knowledge . . . fed with milk:* Cf. 1 Corinthians 3.1–2; Hebrews 5.14; 1 Peter 2.2.

42. *the woman of Canaan:* Matthew 15. Similarly in *Epistola de Lectione*, in Clark and Taylor, p. 237. The woman of Canaan as a figure of the church imploring God's gifts for her children is commonplace. Cf. Bede, *In Matthaeum*, Exp. 3 (PL 92.75).

43. *easily acquired:* Cf. Augustine, *De Quantitate Animae* 33.74: "It is one thing to achieve purity, another to keep it."

44. *ravishing:* Cf. *Scale* 1.8, p. 82.

45. *sensuality:* The body with its complex of senses and emotions. See *Scale* 2.13, p. 213, with note 65.

46. *adversus carnem:* Galatians 5.17.

47. *legem peccati:* Romans 7.23.

48. *legi peccati:* Romans 7.25.

49. *peccatum:* Romans 7.19–20.

50. *freedom (fredom* H): This is written as one word, but cf. *iudicium* (Y) and H's spelling *fredam* at 2.26 (p. 241) and 2.27 (p. 242), which might support "free judgment" as a possible rendering here.

51. *and not be too much concerned with judging them mortal or venial:* For Hilton's unwillingness to fuss about the mortal or venial distinction, cf. *Scale* 1.56, p. 127. He is saying that in any case a generous soul will not want to "measure" sin.

52. *peccata tua:* Matthew 9.2.

53. *non intelligetis:* Actually the old Latin form of Isaiah 7.9, as commonly cited by Augustine (and those who follow him), especially when referring to the necessity of faith as a basis for understanding. See Introduction, pp. 43–44. Curiously, Hilton elsewhere ascribes this text to "the Apostle"—*Epistola de Utilitate* and *Epistola de Lectione* in Clark and Taylor, pp. 142, 229.

54. *Faith . . . understanding comes after:* A quotation from Augustine, *Sermo* 118.1: *Praecedit fides, sequitur intellectus.*

55. *Deum videbunt:* Matthew 5.8.

56. *corda eorum:* Acts 15.9.

57. *Salomonis:* Canticle 1.4. After Bernard, *In Cant.* 25–27.

58. *cedar . . . darkness:* Similarly Bernard, *In Cant.* 26.1.1.

59. *Solomon . . . peaceable:* Similarly Bernard, *In Cant.* 27.1.2.

60. *skin . . . angel:* Bernard takes *pelles* to refer to heaven, citing Psalm 103.2, *Extendens caelum sicut pellem.*

61. *me sol:* Canticle 1.5.

62. *domum tuam:* Mark 2.11. The text is applied similarly in Gregory, *Homilia in Ezekiel* 1.12.11.

63. *extinguere:* Ephesians 6.16.

64. *according to the diverse parts of the soul . . . :* What follows stands close

to William of St. Thierry (Déchanet, p. 178). William describes how some men are "animal" (*animales*); others are rational, and through the judgment of reason and the discretion of natural knowledge can both know and desire what is good; others are perfect, and are led by the Spirit (*spiritu aguntur,* cf. Romans 8.14).

65. *A soul has two parts:* For medievals, *sensuality* is a technical term with a different connotation from that which it has in modern English. The sensuality is that element in man which is common to himself and the animals, which in consequence of the Fall is no longer governed by the reason, because the reason is itself no longer directed to God. Cf. Augustine, *De Trinitate* 12.11.16, citing Psalm 48.13/21. The term *sensualitas* is not actually used by Augustine, but is found in Richard of St. Victor, *Benjamin Minor* c. 5; St. Thomas discusses it in ST 1 q. 81. The two "parts" of reason, *ratio superior* and *ratio inferior,* are not strictly two parts of the reason, but are the one reason performing distinct offices, insofar as it is directed to the right ordering of temporal things (*scientia*), or the contemplation of eternal things (*sapientia*). See Augustine, *De Trinitate* 12.3.3–4.4; 12.14.21–23; St. Thomas, ST 1 q. 79, a. 9.

66. *the dignity of his soul:* Cf. Augustine, *De Quantitate Animae* 34.77: "Among that he has made, nothing is nearer to God (than the soul)."

67. *no rest . . . save God alone:* Cf. Augustine, *Confessions* 1.1.1: *Inquietum est cor nostrum, donec requiescat in te.*

68. *unnaturally . . . unreasonably:* St. Thomas says that all men have a natural desire for God (ST 1, q. 2, a. 1, ad 1).

69. *passing delight of an earthly thing:* Cf. the medieval chapter heading given to Augustine, *De Civitate Dei* 12.8: *De amore perverso, quo voluntas ab incommutabili bono ad commutabile bonum deficit.* ("delight" represents the Latin *delectatio*).

70. *into the likeness of various beasts:* Cf. Psalm 48.13/21, cited at *Scale* 1.43, p. 114. Arising from this, the comparison of various sins—especially the capital sins—to various beasts is a commonplace medieval device. See M. W. Bloomfield, *The Seven Deadly Sins* (Michigan State College Press, 1952), especially the appendix, "Association of Animals and Sins."

71. *Tumidis . . . sulphure:* Revelation 21.8. H reads *tumidis,* supported by Y and by *proude men* below. This differs from the standard Vulgate text *timidis.*

72. *biting of conscience: morsum conscientiae* Y.

73. *non est Deus:* Psalm 13.1.

74. *our Lady's fast:* It was customary in the Middle Ages to fast on Saturdays in honor of our Lady. Cf. *The Book of Margery Kempe,* ed. Meech and Allen (EETS, 1940), p. 162, with note.

75. *auditui:* Isaiah 28.19.

76. *comprehenderunt:* John 1.5.

77. *just as a blind man is all enfolded:* Cf. Augustine, *Enarrationes in Psalmos* 99.5: "He who is said to be blind . . . is present in vain to things that he does not see; indeed he is more properly said to be absent than

present, for where he has no feeling (*sensus*), he is properly said to be absent."

78. *inasmuch as it is: as mikel as is* H; *in quantum est* Y.

79. *et vivat:* Ezekiel 33.11.

80. *they could not well be:* Cf. Y: *non possunt bene esse vel salvari.*

81. *from the lowest to the highest:* Cf. Gregory, *Moralia* 22.19.45; *Homilie in Ezekiel* 2.3.3; similarly *Mixed Life,* in Ogilvie-Thomson, p. 69, referring to Gregory.

82. *a high ladder:* For the soul's ascent to God by introversion, cf. Gregory, *Homilia in Ezekiel.* 2.5.9. St. Bernard's exposition of part of St. Benedict's *Rule* is of course entitled *De Gradibus Humilitatis.* This is the only reference to the "ladder" in Hilton's text, despite the (probably editorial) title of his book. Cf. Introduction, p. 19.

83. *special help:* This refers to the "special grace" of contemplation, which Hilton will describe in the later part of the book.

84. *profiting:* See previous note on 2.5, p. 200 [*beginning, proficient, perfect*].

85. *a soul . . . condition:* A commonplace point; cf. Augustine, *Sermo* 169. 18 (PL 38.926); Gregory, *Regula Pastoralis* 3.34.

86. *a man dragged out of a pit:* Cf. Gregory, *Epistola* 7.37 (PL 77.896).

87. *bodily practices . . . ways and means:* It is commonplace teaching that one has to become detached from pious practices as ends in themselves. John Tauler makes the same point in *Predigten,* ed. Vetter (Berlin, 1909), No. 21, pp. 86–87.

88. *gift:* om. H; *donum* Y.

89. *in Syon:* Psalm 83.8. This verse is also recalled in Bernard, *De Gradibus Humilitatis* 1.2; it is also cited in Bernard, *Sermo in Quadragesima* 6.4, ed. Leclerq, vol. 4, p. 379, = 7.4, PL 183.184. This sermon is a source for other aspects of this part of the *Scale,* see ch. 21, p. 227; 22, p. 231; 27, pp. 243–245. It is a source also for *Ancrene Wisse,* ch. 7. See *Ancrene Wisse, Parts 6 & 7,* ed. G. Shepherd (Manchester, 1972) p. 3, with note.

90. *in hunger, and thirst, in cold:* Cf. 2 Corinthians 11.27.

91. *special healer:* Cf. *Scale* 1.29, p. 100, with note 100.

92. *as he teaches and stirs:* Fishlake renders: *sicut ipse docet et excitat* (Y).

93. *shall not covet any reward but him alone:* Augustine, *De Doctrina Christiana* 1.27.28, speaks of charity as love of God *propter seipsum.* Cf. St. Bernard, *De Diligendo Deo* 7.17: "God is not loved without reward, even if he is to be loved without awareness of being rewarded"; 9.26 goes on to speak of *amor castus,* the love of God for himself and not for his benefits.

94. *He is free, and gives himself where he will:* Cf. William of St. Thierry, in Déchanet p. 344: "But this manner of thinking of God is not in the choice of him who thinks, but in the grace of God who gives; that is, when the Holy Spirit, who blows where he will (cf. John 3.8), when he wills and how he wills, and to whom he wills, gives his inspiration to this purpose. But it is for man continually to prepare his heart." Cf. further Richard of St. Victor, *Benjamin Minor,* c. 73 (PL 196.52): "For

the soul never attains such grace by its own effort. It is the gift of God, not man's desert. But surely no one receives such grace, without great labor and burning desire." There is closely related teaching in *The Cloud of Unknowing*, ch. 34: "And I believe that our Lord as specially and as often—indeed, more specially and more often—will deign to work this work in them that have been habitual sinners, than in some others that (in comparison with them) never grieved Him greatly. And this he will do, because he wants to be seen to be all merciful and almighty, and because he wants to be seen to work as it pleases him, where it pleases him, and when it pleases him" (Hodgson, p. 69, modernization by JC).

95. *perfect love and charity:* Cf. ST 2–2, q. 44, a.1: "The end of the spiritual life is that a man be united to God, which is done by charity."

96. *humility . . . truly as he is:* Hilton is taking up what he has said earlier in *Scale* 1.68, p. 139, on the basis of St. Bernard's teaching.

97. *by grace . . . good works that he does:* The corollary is that one should stop thinking about either one's merits or one's demerits in the face of God's immensity and love. Cf. *Scale* 2.37, p. 272, where Hilton develops this point in the context of the two kinds of humility.

98. *beholding the truth:* Sothfastnes (H); cf. *humilitatis* (Y).

99. *For what is humility but truth?* Similarly *The Cloud of Unknowing*, ch. 34 (Hodgson, p. 69, modernization by JC): "If you were truly humble, you would feel concerning this work as I say: that God gives it freely without our deserving it at all."

100. *this is very hard:* Hilton will describe in chs. 34ff., pp. 263ff., how it is the disclosure of Christ in the life of grace that confers a perfect humility that a person could never attain by himself or herself; this disclosure removes all self-consciousness.

101. *a man who has this sight shall never do less:* There can be no question of Quietism. Cf. ch. 40, p. 281.

102. *There was a man wanting to go to Jerusalem:* The image of the Christian life as a pilgrimage is a familiar one, cf. 1 Peter 2.11. But there is a more specific source here in St. Bernard's *Sermo in Quadragesima* 6 (see on ch. 19, p. 223). The theme of pilgrimage occurs there in nn. 1–2. See further on ch. 21, p. 227; ch. 22, p. 231; ch. 27, pp. 243–245. The man going to Jerusalem, who is attacked by thieves and robbers, suggests the man in the parable of the Good Samaritan (Luke 10.30). In Augustine's exposition of the parable, the Good Samaritan is Christ himself, who rescues the Christian (*Quaestiones Evangeliorum* 2.19, PL 35.1340).

103. *do not willingly stay with it:* Cf. *Scale* 1.38 on not dallying with temptation. But see more particularly St. Bernard's sermon, n. 1.

104. *that is what you long for and what you desire:* Cf. Bernard, *Sermo in Quadragesima* 6, n. 2. "I am indeed dead to all other things; I do not feel them; I do not give any attention to them; I do not care about them." Comparison may also be made with Richard of St. Victor, *De IV Gradibus Violentae Charitatis*, PL 196.1211: *Unum amat, unum dili-*

git, unum sitit, unum concupiscit. There is similar phrasing in the *Cloud*, ch. 7.

105. *Jerusalem . . . sight of peace:* Commonplace. Cf. for example Augustine, *Enarrationes in Psalmos* 64.3.

106. *these two strings:* There is a partial literary parallel in Margaret Porete, *The Mirror of Simple Souls* (Doiron, p. 267, lines 3 ff), referring to the twin strings of faith and love, but this may be due to a common source, unidentified.

107. *only that humility:* Cf. ch. 20, p. 225; and below, ch. 37, pp. 271–273. For the two kinds of humility, there are various parallels, including Bernard, *Epistola* 393.3 (Leclerq, vol. 8, p. 367): "Humility has two feet: the consideration of God's power, and of one's own weakness." Closer is Gilbert of Hoyland, *In Cant.* 15.7 (PL 184.78): "The weaker are made humble by their own vanity; the more perfect by the truth of God." Hilton's teaching here is exactly matched by the *Cloud*, chs. 13–14.

108. *not only as the greatest wretch:* "Perfect" humility does not abolish "imperfect" humility, a point made in the *Cloud*, ch. 14.

109. *forget it:* Cf. Philippians 3.13 f. The *Cloud*, ch. 5, refers to the "cloud of forgetting." Cf. also *Scale* 2.33, pp. 261–262.

110. *Just as a true pilgrim . . . wife and children:* Cf. Matthew 19.27 ff.

111. *set in your heart, wholly and fully:* Cf. *Scale* 1.22, p. 95.

112. *thieves and robbers . . . unclean spirits:* Cf. *Scale* 2.21 above, p. 227.

113. *the degree and state in which you stand* supports the idea that in *Scale* 2 Hilton has in mind a wider readership than in *Scale* 1. Cf. ch. 27, p. 245; ch. 39, p. 278.

114. *prayer: prechynge* (H); emended to agree with *oratio* (Y) and *preiynge* (Rawlinson C. 385 and others).

115. *with a fire and sticks:* Cf. the use of Leviticus 6.12 in *Scale* 1.32, pp. 102–103, with note 112.

116. *practices of your own choosing:* Cf. above, ch. 19, p. 223.

117. *that you have not made a proper confession:* For doubts as to one's salvation, and the remedy, cf. *Scale* 1.21, p. 94. The problem of scrupulosity after confession and absolution is dealt with in *Epistola ad Quemdam Saeculo Renuntiare Volentem* (Clark and Taylor, pp. 265–78). William Flete deals with the problem of doubts regarding absolution or the completeness of one's confession in *De Remediis*, MS. Bodley 43, pp. 145–46.

118. *what with fear and menaces:* Cf. St. Bernard, *Sermo in Quadragesima* 6.2.

119. *fall into sickness:* All this is what Bernard would understand by the *timor nocturnus* (Psalm 90.5), which he takes in *In Cant.* 33.6.11 to refer to the terror that besets beginners, the fear of the unaccustomed strictness involved in turning to God. For Hilton's familiarity with St. Bernard's use of this psalm, as shown in many of his writings both Latin and English, see Clark, "Walter Hilton and the Psalm Commentary *Qui Habitat*," p. 241.

120. *your good deeds and virtues:* The temptation to pride in one's own

achievements suggests the *sagitta volans in die* of Psalm 90.6, as interpreted by St. Bernard, *In Cant*, 33.6.12. Cf. *Scale* 2.37, p. 274.

121. *He makes this desire in you:* The prevenience of grace is a commonplace of Augustinian theology. But comparison is perhaps especially apt with Bernard, *De Diligendo Deo* 7.22: "The cause of loving God is God. I have said the truth, for he is both the efficient and the final cause (*efficiens, finalis*). He himself gives the occasion, he himself creates the affection; he himself consummates the desire."

122. *You do nothing . . . consent to him:* Cf. ST 1-2, q. 111, a. 2, ad 2: God does not justify us without ourselves, because while we are being justified, we consent to the justice of God by the movement of free will. But that movement is not the cause of grace, but its effect. So the whole operation belongs to grace. Similarly ST 1-2, q. 112, a. 2.

123. *a rational instrument:* Cf. ST 1-2, q. 68, a. 3, ad 2.

124. *He goes before you:* Cf. ST 1-2, q. 111, a. 3, on prevenient grace.

125. *secret presence of his power:* "There is one common way in which God is in all things by his essence, his power and his presence; but there is above this a special way in which through grace God is known and loved by the rational creature, and in which he is said not merely to be in the creature, but to dwell in it as in his temple" (ST 1, q. 43, a.3).

126. *tabernacula tua:* Psalm 42.3. Bernard, *In Cant*, 33.6.13, uses this text to refer to the distinction of the true *lux oriens ex alto* from the *daimonium meridianum* of Psalm 90.

127. *praecordiis meis:* Isaiah 26.8-9.

128. *sicut dei:* Genesis 3.5.

129. *natus sum:* Job 3.3. Hilton's exposition at this point is based on Gregory, *Moralia* 4.1.4-6. Gregory relates Genesis 3.5 to the day of false illumination, the day of fallen man which Job cursed, just as Hilton does. Hilton uses Genesis 3.5 in a similar sense in *Epistola de Lectione* (Clark and Taylor, p. 222).

130. *in lumine:* 1 John 2.10.

131. *a good night:* recalling Gilbert of Hoyland, *In Cant*. 1.5 (PL 184.15): "That is a good night, which hides all temporal things with prudent forgetfulness, procuring the time to seek him who is eternal."

132. *luminous darkness:* In itself the phrase is Dionysian, and as such is used in *The Book of Privy Counselling* (Hodgson, p. 154, line 17). But Hilton's use of the term has no apophatic overtones; he uses the Dionysian term in the interests of his own different theology.

133. *lux mea est:* Micah 7.8.

134. *this night . . . easy and comforting:* The *Cloud*, ch. 69, refers to the pain experienced by those who are as yet unaccustomed to God's light.

135. *do not strive too hard:* Cf. *Scale* 1.90, p. 159.

136. *negative:* H reads *noght*.

137. *the true light:* For "light" H has *luf.* Y reads *lumine.*

138. *if your eye . . . answers thus:* Hilton refers to the bodily senses. He does not make a formal distinction between the night of the senses and of the spirit as St. John of the Cross does. See Introduction, p. 49.

139. *blind thinking:* This does not mean the apophaticism of the *Cloud* (cf. *Cloud,* ch. 68), but blind rather means "single-minded."

140. *invisible light:* God's light is so fine that it is invisible. Cf. Gregory, *Moralia* 22.4.6: "If the visible light is recklessly loved, the heart is blinded from the invisible light." This was a commonplace. Cf. Rolle, *Emendatio Vitae,* ch. 12 (MS. Cambridge U.L. Dd v. 64, f. 15 r.): "For if the intellectual eye strives toward the spiritual light, it does not see that light as it is in itself. . . . As when we are standing in darkness we see nothing, so in the contemplation which invisibly illuminates the soul we do not see visible light."

141. *when the night passes and the day springs:* Cf. Romans 13.12.

142. *My soul has desired you in the night:* Isaiah 26.9.

143. *Grow used to staying in this darkness:* For the idea of being able to dispose oneself at will to receive God's gift of contemplation, cf. ch. 27, p. 243; ch. 40, p. 280; ch. 41, p. 285. Richard of St. Victor distinguishes between three ways of experiencing the grace of contemplation represented by the Ark of the Covenant: through the teaching of others; as an occasional gift, through the conjunction of human effort with grace; and as a habitual gift. These three modes are represented by Moses, Bezaleel, and Aaron respectively (*Benjamin Major* 5.1). Richard's teaching is reproduced in the *Cloud,* ch. 73.

144. *to feel at home:* Fishlake (MS. Y) translates *homly* as *familiaris.* Richard of St. Victor speaks of *familiaritas* between God and the soul (*Benjamin Minor,* c. 11; PL 196.8).

145. *orta est eis:* Isaiah 9.2. Bearing in mind the use made earlier of Job 3.3 (see ch. 24), it may be worth noting that *umbra mortis* is a catch-phrase with Job 3.5: *Obscurent eum tenebras et umbra mortis.*

146. *small sudden gleams . . . little crannies:* Fishlake (Y) translates the phrase *smale caues* (H) as *rimas paruulas. Rima* is a familiar word in Gregory the Great for glimmering of contemplation: *Moralia* 5.29.52; *Homilia in Ezekiel* 2.5.16.

147. *the prophet Ezekiel:* What follows is based on Gregory, *Homilia in Ezekiel* 2.5.1. Cf. Ezekiel, Ch. 40.

148. *the midday devil:* This is the *daimonium meridianum* of Psalm 90.6. Richard of St. Victor, *Benjamin Minor* c. 81, speaks of the devil's transforming himself into an angel of light (2 Corinthians 11.14). But Hilton is drawing rather on Bernard's exposition of this verse, as part of his *Sermo in Cant.* 33.5.9. For Hilton's familiarity with this context, see ch. 22, p. 231, note 119. For Bernard the *daimonium meridianum* is evil masquerading as good; it is a temptation that besets especially those who have overcome all worldly temptations, and would be accounted perfect. Cf. *Qui Habitat* (ed. Wallner), p. 21.

149. *as soon as they have forsaken the world:* Hilton is continuing his criticism of immature enthusiasts, found already in *Scale* 1.10. while the reference to "freedom of spirit" later might suggest the heresy familiar on the Continent, with its overtones of pantheism and antinomianism, the reference here to keeping the letter of the commandments

suggests that Hilton has in mind rather those who mistake the avoidance of carnal sins for perfection, ignoring the far more deadly sin of spiritual pride. This accords with the description of the *sagitta volans in die* as pride in *Qui Habitat* (Wallner, pp. 17f.). Cf. also *Scale* 2.37, p. 274.

150. *that heat:* Cf. *Scale* 1.10.

151. *two black rainy clouds:* Similarly *Qui Habitat* (Wallner, p. 23).

152. *from the devil, if it comes suddenly, or from man's own mind, if it comes by study:* Similarly *Of Angels's Song* (Takamiya, p. 13, or Dorward, p. 17).

153. *disobedience to the laws of holy church:* Hilton probably has in mind the effects of the Lollard movement. His emphasis on the spiritual value of the humility involved in the sacrament of penance and absolution is relevant here (cf. ch. 7, p. 201). The related passages in *Qui Habitat* (Wallner, pp. 21–22), and in *Eight Chapters* (Kuriyagawa, pp. 21–22), are more explicitly antinomian, cf. above.

154. *the words that they sow: schewen* H. Emended from Y, which reads *seminant.*

155. *diabolica:* James 3.16, 15; cf. James 1.17.

156. *And so by these tokens:* Cf. Matthew 7.16: "You shall know them by their fruits." The moral test of religious experience is developed in *Epistole de Lectione* (Clark and Taylor, pp. 231f.).

157. *inimicos eius:* Psalm 96.3. Similarly in Bernard, *In Cant.* 31.2.4.

158. *well-assayed and burnt:* Cf. ch. 28, p. 248.

159. *perfect love of Jesus:* Cf. ch. 21, p. 228.

160. *justitiae:* Malachi 4.2.

161. *bring it through grace into custom:* Cf. ch. 25, p. 238; ch. 41, p. 287.

162. *the gate of contemplation:* Cf. John 10.1 ff., discussed below.

163. *to die to the world:* Cf. Galatians 6.14, cited below.

164. *no honor or praise from the world:* This may be a reflection of Hilton's own renunciation of a promising legal career; see Introduction, pp. 14–15. On the other hand, the thought is commonplace, and finds support in Bernard's Lenten sermon already referred to—*Sermo in Quadragesima* 6(7).3.

165. *such blind love ... between a man and a woman:* This is perhaps a recollection of a passage in *Eight Chapters*, ch. 5, (Kuriyagawa, p. 25); in *Eight Chapters* the consequences of such love are more drastic. Hilton is touching here on the *ordo caritatis;* cf. Introduction, p. 41.

166. *delicacies in food and drink:* Cf. *Scale* 1.72, pp. 144–145.

167. *ego mundo:* Galatians 6.14, cited by St. Bernard, *Sermo in Quadragesima* 6(7).3.

168. *it is the gate to contemplation:* Cf. John 10.1ff. In *Scale* 1.91, p. 160, echoing the same context in the Fourth Gospel, Hilton has said that conformity to Christ in the virtues of his humanity is the only door to contemplation. There are similar passages in *The Prickynge of Love*, ed. Kane; see under *Scale* 1.91. The present passage also finds a near parallel in *The Book of Privy Counselling*, Hodgson, pp. 159–60.

169. *according to . . . states they are in:* Cf. *Scale* 2. Ch. 39, p. 278, with the view of an apparently wide readership.

170. *in Deo:* Colossians 3.3. Cited by St. Bernard, *Sermo in Quadragesima* 6(7).2.

171. *possidebit:* Cf. Matthew 19.29.

172. *a good darkness and a rich nothing:* Cf. ch. 24, p. 235.

173. *nescivi:* Psalm 72.22. The *nihilum* refers to poverty of spirit. Cf. above, chs. 21; 22; 23; pp. 229, 231, 233.

174. *abundantly feel the love of Jesus:* Cf. ch. 40, p. 284 on contemplation as "feeling of grace."

175. *Deum suum:* Isaiah 50.10.

176. *At first he shall be as if blind:* Cf. ch. 24, p. 236. There is some similarity here with the *Cloud*, ch. 68 (Hodgson, p. 122): "This nought . . . is full blind and full dark to them that have but a little while looked on it." But the *Cloud* continues: "Nevertheless . . . a soul is more blinded in feeling of it for abundance of spiritual light, than for any darkness or wanting of bodily light." (Text slightly modernized.)

177. *splendoribus:* Isaiah 58.10–11.

178. *Caldeorum:* Isaiah 47.5.

179. *ita et lumen eius:* Psalm 138.12.

180. *He forms . . . he reforms us with us:* After Augustine, *Sermo* 169.13: *Qui ergo fecit te sine te, non te justificat sine te.*

181. *glorificavit:* Romans 8.29–30. *Magnificavit* is a mediaeval intrusion into the Vulgate text. It occurs, for example, in St. Thomas' commentary on Romans.

182. *when he begins to press forward strongly: Eight Chapters,* ch. 2 (Kuriyagawa, p. 17; Dorward, p. 3), refers to temptation and trial which beset the soul after one has begun to make considerable progress. On the relation of this section of Hilton's writing to the pattern set out in *Scale* 1, chs. 36ff., and the relation of both to St. John of the Cross, see Introduction, pp. 48–49.

183. *crooked toward false love of the world:* Fishlake (Y) translates *incurvatus.* "Crooked" is equivalent to *pravus* or *curvus* in contrast to *rectus* in Augustine and the subsequent tradition. See, for example, Augustine, *Enarrationes in Psalmas* 9.15: "When the will is *rectus* it issues in *caritas;* when it is *pravus,* it issues in *cupiditas.*"

184. *rust of impurity:* Similarly in *Eight Chapters,* ch. 4 (Kuriyagawa, p. 22; Dorward, p. 7).

185. *nearly falls into despair . . . forsaken by God:* Similarly in *Scale* 1.38, p. 109, on the basis of William Flete, *De Remediis,* MS. Bodley 43, p. 142. In either case, the insistence that the soul is maintained in union with God at a supernatural level through the infused virtues is in line with Flete (p. 143). It is also in line with the teaching of the *Cloud's* author; see *Book of Privy Counselling,* Hodgson, pp. 167–68.

186. *through both fire and water:* Cf. Psalm 65.12. Flete (p. 147) speaks of the "*ignis probationis.*"

187. *nocebit te:* Cf. Isaiah 43.1–2.

188. *there are many souls newly turned to God:* What follows is a further development from what Hilton has said in *Scale* 1.10–11.

189. *an old cask:* This is based on the parable of the wineskins, Matthew 9.17, and on the application of this in Gregory, *Moralia* 23.11.20.

190. *having pity for all his creatures:* Cf. Wisdom 15.1f.

191. *They are not yet at home: familiaritatem*, Y. Cf. ch. 25, p. 238.

192. *to have knowledge of itself:* Cf. *Scale* 1.42, p. 112.

193. *when the soul is so gathered into itself:* Based probably on Gregory, *Homilia in Ezekiel* 2.5.9.

194. *your soul is not a body, but a life invisible:* A commonplace, deriving directly or indirectly from Augustine, *De Quantitate Animae* 13.22. The same is reproduced in William of St. Thierry, Déchanet, p. 306.

195. *your soul is only a mirror:* Cf. Richard of St. Victor, *Benjamin Minor*, c. 72 (PL 196.51), or else Pseudo-Augustine, *De Spiritu et Anima*, c. 52 (PL 40.818).

196. *in imagination and not in understanding:* The two are contrasted here, just as devotion and contemplation are in *Scale* 1.9.

197. *imagine a wonderful light:* Cf. *Scale* 1.11, p. 84.

198. *our Lord Jesus tempers the invisible light of his divinity:* This is a development of what Hilton has said in *Scale* 1.35, on the carnal and spiritual love of God in Christ, following St. Bernard.

199. *inter gentes:* Lamentations 4.20. The text differs from the standard Vulgate, but is that of the Latin translation from the text from Origen's commentaries, with which St. Bernard was familiar. Bernard uses the text in various passages, including *In Cant.* 31.3.8; 48.3.6.

200. *This was our Lord's teaching to Mary Magdalene:* For Mary Magdalene as the type of the contemplative, see on *Scale* 1.11, p. 85. For what follows, Hilton goes behind St. Bernard to one of the earlier sources on which Bernard's teaching on the carnal/spiritual love is based, Augustine, *Tractatus in Epistolam Ioanni ad Parthos* 3.1–2 (PL 35.1998).

201. *Patrem meum:* John 20.17.

202. *Spiritus Sanctus:* Cf. Acts 2.3. Augustine uses this as one illustration of the temporal disclosure of the Holy Spirit—*De Trinitate* 2.6.11.

203. *veritatem:* Cf. John 16.13.

204. *For if he will give . . . without any labor:* On the unmerited nature of contemplation, cf. ch. 20, pp. 224–225.

205. *sensus vestri:* Romans 12.2. This is a familiar text in such contexts, and with other texts in this chapter is cited by Augustine in many places of the renewal of the *imago Dei* in us. See especially *De Trinitate* 7.6.12; 14.16.22.

206. *spirituali:* Colossians 1.9.

207. *et veritate:* Ephesians 4.23–24; cited by Augustine in, for example, *De Trinitate* 12.7.12; 14.16.22. Cf. also *Scale* 1.86, p. 156.

208. *qui creavit illum:* Colossians 3.9–10. Cited by Augustine in, for example, *De Trinitate* 12.7.12; 14.16.22.

209. *compared to milk:* Cf. *Scale* 1.9, p. 83, with note 28.

210. *the understanding is [the] lady:* After Richard of St. Victor, *Benjamin*

Minor c. 5 (PL 196.5). The soul has two principal faculties: reason and affection. Imagination conveys things belonging to the material and sensible world to the reason, while the sensuality does the like for the affection.

211. *not what he is . . . but that he is:* Cf. St. Thomas, *In Boeth, de Trinitate* q. 1, a.2, ad 1: "Although it remains unknown what he is, yet it is known that he is."

212. *an unchangeable being:* For the epithets, cf. *Of Angels' Song,* Takamiya, p. 10. Fishlake renders "being" as *essentia* (Y). Augustine prefers to speak of God as *essentia* rather than as *substantia,* because etymologically the latter (like Latin *existentia*) implied contingency, that one has an origin outside oneself. Cf. Augustine, *De Trinitate* 5.2.3; 7.5.10. Augustine points out, *De Civitate Dei.* 11.10.3, that God *is* his attributes: "What he has, these things he is, and he is all of them in one."

213. *endless beatitude:* St. Thomas devotes ST 1, q. 26 to the *beatitudo* of God, concluding (a.4) that the beatitude of God includes all that can be desired in every beatitude.

214. *seeing and knowing . . . affections:* It is a commonplace, derived from Augustine (*De Trinitate* 10.1.1) that we cannot love what we do not know, cited by, for example, St. Thomas (ST 1-2, q. 27, a. 2).

215. *It is in faith, because it is still dark:* Cf. 1 Corinthians 13.12.

216. *sicuti est:* 1 John 3.2.

217. *in the light of the sun:* For God as the sun, illuminating us by his light, cf. *Scale* 2.16, p. 218; 2.33, p. 262.

218. *supreme goodness, supreme being and a blessed life:* God's goodness is equated with his being.

219. *of which holy men speak:* This might be taken as a commonplace. But if we have to look for a particular source, it may be that Hilton has in mind Richard Rolle. The latter in his various writings frequently refers to the "door opened in heaven," *ostium apertum* (Revelation 3.8), and relates this to visions of the citizens of heaven, e.g., *Emendatio Vitae,* ch. 12: "Moreover holy and contemplative men behold the glory of the Lord with unveiled face (2 Corinthians 3.18), which happens either when their understanding is opened so that they may understand the scriptures, or when the door of heaven is opened, which is a greater thing, so that with, as it were, all obstacles between their mind and God removed, with the eye of the heart cleansed, they may behold the citizens of heaven" (MS. Cambridge U.L. Dd v.64f. 15r.).

220. *there are many who err:* The *Cloud,* chs. 51 and 57, is likewise concerned to understand the terms "up" and "in" correctly in relation to God.

221. *holy writings:* Cf. *Scale* 1.25, notes 90-91, with references to Hilton's antecedents in his teaching on techniques in prayer.

222. *draw down the sun and all the firmament, forget it:* This suggests the "cloud of forgetting," which according to the *Cloud,* ch. 5, must be put between the soul and creatures. Cf. also *Qui Habitat,* Wallner, p. 33. "Cast all the world under thy feet."

223. *Our Lord is within all creatures:* St. Thomas speaks of God as "in" all things by his presence and power, and dwelling in the soul at a higher level by grace, as in his temple (ST 1, q. 43, a. 3.).

224. *find him within itself or within all creatures:* Cf. *Qui Habitat*, Wallner, p. 32, citing Luke 17.21: "The kingdom of heaven is within you."

225. *Deus lux est:* 1 John 1.5.

226. *videbimus lumen:* Psalm 35.10. Pseudo-Augustine, *De Spiritu et Anima* c. 12 (PL 40.787 f.), holds 1 John 1.5 and Psalm 35.10 together: "As the eye cannot see the sun except in its light, so the understanding will not be able to see the true and divine light except in its own light: Lord, says the Prophet, in your light we shall see light."

227. *ignis consumens est:* Deuteronomy 4.24/Hebrews 12.29. Cf. *Mixed Life*, Ogilvie-Thomson, p. 39.

228. *the love of God burns and consumes all sin:* This is taking up *Scale* 1.31, pp. 101–102.

229. *aeterna sunt:* 2 Corinthians 4.18.

230. *Christum:* John 17.3.

231. *this knowledge . . . is the glory and the end of a soul:* St. Thomas, ST 1, q. 26, a. 3, says that the beatitude of an intellectual nature consists in the act of understanding (*intellectus*), and appeals to Augustine, *Confessiones* 5.4.7, to the effect that beatitude consists in knowing God— *Beatus est qui te novit.*

232. *not only for the sight, but also for the . . . love:* Similarly St. Thomas, ST 2–2, q. 180, a. 7, *in corpore* and ad 1.

233. *the soul cannot come to this knowledge . . . without love:* Cf. St. Thomas, ST 1–2, q. 27, a. 2, ad 2, discussing the question whether knowledge is the cause of love: "Knowledge (*cognitio*) pertains to the reason. . . . For the perfection of knowledge a man must know every single part of a thing. . . . But love is in the appetitive power, which looks at a thing as far as it can. So for the perfection of love it suffices that a thing be loved in so far as it is apprehended in itself." The *Cloud*, stressing this principle, and building on the affective interpretation of the Dionysian writings that derives especially (but by no means only) from Thomas Gallus, opposes love to knowledge: e.g., *Cloud*, ch. 8 (Hodgson, p. 33): "Love may reach to God in this life, but not knowing." Hilton keeps knowledge and love in balance, while accepting of course that in this life we can never know God as he is.

234. *the love that our Lord has for a sinful soul:* For Hilton's tendency to equate grace and charity or love, see already on *Scale* 1.68, p. 138, with note 286. God's love—like grace—is prevenient.

235. *Holy writers say . . . two kinds of spiritual love:* This is a commonplace, though the way in which the principle is applied has varying nuances in different writers. A starting point is Augustine, *De Trinitate* 15.18.32: "Therefore the love (*dilectio*), which is from God (*ex Deo*) and which is God, is properly the Holy Spirit, through whom the love (*caritas*) of God is spread abroad in our hearts" (Romans 5.5); idem., *De Trinitate* 15.19.37: "If in the gifts nothing is greater than charity, and

nothing is a greater gift of God than the Holy Spirit, what follows more directly than that he is Charity (*Caritas*), who is said to be both God and from God?" There are adumbrations of the distinction between uncreated and created love in the early Cistercians, e.g., Bernard, *De Diligendo Deo* 12.35; William of St. Thierry, *Speculum Fidei* (PL 180.395); *Aenigma Fidei* (PL 180.399); *Expos. in Cant.* 1 (PL 180.506). Peter Lombard identified charity itself with the Holy Spirit (*Sentences* 1, dist. 17), but his view was rejected, because it would mean the annihilation of the human personality and of a freely given human response to God; cf. ST 2–2, q. 23, a.2. For a discussion of the varying nuances of the scholastic doctrine of uncreated and created Charity, or uncreated and created Grace, see Karl Rahner, "Some Implications of the Scholastic Concept of Uncreated Grace," in *Theological Investigations*, vol. 1, E.T. (London, 1961), pp. 319–46.

236. *Deus dilectio est:* Cf. 1 John 4.8, *Deus caritas est.*

237. *created love is not the cause:* Hilton is concerned to emphasize the gratuity of God's gift.

238. *He is both the giver and the gift:* Cf. above, same page, note 235. See further Peter Lombard, *Sententiae*, Liber 1, d.18, c.2.

239. *this gift of love:* Hilton's teaching here is partly matched in *Qui Habitat*, Wallner, p. 45.

240. *dilexit nos:* 1 John 4.19.

241. *He loved us much . . . more . . . most:* This is a development from St. Augustine's observation that while the Trinity as such is substantial charity there is a particular sense in which charity is referred to the Holy Spirit, cf. *De Trinitate* 15.17.29.

242. *and less could not suffice for us:* Cf. Augustine, *Conf.* 1.1.1: *Inquietum est cor nostrum donec requiescat in te.*

243. *The making . . . is appropriated:* On the Augustinian, and post-Augustinian theology of appropriation, see *Scale* 1.43, p. 113, note 167 with orientation.

244. *We do nothing at all but submit to him:* Cf. *Scale* 2.24, p. 234, with note 122.

245. *And yet that will is not from ourselves:* Common Augustinian doctrine. See, e.g., Peter Lombard, *Sententiae*, Liber 2, d.26, c.2; d.27, c.4.

246. *then the soul sees:* For the awareness of God, or Jesus, in the life of grace, see *Qui Habitat*, Wallner, pp. 26–27.

247. *power . . . truth . . . goodness:* A variation on the conventional Augustinian appropriation of *potentia, sapientia, bonitas*, to the Persons of the Trinity. Cf. note 167 on *Scale* 1.43, p. 113. Because the Persons of the Trinity co-inhere, and their operation *ad extra* is inseparable, the work of the Trinity and of "Jesus" is interchangeable. The co-inherence of the Persons is common doctrine in Greek and Latin Christendom; for the West, see, for example, Augustine, *De Trinitate* 6.10.12, and the orientation given by Peter Lombard, *Sententiae* 1, dist. 19 cap. 4.

248. *steal his honor:* Pride is an attempted usurpation of God's glory; cf. note 72 on *Scale* 1.20, p. 93.

249. *this love brings into the soul the fulness of all virtues:* See ch. 35, p. 267, and what follows.

250. *shall have the clearest sight . . . heaven:* Cf. *Scale* 1.61, p. 132 on the reward of the vision of God according to one's degree of charity.

251. *it is freely received:* Cf. ch. 20, p. 224.

252. *make themselves love God as if by their own strength:* Similarly in *Of Angels' Song*, Takamiya, p. 13 (Dorward, p. 18); the *Cloud*, ch. 52.

253. *that has the gift of love through the grace-given beholding:* Cf. ch. 34, p. 266.

254. *filii Dei sunt:* Romans 8.14.

255. *so humble and obedient to God:* Here and in what follows, Hilton is recalling the distinction made by St. Thomas between co-operant grace, where there is deliberate conjunction of the human will with grace, and operant grace, where all is perceived as God's work. See ST 1–2, q. 111, a.2. The *Cloud* (ch. 34) reflects the Thomist account of "operant grace" likewise.

256. *at the bidding of reason:* Cf. *Scale* 1.14, p. 87.

257. *turns all these human affections:* What follows seems to be Hilton's own theory.

258. *affections of spiritual love through purchase:* that is, "acquired" (as distinct from "infused") spiritual affections. Fishlake translates: *per adquisitionem* (Y).

259. *ex Deo est:* 2 Corinthians 3.5.

260. *voluntate:* Philippians 2.13.

261. *in imperfect lovers:* Cf. above on the Thomist distinction between co-operant and operant grace.

262. *among all the gifts of Jesus:* This is the familiar distinction between *gratia gratum faciens* and *gratia gratis data*—cf. on *Scale* 1.10, pp. 83–84. For the present passage, cf. also *Qui Habitat*, pp. 46f.

263. *partner in the heavenly heritage:* The reading of H is uncertain: it could be either *percener* (cf. *parcener*, a sharer or partner) or *perceuer* (Underhill's "perceiver"). If we take it as *percever*, OED *s.v. Perceiver* gives two significations: (1) One who perceives (first rec. 1550). (2) One who obtains or receives; a recipient, participator. *obs.* The present passage in the de Worde ed. of 1494 is cited under (2), agreeing with Y *participem* and supporting the translation here.

264. *the soul loves itself and all . . . as itself:* Cf. *Scale* 1.70, pp. 141–142.

265. *the gift of love that makes a distinction:* Cf. *Scale* 1.66, p. 136. The present passage is clearly echoing Augustine, *De Trinitate* 15.18.32.

266. *ego sum Deus:* Psalm 45.11. There is a similar exposition by M.N. in a gloss to the *Mirror of Simple Souls*, explaining how this text is to be understood without any suggestion of Quietism—Doiron, pp. 304f. Cf. Augustine, *Ennarationes in Psalmos* 70.1.18: "What is it—Be still, and see that I am the Lord—but that you should know that it is God

who works in you, and that you should not be puffed up with your own works?" Augustine goes on to cite Matthew 11.28–29.

267. *Then Love brings into the soul the fullness of virtues:* This is the theme, for instance, in Augustine, *Sermo* 70, though it would be too much to say that this sermon is a specific source here.

268. *the common way of charity:* As elsewhere, Hilton equates charity with grace. For what follows, cf. earlier, ch. 35, p. 269.

269. *acquire:* H reads *getynge of vertues.* On this occasion, MS. Y has the colorless *habeant* rather than *adquirent.*

270. *virtues in reason and in will:* Cf. *Scale* 1.14, p. 87.

271. *pays little attention to the struggle for virtues:* This does not, of course, mean that the moral life is unimportant, but that conformity to Christ becomes spontaneous rather than being a self-conscious effort. Cf. William of St. Thierry, Déchanet, pp. 364–66, "And that is perfection and man's true wisdom, when he embraces and contains in himself virtues, not borrowed from elsewhere, but as it were naturally implanted in himself, according to that likeness of God (cf. Genesis 1.26), by virtue of which he is all that he is. Then, just as God is what he is, so in respect of the goodness of virtue the habit of a good will is so bound by affection to the good spirit, that through the most ardent attachment to the unchangeable Good, it seems that it can never be removed from what it is." Idem., pp. 372–74. "Once conformed to this wisdom, reason forms its conscience and orders its life. In the lower matters, which pertain to knowledge (*scientia*), it makes use of its docility and natural capacity. . . . Thus driven from below, and aided from above, advancing to what is right, by the judgment of reason, and by the assent of the will, and by the affection of the spirit, and by its effect in action, it hastens to break out into liberty of spirit and into unity, so that . . . the faithful man is made one spirit with God (1 Corinthians 6.17)."

272. *love slays all sins . . . new feeling of virtues:* Cf. Gilbert of Hoyland, *In Cant.* 15.5: "That fire (referring to Luke 12.49) not only consumes vices, but changes virtues themselves into the affection of sweeter grace."

273. *how love slays sins:* Hilton stands in a wide tradition here. For instance, St. Bonaventure says that the capital sins are removed by the gifts of the Holy Spirit (*In Sent.* 3, dist. 34, p. 1, a. 2, q. 1.). Cf. earlier Gregory, *Moralia* 31.45.87: "Because we suffered captivity with these seven vices of pride, therefore our Redeemer came to the spiritual battle to free us, full with the spirit of sevenfold grace." This tradition is also found in the *Somme le Roy.* Cf. *The Book of Vices and Virtues,* Francis, p. 125.

274. On imperfect and perfect humility and parallel teaching in *The Cloud of Unknowing,* see Introduction, p. 50, with note 236.

275. *It takes no heed of its own unworthiness:* For forgetfulness of one's demerits or merits, cf. *Scale* 2.20, p. 225; cf. the *Cloud,* chs. 13, 16. For similar thought, cf. *Qui Habitat,* Wallner, p. 23.

276. *nihilum ante te:* Psalm 38.6. What follows is the closest that Hilton comes explicitly to the teaching of the *Cloud*, chs. 43 and 44, that in order that God may work freely in the soul one must lay aside all distinct awareness of one's own being as well as deeds, and that this is possible only through the special grace of God. The forgetfulness of one's own being is developed further by the *Cloud's* author in *Book of Privy Counselling*, Hodgson, pp. 156–57.

277. *reputatae sunt ei:* Isaiah 40.17.

278. *the heart . . . made so great and so large:* The expression might suggest the *dilatatio mentis* of Richard of St. Victor, *Benjamin Major*, 5.3 (PL 196.171–2), but in fact is commonplace. Cf. *The Rule of St. Benedict*, McCann, p. 12: "As we progress . . . , our hearts shall be enlarged (*dilatato corde*), and we shall run with unspeakable sweetness of love in the way of God's commandments."

279. *ravished with love of their own honor: Raptus* can have a pejorative sense as well as the good sense it does in, for example, *Scale* 1.8. Cf. *De Imagine Peccati*, Clark and Taylor, p. 76.

280. *pedes meos:* Psalm 24.15.

281. *Scuto circumdabit te veritas eius:* Psalm 90.5. There is a closely related passage in *Qui Habitat*, p. 14, where the "shield" of contemplation is understood as supernatural, infused contemplation, the "spiritual love" of Christ in St. Bernard's sense. Bernard himself, in *Sermo in Ps. Qui Habitat* 5.1, applies the text differently.

282. *non timebis a timore nocturno:* For St. Bernard's interpretation of the *timor nocturnus*, with which Hilton is familiar, cf. *Scale* 2.22, with note 119.

283. *A sagitta volante in die:* Psalm 90.6. In Bernard, *In Cant.* 33.6.12, this refers to pride and vain glory—*inanis gloria.* So also in Bernard, *Sermo in Ps. Qui Habitat* 6.3. In *Qui Habitat*, pp. 17f. it is taken as referring particularly to pride in one's own good deeds and assumption of one's own perfection—matched in *Scale* 2.26, p. 240, with note 149.

284. *Pride comes by night:* Contempt and reproach by others, to which Hilton goes on to refer, is indeed in one sense one of the trials that beset beginners on the spiritual journey, in keeping with the theme of the *timor nocturnus;* sensitivity to such assaults is in one sense a mark of pride, as Hilton says. But the theme of pride is introduced here more specifically as part of Hilton's illustration of the effect of perfect humility in striking down pride, the root sin.

285. *Love works wisely and gently:* Cf. Augustine, *Ennarationes in Psalmos* 31.2.6: "Where charity exists, it must needs work."

286. *For a true lover of Jesus however there is no great difficulty:* Cf. *Qui Habitat*, Wallner, p. 34.

287. *He is not much stirred against them:* Cf. *Scale* 1.70, pp. 141–142 on the love of others "in God" or "for God."

288. *a special grace given to the holy martyrs:* Cf. Pseudo-Augustine, *Sermo de Nativitate S. Laurentii* 206 (PL 39.2127).

289. *contumeliam pati:* Acts 5.41.

290. *hypocrites and heretics who are willing to suffer:* A side-reference to the prosecution of heretics.

291. *the fire . . . high altar of heaven:* Similar Hilton refers to an *ignis alienus* in *Epistola de Lectione* (Clark and Taylor, pp. 230–31).

292. *deceived by the midday devil:* Psalm 90.6. Cf. *Scale* 2.26, p. 239, with note 148.

293. *In the same way, carnal love of father and mother:* This section goes beyond the careful teaching of St. Thomas, ST 2–2, q. 26, aa. 7–8, with its respect for natural ties. But it does accord with the words of St. Bernard, *In Cant.* 50.2.8. For Hilton's familiarity with this context, see *Mixed Life,* Ogilvie-Thomson, p. 8.

294. *except for this: he would rather:* Fishlake softens Hilton's rather severe teaching; his Latin may be rendered: "except that for the sake of natural affection he would rather . . ." (Y).

295. *not only in those . . . at all:* Hilton does not limit the possibility of this degree of grace to vowed religious.

296. *not for the love of itself but for love of God:* The use of creatures is referred to the love of God. On the Augustinian distinction between *frui* and *uti,* see *De Doctrina Christiana* 1.4.4.

297. *discretion:* Standing in a long tradition, St. Bernard refers to discretion as "not so much a virtue, as a certain moderator and charioteer of the virtues" (*In Cant.* 49.2.5).

298. *the best and most costly food under the sun:* This is taking up at a deeper level what Hilton has said in *Scale* 1.72, pp. 144–145.

299. *according to the demands of the state or rank:* Cf. above, p. 278.

300. *song or melody or minstrelsy:* On this occasion not a reference to Rolle's favorite phenomena!

301. *pure, subtle and fit for the work of contemplation:* Hilton is speaking of a habit of contemplation.

302. *it may be called . . . and reforming in feeling:* Similarly in ch. 41, p. 285, Hilton sees the experience of contemplation from many sides, and uses various deliberately commonplace synonyms for it.

303. *a soul that . . . has one, has all:* This matches the interrelation of the virtues, as referred to in *Scale* 1.18, p. 91.

304. *no obstacle in the middle:* Fishlake: *medium impediens* (Y).

305. *at rest from the annoyance of worldly business:* Fishlake (Y): *In quiete est tunc per separacionem a gaudio solicitudinis mundialis.*

306. *far from idleness of the flesh:* Quietism is excluded.

307. *grace loosens the heavy yoke of carnal love:* Cf. Ecclesiasticus 40.1, cited by St. Bernard, *De Diligendo Deo* 13.36, a context with which Hilton was very familiar; cf. *Scale* 1, 88, with note 366.

308. *holy idleness and most busy rest:* Cf. William of St. Thierry, Déchanet, p. 300: *otia negotiosa, quies operosa, caritas ordinata.*

309. *Vox Domini in virtute:* Psalm 28.4.

310. *omni gladio:* Hebrews 4.12. For the use of the text in this context, cf. Cassian, *Collationes* 7.13. The text is also used in Bernard, *In Cant.*

74.2.6. There are many points of contact with this sermon of Bernard in this area of the *Scale*.

311. *dimidia hora:* Revelation 8.1. The text is used in Gregory, *Moralia* 30.16.53, of contemplation, taking "heaven" to refer to the church, and including use of Wisdom 9.15, and a side-reference to Ezekiel 40.5. But compare more particularly *Homilia in Ezekiel* 2.2.14, referring to heaven as the soul of the just.

312. *Heaven is a pure soul:* See above on *Homilia in Ezekiel* 2.2.14. Cf. also Gregory, *Moralia* 29.28.55, including a reference to the text *Anima iusti sedes sapientiae*. The identification of the text is problematic.

313. *confidence in salvation:* Fishlake (Y): *fiduciam*. This is the confidence of which St. John (1 John 4.18) speaks. Cf. St. Bernard, *In Cant.* 7.3.3, referring to *fiducia libertatis* and citing 1 John 4.18.

314. *filii Dei sumus:* Romans 8.16. Cf. Bernard, *De Diligendo Deo* 13.36–14.37; *In Cant.* 37.3.5; 57.2.3–4.

315. *conscientiae meae:* 2 Corinthians 1.12. A commonplace text; cf., for example, St. Bernard, *In Cant.* 25.4.7; 63.2.3.

316. *the soul is raised up . . . above all bodily creatures:* Cf. ch. 33, pp. 261–262.

317. *the . . . use of them:* Cf. ch. 39, p. 278, with note 296 on *frui/uti*.

318. *no error or deceit:* Conformity to God and protection from error lasts for the duration of the contemplative experience. Cf. *Qui Habitat*, Wallner, pp. 36–37.

319. *exaltabitur Deus:* Cf. Psalm 63.7, a familiar text. Among other writers, Richard of St. Victor uses it in *Benjamin Minor* 75; *Benjamin Major* 4.7; 5.4.

320. *ad cor eius:* Hosea 2.14. Another commonplace. Richard of St. Victor uses the text to refer to his second degree of violent love (*De IV Gradibus Violentae Caritatis*, PL 196.1218).

321. *secretum meum mihi:* Isaiah 24.16. Another commonplace, used by, for instance, Bernard and Gilbert of Hoyland; William of St. Thierry, at the conclusion of *Epistola ad Fratres de Monte Dei*, uses the text a little differently from Hilton.

322. *nisi qui accipit:* Revelation 2.17. Another commonplace; cited by, for example, Richard of St. Victor, *De IV Gradibus Violentae Caritatis*, PL 196.1218; *Benjamin Minor* c.36 (PL 196.25). Cf. Gregory, *Moralia* 19.2.4.

323. *Lively feeling of grace:* Cf. *Qui Habitat*, Wallner p. 34. Cf. William of St. Thierry, Déchanet, p. 382: "In that light of truth one indubitably sees prevenient grace."

324. *knows well by experience that he is in grace:* St. Thomas says that a man can know that he is in grace "conjecturally by certain (*aliqua*) signs," and cites Revelation 2.17. But such knowledge is imperfect in this life (ST 1–2, q. 112, a.5). More boldly, he refers to the gift of Wisdom as conferring a lived experience of divine things, *non solum discens, sed et patiens divina* (ST 2–2, q. 45, a. 2), after Pseudo-Dionysius.

325. *it passes away very easily:* The transitory character of contemplation is a commonplace; for Gregory the Great on this point, see for instance

Butler, pp. 81f. See further in ch. 41, with reference more particularly to Bernard.

326. *cor meum vigilat:* Canticle 5.2. Another commonplace. See, for instance, Gregory, *Moralia* 5.31.54; 23.20.38.

327. *maiestatem:* Luke 9.32. Cf. for instance Richard of St. Victor, *Benjamin Minor* 77 (PL 196.55); *Benjamin Major* 5.2 (PL 196.170), both citing the equivalent in Matthew 17.

328. *purity and poverty of spirit:* Cf. Matthew 5.8; 5.3.

329. *because of the corruption of human frailty:* Cf. Wisdom 9.15.

330. *contempletur eum:* Job 34.29.

331. *non respondit mihi:* Canticle 3.1. What follows draws heavily on Bernard, *In Cant.* 74.1.1–4. There is comparable teaching in *The Book of Privy Counselling*, Hodgson, p. 168.

332. *Revertere dilecte mi:* Canticle 2.17. Cf. St. Bernard, *In Cant.* 74.1.1–4.

333. *full of grace and truth:* Cf. John 1.14.

334. *Oleum effusum nomen tuum:* Canticle 1.2. Devotion to the name of Jesus based on this text is a medieval commonplace. St. Bernard devotes *In Cant.* 15 to it. There is also an important tract by Rolle on the Holy Name, based on the same verse. See *Scale* 1.44, p. 115, note 176.

335. *Blessed . . . absence:* Cf. St. Bernard, *In Cant.* 74.1.2; *Restat igitur ut absentem studiose requirat, revocet abeuntem.*

336. *changeability:* This is what St. Bernard knows as *vicissitudo*, on the basis of James 1.17. There is no variableness in God's purpose of love, but the variableness is in our experience of God. In addition to Bernard, *In Cant.* 74, cf. also 17.1.1; 32.1.2. Also cf. Gilson, ch. 5.

337. *anyone who does not recognise the absence of grace:* Cf. St. Bernard, *In Cant.* 17.1.1.

338. *the more stability:* Cf. *Of Angels' Song*, Takamiya, p. 10.

339. *in whom there is no kind of changeability:* James 1.17.

340. *either quite perfect or quite blind:* Cf. *Scale* 2.26, p. 240, on the false assumption of perfection by "enthusiasts."

341. *Iustus ex fide vivit:* Romans 1.17 and Hebrews 10.38, citing Habakkuk 2.4. Hilton is here looking back to *Scale* 2.9. He goes on to make the careful distinction between "feeling" in the meaning of quasi-physical sensations of warmth, and an interior and spiritual awareness. He is taking up at a deeper level points that he has made in *Scale* 1.10–12.

342. *As the soul is the life of the body:* This is an Augustinian commonplace, for example, *Sermo* 161.7.7 (PL 38.881): "Your life is God, your life is Christ, your life is the Holy Spirit." Also Pseudo-Augustine, *De Spiritu et Anima* c. 43 (PL 40.811): "The soul is the life of the body, God is, the life of the soul."

343. *to become one with him:* Cf. 1 Corinthians 6.17, cited at *Scale* 1.8, p. 82.

344. *a heavy lump:* Wisdom 9.15.

345. *the common grace which is charity:* Cf. *Scale* 1.68, p. 138.

346. *quo vadat:* John 3.8. Cf. Bernard, *In Cant.* 17.1.1; 74.2.5.

347. *from excess into sobriety:* 2 Corinthians 5.13; cf. *Scale* 1.9, p. 83.

348. *cold and dry:* Cf. *Scale* 1.4, p. 80.

349. *a great freedom and complete readiness in will:* Cf. *Scale* 2.24, p. 236.

350. *gathered together in itself:* Cf. *Scale* 1.25, pp. 97–98; 1.87, p. 156.

351. *with heart and mouth in full accord:* Similarly St. Benedict, *Rule*, ch. 19, McCann, pp. 68–69.

352. *as sticks nourish the fire:* Cf. *Scale* 1.32, pp. 102–103, with note 112.

353. *in conspectu tuo:* Psalm 140.2. This use of the text is traditional, cf. Cassian, *Collationes* 9.36.

354. *no fly:* A fly (following Y's *moscus*) seems more appropriate to this situation than a flea (H *fle*).

355. *boiling over the fire:* This is probably recalling Bernard, *In Cant.* 74.2.7: "Here the Word has withdrawn, just as if you had withdrawn the fire from a boiling pot"; for other recollection of this area of Bernard, see on *Scale* 2.41, pp. 286, 289.

356. *fatness of devotion:* Normally Hilton relates "devotion" to sensible feelings and ebullience in prayer, rather than to the stillness of contemplation. Cf. *Scale* 1.5, p. 80, on the second part of contemplation. But here he seems to be recalling Bernard once more: cf. Bernard, *Sermo in Ps. Qui Habitat* 9.2: "The word is living and effective (Hebrews 4.12) where it . . . proceeds from the fatness of devotion (*ex pinguedine . . . devotionis*) and the pure intention of the soul."

357. *received by angels:* For the ministry of angels, cf. *Scale* 2.43, p. 293; 2.46, pp. 300–301, with note 403.

358. *solemnitatis vestrae:* Psalm 80.4. Cf. Gilbert of Hoyland, *In Cant.* 18.5: "Blow to us, good Jesus, with the trumpet in the new moon . . . Truly it is an illustrious day, where the divine majesty reveals itself."

359. *without pretense or fantasy:* Cf. *Scale* 2.40, p. 282.

360. *grace of compunction:* Cf. *Scale* 2.7, p. 202, with note 25.

361. *like what he is by nature:* Hilton draws on the Thomist distinction between natural and supernatural to avoid any possibility of being misunderstood in a pantheistic sense.

362. *that your feeling is true:* The same test of religious sensations is applied in *Scale* 1.11, pp. 84–85.

363. *grace . . . love:* For the interchangeability of grace and charity, see note 286 on *Scale* 1.68, p. 138.

364. *one alone:* This implies the Augustinian doctrine of the co-inherence of the Persons of the Trinity, and the inseparability of their operation *ad extra*. Cf. note 247 on *Scale* 2.34, p. 266.

365. *truth and humility:* On their interdependence, cf. *Scale* 2.20, p. 225.

366. *well of wisdom:* Cf. *Scale* 1.4, p. 79, with note 10.

367. *ut intelligerent scripturas:* Luke 24.45. St. Thomas relates this text to the gift of understanding (ST 2–2, q. 8, a. 2). But it is also used by St. Bernard in a context dealing with the transition from the carnal to the spiritual love, *Sermo in Ascensione* 3.3. Hilton seems to be familiar with this sermon; see Clark and Taylor, p. 466.

368. *the harder they are:* Cf. Gregory, *Homilia* in *Ezekiel* 1.6.1.

369. *mystically and heavenly:* A related passage in *Qui Habitat* (Wallner, p. 28) refers only to the moral and mystical senses. For the four senses of scripture, see for example, St. Thomas, ST 1, q. 1, a. 10, traceable to Cassian, *Collationes* 14.8, on the senses of "Jerusalem."

370. *the working of love:* For charity as determining the interpretation of scripture, see Augustine, *De Doctrina Christiana* 1.35.39–40.44.

371. *feci vobis:* John 15.15. The traditional teaching on the transition from servile to filial fear of God, in which fear of punishment gives place to fear of offending God's love, including reference to this text, is found already in Cassian, *Collationes* 11.12–13. See also, for example, Augustine, *Tractatus in Ioannis Epistolam ad Parthos* 9.2–4, and Bernard, *De Diligendo Deo* 14.37. Hilton was very familiar with the last.

372. *in it is hidden the spirit of life:* The Holy Spirit is the "life" of scripture, just as the soul is the "life" of the body. See further on *Scale* 2.44, p. 297, note 385, with reference to Ezekiel 1.20.

373. *white teeth:* Cf. Augustine, *De Doctrina Christiana* 2.6.7, referring to the interpretation of scripture and citing Canticle 4.2, *Dentes tui sicut grex detonsarum.*

374. *they gnaw only the outer bark:* Cf. *Scale* 1.14, p. 87, with note 48.

375. *he does not show them his counsel:* It has been said that preference for the plain "literal" understanding of scripture, as distinct from the overtones and undertones of the "spiritual senses," was a Lollard characteristic. Cf. M. Deanesly, *The Lollard Bible* (Cambridge, 1920), p. 286. For some modification of this, see A. M. Hudson, *The Premature Reformation* (Oxford, 1988), pp. 271 f.

376. *Jesus' finger, which is the Holy Spirit:* For the Holy Spirit as the "finger of God," cf. Augustine, *De Trinitate* 2.15.26, drawing together Exodus 31.18 with Luke 11.20.

377. *He alone has the key of knowledge:* Cf. Richard of St. Victor, *Benjamin Major* 1.1. (PL 196.64). Cf. also Luke 11.52, Christ's words to the lawyers—"You have taken away the key of knowledge"—with Revelation 3.7: "He that has the key of David, he that opens and no one shuts."

378. *ori meo:* Psalm 118.103.

379. *in aenigmate:* 1 Corinthians 13.12. Cf. *Qui Habitat*, Wallner, p. 49: "*huled under a vayle of feir liknes.*"

380. *wisdom and goodness:* The qualities appropriated commonly to the Father, the Son and the Holy Spirit are here ascribed (with other qualities too) to "Jesus." Cf. *Scale* 1.43, p. 113, with note 167.

381. *effect of his working:* Cf. *Qui Habitat*, Wallner, p. 5. God cannot be seen in this life as he is, but he may be known by his effects.

382. *made through grace:* *Lectio* refers not only to scripture, but to the writings of approved theologians. Cf. B. Smalley, *The Study of the Bible in the Middle Ages*, p. 12.

383. *sweet letters:* Cf. Augustine, *Enarrationes in Psalmos* 64.2.

384. *spem habeamus:* Romans 15.4.

385. *sequentes eum:* Ezekiel 1.20. Gregory, *Homilia in Ezekiel* 1.7.11–14, relates this text to the spiritual understanding, which has been the theme of ch. 43. Gregory refers frequently to *spiritus vitae*—the spirit of life. Cf. on ch. 43, p. 294, note 372.

386. *stirs and teaches:* Fishlake (Y): *tangit et instigat.*

387. *me meae:* John 10.27; 14.

388. *or fantasy:* Cf. *Scale* 2.40, p. 282.

389. *beloved spouse:* Cf. Bernard, *In Cant.* 83.2.4: "I have read that God is love (1 John 4.16). . . . It is not that God does not wish honor, who says: 'If I am a father, where is my honor?' (Malachi 1.6). Truly he says that as a father. But if he shows himself as a bridegroom, I think he will change his voice, and will say: 'If I am a bridegroom, where is my love?' For before he said, 'If I am the Lord, where is my fear (Malachi 1.6)?' "

390. *security: securitatem* (Y). Cf. *Scale* 2.40, note 313, with reference to *fiducia.*

391. *it has no time for it:* H's reading not clear, but cf. Y: *non vacat sibi hoc facere.*

392. *and find its goal there:* In chs. 45–46 Hilton will develop the point that even "intellectual visions" are not ends in themselves, but rather means to lead the soul to closer union with Christ. *Of Angels' Song* (Takamiya, p. 12; Dorward, p. 17) makes the same point: that even intellectual visions are secondary to union with God by charity.

393. *anima mea:* Canticle 3.2. Gilbert of Hoyland, *In Cant.* 4.3 (PL 184.27), applies this text in a similar sense. Gilbert's *In Cant.* 4.2, on the limits of faith and understanding is echoed in Hilton's *Epistola de Leccione* (Clark and Taylor, p. 229).

394. *the reprobate:* For the perception of God's justice in reward and punishment, as an anticipation of the Last Judgment, cf. *Qui Habitat,* Wallner, p. 28. St. Thomas says (ST Suppl. q. 94) that part of the joy of the blessed is to see the vindication of God's justice through the pains of the damned. Cf. earlier the *Summa Theologica* that goes under the name of Alexander of Hales, Lib. 1, Pars 1, Inq. 1, Tr. 6, q. 6, c. 8 (Quaracchi, 1924, p. 412).

395. *non erit:* Cf. Proverbs 12.7. Bernard, *Sermo in Dedicatione Ecclesiae* 4.3, relates this text to victory over sin generally.

396. *as the gospel says:* Matthew 8.28–32 and parallels.

397. *his hands are bound:* Cf. Revelation 20.2.

398. *angelos judicabimus?* 1 Corinthians 6.3.

399. *the devil is greatly shamed:* Cf. *Scale* 1.91, p. 159. For the soul's contempt of the devil, cf. generally St. Bernard, *Sermo in Ps. Qui Habitat* 13, on Psalm 90.13, *super aspidem et basiliscum ambulabis, et conculcabis leonem et draconem,* as noted by Sitwell.

400. *the power of the Most High:* Following Y's *altissimi.* H gives *eighest,*

meaning "Most Dreadful," that is God. See Hussey, "Latin and English in *The Scale of Perfection*," p. 475.

401. *the diversity of their orders:* Cf. Bernard, *In Cant.* 62.2.2. G. Sitwell (*Scale*, pp. 309f.) refers to a passage in St. John of the Cross, *Spiritual Canticle*, Stanza 37, on the contemplative's vision of God's secrets. This passage makes use of Canticle 2.13b–14, which Bernard expounds in his *In Cant.* 61–62.

402. *all is spiritual . . . and concerning spiritual creatures:* This is technically known as an "intellectual vision." Cf. *Scale* 1.10, p. 83, note 35.

403. *capient salutis?* Hebrews 1.14. On the ministry of angels in illuminating the soul, cf. *Qui Habitat,* Wallner, pp. 36–37; *Of Angels' Song,* Takamiya, p. 12; Dorward, p. 17. A basis for the account of how the angels "translate" spiritual reality into that which can be apprehended by the bodily senses and imagination can be found in St. Bernard, *In Cant.* 41.3.4 on Canticle 1.10, *Muraenulas aureas faciemus tibi, vermiculatas argento,* citing Hebrews 1.14; cf. also *Sermo in Ps. Qui Habitat* 11.10, likewise citing Hebrews 1.14.

404. *afterward on his blessed divinity:* Cf. Bernard, *In Cant.* 62.2.2–3.4 on the ascent from knowledge of the heavenly hierarchies to the knowledge of God.

405. *auris mea:* Job 4.12. Expounded by Gregory, *Moralia* 5.23.45; 5.28.50–29.52.

406. *revelabit condensa:* Psalm 28.9.

A Select Bibliography

The Scale of Perfection

Editions of Book 1 and Book 2, based respectively on MSS. Cambridge University Library Additional 6686 and British Library 6579, are being made for the Early English Text Society. Professor S. S. Hussey is editing Book 2, and Book 1, edited by the late Professor A. J. Bliss, is to be prepared for the press by Dr. M. G. Sargent.

The Scale of Perfection, edited by Evelyn Underhill (London, 1923), is a light modernization of MS, Harley 6579 and enables the reader to come close to the Middle English. As explained in the Introduction (pp. 54–55), text for Book 1 includes a number of interpolations and alterations, not all of which are noticed as such by Miss Underhill. For Book 2 the text is generally sound, apart from a few minor slips.

The Scale of Perfection, edited by Dom Gerard Sitwell, O.S.B. (London, 1952) is based on the Underhill edition but has helpful notes, some of which derive from the French edition published by Dom Noetinger in 1923.

The Scale of Perfection, abridged and presented by Illtyd Trethowan (London, 1975). The text is taken mainly from Book 2, using the translation made by Leo Sherley-Price for the Penguin Edition of 1957. It has a good and lively introduction.

The Staircase of Perfection, translated, with Introduction, by M. L. del Mastro (New York, 1979).

Unpublished Dissertations

An edition of *The Scale of Perfection*, Book 1, chapters 38 to 52, by Rosemary Birts (Dorward), M. Litt. thesis (Oxford, 1951).

An edition from the Manuscripts of Book 2 of Walter Hilton's *Scale of Perfection*, by S. S. Hussey, Ph.D. thesis (London University, 1962).

Mixed Life

Edited by C. Horstmann in *Yorkshire Writers: Richard Rolle of Hampole, an English Father of the Church, and His Followers*, vol. 1 (London, 1895), pp. 264–92, from the Vernon and Thornton (Lincoln Cathedral) manuscripts.

Edited by S. J. Ogilvie-Thomson from MS. Lambeth Palace 472, Salzburg Studies in English Literature: Elizabethan and Renaissance Studies, 92:15 (Salzburg, 1986). Contains full textual apparatus and theological notes.

D. Jones, ed., *Minor Works of Walter Hilton* (London, 1929). Lightly modernized texts of *Mixed Life, Eight Chapters, Qui Habitat, Bonum Est,* and *Benedictus.*

Angels' Song

Edited by C. Horstmann in *Yorkshire Writers: Richard Rolle of Hampole, an English Father of the Church, and his Followers*, vol. 1, pp. 175–82, from MSS. Thornton and Cambridge U.L. Dd v. 55.

Edited by T. Takamiya, *Studies in English Literature*, English Number 1977, (Tokyo, 1977). Reprinted with F. Kuriyagawa's edition of *Eight Chapters on Perfection* from the Inner Temple MS., under the title *Two Minor Works of Walter Hilton* (Tokyo, 1980).

Ed. R. Dorward, *Eight Chapters on Perfection and Angels' Song* (Fairacres, Oxford: SLG Press, 1983), translated into modern English from the editions of F. Kuriyagawa and T. Takamiya (above).

The Prickynge of Love

Edited by H. Kane, *Salzburg Studies in English Literature: Elizabethan and Renaissance Studies* 92:10, 2 vols. (Salzburg, 1983). Middle English text with full apparatus. Kane is doubtful of Hilton's authorship.

Edited by C. Kirchberger in lightly modernized English version from the Vernon manuscript, as *The Goad of Love* (London, 1952).

Eight Chapters on Perfection

The Inner Temple MS. of Walter Hilton's "Eight Chapters on Perfection," edited by F. Kuriyagawa, *Studies in English Literature*, English Number 1971 (Tokyo, 1971). See under *Angels' Song.*

There are editions of the same work from MS Bibliothèque Nationale, Paris, anglais 41, by F. Kuriyagawa, *Studies in the Humanities and Social Relations*, vol. 9, Tokyo: Keio University, 1967), and from MS. British Library Additional 60577, by T. Takamiya (*Poetica*, vol. 12, [Tokyo, 1981] for 1979).

Ed. R. Dorward: See under *Angels' Song* above.

Qui Habitat

An Exposition of "Qui Habitat" and "Bonum Est" in English, edited by B. Wallner, *Lund Studies in English*, 23 (Lund, 1954). Middle English text with full apparatus. *Bonum Est* is not considered by John Clark to be Hilton's. Wallner has also provided an edition of the Middle English *Benedictus* (Lund, 1957). Cf. under *The Minor Works of Walter Hilton*.

The Minor Works of Walter Hilton, edited by Dorothy Jones (London, 1929) contains lightly modernized texts of *Mixed Life, Eight Chapters, Qui Habitat, Bonum Est*, and *Benedictus* from MS. Lambeth Palace 472. The last two are not believed by John Clark to be Hilton's.

Latin Writings

Walter Hilton's Latin Writings, edited by J. P. H. Clark and C. Taylor, Analecta Cartusiana 124, 2 vols. (Salzburg, 1987). Contains texts of all known Latin works by Hilton, together with the Middle English translation of *Epistola ad Quemdam Saeculo Renuntiare volentem* and the commentary on the lost "Gilbertine" letter.

There is an excellent translation of *Epistola de Lectione, Intentione*, etc., by Joy Russell Smith, under the title "Letter to a Hermit" in *The Way* 6 (London, 1966), pp. 230–41.

Texts of Authors Related to Walter Hilton

Printed Editions

Ailred of Rievaulx, *Opera Ascetica*. CChCM 1. English translations in the *Cistercian Fathers* Series.

Ancrene Wisse, ed. J.R.R. Tolkien, EETS OS 249 (1962).

Anselm of Canterbury, *Opera*, ed. F. S. Schmitt, 6 vols. (Seckau/Edinburgh, 1938–1968).

Augustine of Hippo, *Opera*, CSEL 12; 25; 28; 33–34; 36; 40–44; 51–53; 57–58; 60; 63; 74; 77; 84–85; 88–89; C.Ch. 27–57; PL 32–47.

Augustine Baker, *Holy Wisdom*, ed. G. Sitwell (London, 1964).

Benedict, *Regula* (CSEL 75).

Bernard of Clairvaux, *Opera*, Editiones Cistercienses, Rome 1957–.

Bonaventure, *Opera*, 10 vols. (Quaracchi, 1882–1902).

Cassian, *Opera*, CSEL 13 (1–2).

—— *Institutions Cénobitiques*, ed. J. C. Guy, SC 109 (Paris, 1965).

The Chastising of God's Children, and the *Treatise of Perfection of the Sons of God*, edited by J. Bazire and E. Colledge (Oxford: Blackwell, 1957).

The Cloud of Unknowing, and *The Book of Privy Counselling*, edited by P. Hodgson (EETS OS 218, 1944).

—— *Deonise Hid Diuinite and other Treatises*, edited by P. Hodgson (EETS OS 231, 1955).

—— *The Cloud of Unknowing and Related Treatises*, edited by P. Hodgson, *Analecta Cartusiana* 3 (Salzburg, 1982)—the EETS texts with revised introduction and notes.

—— *The Cloud of Unknowing*, edited by J. Walsh (Paulist Press, 1981)—modernized text, with important introduction and notes. *De Spiritu et Anima*, printed among the Works of St. Augustine. PL 40. Pseudo-Dionysius, *Opera* PG 3.

—— For the various Latin versions of his works, see *Dionysiaca*, ed. P. Chevallier, 2 vols. (Bruges/Paris, 1937, 1950).

English Wycliffite Writings, edited by A. M. Hudson (Cambridge, 1978).

Fasciculi Zizaniorum, edited by W. W. Shirley (Rolls Society 5, 1858).

Gilbert of Hoyland, *Opera*, PL 184.

Gratian, *Decretum, in Corpus Iuris Canonici*, edited by A. L. Richter and E. Friedberg (Leipzig, 1879–1881), vol. 1 of two vols.

Gregory the Great, *Opera*, CCh 140–44; PL 75–78.

Gregory of Nyssa, *De Vita Moysis*, PG 44. Also edited by J. Daniélou as *La Vie de Moïse*, SC 1 (Paris, 1968). There is an English edition in *Classics of Western Spirituality* (Paulist Press).

Guigues II, *Scala Claustralium*, edited by E. Colledge and J. Walsh under the title *Lettre sur la Vie Contemplative*, SC 163 (Paris, 1970).

Hugh of St. Victor, *Opera*, PL 175–77.

John of the Cross, Obras, edited by L. Ruano, Biblioteca de Autores Cristianos 15, 8th edition (Madrid, 1974). The English translation by Allison Peers is available in various editions; see also the English version by K. Kavanaugh and O. Rodriguez (Nelson, 1964).

Margaret Porete, *Le Miroir des Simples Âmes*, ed. by R. Guarnieri in *Il Movimento del Libero Spiritu*, *Archivio Italiano per la Storia della Pietà* (Rome, 1968), pp. 243–382. Also in CChCM, vol. 59.

—— *The Mirror of Simple Souls: A Middle English Translation*, ed. by Marilyn Doiron, with an Appendix on the Glosses, by E. Colledge and R. Guarnieri, *Archivio Italiano per la Storia della Pietà* (Rome, 1968). Peter Lombard, *Sententiae in IV Libris Distinctae* (Spicilegium Bonaventurianum 4-5, Grottaferrata 1971, 1981).

Richard of St. Victor, *Opera*, PL 196.

Richard Rolle, *Incendium Amoris*, ed. by M. Deanesly, Manchester 1915— not a fully critical edition.

—— *English Writings*, ed. H. E. Allen (Oxford, 1931).

—— *Melos Amoris,* ed. by E. J. F. Arnould (Blackwell [Oxford], 1957).
—— *Prose and Verse,* ed. S. J. Ogilvie-Thomson. EETS OS 293 (1988).
—— *The English Writings,* trans. and ed. by Rosamond S. Allen (Classics of Western Spirituality, Paulist Press, 1989).
Henry Suso, *Heinrich Seuses Horologium Sapientiae,* ed. by P. Kûnzle, Spicilegium Friburgense 23 (Freiburg/Schweiz, 1977).
—— Middle English version of part of the above: K. Horstmann, "Orologium Sapientiae or The Seven Poyntes of trewe Wisdom aus MS. Douce 114," *Anglia* 10 (1888), pp. 323–89.
John Tauler, *Die Predigten Taulers,* edited by F. Vetter, Deutsche Texte des Mittelalters 11 (Berlin, 1909).
Thomas Aquinas, *Opera*—Editio Leonina. *Scriptum super Libros Sententiarum* is available in vol. 11 of the edition by Vivès (Paris, 1882).
William of St. Thierry, *Lettre aux Frères du Mont-Dieu* (*Epistola ad Fratres de Monte Dei*), ed. J. M. Déchanet, SC 223 (Paris, 1975).
Other writings on the spiritual life are available in SC, or in the earlier editions by M. M. Davy (Vrin, Paris).
John Wyclif, *De Mandatis Divinis,* edited by J. Loserth and F. D. Matthew (London: Wyclif Society, 1922).
Sermones, 4 vols. edited by J. Loserth (London: Wyclif Society, 1887–90).

Works of Related Authors in Manuscript

Richard Rolle, *Emendatio Vitae,* MS. Cambridge U.L. Dd. v. 64.
—— *Incendium Amoris.* MS. Emmanuel College, Cambridge, 35, should be consulted as well as Deanesley's pioneer edition.
William Flete, *De Remediis contra Tentationes.* Available in many manuscripts; we have used MS. Bodleian Library, Bodley 43.

Secondary Literature: Walter Hilton

Clark, J. P. H.—a series of articles on Hilton's theology, sources and the canon of his writings, in *Downside Review* 95 (1977) to 103 (1985).
—— "Augustine, Anselm and Walter Hilton," in *The Mediaeval Mystical Tradition in England: Dartington 1982,* edited by M. Glasscoe (Exeter, 1982), pp. 102–26.
—— "English and Latin in the 'Scale of Perfection': Theological Considerations," in *Spiritualität Heute und Gestern* 1 (*Analecta Cartusiana* 35:1, Salzburg 1982, pp. 167–212).
—— "Some Monastic Elements in Walter Hilton and in the 'Cloud' Corpus," in *Die Kartäuser und die Reformation,* i (Analecta Cartusiana 108; 1), Salzburg 1983, pp. 237–57.
—— "The Trinitarian Theology of Walter Hilton's *Scale of Perfection, Book Two,*" in *Langland, The Mystics and the Mediaeval English Tradi-*

333

tion: Essays in Honour of S. S. Hussey, edited by Helen Phillips, Wood-bridge, Suffolk, 1990, pp. 125–140.

Gardner, H. "Walter Hilton and the Authorship of 'The Cloud of Un-knowing'," in *Review of English Studies* 9 (1933), pp. 129–47.

———— "The Text of 'The Scale of Perfection'," in *Medium Aevum* 5 (1936), pp. 11–30.

———— "Walter Hilton and the Mystical Tradition in England," in *Essays and Studies* 22 (1937), pp. 103–27.

Hodgson, P. *Three 14th Century English Mystics* (London, 1967).

———— "Walter Hilton and 'The Cloud of Unknowing'—a Problem of Authorship Reconsidered," in *Modern Language Review* 50 (1955), pp. 395–406.

Hughes, A. C. *Walter Hilton's Directions to Contemplatives* (Rome: Gregorian University, 1962).

Hughes, J. *Pastors and Visionaries: Religion and Secular Life in Late Mediaeval Yorkshire* (Woodbridge, Suffolk, 1988).

Hussey, S. S. "The Text of 'The Scale of Perfection', Book 2," in *Neuphilologische Mitteilungen* 65 (1964), pp. 75–92.

———— "Latin and English in 'The Scale of Perfection'," in *Mediaeval Studies* 35 (1973), pp. 456–76.

———— "Walter Hilton: Traditionalist?" in *The Mediaeval Mystical Tradition in England: Dartington 1980*, edited by M. Glasscoe (Exeter, 1980), pp. 1–16.

———— "Editing the Middle English Mystics," in *Spiritualität Heute und Gestern (Analecta Cartusiana* 35:2 Salzburg 1982), pp. 160–73.

Kennedy, D. G. *The Incarnational Element in Hilton's Spirituality, Salzburg Studies in English Literature*, Elizabethan and Renaissance Studies 92:3 (Salzburg, 1982).

Knowles, D. "Walter Hilton," Chapter 6 of *The English Mystical Tradition* (London, 1961), pp. 100–18.

———— and Russell Smith, J., article "Hilton, Walter," in *Dictionnaire de Spiritualité*.

Milosh, J. E. *"The Scale of Perfection" and the English Mystical Tradition* (Madison: University of Wisconsin Press, 1966).

Minnis, A. J. "Affection and Imagination in *The Cloud of Unknowing* and Hilton's Scale of Perfection," in *Traditio* 39 (1983) pp. 323–66.

Mueller, Jane I. *The Native Tongue and the Word: Developments in English Prose Style, 1380–1580* (Chicago: University of Chicago Press, 1984).

Riehle, W. "The Problem of Walter Hilton's Possible Authorship of 'The Cloud of Unknowing' and Its Related Tracts," in *Neuphilologische Mitteilungen* 78 (1977), pp. 31–45.

Ross, E. *Human Creation in God's Image: Richard of St. Victor, Walter Hilton, and Contemporary Theology*, Ph.D. diss. University of Chicago, 1987).

Russell Smith, J. "Walter Hilton and a Tract in Defence of the Veneration of Images," in *Dominican Studies* 7 (1954), pp. 180–214.

———— "Walter Hilton," in *The Month* N.S. (1959) pp. 133–148.

———— See also under Knowles, D.

Sargent, M. G. *James Grenehalgh as Textual Critic*, 2 vols., *Analecta Cartusiana* 85 (Salzburg 1984).

———— "Walter Hilton's 'Scale of Perfection': The London Manuscript Group reconsidered," in *Medium Aevum* 52 (1983), pp. 189–216.

Steele, F. J., *Definitions of the Active Life in Middle English Literature of the Thirteenth, Fourteenth and Fifteenth Centuries* D.Phil. thesis, Oxford University 1979.

Index of Scriptural Citations
and Allusions

References for chapter and verse are to the Latin Bible: *Biblia Sacra iuxta Vulgatam Versionem,* ed. B. Fischer, O.S.B., et al., *Deutsche Bibelgesellschaft,* ed. 3 (Stuttgart, 1983).

Index to Preface, Introduction and Notes

Index to Text

Other Volumes in this Series